# ALASKA
## ADVENTURES IN NATURE

Paul E. Otteson

JOHN MUIR PUBLICATIONS
A Division of Avalon Travel Publishing

John Muir Publications
A Division of Avalon Travel Publishing
5855 Beaudry Street
Emeryville, CA 94608

Printed in the United States of America.
Second edition. First printing March 2000.

Library of Congress Cataloging-in-Publication Data
Otteson, Paul.
    Alaska: adventures in nature / Paul Otteson.
        p.   cm.
    Includes index.
    ISBN 1-56261-487-8
    1. Alaska—Guidebooks. 2. Outdoor recreation—Alaska—Guidebooks.
3. Natural history—Alaska—Guidebooks. 4. Ecotourism—Alaska—Guidebooks.
I. Title.
    F902.3.088    1998
    917.9804'51—dc21
                        97-31273
                        CIP

Editors: Bonnie Norris, Marybeth Griffin Macy
Graphics Editor: Bunny Wong
Production: Scott Fowler
Design: Janine Lehmann
Cover Design: Janine Lehmann
Maps: Julie Felton, Kathleen Sparkes
Printer: Publishers Press
Cover photos:
    Front-©Mike Jones/Photo Network (Canoeing on Rabbit Slough, Palmer Hay
        Flats State Game Refuge)
    Back-©Paul Otteson (Sunset in the Alaska Range)
    Title page photo: ©Paul Otteson (Denali National Park)

Distributed to the book trade by
Publishers Group West
Berkeley, California

# CONTENTS

# CONTENTS

# CONTENTS

# ABBREVIATIONS USED IN THIS BOOK

**BL:** Backcountry lodge
Rustic, casual accommodations located in wilderness areas, miles from the nearest road or town. Meals, services, and a range of optional activities are typically provided.

**RH:** Roadhouse
Homes away from home in rural Alaska, roadhouses offer travelers a number of services under one roof, typically some combination of lodging, meals, libations, supplies, and gas.

**RT:** Round-trip time
Time needed to complete a given trail, hike, or travel route

**Alaskajourney.com**
Visit the author's website at www.alaskajourney.com for the latest updates to the information offered in the following chapters. The site also features a large collection of Paul's photographic images from throughout the state, as well as links to other useful Alaska web pages.

# DEDICATION

*As with the first, this second edition is dedicated to Mary, my wife and dearest friend, and to the state that brought us together—Alaska.*

# ACKNOWLEDGMENTS

Thanks to the following businesses for their support: the Alaska Marine Highway System; the Alaska Railroad; Alaska Airlines; Northwest Airlines; Cruise West; Reeve Aleutian Airways; Era Aviation; Temsco Helicopters; Uyak Air; Homer Air; Baker Aviation; Alaska Flyers; Westmark Hotels; the Nugget Inn in Nome; the Nullagvik Hotel in Kotzebue; and the unexpectedly nice Pacifica Guest House in Bethel.

Thanks to the many fine folks who make my Alaska journeys wonderful: the Dippes, Denmans, and Heapheys—my family in Anchorage; Cheri King—our Ruth Glacier leader; Mike Doncaster and David Endicott—for their help and friendship in Deadhorse; Walt and the Waldo Arms in Kaktovik; Richard Beneville—Nome's greatest asset; and many others.

And thanks to all my Denali friends—Tony, Gooch, Cliff, Jersey, Gary, Randy, Page, and so many more; Ross Houghton—my travel partner, all around good guy, and photographer par excellence; and Todd Stritter—for starting it all.

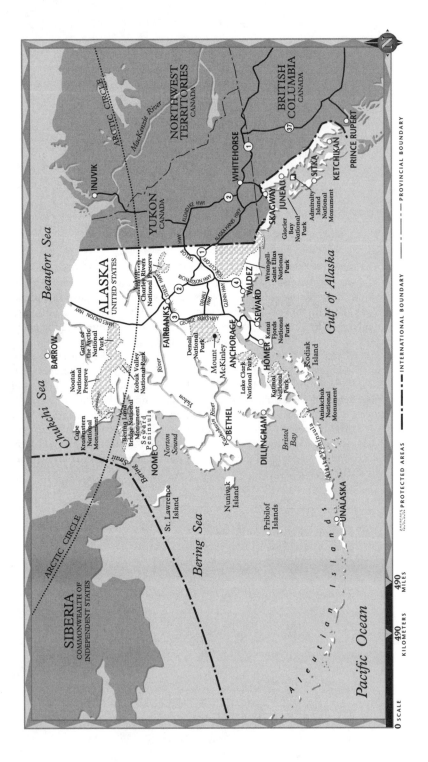

SIBERIA
COMMONWEALTH OF INDEPENDENT STATES

ARCTIC CIRCLE

Chukchi Sea

Beaufort Sea

Bering Strait

St. Lawrence Island

NOME

Norton Sound

Nunivak Island

Pribilof Islands

Bering Sea

Pacific Ocean

Aleutian Islands

UNALASKA

Alaska Peninsula

Bristol Bay

DILLINGHAM

BETHEL

Kuskokwim River

Yukon

River

Cape Krusenstern National Monument

Bering Land Bridge National Monument

Seward Peninsula

Noatak National Preserve

Kobuk Valley National Park

Gates of the Arctic National Park

BARROW

JAMES DALTON HWY

ALASKA
UNITED STATES

Yukon-Charley Rivers National Preserve

STEESE HWY

FAIRBANKS

TAYLOR HWY

ELLIOTT HWY

Mount McKinley

Denali National Park

DENALI HWY

GEORGE PARKS HWY

ANCHORAGE

Lake Clark National Park

Katmai National Park

Kodiak Island

Aniakchak National Monument

HOMER

Kenai Fjords National Park

SEWARD

GLENN HWY

RICHARDSON HWY

VALDEZ

Wrangell-Saint Elias National Park

Gulf of Alaska

Glacier Bay National Park

SKAGWAY

JUNEAU

Admiralty Island National Monument

SITKA

KETCHIKAN

PRINCE RUPERT

BRITISH COLUMBIA
CANADA

WHITEHORSE

YUKON
CANADA

KLONDIKE HWY

ALASKA HWY

HAINES HWY

INUVIK

MacKenzie River

NORTHWEST TERRITORIES
CANADA

ARCTIC CIRCLE

0 SCALE

490 KILOMETERS

490 MILES

············· PROTECTED AREAS

––·––·– INTERNATIONAL BOUNDARY

– – – – PROVINCIAL BOUNDARY

# WHY ALASKA?

To travelers from more populated areas of the world, Alaska can seem like another planet. It is otherworldly in its difference, with its vast wilderness, free-roaming wildlife, and splendid scenery. But the call of the wild is also a call to our roots—to a rich fabric of nature that speaks to our primeval past. That other world is also an ancient home. All it takes to answer the "why" question is a visit to the state. There is simply no comparable travel destination on Earth.

A more important question might be, "What's the best way to see Alaska?" Tourists make a mistake when they treat the state as they might treat Washington, D.C., or Yellowstone. In Alaska, it is less appropriate to carry a "must-see" destination list and drive from sight to sight or viewpoint to viewpoint. The state is so richly endowed with stunning mountains, awesome glaciers, and impressive wildlife that, in a way, there's no place to go—you're already there!

If you're wise, you won't come to Alaska to collect snapshots and T-shirts, but to seek experience. Head into the wild country. Feel the power of a land that is geologically violent, climatologically raw, and biologically inhuman. Nose your kayak into bergs of a Kenai Fjords glacier, hoping you're not a little too close to the calving river of ice that sloughed them off. Listen to the motor of a floatplane fade into the distance, the pilot having promised to retrieve you a week later from a lonely gravel bar, 50 miles away across the Brooks Range.

1

Paul Otteson

*Arctic Circle marker on the Dalton Highway*

Leave your tentsite for a sunset hike in the Wrangells, knowing that a grizzly sow and her cubs might be trundling silently through the alders just over the next rise. If your Alaska visit is likely to be a once-in-a-lifetime event, come not as a tourist, but as an explorer.

Then again, major wilderness adventures are not for everyone; most Alaska travelers will want access to civilization for some or all of their time in the state. If a less ambitious course suits you, the shift from tourist to explorer can involve safe and comfortable decisions. Maybe you stay at a backcountry lodge instead of a bus-tour hotel. Perhaps you take a smaller tour boat into a less-visited fjord. You could see your bears on the secluded Katmai south coast instead of booked-solid Brooks Camp. Opt for a two-hour raft ride on the Nenana instead of browsing the gift shops at Denali. Enjoy a morning walk in the White Mountains on your way to Circle Hot Springs. Even if scaling Mount St. Elias or canoeing the Yukon is not for you, find your personal explorer's edge and step toward it.

More than anything else, it's important to extend your vision beyond a normal frame of reference—Denali is a perfect example. How do you "see" the mountain that ranks as the largest in the world from base to summit? It really isn't enough to have the clouds lift so you can snap a picture from an overlook. I've observed that mountain from various angles, at different times of the year, from great distance and near its base, but I still can't quite "see" it—it's just too big. It cannot easily be translated from vast reality into mental image. I know it's there, though—looming and presiding, spilling glaciers and rejecting climbers, seizing the atmosphere and wrapping itself in brooding mists. Hundreds of square miles cower under its sway.

The wise visitor remembers that Alaska is not a convenient collection of Kodak moments. It's a vast wild country where the miles are long and expensive, the conditions sometimes a challenge, and the best features hidden far from bus and cruise-ship windows. For a guaranteed good view of bears, eagles, whales, the northern lights, and calving glaciers, you'll need to buy that $30 video in the gift shop. If that bothers you, rethink your trip. Better yet, open your eyes a little wider, grab your paddle or lace up your boots, and leave civilization behind.

All of the advice in this book is geared toward those who seek a deeper experience, who want to be filled with the strength and spirit of the natural world—who, in other words, are *coming home to Alaska*. Answering the "why" question is intellectually easy. Following up that answer with a well-designed journey is the challenge.

# How to Use This Book

**Appendix:** Use it as an information resource for Alaskan transportation options, guides, tour companies, rentals, and native and state government agencies.

**Details:** Detailed, easy-access reference information follows the introduction of each significant community, park, forest, or wilderness area.

**Temperatures:** Ranges indicate average highs and lows; extremes are noted.

**Road routes:** Major road routes are described in milepost fashion. Road conditions are provided; roadside accommodations and attractions are listed by the highway mileage point at which they're located.

3

*Valdez*

# ALASKA: AN OVERVIEW

2

Alaska is a story long in the telling. Despite the challenge of climate and mountains, it's widely held that this was the first place humans lived in the Western Hemisphere. An accident of nature made this possible, but it took a hardy people to take the high road to the Americas. The Eskimos, Aleuts, and Indians who have been here longest have a unique subsistence heritage that has only recently been awkwardly thrust into the modern world.

While many non-native Alaskans trace their roots back to Russian trappers or early gold seekers, most are first-, second-, or third-generation residents with various roots and a vigorously adopted "Alaskanism." Established towns and cities are fairly balanced in gender representation, but the seasonal and itinerant work force is largely male, somewhat skewing the total population. Alaska hosts numerous and often caricatured individualists or "end-of-the-roaders" who deliberately sought the fringes of society to begin a self-reliant life in a land of challenge.

The traveler will get the feel of Alaska almost immediately, discovering how land and people fit each other. Officially 586,412 square miles in land area (656,424 with state waters), Alaska is 3½ times larger than California, while having less than 2 percent of its population. Out every door is a short route to wilderness. Any family can wake to a bull moose browsing in the yard. People care for

# Beringia

*Alaska's landscape and natural history have been heavily influenced by recent ice ages. Ice-age cycling results in sea-level fluctuation, repeatedly exposing and submerging areas of the continental shelf. The most recent rise flooded coastal glacier valleys, creating Alaska's many fjords. During past ice ages, Asia and North America were connected by Beringia, or the "Bering land bridge." Much more than a narrow bridge, the exposed land included all of the seafloor of the Bering Strait and Chukchi Sea, and much of the Bering Sea. This lost land is now under more than 200 feet of water.*

*When exposed, Beringia provided a contiguous area of grass-and scrublands for wildlife migration. Eurasian species are thus closely related to their Alaskan and Canadian cousins. The herbaceous plants of the tundra and the birch, aspen, and spruce of the taiga are also very similar through-out the world's northern latitudes.*

each other easily when the need arises, enjoying stronger bonds of community than individualist caricatures would suggest.

## NATIVE PEOPLES

The first humans to arrive in North America came across Beringia in several waves of migration from Asia. The migrations occurred between 30,000 and 10,000 years ago, and possibly as early as 40,000 years ago. Humans moved south from Alaska along the coast, and perhaps made their way across an ice-free, overland corridor between the coastal mountains and the continental interior. As of 17,000 years ago, native peoples had spread throughout North America; by 10,000 B.C. they had reached the southern tip of South America.

Along with contemporary species, the earliest Alaskans found a land populated by mastodons, woolly mammoths, saber-toothed cats, giant sloths, and cave bears. There is still some dispute over the demise of these species, but many hold that their extinction was a direct result of competition with humans.

Currently, native peoples in Alaska have a combined population of less than 100,000. Twenty different languages in 4 language families are spoken today, though a few languages are nearly extinct, especially Eyak. Language-based native organization is as follows:

## ESKIMO-ALEUT
Aleut—Outer Alaska Peninsula, Aleutians, Pribilof Islands
Eskimo
   Alutiq (Sugpiak)—Alaska Peninsula, Kodiak, Kachemak, Prince William Sound
   Central Yupik—Yukon and Kuskokwim Delta, north Bristol Bay
   Siberian Yupik—St. Lawrence Island
   Inupiaq—Seward Peninsula, Kobuk Valley, North Slope

## ATHABASKAN-EYAK-TLINGIT
Tlingit—Southeast, Yakutat
Eyak—Copper River Delta area
Athabaskan
   Ahtna—Copper Basin, Chitina Valley, Talkeetna Mountains
   Tanaina—Cook Inlet, Susitna Valley, Lake Clark region
   Ingalik—Anvik, Shageluk, central Kuskokwim
   Holikachuk—Upper Innoko River Valley
   Koyukon—Central Yukon, Koyukuk, lower Tanana Valleys
   Upper Kuskokwim—Upper Kuskokwim Valley
   Tanana—Nenana, lower Tanana, Salcha Valleys
   Tanacross—Upper Tanana, Tok, Tanacross, Dot Lake
   Upper Tanana—Upper Tanana Valley, Northway, Tetlin
   Han—Upper Yukon, Eagle
   Kutchin—Yukon River, Porcupine River, Fort Yukon, Arctic Village

**HAIDA**—South Prince of Wales Island, Hydaburg
**TSIMSHIAN**—Duke Island, Annette Island, Metlakatla

Some of America's earliest civil-rights battles were fought by native Alaskans demanding land rights and equal treatment under the law. In 1971, after oil was discovered in the Arctic, the sweeping Alaska Native Claims Settlement Act (ANCSA) was enacted—in part to settle the many small claims quickly to assure unobstructed access to the oilfields. ANCSA promised cash payments and deeded approximately 10 percent of Alaska lands to 12 native corporations. All Alaska natives are members of one of the corporations, each of which encompasses a contiguous geographical region of the state. Smaller village corporations were established in permanent native settlements.

The corporation structure allows native groups to own and administer their land, resources, and revenues. By most accounts, it is a substantial improvement over the reservation system in the lower 48. Corporations can deal effectively with the larger economy while fairly representing shareholders.

The Arctic Slope Corporation is an example of financial success. The corporation receives a share of Prudhoe Bay oil revenues in addition to direct ANCSA payments. Members currently have a life reminiscent of a wealthy OPEC state in which the corporation pays for all basic services, from education to health care, and provides a monthly stipend to members. The total value to each individual is upwards of $30,000 per year. Other corporations don't currently fare as well.

## EXPLORATION AND SETTLEMENT

Danish explorer Vitus Bering, for whom the Bering Sea and Strait are named, was probably the first European visitor to what is now Alaska. Sailing for the Russians, he landed on St. Lawrence Island in 1728. In 1741 he extended his explorations along the Southcentral coast, bringing a Russian party under Aleksei Chirikov to Kayak Island in eastern Prince William Sound. Bering and others died on the journey, but members of the party returned to Russia with otter pelts.

Russian trappers followed up on the discovery and were soon at work depleting the otter population as they would all along the coast, as far south as California. In 1784 Grigory Shelekhov (or Shelikof) founded the first permanent Russian settlement on Kodiak Island. Shelikof Strait is named for him, as Cook Inlet is named for Captain James Cook, who visited the region on his travels in 1788.

Czar Paul I chartered the Russian-American Company in 1799 to control the otter trade, appointing Alexander Baranov as its head.

Baranov established a settlement at the present site of the town of Kodiak, then moved on to found New Archangel, later renamed Sitka, in 1799. The Tlingit Indians burned Sitka in 1802, but it was rebuilt two years later and served as the capital of Russian Alaska until it was sold to the United States. During the ensuing period, the Russians founded a number of settlements, surveyed mineral wealth, experimented with agriculture, and established trade routes.

In 1867 United States Secretary of State William H. Seward reached an agreement for the purchase of Alaska from the Russians, who sought to secure Alaska in the hands of an ally rather than lose it to the British. The state was formally turned over to the United States on October 18, 1867, in a ceremony on Castle Hill in Sitka. The purchase quickly became known as "Seward's Folly," his critics contending that it was a waste of money. The U.S. War Department, Treasury Department, and Navy administered the land until a civil government was established in 1884.

Seals, whales, and otters were harvested throughout the late nineteenth century, continuing the decline in populations of each. Fur seals were particularly hard hit. When the government began fur-seal protection in the early 1900s, numbers were just over 100,000. The population today is estimated at 2.5 million. Salmon fishing also grew in importance during this period. Despite this modest economic activity, Alaska remained almost wholly undeveloped.

Enter gold! Prospectors were working several modest claims in Alaska in the late 1800s, but it was news from Canada in 1896 that really got things going. That year, gold was discovered in Rabbit Creek, a tributary of the Klondike River which flows into the Yukon River at Dawson City. About 30,000 people came to the Yukon in the Klondike Gold Rush of 1897–98, most arriving via the instant boom towns of Skagway and Dyea. Over Chilkoot Pass on the Chilkoot Trail they went, then down the Yukon to the gold fields. As with all such rushes, the early birds and big investors struck it rich while most just squeaked by or failed altogether. By 1910 the all but exhausted claims had produced $100 million worth of gold.

With the ports of Valdez and Skagway opened and regular sea traffic established, intrepid prospectors pushed inland. Gold was discovered again on a beach on the Seward Peninsula in 1899, ushering in Nome as a new boom town and chief city of the Bering coast. In 1902 it appeared yet again, this time in the rivers that fed the Tanana and Yukon near Fairbanks and to the north. Gold was discovered in

*Juneau*

the feeders of the Iditarod River in 1906, at the edges of the Kuskokwim Mountains near the town of Flat. A year later, the hills south of Ruby on the Yukon River divulged their golden secret.

Juneau was made the capital of Alaska in 1900 and, in 1912, Alaska became an official U.S. territory. By then, the slogan "Seward's Folly" had been turned back against the original critics. In the 1920s aircraft slowly began to supplement riverboats and dogsleds as modes of transportation into the bush. The Alaska Railroad from Seward to Fairbanks was completed in 1923. The thirties saw the establishment of agriculture in the Matanuska Valley. Still, development was expectedly slow, limited by difficult transport, harsh conditions, and the fading of the gold boom.

## MODERN ALASKA AND A LEGACY OF WAR

In 1942 the Japanese attacked the Aleutian Islands, bombing Dutch Harbor and occupying the islands of Kiska and Attu. In a breathtaking effort that same year, the United States built the entire 1,523-mile Alaska Highway from Dawson Creek, British Columbia (not to be confused with Dawson City, Yukon), to Delta Junction, Alaska. They also built another 500 miles of road, including the Haines Highway (Haines to Haines Junction) and Glenn Highway (Tok to Anchorage).

The islands were retaken in 1943, but the accompanying military build-up persisted throughout the Cold War. Several bases are active today, including Fort Richardson and Elmendorf Air Force Base near Anchorage, Fort Wainwright and Eielson Air Force Base near Fairbanks, and Fort Greely near Delta Junction.

Alaska's population nearly doubled in the 1940s, reaching 130,000 by the end of the decade. Since then, the lure of various economic booms has combined with intermittent periods of widespread unemployment to keep the state growing in fits and starts. News of jobs attracts people to Alaska, but—like the Klondike gold rush that set the tone—many don't find what they expected and in time must turn their efforts elsewhere.

Five types of economic activity generate revenue of consequence for the state and its citizens. Two of them, oil and the military, were recently in decline. Mining offers steady work for many, but grows reluctantly in the modern environmental era. Fishing and tourism fluctuate annually in their revenue-generating potential and are easily affected by circumstances beyond anyone's control.

When the economy is growing, jobs pay well and often go wanting. Anyone willing to work hard in fishing, construction, mining, and oil production can ride the coattails of a minor boom, socking away a lot of money in a short period. When the booms fade, workers must leave the state for greener pastures or head for that paid-for cabin just off the highway to hunker down and wait for the next opportunity to knock.

This boom-to-bust cycling is an integral aspect of life in Alaska. Even when larger trends are on a steady rise, the annual cycles of the tourist and fishing industries persist. In May hundreds of businesses open, construction projects get underway, and thousands of seasonal workers stream into the state. In September you can almost feel people drain away. Each day on the highway offers longer intervals between vehicles. When the northland gets dark and cold, the economy goes into partial hibernation. The vivid rhythms of the seasons are a part of Alaskans' lives in a way that other Americans could never appreciate. Even those who live in places where the seasons bring great change cannot imagine frozen Deadhorse, where the winter sun doesn't rise above the horizon for two months.

11

Alaskans love their land. They feel a sense of ownership for their state and its issues like no others. Challenge and struggle are a part of the lives of even the wealthiest among them, and they know at all times that local economies are a step away from disaster. That step could be a volcano or a congressional decision, an earthquake or an oil spill. There is nothing casual about choosing the Alaskan life.

## PUBLIC LANDS AND WILDERNESS

Four major events since World War II have shaped the status of land use and wilderness preservation in Alaska. The first occurred when Alaska gained statehood in 1958. As part of the transition, the federal government promised 28 percent of the land to the state to do with it as it saw fit. Second was the discovery in 1968 of huge oil and gas deposits on the North Slope. New infrastructure and a flow of revenue brought a burst of development. Third on the list was the signing of the Alaska Native Claims Settlement Act in 1971, with 10 percent of Alaska land going to native corporations. With the rights of corporate landholders, resource exploitation ensued—particularly the clear-cutting of forests on the south coast.

Last and perhaps most important was the remarkable Alaska National Interest Lands Conservation Act (ANILCA), shaped, supported, and signed into law by President Jimmy Carter on December 2, 1980. ANILCA doubled the size of the U.S. National Park and National Wildlife Refuge systems, adding 97 million acres. The act also set the stage for the final selections of federal parcels by the state and native corporations—a process that is still not complete. When all the dealing is done in a few years, about 62 percent of Alaska will remain in the federal public domain—owned and stewarded, if you're a U.S. citizen, by *you*.

The most remarkable feature of ANILCA is that the selection criteria used to secure federal parcels was based largely on conservation of critical habitat and scenic wonders. Fifty-seven million acres of designated wilderness (the equivalent of two dozen Yellowstones) presently exist within the larger system of BLM lands and 37 national parks, preserves, forests, monuments, and wildlife refuges. Twenty-six National Wild and Scenic Rivers preserve hundreds of miles of free-flowing waters and riparian environment. The final decision on the Tongass National Forest Management Plan, made in April 1999, protects more wilderness area and river miles.

# PRESERVATION, DEVELOPMENT, AND THE FUTURE

Alaskans call their state "the last frontier," and with good reason. To this day, fortune seekers, homesteading pioneers, and other searchers are pushing back the limits of the wild country to carve out a life in difficult conditions. The state offers great deals on land in remote locations.

With the major issues of land distribution behind, the stage is now set for decisions regarding how that land is used. Manufacturing may be growing as a part of the economy, but the exploitation of natural resources and the improvement of infrastructure are still the state's primary development goals. Three recent and current issues highlight the kinds of choices that confront individuals, businesses, native corporations, state, and nation.

## Tongass Timber

Most of Alaska's panhandle (the Southeast) is federal public land, almost all of which is managed by the U.S. Forest Service as the Tongass National Forest. Of the 10 million forested acres, about 8.5 million acres are old-growth Sitka spruce and western hemlock. Much of this forest is suitable for use as lumber and pulp—but is equally suitable as habitat and scenic land. So far, only a small percentage of the old growth on federal public lands has been harvested.

In the recent battle over the new Tongass Land Management Plan, timber companies and the Alaskan congressional delegation went head to head with the Clinton administration, environmental groups, and the tourist industry over the future of the forest. Virtually every key pro-exploitation legislative effort was defeated. It became clear that government subsidies to timber interests were doomed and that long-term contracts due to expire would not automatically be renewed. Policies were strengthened against road building and for the protection of habitat and "viewshed." With the final decision on the plan in April, 1999, it appears that the integrity of Tongass wildlands will stand for another decade.

But this strong new sentiment of preservation is no small thing to the towns of the Southeast. The economic backbone of several communities is at stake, particularly Ketchikan, where a polluting pulp mill—the last remaining in the panhandle—was closed in March of 1997 due to falling pulp prices and tough regulations. Towns like Sitka have recovered strongly from the closing of large mills, but the

changes in community character and job opportunities were bitter pills to many residents. The fate of Ketchikan remains to be seen.

## ANWR Oil

While the mountainous regions of the vast Arctic National Wildlife Refuge (ANWR, pronounced "AN-wahr") are protected as designated wilderness, the coastal plain along the shores of the Arctic Ocean is "standard" refuge land and legally open to some development. There is a strong indication from very limited explorations that a substantial amount of oil lies beneath the plain, much of it accessible from proposed drilling pads on native and public lands. Congress has prevented development from proceeding by blocking exploration on federal land and prohibiting road building and industrial transport between the state lands around Prudhoe Bay and the Arctic Slope Corporation land.

Three entities stand to gain tremendously from ANWR oil development. The oil companies (British Petroleum, Chevron, Exxon, and Arco) are poised to leap into action, their Prudhoe Bay experience erasing many uncertainties about profitability. The Arctic Slope Corporation and smaller native corporations could score big via fees, royalties, and native hiring rules. The state of Alaska will also benefit hugely, certainly because of job opportunities for residents, but also because the biggest cut of government income goes to the state.

As the production of the Prudhoe Bay–area fields continues its steady decline, the pressure for ANWR development gradually builds. Advanced technologies offer the chance to extract the most oil with the least impact. A list of promises and stringent regulations are in place to ameliorate damage. Guarantees to remove every trace of intrusion once the oil is gone could be inked in an instant. Everyone concerned has beaten the issue to death—development is only a shift in the economic and political winds away.

From an Alaskan, or even an American, perspective, it's hard to argue with those who would have the oil out, but I have no trouble drawing the line and saying "no more" (though it's hardly my line to draw). Alaska is what it is because of what *hasn't* happened to it yet—it is perhaps the last place on Earth where wilderness that is vast and vital has a chance to survive. That is enough for me, though it is never enough across the committee table. Tenuous arguments about the fragility of the tundra and behavior of the Porcupine caribou herd are all that substantially forestall the decision to develop ANWR. Vastness, vistas, and wholeness are not yet accepted as sufficient values for wildland preservation.

## ROADS TO NOWHERE

Starting with the construction of the Glenn, Haines, and Alaska Highways in 1942, each of the state's major road-building projects has changed the face of Alaska forever. Some roads, such as the Richardson Highway linking Fairbanks with the port of Valdez, began as winter roads and early overland routes. Others, like the Dalton, were sliced new through raw wilderness that had never known regular human travel. Today road building is an issue that enflames passions and brings otherwise pleasant conversations to an abrupt end. "Why shouldn't I be able to drive to Nome?" the proprietor of the resort at Circle Hot Springs asked me, pointing out that you can get anywhere from everywhere in the lower 48. Why indeed?

The answer, increasingly, is that the American public will not allow the construction of any more roads across federal lands. Of course, that largely unaware public is represented by congress-people and appointed Department of the Interior heads who change with fair frequency. So while well-loved national parklands are probably safe, obscure BLM parcels that never get a visitor are continuously at risk.

In a recent effort, Alaska tried to use the wording of old law to claim that footpaths, snowmachine trails, and other regularly uti-lized minor transit corridors qualified under states' rights as emi-nent domain property. The state claimed to have the legal right to improve those passages any way it saw fit, including establishing a roadbed that could accommodate semis and RVs.

Local, short-term thinking in Alaska is common and hard to argue with, but we shouldn't forget that the incremental develop-ment of wildlands represents the incremental end of the wildness. In the end, it is a matter of values. The extra push for development in Alaska is a response to both opportunity and current instability. Visitors should consider reminding Alaskans that nearly two-thirds of the state is owned by all Americans—but remind them gently.

Columbia Glacier

# CONSERVATION AND RESPONSIBLE TOURISM

**3**

In many locations throughout the world, the challenge of environmental awareness and responsible tourism is clear and critical. Battle lines are easily drawn between exploitation and preservation. Species are rare and threatened, habitat is encroached upon from all sides, everyone from developers to subsistence farmers is eager for economic opportunity, and environmentalists are desperate for money and publicity. Even in the lower 48, wildlands and habitats that recently enjoyed wide margins of security are now shrinking islands in a growing flood of freeways and sprawl. Not so Alaska—not yet.

In part, Alaska represents the best we have managed so far in environmental foresight and planning. ANILCA (see page 12) was a watershed in environmental legislation. The Tongass National Forest Management Plan is an exacting agreement laden with protections for air, land, water, wildlife, and scenic value. Even the generally pro-development state government has set aside over 3 million acres to parks and preserves for critical habitat, scenic value, and recreational uses—over one-third of all the state park land in the United States.

In many ways, however, it has been relatively easy to parcel out huge chunks of the state for preservation. With extensive public ownership, a small population, limited infrastructure, and the high cost of resource exploitation, the challenges to preservation sometimes seem faint and remote. Besides, there was enough to go

around to all concerned—at least enough so that any demands for greater allotments by private, native, and state concerns seemed like pure greed.

Alaska has many rough edges that can disturb the environmentally aware traveler with sensibilities developed elsewhere. Many Alaskans and others see the state as a land of raw potential for exploitation and development. Tourists represent a threat to a way of life, even as they provide needed jobs and revenue. It is no easy thing to determine what "responsible tourism" means in the context of Alaska. Small decisions about intrusion and impact are easy enough to make, but the larger choices are less clear: Do the tourist dollars that support the Alaskan economy get used to nibble away at the very wonders the tourists come to see? How many visitors does it take to remove the wildness from wilderness? Should people visit Alaska at all?

My short answer to these and other questions is, "Go!" Tourist money feeds the consuming, exploiting economy, but it also steers it. The sentiments of Alaska's population are shifting with time toward preservation and careful management. Because of the influx of tourists and their dollars, environmental awareness has never been higher in the state—even more so because of that new visitor on the scene: the "ecotourist."

## ECO-WHAT?

The term "ecotourist" has been popularized recently, mainly by private companies and organizations interested in tapping the purses of those with contemporary, "politically correct" attitudes. The label applies either to a new type of get-into-nature adventure for the typical tourist, or to a nonintrusive "style" of tourism—such as watching whales without disturbing them, or taking a quiet kayak to the glacier instead of a cruise ship. At best, the label is assigned accurately by a tour company, enabling the consumer to choose an option that is enriching and sensitive. At worst, it is a public relations ploy that relies on a phony veneer of credibility.

In reality, "ecotourism" is nothing more than a new label for a well-established approach to travel. In fact, I think "eco-traveler" is a better term than ecotourist, because "travel" implies independence and spontaneity—qualities which suit an overall approach to an Alaska trip. "Eco-travel" also seems to lay responsibility for environmental awareness on the traveler, not so much on the tour provider.

To the extent that eco-travelers are less intrusive visitors who have a minimal impact on the environment, all of us should strive to fit the image. If the following characteristics apply to you, it makes sense to use the "eco-" prefix:

1. The eco-traveler seeks natural destinations and activities when traveling, prioritizing real parks over theme parks, hiking over shopping.
2. The eco-traveler strives to have a minimal impact on the environment. Animals are not disturbed or fed, plants are not removed or damaged, and signs of human passage and presence are kept to a minimum.
3. The eco-traveler studies destinations in advance, learns from the travel experience, and brings this new understanding into the future. She takes active stands on environmental issues and avoids habits of consumption that degrade the natural world.
4. The eco-traveler maintains an attitude of respect not just for wildlife and habitat but for the history and culture of local people. The presumptions and simplistic judgments of the thoughtless visitor are avoided in favor of genuine human interaction.

The eco-traveler is well advised to take ecotours within the larger Alaska travel experience. Tours that facilitate independent choices are the best of the bunch. Heli-hiking or backcountry-lodge weekends enable independence while cruise/bus package tours stifle it. Elderhostel offers an education while big-ship cruises offer scenic morsels (albeit tasty ones). Perhaps the best way to think of this book is as an overall guide to eco-travel that includes numerous options for ecotourism.

## THE CHALLENGE OF ECO-TRAVEL

The visitor to the 49th state is confronted with a different set of responsibilities and expectations than those found in other natural destinations. Some are specific—like what to do with human waste on a glacier trek or how to discourage a grizzly from breaking a wild routine for the sake of a Snickers bar. Others derive from larger issues and involve an understanding of the Alaskan culture.

The following two topics provide food for thought and a look into the unique challenges of eco-travel in Alaska.

## HUNTING, TRAPPING, AND WILDLIFE HARVESTING

In the urban and suburban regions that are habitat to most of us, hunting as a pursuit has come to seem anachronistic—even primitive. Most eco-travelers no longer identify with hunting and have little exposure to those who value or participate in it. Often, they are anti-hunting, let alone out of touch with it. If you are such a person, Alaska offers a learning experience.

"Wildlife harvesting" is very much a part of the Alaskan culture and subsistence lifestyle. Game is not "killed" by hunters, but "taken." Herds of caribou are "managed" to prevent any in the herd from starving during hard winters. Whales and marine mammals are harvested in small numbers by natives living in coastal communities. Trappers set their lines to bring in the furs of fox and other small mammals. Salmon and other fish are pulled from the oceans, rivers, streams, and lakes in unbelievable numbers. Many thousands of Alaskans depend, at least in part, on their harvest of wildlife for food and income.

To the non-hunter, the language of hunting may seem like a denial of the raw emotions of killing and death. You may picture an agonized moose collapsing in the bush after a bullet rips through its gut, suffering for minutes as it waits for the killing shot, but you won't hear that aspect expressed over coffee at the roadhouse. To the anti-hunter, the hunting culture can seem arcane. Can you engage meaningfully with people for whom wildlife harvesting is a way of life?

I am not a hunter, but I no longer wince at the stories. Though habitat sometimes suffers a bit from motor-vehicle use, subsistence hunting in Alaska is no threat to animal populations. Trophy hunting is a different story, perhaps, but I have come to know several people involved in it and have been struck by their convictions. Some of them, at least, have a deep respect for the land and wildlife. Any stereotypes and caricatures you have may collapse if you choose to get to know such folks.

The brown bear you photograph on Kodiak Island may be shot dead a month later—the pilot who flies you in for a view may be the same one who shuttles a hunter in for the kill. You may overhear the tale in a roadhouse from one who stalked a bear, shot it for sport and a trophy, skinned it, removed the skull and claws to show the fish and game officers, and left the carcass in the bush for scavengers. The eco-traveler to Alaska is likely to interface with a very real, active, and accepted culture of sport hunting and wildlife "harvesting." How will you react?

## THE *EXXON VALDEZ*

Twelve million gallons (258,000 barrels) of oil is a lot of oil. When it began draining out of the damaged hull of the *Exxon Valdez* and into Prince William Sound on March 23, 1989, a sequence of events followed that serves as a lasting lesson to all concerned. Brazen and idiotic corporate dissembling and cover-up were followed by a backlash response that featured plenty of mistakes. After delays and lack of preparedness exacerbated the initial problem, an awkward but huge and swift response was mounted. At the peak of activity, 11,000 people, 1,400 vessels, and 80 aircraft were at work cleaning up the oil and trying to protect critical sites.

The chief damage of the spill was its impact on wildlife populations. As many as 5,000 sea otters, 300 bald eagles, 350 harbor seals, 13 killer whales, and perhaps one-third of a million seabirds died as a direct result of the oiling of waters and 1,500 miles of coastline. These and other species were also indirectly affected with nonlethal injuries, habitat degradation, and feeding and reproductive disruption. Salmon and herring fisheries suffered, as did plant and animal species living in shallows below low tide. Certain populations of plant and invertebrate species in heavily oiled intertidal-zone areas were devastated.

The whole event exposed the financial fears of a corporate giant, the economic fears of Alaskans, and the environmental fears of all who want a better world. Most of all, however, it revealed the power of life, given time, to heal itself and carry on. It is a lesson to travelers as well. So many of us have been attuned to the fragility and growing rarity of species and ecosystems throughout the world that we may have forgotten there is another side.

In the zeal to "do something" about the *Exxon Valdez* spill, well over a billion dollars was spent by Exxon ($900 million in a court settlement alone), much of which, from several perspectives, was wasted. Painstaking cleaning of oiled birds and mammals saved only

a few, and many of those, it appears, died shortly thereafter. Hundreds of tons of absorbent material used to sop up oil from the seas and beaches went into landfills or were incinerated, creating problems of a different sort. It's estimated that more oil was burned by ships, planes, and vehicles in the clean-up than was spilled. The miles of shoreline that were scrubbed by pressure hoses are in worse shape biologically (in some respects) than stretches that were left alone.

Today, more than a decade after the spill, signs of disaster are few and obscure. In general, wildlife populations have recovered. Oil still found ashore is often that driven deep into the beaches by high-pressure cleaning hoses. Chemical analyses of air, water, plants, and animal tissue show limited and diminishing effects. People can be confident that their efforts contributed positively to this healing in general, but the more vivid impression is that of the marine and coastal environment healing itself—thanks in large part to rough weather and natural chemical processes. Strong overall numbers within species have supported recoveries of many local populations—though harbor seals, sea otters, certain salmon runs, Pacific herring, and several bird populations still show regional lack of recovery.

But that is the nature of healthy, wild systems! The land and wildlife of Alaska have been challenged time and time again—with glaciation, volcanoes, tsunamis, war, rapacious mining, over-hunting, over-trapping, and over-fishing, as well as a major oil spill. Because it is vast and wild, however, the power of life to accommodate and respond has so far been sufficient for full, if scarred, recoveries.

## THE REAL CHALLENGE

The details of ecologically sensitive travel are second nature to many of us. We don't feed the animals. If we pack it in, we pack it out. We put fires dead out, take only pictures, and leave only footprints. But the traveler in Alaska has a greater responsibility—that of fighting for the continued existence of the wilderness itself.

Americans have a remarkable inheritance in their public lands. There are those who think of them as "federal" or "government" lands, but the truth is that the lands are ours—though we are more stewards than owners. Even non-citizen visitors share the responsibility of stewardship of American public lands, for the legacy we leave to future generations is ultimately one for all people. The risk for Alaska lies in its very value. It is remote, difficult to encompass, and hard to be aware of from far away. A road here, a power line there, a new mine over the hill; before you know it, the wilderness has been nickeled and dimed out of existence.

While in Alaska, it's hard not to be a responsible tourist. Unlike fragile natural destinations in poor countries, the regulations that govern the activities of tourists and tour operators alike are thoroughly developed and assimilated. Due to the economic importance of tourism, Alaska is quick to incorporate modern travel ethics and sensibilities. The real challenge is to help permanently secure the future of the larger wilderness. Alaska is truly America's last frontier. "Last" means either the last to fall or the last to remain. It's our call.

## THE ALASKA WILDERNESS RECREATION AND TOURISM ASSOCIATION

Many guides and outfitters serve travelers with outstanding, nonintrusive, environmentally sensitive options. Such companies are often members of the Alaska Wilderness Recreation and Tourism Association, or AWRTA (AR-ta). This nonprofit umbrella organization promotes "sustainable recreation and tourism for a quality future." Members are strongly encouraged to adopt AWRTA's ecotourism guidelines and subscribe to the organization's larger goals.

Many AWRTA-member businesses are included in the regional and appendix listings in this book. You may want to contact AWRTA directly for specific assistance and current information, especially if you are planning to book tours or adventures in advance. They are a good one-stop information source.

AWRTA members are likely to pay a bit more than lip service to environmental ethics, though *you* are ultimately responsible for the impact of your visit. It's also true that most non-member companies are decent, honest, knowledgeable, and fully aware of the environmental implications of their activities.

Contact AWRTA at 2207 Spenard Road, Suite 201, Anchorage, AK 99503, (907) 258-3171/info@awrta.org, www.alaska.net/~awrta.

*Two young grizzlies at play*

# WILDLAND AND WILDLIFE

## 4

The primary attractions for most visitors to Alaska are its vast wilderness and amazing natural features. With fewer than one person per square mile and most residents concentrated in population centers, huge areas of the state are virtually empty of humans and their activities. You can step out of the Katmai Wilderness Lodge on the south coast, hoist your pack, and head for the North Pole—knowing as you do that you need not meet a single human, cross a single road, or walk under a single power line. Of course, you'll want good maps, food caches, mosquito repellent, the zeal of a missionary, a copy of Michener's *Alaska*, amazing luck... and maybe a gun.

It's hard to fully grasp the scope of Alaskan wilderness. Only in the southcentral region of the state is the pattern familiar. Here, definable wild regions are segregated by highway arteries beaded with towns, most of which are tiny and far apart. Elsewhere, lonely roads head away from the population centers, piercing the larger wilderness, only to end at a wide river, coastal town, or cluster of lodgings. Beyond these points, human habitation is accessible only by foot, horse, air, boat, dogsled, or snowmachine. Small road systems exist around Nome, Kodiak, Juneau, and a number of other towns, but they do not connect with the continental grid.

Despite the wildness, there is a persistent illusion of civilization

# Alaska's Regions

*You can expect to see state and private tourist literature that refers to the following five regions. These regional designations are used throughout this book as well, though not necessarily as headings for the regional chapters, which are more specific in scope.*

**Southeast Alaska:** *Panhandle, Coast Range, St. Elias Mountains, Yakutat Bay, Juneau, Sitka, Ketchikan, Skagway, and Haines.*

**Southcentral Alaska:** *Wrangell Mountains, Chugach Mountains, Talkeetna Mountains, Prince William Sound, Copper Valley, "MatSu" region, Cook Inlet, Kenai Peninsula, Alaska Range, Anchorage, Palmer, Kenai, Seward, Homer, and Valdez.*

**Southwest Alaska:** *Kodiak Island, Alaska Peninsula, Aleutians, Bristol Bay, Yukon Delta, Lower Kuskokwim Valley, Kodiak, King Salmon, Dutch Harbor, Bethel, and Dillingham.*

**The Interior:** *Yukon Valley, Tanana Valley, Upper Kuskokwim Valley, Fairbanks, Fort Yukon, Tok, Circle, Eagle, Galena, and McGrath.*

**Far North:** *Brooks Range, Seward Peninsula, North Slope, Nome, Kotzebue, Barrow, and Deadhorse.*

that affects many travelers to Alaska. When you're on a road, behind a train or bus window, or gathered with others on a ferry deck, your view is always half civilized. Often, it takes a jolt to shake you from a secure perch—as when your vehicle breaks down at night on the road to Prudhoe Bay, or the plane that is to pick you up from a backcountry cabin is delayed by weather. Perhaps a bull moose galumphs suddenly into your headlights, or a bear ransacks your tent. None of these events are on many wish lists, but it's important to know that Alaska can challenge your self-reliance at many points. When you push your own frontier, it might push back.

# THE LAND:
# REGIONS AND CLIMATE

Alaska is basically a mountainous state—the northernmost end of
the continuous cordillera that stretches down through the Americas
to the tip of Cape Horn. Several major mountain ranges cross
portions of the state, all running roughly parallel to the Pacific
Coast. Between the major chains are lesser mountains, broad
valleys, and interior basins. Coastal plains are found in the north
and west.

In understanding the lay of the land, I find it helpful to distinguish three broad geographic regions that have clear identifying
characteristics. The following sections examine each of them.

## THE COAST RANGES AND ISLANDS

Mountain ranges and mountainous isles stretch along Alaska's
south coast in a swath 50 to 200 miles wide, dominating the
landscape and creating a rugged and wild menu of wilderness-
experience possibilities. Every one of Alaska's many peaks above
10,000 feet and all of its volcanoes are found within 200 miles of
the Pacific (most are much closer), as are nearly all of the state's
glaciers. Comparatively warm ocean currents influence the maritime climate, moderating temperatures and raising precipitation
levels.

Due to heavy tectonic activity, volcanoes rumble, steam, and
blow here with great geologic frequency. Amazing destinations like
the Valley of 10,000 Smokes in Katmai National Park and the 6-
mile-wide Aniakchak Caldera in Aniakchak National Monument
are the results of this volcanism.

Perhaps more telling of the tectonic activity in the region is the
fact that the strongest earthquake ever recorded in the Western
Hemisphere (by some estimates) occurred here on March 27,
1964. Anchorage and numerous coastal Alaskan towns were devastated by the quake that has been estimated at anywhere from 8.4 to
9.2 on the Richter Scale. Hundreds of miles of coastal lowlands
subsided as much as 6 feet, while mountain ridgecrests may have
risen just as much. Tsunamis from the event caused massive
destruction throughout the region.

## THE INTERIOR

Walled off to the south by the Alaska Range and Wrangell Mountains, and to the north by the Brooks Range, Alaska's vast Interior encompasses more than half the state. The region is dominated by the Yukon River, which flows east to west from the Yukon border to the Bering Sea.

Between the Yukon and other rivers are wide ranges of low mountains and high hills. Combined with difficult river crossings, boggy flats, extreme temperatures, and mosquitoes, these rugged hills have helped to slow development in the region—though they didn't stop the miners looking for gold.

The Interior receives substantially less precipitation than the coastal mountains and basins. Temperatures vary widely, with winter lows occasionally reaching -70°F, while summer highs may climb into the 80s. Not surprisingly, access to remote areas is difficult, though it opens up in the winter to snowmachine traffic.

The main features of the Interior are vast spruce forests and sprawling wetlands. Stands of aspen and birch precede new spruce growth in recovering fire areas. White spruce dominates higher and drier areas, while the very similar black spruce is found in the boggy flats.

## THE FAR NORTH AND ARCTIC COASTS

North and west of the Interior forests, the land along the shores of the Arctic Ocean and Bering Sea is stark and wide. In the west, coastal areas and valleys have short, warmish summers and long, cold winters. In the north and northwest, the Arctic climate features colder temperatures, only slightly moderated by the proximity of the oceans. High winds and extended winter darkness produce bitter windchills.

The landscapes of the Far North and Arctic Coast are heavily influenced by the permafrost that underlies 80 percent of Alaska. Where the layer is continuous in the Far North, the ground is frozen solid to a depth of up to 2,000 feet—though usually much less. Summer thawing occurs only in the uppermost inches and feet, allowing a thin layer of soil to support lush plant life atop of what is basically a giant ice cube.

The melting of surface layers, as well as the nonporous qualities of the layers beneath, creates lakes and pools in the poorly drained permafrost. Refreezing causes the soil to buckle, creating domes called "pingos" and polygon-patterned networks of low dikes. In some locations, pingos rise as much as 200 feet above the surrounding flats, demonstrating the power of the freeze/thaw cycle.

Since permafrost often underlies slopes and hillsides as well as flats, many Far North or Arctic Coast walking routes that look open and easy from a distance turn out to be slogs through sopping tundra. In general, the presence of forest and brushy ground cover is a sign of more stable, better-drained soils.

# ALASKAN WILDLIFE

Foremost in the minds of many people when thinking of Alaska is the state's fabulous wildlife. This is still a place where the ecosystems are intact and the migration routes uninterrupted. In the lower 48, the accidental introduction of hundreds of exotic plant and animal species has changed the face of nature forever. Not so in Alaska, where the progression has been comparatively untainted since the last ice age. In addition, the free interaction of healthy animal populations remains virtually unhindered by barbed wire, tract homes, or interstate highways.

Surprising to many is the fact that, in many areas, the population density of certain well-known species is really quite low. Large animals need a large territory, particularly where conditions for survival are difficult. Harsh conditions and a short growing season limit populations in many areas. Fortunately, wildlife viewing of the most popular species is relatively easy due to the prevalence of open terrain, good understanding of animal habits and migration routes, and access to locations where wildlife concentrates.

## BEARS

All three bear species found in North America are found in abundance in Alaska. Observing any of these beasts browsing, preying, fishing, or mating can be the highlight of a visit, and the chances to do so are many. Money buys "guaranteed" opportunities, but with a little planning and persistence, the chance for sightings is high for any traveler.

Black bears are the smallest of Alaskan bears, weighing up to 400 pounds and reaching 6 feet in length from nose to tail. They

are often distinctly black, but can also range in color from dark brown to medium brown and cinnamon. Blacks are easily distinguished from brown bears by their size, lack of shoulder hump, and more dog-like snout and forehead. More than 50,000 black bears live in Alaska's coastal and Interior forests, but are seen less frequently than grizzlies if at all by many tourists. Look for them in clearings and at the forest edge. They are often sighted along the Cassiar Highway in northern British Columbia and on Prince of Wales Island west of Ketchikan.

Polar bears live mainly solitary lives on the polar pack ice off the coast of the North Slope and Seward Peninsula. They live primarily on seals and seal pups that are vulnerable to attack when they're not in the water. Polars come ashore in the summer to mate, returning to the pack ice when the ocean margins freeze in November. While ashore, they may seek food in inhabited areas—usually when they smell human-produced odors from garbage, cooking, or hunting. They are fantastic swimmers and travelers of the pack ice, able to rapidly cross ice and water, pull themselves onto bergs in one fluid motion, then leap from the far side with graceful dives.

Easily the most dangerous of all bears, polar bears cause more injuries to humans per encounter than the others. Unlike grizzlies and blacks, polars are pure carnivores functioning in environments with very little distraction and cover. Your presence and movements can challenge them for a variety of reasons, including hunger. Before exploring the Arctic Ocean coast and ice pack, talk to locals and outfitters about recent bear behavior. As with any bear, it is highly unlikely that you'll have any problems, but follow prevention and reaction advice with care.

*Ursus Arctos*, the Alaska brown bear or grizzly, is the world's largest land carnivore and the undisputed king of beasts in the North. About 40,000 live in the state, as compared to a total population of fewer than 400 in the lower 48. They are found everywhere in Alaska except the Aleutians and several islands in the Bering Sea, Southcentral, and Southeast. The greatest concentrations are in the mountainous islands and coastal foothills of the south coast.

Premier areas for viewing brown bears include Admiralty Island and other locations in the Southeast, Kodiak Island, and the Katmai region west of Cook Inlet. The easiest and least expensive viewing access (no flights involved) is along the park road in Denali National Park, though viewing here cannot be "guaranteed" as it can in coastal regions. Elsewhere, a sharp eye and a little luck can reveal a bear going about its business just about anywhere you go.

It is largely agreed upon that the brown bears of the coastal regions and the inland grizzlies are the same species, though they can certainly appear different to even the casual observer. Salmon-fed browns can be huge, some males reaching over 1,500 pounds, with fur that ranges from medium to dark brown. They may seem a bit more vertical—less "stretched out" than their inland kin—and the fur around their faces sometimes seems to frame the eyes and snout, almost owl-like. Coastal browns gorge on high-protein, high-fat salmon for much of the feeding season, enjoying a consistent and easy feast of plenty.

Denali and other Interior bears are considerably smaller in maximum size, occasionally reaching 1,000 pounds. They have been known as grizzlies rather than brown bears, and include a sub-category of barren-ground grizzlies that live mainly above or beyond the treeline. Their fur tends to be lighter, almost blond on occasion, and may feature more distinct "grizzling"—the lighter tips of the fur which shimmer and ripple when the bears move. Interior grizzlies face a harsher climate and a diet much lower in animal fat and protein than their coastal kin. They roam relentlessly, consuming mainly berries, roots, shoots, and various plants. When possible, they will feast on ground squirrels, moose calves, caribou—on anything nutritious that they can catch.

## Bear Safety

Studying grizzlies and their behavior toward human visitors leaves me with only one certainty: They are unpredictable and potentially extremely dangerous. When observing bears, remember that your safety is ultimately up to them. You cannot outrun or out-battle any healthy adult bear should it decide to attack. They can maim or kill with one swipe of a paw. Religiously adhere to the following guidelines, remembering that even doing so does not guarantee your safety:

**1. Adopt a bear-repelling profile of behaviors**—Make noise when you hike by tying a bell to your pack or singing or talking loudly. Set up your camp away from roads, trails, animal carcasses, flocks of scavenger birds, known bear haunts—anywhere that would attract or provoke a bear in the area. Cook, clean, and store all food well away from your campsite. Use bear-proof containers to store food and fragrant items.

31

**2. Be part of a managed situation**—Keep dogs leashed and the leash in your hands. Watch out for children, keeping them still, quiet, and with you when observing bears. Avoid observing with groups of people if any of them are behaving inappropriately—especially if they have food or are stupid enough to try to feed bears. Follow any official advice offered for the particular location you visit and activity you're involved in.

**3. Never approach a bear**—particularly a mother with cubs (any pair or trio of bears with one apparent leader is a mother with cubs, regardless of size). Two hundred yards downwind of a lone, foraging bear is more than close enough—though you can get much closer to salmon-fishing browns in designated viewing areas.

**4. If a grizzly becomes aware of your presence and sniffs or approaches (either because you surprise it or pass upwind) do not run!**—As to what you should do, opinions vary a bit. My interpretation of the consensus is that you should hold your ground, identify yourself as human by talking calmly, loudly, and firmly, and wave your arms. Face the bear and stay vertical (don't bend over), and back slowly, diagonally away.

**5. If a grizzly charges, do not run!**—Hold a frozen, face-on, vertical but submissive posture and keep talking until the last possible instant, then drop to the ground in a fetal position or flat on your stomach, with your arms protecting neck and face. Play dead, remaining very still until you are certain the bear has moved well away and is no longer interested in you. Bear charges are often bluffs. Premature rapid motion or fleeing on your part will trigger a predatory response from the bear that all but assures a biting and/or mauling.

In general, this advice applies to all bears—though by most accounts, you can take a firmer, louder approach with black bears and should fight blacks vigorously in the rare instance of attack. Remember that people die from bear attacks in Alaska only once every four or five years on average. Compare that to two per year dying from dog attacks and several in car accidents. I've never had a negative encounter with any of the many bears—black, brown, or polar—that I've observed.

## WOLVES

Alaska's approximately 7,000 timber wolves are spread throughout the state. Individuals can reach 175 pounds and over 6 feet in length from nose to tip of tail. They live in packs of up to 35 individuals (but generally fewer than 10) in territories ranging from 50 to 5,000 square miles (including nomadic range). A dominant or "alpha" male leads the pack and marks the territory, with the alpha female occupying a secondary leadership role. The pack maintains a complex social hierarchy with posturing and vocalizations. Mating is for life.

Alaskan wolf packs occupy a centered hunting range during the period when pups are born and restricted to the den. At other times of the year, packs may become nomadic, following concentrations of their primary prey, often caribou. Wolves are opportunistic carnivores, eating whatever they can catch, but focus pack efforts on large grazing animals, including caribou, moose, and musk ox.

Wolves are the subject of controversy in Alaska and are still actively trapped and hunted. The Alaska Board of Game allows hunting on the grounds that wolves compete for caribou with sport and subsistence hunters—which is certainly true, though simple math shows that it's slim competition indeed. Battles over how and where wolves can be killed have made news in the last several years and will continue to do so.

Public lands offices and park headquarters maintain current information regarding where wolves can be observed. Their large territories, mobility, relative scarcity, and general shyness make sightings difficult without a targeted effort. A pack has been active in Denali recently, making the park the best viewing choice for roadbound travelers.

## LESSER CARNIVORES AND SMALL MAMMALS

Several other species of carnivores and small mammals are found throughout the state, though few are regularly seen by tourists—mainly because they are speeding from scenic site "A" to scenic site "B" and don't slow down to look around. Keep your eyes open, have those binoculars handy, and stop now and then for a walk or a long look out over the landscape.

In addition to the animals listed below, badgers, skunks, muskrats, rabbits, squirrels, lemmings, voles, mice, and shrews are also found in various habitats.

Unlike bears, animals including voles and arctic ground squirrels are true hibernators, sinking into a deep stupor for the duration of winter in their burrows. Bears, on the other hand, simply sleep

# Midnight Sun and Northern Lights

*The Arctic Circle, latitude 66°33', runs through the northern half of the Interior, passing close to Fort Yukon, Alatna, Selawik, and Kotzebue. Every point north of this line has at least one day per year when the sun does not rise above the horizon, and one day per year when it is visible all day. Thus, it is possible to see the fabled midnight sun throughout the Far North.*

*In Barrow, the northernmost point in Alaska, the sun doesn't set for almost three months (mid-May to mid-August). The small influx of tourists to Barrow who hope to see the midnight sun bring revenue to the town—some consolation for the long winter days when old Sol can't break the horizon. You can see the midnight sun with well-timed visits to spots south of the Brooks Range, but it's an iffy thrill and hardly enough on its own to justify a journey. Consider enjoying the 10 or 11 p.m. sun further south around solstice time.*

longer and more deeply. When the weather is encouraging, some may come out of their dens to browse for food.

**Beaver**—Beavers are common in Alaska's forests and brushy upland valleys. Look for their dams and lodges anywhere you see standing water in gently sloping sections of valleys and basins.

**Fox**—Red fox are common in forested areas, particularly in the warmer south. The beautiful arctic fox is found on the tundra of the Far North. It is still trapped in winter for its thick, soft, snow-white fur.

**Lynx**—Your glimpse of a lynx will be a thrill long remembered. Secretive and solitary relatives of the bobcat, they feed primarily on snowshoe hares, though they will pursue other prey (including domestic pets) when the hare population is in decline.

**Marmot**—These chubby, rock-dwelling rodents live in exposed

*A much more wondrous feature of the Alaskan night is the aurora borealis, or northern lights. When solar activity radiates storms of particles through space, they strike the Earth's upper atmosphere in patterns shaped by magnetic fields, displaying glowing, shifting curtains of light and color—a phenomenon peculiar to a wide band of the polar latitudes. The lingering twilight of summer months masks the effect, but when shadows get long in the fall, the hypnotic northern lights can be observed in all of their splendor.*

*Lodges and tour companies that operate in the colder months sometimes offer special northern-lights packages, perhaps featuring a snowmobile ride to a high and open observation spot, with a warm bed and hot buttered rum waiting upon return. Look for a shimmering in the northern night sky (possibly overhead, or even to the south!) at the darkest hours of your visiting period. Check periodically if you don't spot it on the first try, since the lights ebb and flow in coverage and intensity.*

high country with hideouts and vantage points among the boulders. Their distinct whistle announces the approach of potential danger (also making them easy to find).

**Marten, Mink, and Weasels**—Several members of the long-bodied, short-legged weasel family are found in Alaska. The smallest is the least weasel (less than 2.5 ounces), the largest is the wolverine. All feed primarily on smaller mammals, such as voles and mice, helping to control their population. Pine martens and mink are trapped for fur.

**Porcupines**—Found throughout forested regions, slow-moving porcupines are the nemesis of curious dogs and wolf pups. They are common members of the roadkill roster in certain areas—and they do not "shoot" their quills.

**River Otters**—Members of the weasel family, river otters are common residents of river valleys and coastal environments in southern and southeast Alaska. They feed on fish, shellfish, amphibians, and small mammals.

**Wolverines**—Closely related to badgers, these rarely sighted, nocturnal predators live largely solitary lives in Alaska's forested hills. Reaching 70 pounds, they are tenacious in defending themselves and their territory.

## MOOSE, CARIBOU, DALL SHEEP, AND OTHER LARGE HERBIVORES

Alaskan moose are found in forested areas, usually near bogs, streams, and standing water where they can find willow shoots— their food of choice. The biggest populations are found in the basins south of the Alaska Range and on the Kenai Peninsula, though they are also common in the Interior. Larger than their counterparts in the lower 48, a big bull moose can reach over 1,500 pounds with antlers 6 feet across. As members of the deer family, male moose grow new antlers every year, the heavy racks losing their felt and reaching full size around the September rut. One or two calves are born to females in May. Look for solitary moose or small, spread-out groups in boggy areas and near the roadside, but don't approach them—particularly males during the rut and females during calving season. Unlike the rule for bears, if a moose charges you, run!

Alaska's nearly 1 million caribou are members of about 30 separate herds, including a dozen major ones, each of which has distinct and relatively unchanging migratory routes and calving grounds. Male caribou can reach 500 pounds while females are considerably smaller. This helps to distinguish them since, unlike any other member of the deer family, the females grow antlers. During the summer, the herds disperse somewhat and concentrate on feeding. Caribou can be seen singly or in groups of various size in more open terrain, often walking or running. In insect-heavy areas, look for the occasional caribou sitting on a patch of late-melting snow to escape the torment.

Dall sheep are close relatives of the bighorn sheep found in the Rocky Mountains and coastal ranges to the south, their white fur distinguishing them clearly from their tan cousins. During the summer months, males tend to live higher in the mountains, separate from the small herds of females and kids; you may see the distinctive curved rams' horns less often than the ewes' more delicate version. The dominance ritual of rams smashing horns in a head-on collision is easier to hear than see during the fall rut. Look for Dall sheep in the higher reaches of the Alaska, Wrangell, Chugach, St. Elias, and Kenai Ranges. The Denali Park Road, Sheep Mountain on the Glenn Highway, and the Seward Highway along Turnagain Arm are three good areas to see them.

Other hoofers are found in various parts of the state. Mountain goats reach their northern territorial limit in the high southern crags of the Kenai, Chugach, and St. Elias Ranges, their goat-like faces and horns, shaggy white hair, and incomparable climbing ability distinguishing them from Dall sheep. Reindeer are essentially domestic caribou. They were brought to Alaska from points west and live in herds managed by Arctic Coast native peoples. Once extinct in the state, wild populations of shaggy musk ox can be seen on Nunivak Island and a few areas of the North Slope. A captive herd is kept for fur and breeding near Palmer. Bison are found in a managed herd near Delta Junction, while 1,200 elk roam Afognak and Raspberry Islands near Kodiak. Populations of the small Sitka black-tailed deer browse the wooded areas and mountainsides in the Southeast, Kodiak, and around Prince William Sound.

## BIRDS

When you see your fiftieth bald eagle perched atop a Sitka spruce, diving for fish in the harbor, or soaring over the channels of the Southeast, you *might* begin to take them for granted (I still don't). Eagles are most easily seen from a kayak or the deck of a boat in the sheltered waters of the Southeast, Prince William Sound, and Kenai Fjords. They can also be found within several miles of forested areas up into the Alaska Range, and even further north and west. They gather around late-run salmon streams as things begin to freeze up for an autumn feast—up to 4,000 can be found in or near the Alaska Chilkat Bald Eagle Reserve north of Haines from late September into December.

Other birds of prey include golden eagles, peregrine falcons, gyrfalcons, and hawks. Snowy owls can occasionally be seen perching regally or flying silently in the twilight. The scavenging,

opportunistic raven, the most widespread bird on the continent, is found in many terrains.

Fifty million migratory birds nest in Alaska, most on Pacific Ocean and Bering Sea islands, protected coastlands, or in the vast refuges of the Interior. Several types of geese are commonly seen, including Canada, snow, and emperor. The once rare Aleutian Canada goose, smaller cousin of the regular Canada goose, now thrives in the Southwest. Beautiful trumpeter swans, weighing upwards of 35 pounds, can be observed near Nome and along the Parks Highway and other roads. Many types of ducks are easily seen, including the spectacled eider.

Seabirds include the ubiquitous gulls, terns, murres, kittiwakes, and cormorants. Coastal ferries and tour boats offer good looks at rookeries that often host odd collections of reluctant neighbors. One of the more interesting residents is the puffin. With its colorful, triangular beak, bright orange feet, slicked-back white-streaked head feathers, and wave-dodging flight, they are very popular with wildlife viewers.

The willow ptarmigan is a common game bird. This none-too-bright bird needs the year-round camouflage it enjoys, its feathers

Paul Otteson

*Bear at Katmai National Park*

turning from mottled brown to pure white as the winter snows fly. Once seen, it's easy to get close enough to observe individuals or small groups, perhaps as one offers a mock broken-wing diversion, or a male displays his puffed-chest, cooing courtship dance. If you're driving, stay in your car. Ptarmigans, like many other animals, fear your vehicle far less than they fear you.

Many tour companies emphasize bird observation, some offering exclusive birding adventures. Details are offered in the regional chapters and appendix.

## SEA MAMMALS

Both gray whales and humpbacks reach the northern end of their annual migration in Alaska's waters. Grays come up from California to feed in coastal waters, while humpbacks arrive from Hawaii. The lucky traveler will see a whale breach, rising from the deep at great enough speed to lift its bulk completely from the water before it crashes again into the sea. It's an unforgettable sight.

Humpbacks are commonly seen rolling through the water by travelers in the Southeast, puffs of mist spouting from their blowholes. Typically, they spout three or four times before diving deep, exposing their unmistakable tail flukes as they do so. As baleen whales, they filter tiny krill out of the water, often driving them together in a spiraling tube of bubbles before rising through the tube with baleen exposed.

Minke whales are common in Alaska waters, as are killer whales or orcas. The 6-foot, black dorsal fins of a pod of killer whales (really members of the dolphin family) are an impressive and slightly disquieting sight, though they feed on fish and the occasional seal or otter, not on humans. White beluga whales (also really dolphins) are seen in large pods in the shallows of Cook Inlet where they live, presumably to avoid deep-water predators. Belugas are sometimes beached at low tide, usually with no ill effects. Bowhead whales are found in the Bering Sea and Arctic Ocean waters. Dall and harbor porpoises are commonly seen racing along in the bow waves of ferries or heading rapidly across a channel.

Seals are frequently observed bobbing in a harbor or lying about on rocks or beaches. Once-threatened fur seals are now strongly represented, with the biggest concentrations found on the remarkable Pribilof Islands in the Bering Sea. The still-threatened

Steller's sea lion hangs on in Alaska in moderate numbers, but suffers from competition with commercial fishers and does not yet enjoy stability. Walruses can be seen at several places along the Bering Coast, particularly in the Walrus Islands State Game Sanctuary (permit required) near Togiak on Bristol Bay. Sea otters, once hunted to near extinction, are now fairly common residents of the calmer waters along the south coast. A recent decline in their numbers has caused concern. Look for them floating on their backs in the waves, preening or cracking shellfish.

# FLORA

The vegetation patterns of Alaska are quite complex, but three basic categories dominate the Alaskan landscape: tundra, taiga or boreal forest, and coastal forest. The Alaska Field Office of the U.S. Geological Survey identifies 20 distinct "ecoregions" that demonstrate a unique combination of climate, landform, and vegetation. A view of the ecoregions is very helpful in understanding the details of vegetation and habitat of specific destinations. Complete information is available on-line at www-eros-afo.wr.usgs.gov/ecoreg/ecoregmap. html, or via the USGS (see appendix).

About half of Alaska is covered with tundra—mixed short vegetation featuring mosses, lichens, grasses, and dwarf shrubs. Alpine tundra is found above treeline in all of Alaska's mountain ranges, usually changing from thick scrub and deep spongy tundra to thinner, shorter plants on high slopes and ridges. Arctic tundra usually overlies permafrost. It varies in wetness, thickness, and plant profile due to a number of factors, including climate, soil, freeze-melt schedules, drainage, and elevation. The short growing season in tundra areas results in a sudden profusion of growth and blooming when summer arrives. Beautiful wildflower displays are characteristic of drier, higher zones.

Taiga or boreal forest is found throughout much of the Alaskan Interior, Matanuska-Susitna (known as "MatSu"), and the Copper River Basin. It is characterized by forests and groves of white spruce, black spruce, aspen, and birch, interspersed with tundra-topped hills, tundra plateaus, and wetland flats and bogs. Muskeg, a transitional vegetation zone between wetland and dryland, is essentially a tufty, wet peat bog that may support scraggly black spruce. Fire is important in shaping the distribution of vegetation in the taiga, with a natural succession of plants in burned zones proceeding from fireweed, through birch and aspen, and finally to spruce. The boreal forest grows to about 3,000 feet in elevation in the east, though the maximum elevation declines moving west and north toward treeline.

Alaska's coastal forest, dominated by Sitka spruce and western hemlock, is found in temperate, well-watered, and well-drained coastal regions from the panhandle through Prince William Sound, and as far west as Afognak and northern Kodiak Island. Rain-forest conditions exist in several areas unsheltered by mountains, with old-growth trees growing to great heights.

*Sailing near Juneau*

# SPECIAL INTERESTS AND ACTIVITIES

5

Alaska features museums (good ones), arts offerings, festivals, sports competitions, tram rides, and even a theme park of sorts (Alaskaland in Fairbanks), but most tour and travel offerings get you to the wildland and wildlife—sometimes wildly! Advanced-level rafting excursions will tumble you down a river. Flightseeing on a windy day offers a stomach-challenging roller-coaster ride. Floatplane bear viewing sets your heart racing as a thousand-pound brown swims by a dozen feet from where you stand.

The following sections introduce some of the wonderful alternatives on your Alaska menu. For information on outfitters for these activities, see the appendix.

## FISHING

About half the time I tell someone I'm going to Alaska, I am asked in return if I'm going fishing—with good reason! Alaska has amazingly rich fisheries and a well-managed balance of subsistence, commercial, and recreational fishing opportunities. Deep-sea, shoreline, river, and lake fishing can put you in close contact with the outdoors and with the spirit of Alaskans. Trout, grayling, arctic char, and others are common sport fish. Deep-sea halibut fishing is popular with the bold and strong of stomach.

The favorite Alaskan fish of all is the salmon. Five types return by the millions to clear running coastal streams and rivers on a clockwork schedule, spawning in the clean gravels of the shallows. Each type has two names to confuse the uninitiated:

**King/Chinook**—These biggest and least numerous of Alaskan salmon are found only in larger streams and rivers, arriving to spawn from late May through July. The Kenai is by far the river of choice, with other easily accessible runs found in the Susitna and Copper Rivers. Catching 30-plus pounders isn't uncommon—the largest ever caught was over 126 pounds.

**Silver/Coho**—Known for their activity and aggression, silvers pick up when king season fades, generally showing up to spawn in fresh water from July to October. They are found all along the Alaskan coast and occasionally reach 35 pounds.

**Pink/Humpback** ("humpies")—Rarely exceeding 10 pounds, humpies are the smallest of Alaska's salmon. They spawn from late June to mid-October, usually not far from saltwater.

**Red/Sockeye**—Reds are unique in their habit of spawning in streams that flow from lakes, or in lakes themselves. Their spawning runs go from late May to mid-August. Many consider reds to be the tastiest of them all.

**Chum/Dog**—Rarely taken by sport fishermen, chums are called dog salmon because of their traditional use in feeding the dogs. The best of the freshwater chum are found in the Yukon River.

To some extent, fishing disrupts the natural environment, threatening wild fish populations by introducing hatchery fish, degrading riverbanks and riparian habitat, and tampering with a food chain that ultimately supports bears, eagles, and sea mammals. Fortunately, Alaskan fisheries are rich and strong. Federal and state management practices are generally good and work to preserve a healthy food chain. When you watch brown bears gorge on salmon as, by the thousands, they flounder and die in the spawning streams, your impressions of this form of wildlife harvesting may change. Besides, hooking that 30-pounder is a blast!

## FRESHWATER SPORTS: CANOEING, KAYAKING, AND RAFTING

Lake and river adventuring continue to increase in popularity in Alaska, though only a few options offer road access for both put-ins and take-outs. Those that do are well served by guides and outfitters, while the legion of bush pilots operating throughout the state will drop you off or pick you up just about anywhere else—for a price.

There is a great tradition of exploring the backcountry of Alaska via lakes and rivers. "Canoe" and "kayak" are both Native American words, as well as original native watercraft. The kayak is the traditional Aleut craft, used in both rivers and coastal waters. The Yukon, Tanana, Kuskokwim, Kobuk, Noatak, and other rivers were commonly used by trappers and prospectors. Today, 26 National Wild and Scenic Rivers are designated in the state with more pending. Many of these and several other lake, river, and portage routes are well established and served by outfitters.

Whether you take a two-hour excursion or a multiday float trip, river rafting is a wonderful choice for those interested in guided whitewater fun. Numerous outfitters offer a variety of options, particularly on the upper reaches of rivers paralleled by roads. The most popular run is on the Nenana River near Denali National Park, which is served by a half-dozen rafting companies.

Specific watersports recommendations are found in the regional chapters while outfitters, tours, guides, and rental outlets are listed by region in the appendix. Public-lands managers often have listings of approved or recommended guides and outfitters for areas within parks, preserves, refuges, and forest lands. It is highly recommended that you consult them directly when planning a trip.

## FLIGHTSEEING

One of the best ways to get a good look at the wonders of Alaska is from the air—and dozens of small and medium-size flying services will take you just about anywhere you want to go. In the main tourist areas, pilots fly regular routes with optimal viewing and you pick from a menu of standard tours of varying lengths. For custom tours, one-way bush flights, drop-offs, and pick-ups, fees are usually based on an hourly rate—typically from $200 to $400 per hour. If you tag along on a mail or supply flight, you may pay a standardized "seat rate" ranging upwards from 25 percent of the equivalent hourly plane rate. Flying in the Alaskan bush is pricey.

But it's worth it! Imagine soaring between the 5,000-foot walls of the Great Gorge over 50-mile-long Ruth Glacier, breaking out into the open over the vast icefield of the Don Sheldon Amphitheater,

and gazing at the suddenly visible Denali—so close you can touch it. You have no sense of scale until you spot the tiny tents of mountaineers clustered on the snow. Then the pilot circles and drops, setting the plane down on skis. You step out into the icy wilderness—for five minutes or five days—splendid indeed!

Helicopter flightseeing is a relatively new and expanding opportunity. In a helicopter, you get a great view and the chance to observe wildlife without flying in a fast circle. The hourly rate for a helicopter is in the same expensive range as that for planes. Read about heli-hiking in the Hiking section below—it's a great way to access the high ridges without working at it.

Good pilots love what they do—and to fly in the Alaskan bush, pilots have to be good. Piloting ski- and floatplanes requires special certification, while landing on riverside gravel bars takes guts and experience. You can count on being flown by a competent, interested pilot who will gladly point out wildlife and special features of the landscape. Your interest and courtesy will be appreciated and responded to. Some of the flights I've taken have been better than others, but all have been rewarding. Air services are listed by region in the appendix.

## HIKING AND BACKPACKING

Wilderness travelers on land can choose from hundreds of lonely valleys, trackless ridges, miles-long glaciers, and unnamed summits for everything from half-day hikes to summer-long treks—though comparatively few miles of developed trails exist in the state. Because of this, the longer routes that do exist are relatively heavily traveled. The great majority of trails are less than 10 miles long; many are only two or three. Several are concentrated near Anchorage, Fairbanks, on the Kenai Peninsula, near Palmer and Cordova, close to Juneau, and elsewhere in the Southeast. Areas with one or two longer trails or old roads of note include the Wrangells, Denali State Park, and the White Mountains north of Fairbanks. The Chilkoot Trail near Skagway follows the historic gold-rush route over Chilkoot Pass and into Canada. Huge parks like Denali and Gates of the Arctic in the Brooks Range are almost pathless.

Walkers in regions without trails have used natural alternatives successfully for thousands of years. River gravel bars offer routes of variable utility through forested and wet tundra country in the foothills. Exposed ridges and other well-drained tundra or grassland

Anchorage Convention and Visitors Bureau

*Explore Alaskan backcountry by raft.*

terrain is often simple to traverse, especially since it's easy to see landmarks and select routes wisely. Brushy areas get more difficult to cross as the vegetation thickens in the summer. Glacier and ice-field walking requires skill, equipment, and care, but often allows relatively easy passage to marvelous high-country locations. When snow is on the ground, the land opens up in all directions for cross-country skiers, snowshoers, and snowmobilers.

As with other options, access is often the biggest hurdle to back-country exploration. Some great but expensive options enable hikers and backpackers to pick their zone of choice with few hassles.

## HELI-HIKING AND DROP-OFFS

With so much of Alaska inaccessible by road, the only way to explore it on foot is to get dropped off at a remote location, then picked up at a later date. Sometimes, a road can be at one end or the other of a hike, making only one air or boat shuttle necessary, but for many areas and schedules, two shuttles are required. Boat, airplane, and helicopter are the three choices.

Boat shuttles on navigable rivers are usually used by hunters, fishers, and visitors to remote towns and villages, especially in the Interior along the Yukon and its feeders. The bottomlands along rivers are often boggy and thickly vegetated, making them poor choices for beginning or ending a hiking trip. On the other hand, kayakers can enjoy a three-day trip down the wild Charley River, flying into a drop-off point, then getting picked up at the point where the Charley meets the Yukon for an upriver boat shuttle to Eagle.

Small-plane drop-offs and pick-ups are a particularly good idea for very remote hikes in areas like the Brooks Range. A bush pilot will fly you to a small airstrip, lake, glacier, or gravel bar, dropping off you and your gear. By arrangement, the same pilot or company will pick you up days later. Your task is to show up at the pick-up spot at the scheduled hour. There are, of course, safety and rescue contingencies followed by pilots in case you aren't where you are supposed to be on time. Several walking routes involve hiking to or from a town or highway, making only one air or water shuttle necessary, thus cutting the cost in half.

Heli-hiking is an expanding opportunity. Shuttling to the beginning point of a hike via helicopter opens up many more possibilities for routes, though helicopter mileage range is limited in comparison to planes. A helicopter can set you down in high-country meadows, lake basins, and ridgetops—the best places to land for lofty day hikes and longer-term, well-supplied base camping. Many companies have great suggestions and flight packages that are within the range of those with moderate to high budgets.

## SEA KAYAKING

A marvelous choice for exploring the ins and outs of the Alaskan coastline is to venture forth in a sea kayak. For every area you might want to put-in and explore, there will be a rental and/or guided-trip company to set you up. Drop-off and pick-up plans can get you into the most remote and beautiful stretches. Though some skill is required, the many sheltered waters of Alaska's coast offer wonderful options for the novice. Sea kayaks on calm waters are markedly easier to manage than their riverine kin.

The best-loved kayak areas all offer plenty of opportunity for solitude, though in peak season in popular areas, kayakers may find it hard to get away from cruise ships and tour boats. The parks and wilderness areas of the Southeast probably get the thickest traffic. Other popular areas are found in Icy Bay, Prince William Sound, Kenai Fjords, and Kachemak Bay. There are maintained campsites and reservable wilderness cabins in a variety of public lands. Elsewhere, secluded beaches, meadow margins, and openings in the trees abound.

Most of the following locations are well served by guides and rental companies. All offer outstanding scenic settings and wildlife-viewing opportunities. Locations are followed by towns that serve as the best bases for exploration.

### Southeast
Misty Fiords National Monument/Ketchikan
Stikine-Leconte Wilderness/Petersburg
Admiralty Island National Monument/Juneau
Tracy Arm–Fords Terror Wilderness/Juneau
South Baranof Wilderness/Sitka
West Chichagof-Yakobi Wilderness/Sitka
Glacier Bay National Park and Preserve/Gustavus
Yakutat Bay and Russell Fiord Wilderness/Yakutat
### Southcentral
Columbia Glacier (Prince William Sound)/Valdez
College Fjord (Prince William Sound)/Whittier Icy Bay/Yakutat/
Kenai Fjords National Park/Seward
Kachemak Bay/Homer
### Southwest
Kodiak National Wildlife Refuge/Kodiak
Katmai National Park (south coast)/Kodiak

With an official 33,904 miles of coastline (80 percent around islands), most of which is rugged and much of it sheltered, the possibilities are endless—you can find any number of gorgeous spots to be totally alone with eagles, whales, bears, and glaciers. Regional chapters describe options and the appendix lists outfitters, tour providers, and rental companies.

Be aware that travelers by sea sometimes take their interface with land a bit too casually, particularly with regard to bears. In many areas, grizzlies browse the shoreline for food and use the relatively open margins along the sea for transit. As with any bear area, it is not likely that a clean camp with chatty, smelly (to a

bear) people will be of interest to a grizzly, but don't let your sea and glacier adventure dull you to land-based precautions.

On the Arctic Coast, polar bears come ashore in numbers in the summer and may be attracted by the smells associated with cooking, hunting, and garbage disposal. Keep that kayak camp clean and talk with experts about your plans!

## TRAIL RIDES AND HORSEPACKING

Outfitters for horseback riding are often found near tourist centers such as Denali, or associated with backcountry lodges. Many are oriented toward serving hunters and fishers, providing remote access, pack animals, and an adventure in the pioneer spirit. More and more, however, horsepack trips are designed for campers and wildlife observers, as are shorter rides, from an hour or two to all day. Most available rides are guided, though renting horses may be possible.

Remember that riding a horse is not like riding a bus. If you're not used to horses, proceed with caution. Explain your novice status to the outfitter in all humility to make sure you get that reliable old beast that plods along like a Toyota on the hoof.

## WILDERNESS STAYS: LODGES AND BACKCOUNTRY CABINS

A growing number of people are enjoying stays in cabins and lodges miles from the nearest road or town. With a secure base of operations, you can enjoy days of in-your-face wilderness experience, retreating to a place of comfort when the hour grows late and your bones need rest.

Wilderness lodges are run like inns and have various features. Many offer package deals handled by the lodge, a tour company, or travel agents, and fly their patrons and supplies to a nearby lake, cove, river, or landing strip. They are always rustic and casual, and meals, service, and a range of optional activities are typically provided. Some lodges are associated with specific pursuits, like hunting, fishing, or bear viewing. Other offerings include horsepacking, hikes, bird watching, glacier access, northern-lights viewing (winter), or just plain relaxing. Some can be used as destinations, supply stops, or starting points for river travel, sea kayaking, or hikes. A few backcountry lodges are noted in the regional chapters while others are listed in the appendix.

The National Forest Service, National Park Service, Bureau of Land Management, and Alaska Department of Natural Resources (Alaska State Parks and Wilderness Parks) all maintain backcountry cabins, most of which are very cheap to rent. Though they vary somewhat, they are typically one- or two-room rustic boxes located at or near a water source. Cabins come equipped with bunks, an outhouse, and a wood or fuel stove. They can be reserved for a block of time through the appropriate agency, and the more popular ones are booked well in advance during peak times. Most cabin locations are associated with plane landing sites and walking or water routes. They range in price from free to $45 a night or so. You'll find more detailed information in the regional chapters.

Cabins in the Tongass and Chugach National Forests can be reserved with a credit card by calling (877) 444-6777 (toll-free call), via www.reserveusa.com, or at a number of forest service visitor centers and district offices (see appendix). Tongass cabin information is available at www.fs.fed.us/r10/tongass/recreation/cabin_ info/ cabin_info.html. Check on Tongass cabin availability by calling 586-8751. Call 271-2737 for Chugach cabin availability information.

Eight national wildlife refuge cabins are found on Kodiak Island, all usually reached by floatplane. Visit www.nps.gov/aplic/ cabins/nwr_cabins.html for information. Reserve through: Kodiak National Wildlife Refuge, 1390 Buskin Road, Kodiak, AK 99615, 487-2600.

The Bureau of Land Management maintains cabins in the White Mountains near Fairbanks. Contact the BLM Land Information Center, 1150 University Avenue, Fairbanks, AK 99709, 474-2250.

Three National Park Service cabins are located along the coast of Kenai Fjords National Park. Visit www.nps.gov/aplic/cabins/ nps_cabins.html for information. For reservations and information, contact Kenai Fjords National Park, P.O. Box 1727, Seward, AK 99664, 224-3175.

Visit www.nutmeg.state.ak.us/ixpress/dnr/parks/index.dml to learn about the more than 40 cabins maintained by the state of Alaska. Reservations can be made through the DNR Public Information Center, 3601 "C" Street, Suite 200, Anchorage, AK 99503, 269-8400; or in person at several regional offices.

*A DC-3 prepares for takeoff.*

# NORTH TO THE 49TH STATE

6

Many visitors fly to Alaska, but the magic of the north doesn't begin at the state border. The Canadian provinces of Alberta, British Columbia, and the Yukon offer wildlife, scenery, and history of their own, as do the states of the northern and western United States. Because of this, others make the excellent choice of reaching Alaska via the Earth's surface. It can be done by car, bus, ferry, and, in part, by train. These four modes of transport may be combined in several ways. Alaska is best appreciated when you sense its remoteness by taking the long road to get there.

## GETTING TO AND AROUND ALASKA

When it was first constructed in 1942, the Alaska Highway (once known as the Alcan) was a slow, gravel road, intended for military convoys and supply trucks. Roadhouses and service stations were few and far between. Travelers needed to carry extra gas cans, two or more spare tires, and survival gear. Various screens and panels were used to protect headlights and windshields from destruction by flying gravel thrown up by passing trucks. Personal vehicles

ready for an Alaska journey often resembled a cross between an armored personnel carrier and the Beverly Hillbillies' truck.

Today, the primary route to Alaska is all but completely paved. Nowhere will you have to go more than a hundred miles between fueling points (except at night and in the winter). On many segments, tight curves have been smoothed and lanes have been widened. The traffic is thick enough with good-hearted people that your chances of getting stranded are slim. For a long time, the Alaska Highway was the only driving route to Alaska. Today it's possible to drive to Anchorage almost completely via alternate and equally wonderful routes, all of which offer plenty of scenic beauty and long miles.

"Progress" aside, a drive to Alaska should not be taken lightly. The miles are long and still quite empty. Carrying two spare tires (or at least a can of a fix-a-flat product) and a 5-gallon gas can is prudent. A heedless moose can still trundle onto the road and end your trip. Perhaps the biggest consideration is the amount of time it takes to reach Anchorage—four long days from Seattle, eight from Miami. If you plan to drive round trip, you'll want to allot at least three to four weeks for the whole journey.

## ALASKAN ROADS

Not much changes when you reach Alaska—except perhaps that you drive a little more slowly and stop more often. There are numerous towns and roadhouses that offer lodging. An extensive network of state recreation sites and areas offers public camping, as do the larger parks and private businesses. Highway services and vehicle repair are found at reasonable intervals on main routes. Just never forget that you are in Alaska, and that an 800-pound grizzly is no friendlier looking for a burger in a campground than it is in the middle of nowhere. Keep a clean camp and watch your pets and kids.

You may want to put a ferry link into your car tour. In the Southeast, the mainland highway system connects with the Alaska Marine Highway System ferries in Prince Rupert, Hyder, Skagway, and Haines. Prince William Sound, the Southwest, and the Aleutians can be accessed from Valdez, Whittier (via the train shuttle), Seward, and Homer—though there's little reason to take your vehicle to the Southwest. A new once-a-month ferry now links the Southeast with Prince William Sound and points west.

You can rent cars in many places, but the option is particularly

# Milepost Guides

*In rural Alaska (which is most of Alaska), addresses and locations are commonly expressed in relation to the closest highway mileage point as measured in tenths of miles. Thus, the Chistochina Trading Post can be found at Mile 32 of the Tok Cutoff, while the Clam Gulch State Recreation Area is located at Mile 117.4 of the Sterling Highway. Alaska's most famous vehicle travel guide,* The Milepost, *charts every turnout, viewpoint, and bump in the road in milepost order.*

*In the regional chapters of this book, every major road route outside of a metropolitan area is described in milepost fashion with roadside accommodations and attractions listed in ascending order of the highway mileage point where they're located. Obviously, if you're driving in the opposite direction—counting down the mileposts—you'll need to read these sections in reverse. As a supplement to these listings, you should carry the Alaska Atlas and Gazetteer, published by DeLorme Mapping and available at many map and bookstores, particularly in the western United States.*

valuable away from the main highway grid in places with small road systems like Ketchikan, Kodiak, and Nome. Some travelers fly to Anchorage and rent a car or small RV. See the appendix for rental-company listings.

## FLIGHTS

Alaska Airlines is the primary carrier serving Alaska. Numerous routes link all of the important towns and cities within the state, while several flights daily connect Alaska with points throughout the western United States. Teamed with partner Horizon Air, excellent connections are possible to and through Alaska from scores of points throughout the west. Alaska Airlines also offers a variety of tours and packages, including a number of excellent winter options. Visit www.alaskaairlines.com or call (800) 426-0333 for reservations and information.

The best routing and scheduling from the midwestern and eastern United States is offered by Northwest Airlines, www.nwa.com, (800) 225-2525. Northwest and partner KLM have great international routing, while Alaska, Horizon, Northwest, and KLM also have a frequent flyer mileage-sharing agreement.

Other carriers with a flight to Alaska include Delta, United, Continental, and Reno Air. Reeve Aleutian Airways makes a great alternative for flights in the Southwest. PennAir, Era, and smaller companies complete the picture (see appendix for complete listings).

## RAIL TRAVEL

Rail travel has always been a favorite of mine. Gaze out the window as you relax with a sandwich and cool drink in the lounge car. The world rolls by outside as the rhythmic rocking and clacking melts anxiety to nothing. Though you cannot travel by rail all the way from the lower 48 to Alaska, there are several links that can be incorporated in a larger scheme.

Amtrak routes can be linked with Canadian rail routes at several points. From Seattle, the Mt. Baker runs once-daily to Vancouver, as do three Amtrak Thruway buses. All stop in Bellingham, enabling rail travelers to connect directly with the once-weekly ferry to Ketchikan, Juneau, and other points. From the Rockies and upper midwest, you must put a bus link in your itinerary to hook up with Canadian trains, perhaps motoring from Shelby, Missouri, to Edmonton, or Grand Forks, North Dakota, to Winnepeg. U.S.– Canada rail connections in the east are possible from New York to Montreal via the Adirondak, from New York to Toronto via the Maple Leaf, and from Chicago to Toronto via the International.

All run once-daily; other connections are possible by including an Amtrak Thruway bus link. Call (800) USA-RAIL for information, or visit Amtrak's website at www.amtrak.com.

Canada's **VIA Rail** offers the Canadian, which runs three times per week from Toronto to Vancouver, passing through Winnipeg, Saskatoon, Edmonton, Jasper, and Kamloops—though not Calgary— on the way. Call (888) 842-7245 for Via Rail bookings (free call), or visit the Via Rail website at www.viarail.ca for information and reservations.

**VIA Rail** offers the Skeena through Prince George to Prince Rupert from the junction with the trans-Canada line in Jasper. **B.C.**

**Rail**'s "Caribou Prospector" runs from North Vancouver to Prince George, (800) 663-8238 outside B.C., (800) 339-8752 in B.C., www.bcrail.com/bcr. The two trains only run three days a week, but have coordinated schedules enabling an efficient trip between Vancouver and the ferry connections at Prince Rupert. Trains leave Sunday, Wednesday, and Friday morning for the 36-hour trip, including 10 hours for an overnight and train switch in Prince George. The Caribou Prospector one-way fare is $200 including meals, while the VIA train from Prince George to Prince Rupert is $70 to $90 economy and $190 "totem class" including meals.

The tracks of the Alaska Railroad run from Seward to Fairbanks. Every morning from mid-May to mid-September, a train departs Fairbanks for Anchorage, and Anchorage for Fairbanks, both stopping along the way in Denali Park, Talkeetna, and Wasilla. Several other flag stops are possible. The one-way fare from Anchorage to Denali is $102 ($84 in shoulder season). Anchorage to Fairbanks is $154 ($120 shoulder), while Fairbanks to Denali is $54 ($44 shoulder). Both trains depart at 8:15 a.m. and arrive at 8:15 p.m.

The southbound Coastal Classic departs Anchorage for the 4 ½-hour trip through Portage to Seward at 6:45 a.m. It then departs Seward for the return at 6 p.m. ($50 one-way, $86 round-trip). The same train becomes the Seward Swing for a midday Seward-Portage-Seward round-trip (departs 11:30 a.m. from Seward, 2:45 p.m. from Portage; $34 one-way, $60 round-trip). A new train, the Glacier Discovery, departs Anchorage for Whittier at 9 a.m. (departs Whittier on the return at 5:45 p.m.; $26 one-way, $52 round-trip). With the opening of the new road, the auto-shuttle trains between Portage and the ferry pier at Whittier are ceasing regular operation.

For further information contact the Alaska Railroad Corporation, 411 West 1st Avenue, Anchorage, AK 99501, (800) 544-0552, 265-2494, www.akrr.com, reservations@akrr.com.

## BUS TRAVEL

**Greyhound** can connect you via any number of routes in the United States and Canada, getting you as far as Whitehorse in the Yukon, or Prince Rupert, British Columbia. From Prince Rupert you can catch an A.M.H.S. ferry, while from Whitehorse, the Yukon & White Pass Railroad offers a bus/train trip to Skagway (see Skagway in chapter 7); or you can connect with Gray Line's

Alaskon Express (see below). Greyhound offers a variety of packages and passes that might save you money. For information and reservations for the United States and Canada, call (800) 231-2222 or visit their website at www.greyhound.com. For information on Greyhound Canada alone, call (800) 661-8747 or visit the Greyhound Canada website at bus.greyhound.ca.

Greyhound does not serve Alaska; however, **Gray Line of Alaska**, (800) 544-2206, carries fare-paying passengers as well as the package-tour variety. Their Alaskon Express buses run from Skagway or Haines to Fairbanks or Anchorage for around $200—less for points between. Eastbound buses leave at 7:30 a.m. on Sunday, Tuesday, and Friday; westbound at 7:30 a.m. Sunday, Tuesday, and Thursday. The buses stop for the night in Beaver Creek (accommodations extra). Alaskon Express can be linked with Greyhound in Whitehorse.

For connections to the B.C. Ferries terminal in Port Hardy or B.C. Rail Station in North Vancouver, contact Greyhound.

## FERRY TRAVEL

The best way to travel to and through coastal Alaska is undoubtedly via the ferries of the **Alaska Marine Highway System**. You can catch the ferry in Bellingham, Washington, 80 miles north of Seattle, for a three-day ride to the highway connections in Haines or Skagway. Many people who drive to Alaska catch the ferry in Prince Rupert, B.C., thus saving some money and enjoying British Columbia by road. In May of 1998, the A.M.H.S. initiated monthly service between the Southeast and Prince William Sound, making it possible to travel by sea all the way from Bellingham to Unalaska and Dutch Harbor in the Aleutian Islands.

The ferry is a great alternative to cruise ships and tour boats. Though ferries don't normally go out of their way for scenic spots, there are some notable exceptions. In the Southeast, ships pass through several narrow channels where seals, otters, eagles, and porpoises can be seen. In Prince William Sound, the Valdez to Whittier route stops in the mouth of Columbia Bay for a long look toward Columbia Glacier. Almost anywhere along the ferry routes, captains will point out whales and other wildlife sightings, occasionally shifting course or slowing down to allow better viewing.

Budget ferry travelers can buy a basic fare, then sleep in the recliners, on the floor, or—best of all—on the upper deck under the

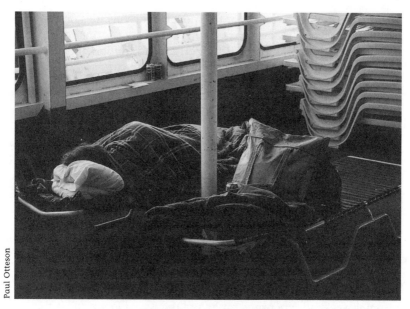

Paul Otteson

*Napping on the Alaska Rail*

stars or in the solarium. Deck chairs fold flat into comfortable cots. Just position yourself away from doors and foot traffic and let the thrumming engines ease you to sleep.

Those with bigger budgets can reserve full-service cabin accommodations and enjoy relative luxury while their vehicle relaxes on the car deck. When comparing the cost of the total ferry experience to that of driving or flying, make sure to include the scenic and relaxation value in the equation. If you like nothing better than gazing over deck rails or out observation windows as the world unfolds before you, the ferries are for you. For current fares, schedules, and reservations, contact the Alaska Marine Highway System, (800) 642-0066, fax (907) 277-4829, www.dot.state.ak.us/external/amhs/home.html

Some of British Columbia's coastal B.C. Ferries routes might be of interest. A ferry leaves Port Hardy on Vancouver Island for Prince Rupert every other day while the A.M.H.S. from Bellingham only runs once a week. Port Hardy can be reached via Greyhound from Victoria (see Bus Travel, above). Victoria, in turn, can be reached by B.C. Ferries from Vancouver or private service from Seattle. It should be noted that Victoria is one of the most wonderful cities on the continent and is worth a day or two itself.

Call (604) 669-1211 for B.C. Ferries information and reservations, or visit their website at www.bcferries.bc.ca.

# WHEN TO GO

The rhythms of the Far North reach extremes that distinctly shape the travel and tour season. In May, young people begin arriving to work in the many businesses that are all but closed through the long winter. Most climbers schedule summit attempts in May and June—the short window between winter weather and avalanche season. Booking for cruises, ecotours, scenic flights, ferry tickets, and hotel rooms rise and fall in a bell curve, starting from near zero in early May, peaking to sold out in July and August, and dropping back to nothing by the end of September.

If you wish to fish (or to avoid the fishing crowds), early- to midsummer weekends are prime times and the Kenai Peninsula is the main location. These are also good times to view bears that concentrate along certain falls and cascades to enjoy their own salmon harvest. To avoid active hunting, inquire about the carefully managed seasons, most of which occur after August.

Though almost all highways to and through Alaska stay open yearround, harsh conditions and the closure of many roadside businesses make off-season driving in several areas problematic. The ferries run less frequently from fall through spring, and most backcountry lodges are boarded up seven or eight months of the year. Flightseeing companies shut down and bush pilots face harsher conditions.

Travelers can face difficult weather in the off season, but the most noteworthy feature of the winter months is that it gets dark! On September 22, every place on Earth has a 12-hour day and a 12-hour night. On September 23, Fairbanks has 11 hours and 53 minutes of sunshine; on the 24th, it's 11 hours and 46 minutes. Hang around for nine days, and you lose an hour! By the time the winter holidays roll around, the sun in Fairbanks makes only a reluctant appearance, teasing the hem of the sky from about 10:30 a.m. to 1:30 p.m. then disappearing again. The lingering dawn and twilight are little consolation.

Only the rare traveler will opt to experience Alaska's winter wonders, but it might be wise for all visitors to avoid the tour-heavy months of July and August. Consider the shoulder season for your visit, particularly the late summer and very early fall. In early September, availability of rooms and tours is on the rise and prices are dropping. Ferries and flights into the state are easy to book. The mosquitoes and the other biting bugs are fading fast, and the fall colors in parts of the Southcentral and Interior regions are spectacular. Areas where hunting is in progress are poor choices for backcountry exploration at this time, but most of the national parks and many other key destinations are free of the activity.

# PACK SMART

Beyond the most obvious items—camera and binoculars—functionality should take precedence when packing for an Alaskan journey. Highly variable weather conditions and the wide range of possible outdoor activities call for a broad but thoughtful approach.

Although Alaska has civilized centers of population, it can often be inconvenient and sometimes impossible to find a needed piece of equipment. Smaller towns have more available than you might expect, but key items may be out of stock for days at a time—especially if supplies arrive only by air or sea.

If you are planning to get completely away from supply points for a time, you'll want to plan with great care. Make sure you know exactly what a guide or outfitter supplies. Check with backcountry lodges about what you should bring before you climb into the bush plane. Self-contained backpackers and kayakers should use a comprehensive checklist to assure preparedness.

## CLOTHING

Alaska can be wet, windy, and chilly at any time of the year. Choose activity-related gear that is rugged and casual. Very few establishments expect any kind of formal, or even business-level, garb from their patrons. Scuffed boots and grubby Gore-Tex are de rigueur in the finest hotel lobbies (both of them).

The best approach is to think in layers. Have a fleece to go over your flannel when the wind blows and a waterproof jacket to go over the fleece when it's wet. If you're pushing the edges of the travel season, or planning high-altitude or Far North travel, add another warm layer, plus gloves, stocking cap, and long underwear. In the summers, expect rain at anytime along the coast and in the mountains; moderate temperatures near the sea; extended warm spells in the Interior; wind in the Aleutians, Arctic Coast, and North Slope; and crisp nights everywhere.

Alaska is at its best when the weather is wild. Pack smart so you aren't driven indoors against your will. On the other hand, the summer can bring hot weather.

Consider, too, the lowly mosquito and its various biting cousins, including flies, gnats, and no-see-ums. They appear in the spring and fade in the fall, but seem to rise from the dead to find your exposed skin, even in the off season. They're found everywhere in Alaska, except over snow and ice, though they're densest in or near boggy areas. Baggy pants and a loose, long-sleeved shirt over a T-shirt provide good protection. Long hair and a hat help head and neck, as does a careful dose of DEET. Some folks like a hat with a veil of mosquito netting. Other swear by Avon's Skin-So-Soft as repellent. Alaska has no ticks, poison ivy or oak, dangerous spiders, or snakes (or any reptiles for that matter).

Footwear is very important. Hiking boots are a good choice. Both on and off trail, wet, boggy, and muddy conditions are common—fully waterproof rubber boots or a pair of waterproof hiking boots should be basic gear. At the least, plan on maintaining the water-shedding qualities of your boots with appropriate surface treatment. A second pair of walking or athletic shoes are good for general knocking about. Backpackers may want to carry Tevas or another type of rubber sandal for crossing the many streams and rivers. Gaiters keep mud and debris out of boot tops and keep pant legs dry.

## CAMPING GEAR

Selecting camping gear involves three notable considerations—cold, wet, and mosquitoes. When deciding what to pack, make sure you have adequate protection against all three.

Cold is the toughest thing to plan for, since it may not be—cold, that is. Every night of your five-day trek through the Alaska Range may be mild, even balmy—or may not. When combined, your tent, sleeping bag, pad, and clothes should be warm enough for 30°F to 40°F nights, even in mid-summer. On the other hand, a well-ventilated tent and light, breathable bedding can enable a good

## Alaskans: Your Greatest Travel Resource

*Imagine, if you will, the difficulty of documenting a state with fewer road miles than Vermont and fewer residents than Columbus, Ohio, but as large as six Nevadas. As you drive or ferry through the state on your way from noted location A to noted location B, you will pass by hundreds, even thousands of square miles of unreferenced wilderness. The organized words in this book will get you informatively from A to B, but only on-site investigation can reveal the mysteries of the wildest of wild Alaska.*

*Talk to Alaskans! They are used to the idea that fierce independence is best sustained by mutual support. Everywhere you go, someone will know about that peak or river or will know someone else who does. They have fished and hunted the land, walked the ridges and riverbanks, canoed the backwaters and snowmobiled among the spruce trees. Each has a turf and territory they know well—that is not a "wilderness" to them. The adventurous explorer who doesn't learn from those who've gone before is foolish. And in the wilderness of Alaska, foolishness can be very costly indeed.*

night's sleep when it's warm or rainy. Car travelers can pack a variety of stuff; backpackers should plan carefully.

Preparing for rain and dampness shouldn't be taken lightly. If you and your gear get wet on a long hike and the evening turns chilly, anything from discomfort to hypothermia can result. At the least, make sure that you can get into a dry sleeping bag that will stay dry throughout the night in a tent or bivvy sack. Better yet, make sure your headgear, outerwear, footgear, and pack cover all repel water efficiently.

Be prepared for a little gnat known descriptively as the no-see-um. Old-style netting, as well as the screening and netting still found in some vehicles, cheap backpack tents, and family-style tents

will not keep them out. Make sure that there is a layer of no-see-um netting between your sleeping skin and the world outside.

The other thing to be aware of is the sly speed of mosquitoes. Crack a car window for 30 seconds to take a picture and 20 relentless mosquitoes might slip in. Make sure to keep your tent screening closed *completely* and *at all times* so you don't spend your first night-time hours hunting the villains with a flashlight.

A fourth consideration is specific to certain regions, but is nonetheless vital: wind. Winds can be fierce enough to blow down many types of tents, as well as blow body heat away and rain into your sleeves. The best-known wind areas are the exposed, relatively flat areas of the ocean coasts (Aleutians, Arctic Coast, North Slope), high mountain areas, and certain other areas where sweeping slopes, valleys, and lowlands seem to concentrate the breeze, particularly in non-forested terrain. Consult the appropriate area expert when devising backcountry and sea-kayak routes.

# COST

Make no mistake, travel to and through Alaska is generally more expensive than anywhere else in the United States—in part because the cost of living is among the highest, but mainly because most tour and travel options are logistically "big." The next destination on a high-budget itinerary is often many miles from the previous place, and your group has to fly there and back in a plane that costs $300 per hour. Food, lodging, and provisions in remote locations can rise in price to double what you're used to (and beyond). If money is an issue and you'll be covering a lot of miles, plan your itinerary one fare, fee, and rate at a time.

The flip side of this is that Alaska is a great place to just "be." If you stick around a town or park for a few days, the cost of moving around is diminished. In the heavily traveled areas of the state, food and lodging may actually seem cheaper because so much of it is rustic. Along the highways, hitchhiking is easy (though not officially endorsed by this author), camping ranges from free to competitive, gas and groceries are 10 to 20 percent above average, and park admissions are the same you'd see anywhere. If you stay out of small planes and near the road, you can stretch those dollars with great success.

## SEASONAL WORK

There are numerous opportunities for those who want to work to support their trip. The jobs tend to be menial, but pay relatively well. Fish canneries, for example, are always looking for people (in season). See the appendix for state and local information contacts.

The bold might consider a better-paying job working on a fishing boat. Openings, however, can be hard to find. Statistically, crewing is also by far the most dangerous of all seasonal work and the quality of employers varies widely.

The major hotel and tour companies hire many employees for the summer. One of the biggest concentrations of jobs is in the "town" of McKinley Park—a short commercial stretch along the George Parks Highway a mile north of the Denali National Park entrance. Princess Cruise Lines and Aramark both operate large hotels, and there are several smaller operations. Summer employees receive low wages for various types of unskilled and semi-skilled work. Cheap room-and-board contracts are offered.

There are several advantages to working in the tourist industry. Some jobs are interesting, such as assisting with rafting trips or crewing on a tour boat. Many young people and outdoor enthusiasts are concentrated in tourist areas as employees, thus providing great opportunities for friendship, adventure, and partying.

Volunteering and service opportunities also exist. The great advantage of maintaining a trail, assisting in a native village, helping on an archaeological dig, or teaching with Elderhostel is in the people you meet and work with.

# PARKS, PRESERVES, REFUGES, AND DESIGNATED WILDERNESS

A truly unique blend of ownership, land use, and surface and mineral rights is found among the public lands of Alaska. Many designated federal areas are shown on maps as contiguous, but in reality have significant inclusions of private, state, or native lands. This is particularly true of certain national wildlife refuges, most notably the Yukon National Wildlife Refuge, which includes vast tracts of native corporation lands. Though the lands are so wild and empty as to make the point almost moot, travelers should not expect all public land areas to be pristine, or even unpopulated.

National preserves are almost unique to Alaska. The designation was created as way of adding and expanding national parklands while maintaining  traditional use patterns. Many things are allowed in preserves which are generally forbidden in parks, including hunting and motorized-vehicle access. In fact, other than enhanced management and administration, nothing has really changed on many of these lands. Indeed, subsistence hunting is still allowed in certain parts of national parks—something you would never see in the lower 48.

Designated wilderness areas are found in national parks, preserves, wildlife refuges, and forests. Here again, the designation often means something very different than what it means in other states. Hunting is often allowed, as are certain types of motorized-vehicle access. Cabins and a few backcountry lodges are located in a number of wilderness areas. Again, expect the boundaries on the map to mean less in Alaska than they may elsewhere.

# FOOD AND LODGING, ALASKA STYLE

In general, accommodations in Alaska are a notch below what you'll find elsewhere. There are very few luxury hotels, and even the best of them host primarily a business or cruise-tourist clientele. Midgrade chain or independent motels are found in Anchorage, Fairbanks, Juneau, and a few other large towns. Smaller communities and tourist centers generally feature independent accommodations that are basic at best, though Alaskan moteliers keep the sheets as clean as anywhere else. Reservations are strongly recommended statewide during July and August. The rate ranges described in the listings were accurate at the time of publication. Note that many areas have additional bed taxes of up to 10 percent.

In remote locations and areas where seasonal workers need housing, you may find lodgings that utilize "Atco units"—essentially pre-fab boxes akin to mobile homes. Atco units are delivered to remote locations by truck, ship, and even large snowmachine. They can be linked like dominoes and even stacked to provide the basic cubic footage that can then be jazzed up into a motel.

# Area Code 907

*The area code for all of Alaska is 907. In the following sections, any number without the area code noted is a 907 number.*

Alaska has, perhaps, more bed-and-breakfast choices per capita than anywhere else in the nation. Many B&Bs are family homes, operating only during the travel season. Most are rustic or "family-style." Commonly, only one or two rooms are available, and guests may cross paths with junior and the family dog. Because of the sheer number of B&B offerings, especially in popular destinations, chapters include a central reservation number wherever B&Bs have banded together.

For a true Holy Grail–type quest, try looking for fine cuisine in the 49th state. The restaurants in Anchorage and Juneau aside, your finds will be truly rare. Even in the major centers, the best of the best would be no more than average elsewhere. As for most roadhouse-grade grub, it hearkens back to the Route 66 truck-stop fare of yore. On the other hand, the splendid simplicity of hearty food fits Alaska perfectly.

## ROADHOUSES

Once common along Alaska's transport routes, roadhouses offered travelers every needed service under one roof. Lodging, a bar, a restaurant, a store, and later, gas, were typically available at these isolated, oases, often located an average day's travel from one another. While today's "average day's travel" makes many roadhouses obsolete, they persist in both actuality and spirit throughout the state—though the word "roadhouse" may not appear on any sign. There are still many towns shown on the map that are no more than a roadhouse with a few scattered homes nearby.

## SALMON BAKES

You'll see the sign and wonder what's up. Yes, the salmon is hot and ready, as typically are halibut, ribs, and other goodies. The mood is often rustic, almost picnicky, with heaping side dishes you'd find at a family-reunion potluck. The fixed price includes the works—even soft drinks, coffee, or tea.

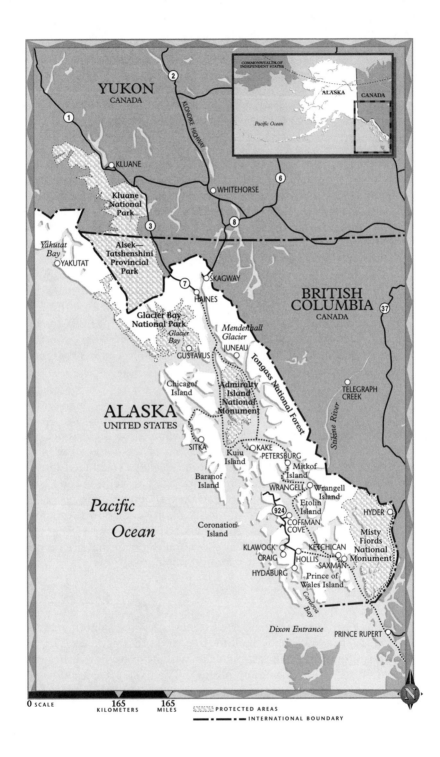

YUKON
CANADA

② ① ⑥

KLONDIKE HIGHWAY

COMMONWEALTH OF
INDEPENDENT STATES

ALASKA   CANADA

Pacific Ocean

○ KLUANE

WHITEHORSE ○

Kluane
National
Park

③ ⑧

Yakutat
Bay

Alsek—
Tatshenshini
Provincial
Park

○ YAKUTAT

⑦ ○ SKAGWAY

○ HAINES

BRITISH
COLUMBIA
CANADA

③⑦

Glacier Bay
National Park
*Glacier
Bay*

Mendenhall
Glacier

○ JUNEAU

Tongass National Forest

GUSTAVUS ○

ALASKA
UNITED STATES

Chicagof
Island

Admiralty
Island
National
Monument

TELEGRAPH
CREEK ○

Stikine River

○ KAKE

Kuiu
Island

PETERSBURG

Mitkof
Island

SITKA ○

Baranof
Island

WRANGELL ○ ○ Wrangell
Island

Pacific

Ocean

⑨②④

Erolin
Island

COFFMAN
COVE

HYDER ○

Coronation
Island

KLAWOCK ○

CRAIG ○

KETCHICAN ○

HOLLIS ○

SAXMAN ○

Misty
Fiords
National
Monument

HYDABURG ○

Prince of
Wales Island

*Cordova Bay*

Dixon Entrance

PRINCE RUPERT ○

0 SCALE

**165**
KILOMETERS

**165**
MILES

PROTECTED AREAS

INTERNATIONAL BOUNDARY

N

# SOUTHEAST ALASKA

## 7

The Alaskan panhandle, generally referred to as the Southeast, is a region of lushly forested isles, sinuous fjords, jagged coastal mountains, and glaciers. It stretches from the Dixon Entrance—the large inlet just north of Prince Rupert, British Columbia—to Yakutat Bay on the St. Elias coast. This northern limit reflects the extent of the Tongass National Forest, which encompasses most of the region. Long a favorite destination for cruise ships, the area is one of the loveliest in the state.

Humpback whales roll through the waters, lofting their tails before diving deep. Eagles perch on the tops of the tall evergreens, their white heads serving as beacons of identification to the sharp-eyed. As your ferry, cruise ship, tour boat, or kayak rounds a point, yet another great glacier becomes visible. Abundant waterfalls, misty clouds, and ephemeral rainbows paint the landscape with motion and color.

Four roads link Southeast towns with ferry connections to highway routes in Canada. In British Columbia, Prince Rupert is reached via B.C. 16 from Prince George, while Highway 37A connects the Cassiar Highway to Stewart and its tiny neighbor, Hyder, Alaska. From the Yukon, the Klondike Highway crosses from near Whitehorse over White Pass into Skagway. Haines is reached on the Haines Highway via Kluane National Park, British Columbia's Alsek-Tatshenshini Wilderness Park, and the Chilkat River. In summer, ferries serve Prince

Rupert, Haines, and Skagway several times a week. The Hyder-Ketchikan ferry runs weekly (see chapter 6 for details).

Though every town of the Southeast is unique, most share a common heritage. Camps and villages of the native Tlingit Indians grew into many of today's larger settlements. Resource exploitation—whether of otter pelts, fish, timber, or gold—led to the creation of virtually all the modern towns. Southeastern communities share a dependence on the calm water routes of the Inside Passage for transportation and supplies.

Today, all of the larger towns are bound together by tourism as well. Most visitors to Alaska travel in the Southeast—and wisely so! In prioritizing areas to explore, the Southeast should be at or near the top of most lists. People familiar with the islands and mountains of the Pacific Northwest will find the landscape somewhat similar, though much wilder and greater in scale. For the rest of us, the Alaskan Southeast will seem stunningly different. For all, it's some of the best the Earth has to offer.

Information on many of the sights featured in this chapter can be obtained from the **Southeast Alaska Discovery Center**, 50 Main Street, Ketchikan, AK 99901, 228-6214, akinfo/r10_ketchikan@ fs.fed.us, www.fs.fed.us/r10/tongass/districts/discoverycenter.

## TONGASS NATIONAL FOREST
*Location/Size:* Encompasses most of the Alaskan panhandle. 17 million acres; wilderness, 5.7 million acres (before new plan).
*Main Activities:* Kayaking, hiking, wildlife observation, bear viewing, eagle viewing, whale watching, birding, flightseeing, boat tours, fishing.
*Gateway Towns/Getting There:* Ketchikan, Petersburg, Wrangell, Sitka, Juneau, and Haines. Vehicle and foot access via A.M.H.S. ferries, scheduled air service from Anchorage (via Juneau to smaller towns), vehicle access to Haines via Haines Highway from Alaska Highway. Forest access by hiking and backpacking from towns, charter-plane air service, boat drop-offs, and shuttles; sea-kayak and tour-boat access to many points; ferry access.
*Facilities, Camping, Lodging:* Information centers in Juneau, Ketchikan, and Sitka; bear-viewing facilities at Anan and Pack Creek; numerous Forest Service roads on several islands. Numerous reservable backcountry cabins and several designated campgrounds.
*Headquarters and Information:* 648 Mission Street, Ketchikan, 228-6202; Forest Service Information Center, 101 Egan Drive, Juneau,

*586-8751; Southeast Alaska Discovery Center, 50 Main Street, Ketchikan, 228-6214; see appendix for several ranger district offices.*

Encompassing almost the entire panhandle, America's largest national forest is also its most magnificent. The beautiful Inside Passage—a maze of interconnected channels and sheltered waters—provides travel routes among forested isles, sparkling peaks, massive glaciers, and windblown waterfalls. The forest lands are rich in wildlife, including large numbers of brown and black bears, Sitka black-tailed deer, moose, lynx, and mountain goats. Humpback whales share the waters with seals, otters, and porpoises. The largest concentrations of bald eagles in the world soar along the shores or perch high atop the old-growth Sitka spruce and western hemlock.

Water is the defining feature of the Tongass. The frequent rains feed thousands of streams and waterfalls. Snows pile layer upon layer onto the icefields of the coast ranges and St. Elias Mountains. The icefields, in turn, squeeze scores of glaciers through precipitous defiles toward the sea. Rainbows are there one minute and gone the next as squalls blow past gaps in the cloud cover. The weather can indeed be broken and fitful as the clouds driven in from the Pacific by the prevailing westerlies run up against the ragged landscape.

The Tongass includes two major national monuments and several designated wilderness areas, all offering potential rewards to the explorer. Admiralty Island National Monument and Misty Fiords National Monument earn descriptive sections of their own in this chapter. Larger wilderness areas are written up with the communities that serve as the best gateways. Smaller designated wilderness areas are described below. Information, cabin reservations, and certain permits can be obtained through Tongass National Forest offices. Adjustments in the final Tongass management plan may result in the expansion of some of the following areas.

## Smaller Wilderness Areas in the Tongass

**Chuck River Wilderness (74,298 acres)**—Essentially stretching Tracy Arm–Fords Terror Wilderness to the crest of the divide between Endicott Arm and Stephens Passage, Chuck River protects the south shore of Endicott Arm and the inner two-thirds of Windham Bay. Also protected is much of the Chuck River watershed south of Windham Bay (see Tracy Arm–Fords Terror Wilderness, below).

**Coronation Island Wilderness (19,232 acres)**—Coronation Island, Warren Island, and the Maurelle Islands are a rugged trio of designated wilderness areas spread across Iphigenia Bay, west of the northern half of Prince of Wales Island. Each is windswept and rugged, exposed to the open ocean, and difficult to reach. Sitka, Kake, and Hollis are the closest towns with regular ferry service, all at least 50 air miles away. Floatplane, chartered boat, or serious kayaking are the only ways to reach these wild destinations. During much of the year, floatplane access is difficult or impossible due to rough seas.

**Endicott River Wilderness (98,729 acres)**—Contiguous with Glacier Bay National Park, the wilderness protects all of the Endicott River watershed, which drains eastward from the Chilkat Mountains into Lynn Canal, north of Juneau. From its mouth, the Endicott and its many tributaries branch upward through wet, forested, 15-mile valleys to the open peaks and passes of the divide. The source of the Endicott is in a wide, boggy flat that gives way gently through Endicott Gap to Main Valley, which drains into Adams Inlet of Glacier Bay. Haines, Juneau, and Gustavus are the nearest towns with regular ferry service. Access is by chartered boat, small plane, or sea kayak, and then on foot.

**Karta River Wilderness (39,889 acres)**—Five backcountry cabins and several miles of trail are found between Karta Bay and Salmon Lake in the center of Prince of Wales Island. The peaks around this protected watershed reach 3,800 feet. Hollis receives regular ferry service and is a 25-mile charter boat or kayak trip from the trailhead. Overland (no official trails) access is possible from the south or north via Forest Service roads—some of the many that lace this most heavily exploited of the Southeastern isles. Fishing, exploring, and camping are good options here.

**Kuiu Wilderness (60,851 acres)**—Along with Tebenkof Wilderness to the north, the Kuiu Wilderness protects a large portion of Kuiu Island. Deep bays and inlets provide ideal waters for extended kayak trips. A 3-mile portage connects Affleck Canal in the south with Tebenkof Bay to the north, and also connects the two wilderness areas. Kayak access to hidden coves can be combined with bushwhacking hikes to exposed 2,000-foot summits. The closest town with regular ferry service is Kake on Kupreanof Island, 45 air miles to the north. Access is by floatplane, chartered boat, or extended kayaking. There are no cabins or interior trails.

**Maurelle Islands Wilderness (4,937 acres)**—Numerous

small islands and tiny islets beckon the adventurous kayaker (see Coronation Island Wilderness, above, for details).

**Petersburg Creek–Duncan Salt Chuck Wilderness (46,777 acres)**—This popular wilderness lies directly west of Petersburg and is easily accessible by trail after a short crossing of the Wrangell Narrows. The watershed of Petersburg Creek is protected, as is a small divide and the corresponding basin to the west, which includes the North Arm of Duncan Canal and "Salt Chuck," a 4-mile-long tidal flat. Western boat or air access is possible via Duncan Canal. The wilderness and surrounding non-wilderness land has several miles of trail, a difficult 15-mile portage from Petersburg to Duncan Canal, and three backcountry cabins.

**Pleasant-Lemesurier-Inian Islands Wilderness (23,096 acres)**—Essentially contiguous with Glacier Bay National Park to the north, this three-unit wilderness preserves the forested isles of Icy Strait. Gentle Pleasant Island, directly south of Gustavus, is the largest of the three units. Lemesurier Island, the middle of the three, is steeply sloped with a 2,180-foot peak in the middle. The Inian Islands are further west, receiving the brunt of wave action from the open ocean, but offering several sheltered channels to kayak explorers. Gustavus is the obvious gateway of choice, with access by charter boat or sea kayak. There are no cabins or trails.

**South Etolin Wilderness (83,371 acres)**—South of Wrangell, the southern third of Etolin Island and surrounding smaller isles are preserved in this lovely wilderness. The many passages and small islands make an ideal region for sea kayaking, set as they are between the sheltered waters of Clarence Strait and Ernest Sound. South Etolin's interior features several high-country lakes and exposed peaks that reach 3,700 feet, though access is difficult. Wrangell is the closest town with regular ferry service. Access is by floatplane, chartered boat, or multiday kayak trip.

**South Prince of Wales Wilderness (90,996 acres)**—The watershed that drains into Klakas Inlet of Cordova Bay is protected, as are scores of small islands and peninsulas on the southwest coast of Prince of Wales Island. Steep cliffs and rugged headlands are found at the wilderness' and island's southern tip which confronts the open ocean of the Dixon Entrance. The ruins of a village and cannery can be visited, though there are no interior trails or backcountry cabins. The closest town with regular ferry service is Ketchikan. Taking the local ferry from Ketchikan to Hollis allows

road access to Hydaburg and a 25-mile kayak or charter boat trip through sheltered waters to the wilderness.

**Tebenkof Bay Wilderness (66,839 acres)**—Contiguous with Kuiu Wilderness to the south, Tebenkof Bay offers excellent kayaking in the sheltered waters along the intricate coastline (see Kuiu Wilderness, above, for details).

**Warren Island Wildernesses (11,181 acres)**—About 10 miles long and 5 miles wide, this empty isle has 2,329-foot Warren Peak as its exposed summit (see Coronation Island Wilderness, above, for details).

## HYDER, ALASKA, AND
## STEWART, BRITISH COLUMBIA

*Location/Climate: 80 miles northeast of Ketchikan at the head of Portland Creek. 78"/yr. precip., 25°F –57°F.*

*Population: Hyder—138 (1 percent native); Stewart—2,300.*

*Travel Attractions: Misty Fiords National Monument access, Portland Canal, mining roads and ruins, hiking, alpine access, glacier access, river running, kayaking.*

*Getting There: Vehicle access via B.C. Highway 37A, from Cassiar Highway; weekly ferry service from Ketchikan; charter and regular small-plane air service.*

*Information: Stewart Chamber of Commerce, P.O. Box 306, Stewart, B.C. VOT 1WO, (604) 636-9224; Stewart Museum, 6th Street at Columbia, (604) 636-2568; Hyder Community Association, P.O. Box 149, Hyder, AK 99923, (604) 636-9148.*

Located at the head of the 70-mile-long Portland Canal, the towns of Stewart and Hyder are accessible by A.M.H.S. ferry or by the beautiful, 41-mile B.C. Highway 37A, which connects to the Cassiar Highway at Meziadin Junction. The ferry route passes along the Alaska-Canada border with the designated wilderness of Misty Fiords National Monument to the east and the similarly wild country of British Columbia to the west.

Stewart is the real town of the two with a population of about 2,300, while Hyder, with its 138 official residents, bills itself as "the friendliest ghost town in Alaska." Canadian currency is the standard on both sides of the border. Police, phone, and school services for both towns are based in Canada. There is no border station between the two towns, which are separated by about 2 miles of roadway.

Hyder is located on the Salmon River near the point of land where the Salmon meets the Bear River at the head of the Portland Canal. Stewart lies a bit to the north on the shores of the Bear.

Both towns exist because of mining. Hyder sprouted as a supply point for miners working lodes discovered on Canada's upper Salmon River in the late 1890s. More veins were located in the region and Hyder grew through the boom years of the 1920s. Until it closed in 1948, the Premier Mine was the largest gold mine in the country. Large-scale mining continued until 1984, but has ceased in the region for the present. Stewart now serves mainly as a timber processing and shipping point, while Hyder depends largely on tourism.

While in the area, consider a visit to **Bear River Glacier**, 23 miles from Stewart on Highway 37A. The road takes you close to a berg-dotted lake at the foot of this outstanding river of ice. Four miles north of Hyder by road, **Fish Creek** offers fishing for record chum salmon and good bear-viewing possibilities.

In town, you can enjoy the mining-heritage exhibits and get area information at the **Stewart Museum**. Call the **Stewart Forest Service office** for information on area trails, (604) 636-2663. See the appendix for outfitters and tour providers.

## Where to Stay and Eat in Hyder and Stewart

**Bitter Creek Cafe**, 5th Avenue, Stewart, (250) 636-2166. Salads, pasta, seafood, pizza, Mexican.

**Grand View Inn**, Hyder, (250) 636-9174. Motel, kitchenettes, $50 to $60 (U.S.).

**King Edward Hotel and Motel**, 5th and Columbia Street, Stewart, (250) 636-2244. Coffeeshop, dining room, kitchenettes, TV, phones, $60 to $105 (Can).

**Rainy Mountain Bakery & Deli**, Stewart, (250) 636-2777. Deli, coffeeshop, courtyard.

## MISTY FIORDS NATIONAL MONUMENT

*Location/Size: East of Ketchikan in far Southeastern Alaska; 2,142,243 acres.*
*Main Activities: Sea kayaking, fishing, backcountry camping, hiking, backpacking, flightseeing, boat tours.*

*Gateway Towns/Getting There: Ketchikan/via scheduled air service from Juneau; via scheduled ferry service from Prince Rupert, B.C.; Wrangell; or points north. Monument access by floatplane from Ketchikan and elsewhere; tour and charter boat from Ketchikan; sea kayak; by road and foot from Hyder; possible foot access from kayak anchorages.*
*Facilities, Camping, Lodging: No park facilities. Primitive camping, some traditional campsites on west-central lakes; several reservable backcountry cabins, primarily in west-central lakes area.*
*Headquarters and Information: Headquarters, 3031 Tongass Avenue, Ketchikan, AK 99901-5743, 225-2148, www.fs.fed.us/r10/ketchikan/mfnm/misty.htm; Southeast Alaska Visitor Center, 50 Main Street, Ketchikan, AK 99901, 228-6220.*

At over 2 million acres, Misty Fiords is the largest national monument in the United States (the National Forest Service spells "fiord" with an "i" instead of a "j"). It is a land of sinuous fjords, long, twisting valleys, and exposed ridges. Most of the monument is very rugged, with 3,000- to 4,000-foot ridges rising steeply from the margins of glacier-cut, U-shaped valleys. In the northeast the peaks are higher and host numerous small glaciers, while to the southwest the terrain is somewhat gentler. As is true in most of the Southeast, the lowlands and slopes up to about 2,500 feet are covered with a forest of old-growth Sitka spruce and western hemlock.

The monument is located in far southeastern Alaska, bounded to the east and south with the Canadian border. It is largely on the mainland, though it also includes a sizable chunk of Revillagigedo Island—everything east of a major divide. Behm Canal thus passes wholly through designated wilderness for much of its length, offering wonderful possibilities for exploration by water.

A large portion in the center of Misty Fiords is non-wilderness, primarily because of the existence of a mine that continues to operate as part of an agreement written into ANILCA. Another area near Hyder is non-wilderness due to past and possible future mining activity, but the rest of Misty Fiords is deserving of true wilderness status and is designated as such.

Water is a primary feature of Misty Fiords. Rugged adventurers can enjoy kayaking deep into the interior, then follow challenging routes up onto the open ridgecrests. Numerous lakes open out in valley basins, inviting wilderness camping and fishing. With some areas receiving upwards of 150 inches of rain per year, rushing streams are plentiful, as are waterfalls, wet meadows (muskeg), and boggy flats.

Perhaps the most amazing of Misty Fiords' features is the 100-mile-long pairing of Pearse Canal and Portland Canal, an astonishingly uniform fjord system that runs from Hyder to the open ocean. The main channels of a riverine glacier system in the last ice age, the Pearse/Portland now serves as the eastern boundary of the monument as well as the U.S.-Canada border. Weekly summer ferry service from Ketchikan to Hyder follows the Portland Canal, though a relative few use the route for travel, recreation, and monument access. Consider joining those few.

Misty Fiords has several reservable backcountry cabins available, most located on lakes in the popular west-central portion of the monument on either side of the Behm Canal. A few short portage-, fishing-, and cabin-access trails link saltwater-access points with some lakes, while others must be reached by floatplane. Ketchikan is the main gateway town, offering a variety of outfitters and tour companies as well as being an important stop in the Alaska Marine Highway System.

## KETCHIKAN

*Location/Climate:* 235 miles south of Juneau, 679 miles north of Seattle, on the southwest coast of Revillagigedo Island. 154"/yr. precip., 29°F–59°F.

*Population:* 8,557 (15.7 percent native, mainly Tlingit, Tsimshian, Haida); Ketchikan Gateway Borough (includes Saxman and surrounding area), 15,082 (13.7 percent native).

*Travel Attractions:* Misty Fiords National Monument access, ferry link, historic town, Creek Street, Totem Heritage Center, Southeast Alaska Visitor Center, Community of Saxman.

*Getting There:* Scheduled air service from Juneau, Seattle, and other points; scheduled ferry service from Juneau and Prince Rupert.

*Information:* Ketchikan Visitors Bureau, 131 Front Street, Ketchikan, AK 99901, (800) 770-3300, 225-6166, kvb@ktn.net, www.visit-ketchikan.com.

Ketchikan is located beside the Tongass Narrows on the southwest shores of Revillagigedo Island—named by Spanish explorers who visited the region briefly in the 1700s. Tongass and Cape Fox

Tlingit Indians had long used the area near the mouth of the Ketchikan Creek as a fish camp. They called it "Kitschk-him," which translates to "thundering wings of an eagle." Fish and timber resources attracted settlers in the late 1800s and the town quickly grew. By 1936, seven canneries were in operation producing 1.5 million cases of salmon annually. Spruce logging grew in importance in World War II. The huge and infamous Ketchikan Pulp Company mill was built for $55 million in 1954.

Today Ketchikan is the largest community in the southern panhandle. This wet, blue-collar version of Juneau has plenty to offer both typical tourists and outdoor enthusiasts. The town attracts cruise-ship activity and is a major stop on the Alaska Marine Highway. Visitors enjoy the compact town center and important native sites. Those with access to a vehicle or bike can tour the roads to the north and south, gaining access to Forest Service roads and trailheads.

The town and roads of Ketchikan are actually on a modest, isolated thumb of the largely wild Revillagigedo Island, bounded by Clover Passage to the north, the Tongass Narrows running from northwest to southeast, and the George Inlet to the east. This 100-plus-square-mile thumb is a microcosm of the Southeast. There are wild, rain-forested valleys, forest roads leading to clear cuts, barren summits, isolated lakes, and a busy coastal town. Forest Service campsites are a hike, paddle, or drop-off flight away, while a vast wilderness is just around the corner.

Take the North Tongass Highway 5 miles north of town to Ward Cove to see what was the largest year-round manufacturing facility in Alaska—the Ketchikan Pulp Company mill. Its closure in March of 1997 ended pulp milling in the Southeast. To attract attention in a local cafe, loudly discuss the environmental damage caused by the release of poisonous fumes and effluent from the pulping process. Almost 1,000 jobs went with the mill, and they didn't go quietly. New sawmill jobs may pick up some of the slack.

Three miles southeast of Ketchikan on the Tongass Highway is the largely native community of **Saxman** (population 402; 77 percent native, mainly Tlingit), center of the Cape Fox Village Corporation. Just above the road is an interesting totem park and tribal house, as well as the Cape Fox store and Saxman Arts Co-op where art and craft objects can be purchased. The Beaver Clan youth demonstrate tribal dances and stories, and master totem carvers can be observed at work. Call 225-5163 for information.

A walking-tour map for Ketchikan is available in several locations, including the Ketchikan Visitor Information Center and the Southeast Alaska Visitor Center (see details above).

## Things to See and Do in Ketchikan

**Creek Street**—Following Ketchikan Creek between the small boat harbor and Park Avenue, this boardwalk lane raised on pilings was once the red-light district in town. Now gift and other tourist-related shops line the way. A short, free tram climbs to the Westmark hotel on the hill (ride it for fun and a view). This is certainly the town's biggest camera click and offers pleasant browsing.

**Deer Mountain Tribal Hatchery**—Next to City Park and the Totem Heritage Center, the hatchery is a salmon- and steelhead trout–raising facility. A new raptor center features birds that cannot be returned to the wild. 429 Deermount Street, 225-5158. Open May 15–September 30.

**Southeast Alaska Visitor Center**—As one of Alaska's interagency, public lands information centers, this is much more than a place to get pamphlets and information with a smile. It's my favorite of Ketchikan's offerings; the exhibits here are outstanding. Detailed information is available for trip planning and wilderness

Paul Otteson

*Creek Street in Ketchikan*

access throughout the Southeast. 50 Main Street, Ketchikan, AK 99901, 228-6214.

**Tongass Historical Museum and Public Library**—This inauspicious museum offers regional and local heritage exhibits, including the tale of the town of Loring, Ketchikan's predecessor. Outside are three historic Tlingit totems, including the Chief Johnson Totem Pole, an exact replica of a turn-of-the-century pole raised by Tlingit Chief Johnson (carved by Israel Shotridge). 629 Dock Street. Open daily May 15–September 30 8 a.m. to 5 p.m.; Wednesday–Sunday winter; $2.

**Totem Heritage Center**—Original and replica totem poles are displayed indoors and out at this national landmark center. Also featured is the *Drums of the Northwest Coast* collection, a *Fish Camp Life* exhibit, and other exhibits and presentations relating to the arts and culture of the Haida, Tlingit, and Tsimshian peoples. 601 Deermount Street (10-minute walk from downtown), 225-5900, fax 225-5901. Open daily May 15–September 30 8 a.m. to 5 p.m.; winter Tuesday–Friday afternoons; $5 (includes hatchery).

## Recommended Hikes near Ketchikan
A number of maintained trails are easily accessible from town via the Tongass Highway. Several short paths are found near fishing lakes and campgrounds. Two of note are:

**Deer Mountain Trail** (10 miles, 2,000' gain)—This rugged route through the high country is Ketchikan's best. The trail climbs directly from town for 2.5 miles to the Forest Service cabin near the summit of Deer Mountain. From here, the route winds through open, rocky terrain with small lakes and a couple of 3,000-foot summits, then drops to Silvis Lake and the trailhead at the end of the Forest Service road. It's 15 miles back to town by road. Through trail—overnight.

**Perseverance Trail** (2.3 miles, little gain)—This moderately easy route is mostly boardwalk through mixed muskeg and forest. The trailhead is near Ward Lake on the Ward Lake Road. RT—3 hrs.

## Where to Stay in Ketchikan
**The Gilmore Hotel**, 326 Front Street, 225-9423. $64–$74 (winter), $70–$130 (summer), suites more. On National Historic Register, waterfront views, private baths, cable TV. Features good food and drink at Annabelle's Keg & Chowder House.

**Inside Passage Bed-and-Breakfast**, 114 Elliot Street (on the stairway), 247-3700. $60–$70 (rooms), $85 (apartment, 3-day minimum stay). Two rooms share one bath, one-bedroom apartment, breakfast.

**Ketchikan Reservation Service**, 412 D-1 Loop Road, (800) 987-5337, 247-5337, krs@ktn.net. B&Bs, hotels, rental cars, charters, tours.

**The New York Hotel and Cafe**, 207 Stedman Street, 225-0246. $60 and up (winter), $70 and up (summer). Small, charming, restored hotel near Creek Street; full baths; cable; 1920s decor.

**Settler's Cove State Recreation Site**, North Tongass Highway (end, 15 miles north of town) on Clover Passage.

**Tongass National Forest Campgrounds**
Two campgrounds, **Signal Creek** and **Three Cs**, are located on Ward Lake Road north of town.

**Westmark Cape Fox Lodge**, 800 Venetia Way, (800) 544-0970, 225-8001. $109 and up (winter), $131 and up (summer). The nicest hotel in town; ride the short tram up to lobby from town center.

### Where to Eat in Ketchikan
**Annabelle's Keg & Chowder House**, 326 Front Street, 225-9423. Moderately priced lunch and dinner. Seafood, pasta, chowder, salads, sandwiches, espresso.

**Papa's Ketchikan Cafe & Pizza**, 316 Front Street, 247-7272. Tasty lunch and dinner, pastas, sandwiches, pizza, burgers.

**Pioneer Restaurant**, 124 Front Street, 225-3337. Breakfast, lunch, and dinner.

**Pizza Mill**, 808 Water Street, 225-6646. Pizza, burgers, subs, Mexican. Open late.

## PRINCE OF WALES ISLAND
America's third-largest island is of particular worth to those interested in native communities, sea kayaking, and driving. The island

offers more road miles than any other region in the Southeast and can be explored in vehicles as cumbersome as an RV. The main communities each have their attractions, though all are off the beaten track. Access to the island is by scheduled small aircraft, floatplane, or charter boat, most of which are based in Ketchikan. An A.M.H.S. ferry connects Ketchikan with Hollis about once a day, enabling vehicles to reach the island.

Most of the island is part of the Tongass National Forest, though there are also large inclusions of native corporation and private lands. There are two small designated wilderness areas, as well as three other island wildernesses on the Pacific north coast (see Tongass National Forest, above). The final decision on the Tongass Management Plan in April, 1999, completed protection of wilderness study areas and other forest lands, but the island will remain one of the most exploited areas in the Southeast. Still, the relatively slow pace of timber harvesting on federal lands and the regenerative powers of a rain-forest climate ensure that visitors will experience a lush and wild landscape in most areas.

Five national forest campgrounds are accessible by road on Prince of Wales Island. They are Exchange Cove in the far northeast on National Forest Road #30; Eagle's Nest on Thorne Bay Road just east of the Prince of Wales Road junction; Lake Number 3 near Salt Chuck on National Forest Road #2030; Staney Creek Bridge on National Forest Road #2050 west of Prince of Wales Road; and nearby Horseshoe Hole at the ocean end of National Forest Road #5034. All five are listed as no-fee campgrounds with no drinking water.

## Island Towns

Five coastal towns of consequence are found on the island, as are several smaller communities. All are accessible by floatplane or small-plane air service, or by road from the ferry terminal in Hollis. For information, contact the Prince of Wales Chamber of Commerce, P.O. Box 497, Craig, AK 99921, 826-3870.

**Coffman Cove** (population 254, 7 percent native)—Located about 50 miles northeast of Klawock by various roads, Coffman Cove was first settled as a logging camp in the 1970s. There is access across Clarence Strait to the south Etolin Wilderness. Gas and general supplies are available, but there are no accommodations or outfitters.

**Craig** (population 1,946, 22.9 percent native)—Located 31 miles from Hollis, Craig has three hotels and a variety of travel services. Commercial fishing and fleet support services occupy most residents. Charter air and boat services are available, as are canoe and kayak rentals (see appendix). With the sheltered waters of Prince of Wales Island's west coast at hand, Craig makes a good base for exploration of the bays, channels, and outer islands. For information, contact City Office, Craig City Hall, 826-3275, tbriggs@eagle.ptialaska.net; U.S. Forest Service office, 826-3271.

**Hollis** (population 106, 2.7 percent native)—Once an important mining camp and later an important logging camp, Hollis was rejuvenated once again with the development of the ferry terminal and state land sales to potential new residents. Logging and ferry jobs occupy most residents. Travel services are limited.

**Hydaburg** (population 406, 89.1 percent Haida)—This

# Caves and Karst Formations

*Limestone-based karst formations are found in several areas of the Southeast, particularly on Kuiu, Chichagof, and Prince of Wales Islands. Karst landforms are created when acidic groundwater acts upon limestone and marble, sometimes resulting in cave systems. The acid in the area comes mainly from peat bogs that form in rain-soaked flats and gently sloping hills. The limestone originated as layered deposits of calcium-rich invertebrate shells on the sea floor, later uplifted by tectonic action.*

*Over 500 caves in the larger region have been mapped and studied by scientists so far, with many more remaining to be found and investigated. Two such caves have become visitor attractions on Prince of Wales Island. The Forest Service offers tours of **El Capitan Cave**, while **Cavern Lake Cave** is accessible by trail from a Forest Service road. Both sites are reached from Prince of Wales Road, via Thorne Bay Road from Thorne Bay, or via Big Salt Road from Klawock. Get detailed information from the Forest Service before setting out.*

largely native community grew from the combined populations of three older Haida villages around 1911. Most residents are occupied by commercial fishing, construction, and timber harvesting. Of particular interest in town is the **Totem Park**, developed by the Civilian Conservation Corps (CCC) in the 1930s. The park contains a fine collection of new and restored Haida totems. Hydaburg is a good put-in point for long-distance kayakers intending to explore the South Prince of Wales Wilderness. The town has a cafe. Limited lodging opportunities are not far away.

**Klawock** (population 759, 54.3 percent native)—Site of a traditional Tlingit fish camp, Klawock is where Alaska's first salmon cannery was built in 1878. Fishing and timber-related jobs occupy most residents. Nearby lodges cater to sport fishers, while in-town services are limited. Boat charters and rentals are available (see appendix).

**Thorne Bay** (population 650, 1.2 percent native)—Basically a non-native logging town, Thorne Bay is located on the bay of the same name along Clarence Strait on the island's east side. Most residents are involved in timber harvesting or forest management. Thorne Bay Road connects the town with Klawock. The road is a good way to cross the island and, via Prince of Wales Road and Forest Service roads, gain access to its northern end.

## WRANGELL

*Location/Climate:* 80 miles north-northwest of Ketchikan, 150 miles south-southeast of Juneau. 82"/yr. precip., 29°F–57°F.
*Population:* 2,758 (20 percent native, mainly Tlingit).
*Travel Attractions:* Access to Stikine River and Stikine-Leconte Wilderness, Tlingit totems, Wrangell Museum, genuine Alaska.
*Getting There:* Scheduled air service from Juneau; scheduled ferry service from Ketchikan, Juneau, and other points.
*Information:* Chamber of Commerce, P.O. Box 49, Wrangell, AK 99929; Visitor Center, in the Stikine Inn 1 block from ferry dock, 874-3901, (800) 367-9745, chamber@seapac.net, www.wrangell.com. Open when cruise ships and ferries are in port, longer in summer.

Wrangell is a working town with relatively little in the way of travel attractions. It claims to be the third-oldest Alaskan community, the gateway to the Stikine River, and the only Alaskan town to have been ruled by four different nations: Tlingit, Russia, Britain, and the United States. Tongass logging, commercial fishing, and fish processing occupy most of the work force, while others are involved in mining transshipment and tourism. Those staying in Wrangell can enjoy a friendly, working, genuine Alaskan town with local attractions including short hikes and a history museum.

One interesting feature of Wrangell is the garnet business, engaged in by local scouts. The Boy Scouts of America own **Garnet Ledge**, a formation about 8 water miles from town at the mouth of the Stikine River where garnets are found in abundance. A reservable Forest Service cabin near the ledge is one of six such cabins found at the mouth of the river. The scouts and their siblings sell garnets at the ferry terminal.

Wrangell is a good base for visits to the Stikine-Leconte Wilderness and Anan Bear Observatory. The 18-mile **Zimovia Highway** runs a third of the way down the west shore of Wrangell Island and links to national forest roads that wind across much of the island. A few short area trails lead to lakes and overlooks. The local summit of **Mount Dewey** can be reached by a steep, half-mile trail from 3rd Street.

## Things to See and Do in or Around Wrangell

**Anan Bear Observatory**—The Anan Creek Trail (.5 mile) follows Anan Creek from Anan Lagoon to the observatory where black bears feed on spawning pink salmon (humpback salmon or "humpies") in July and August. Brown bear and bald eagles may also be seen, and seals frequent the lagoon. The observatory is staffed from mid-June to mid-September; no reservations necessary. Anan is about 30 water miles southeast of Wrangell at the head of Bradfield Canal. Access is via floatplane, sea kayak, or charter boat (see appendix).

Check with the Wrangell Ranger District office for current schedule and information, 525 Bennett Street, 874-2323. They also have information on reserving backcountry cabins at Anan and elsewhere in the district.

**Petroglyph Beach**—Head north from the ferry terminal on Stikine Avenue a little more than half a mile to reach a small parking area and access to the shore. A boardwalk provides access to several good petroglyphs that face the water above the high-tide line. The carvings are of unknown origin, but may date back 8,000 years.

**Shakes Island and Tribal House**—At the south end of Front
Street near the floatplane harbor, a boardwalk leads out onto Shakes
Island. There are several fine totem poles here, as well as a replica
of a tribal house with interesting artifacts inside. The site is listed on
the National Register of Historic Places. Open irregularly in summer; call for hours or drop by, 874-3747.

**Wrangell Museum**—Regional heritage exhibits and artifacts
are found at this museum, just down the street from the ferry dock.
318 Church Street, Wrangell, AK 99929, 874-3770. Open weekdays 10 a.m.–5 p.m., Saturday 1 p.m.–6 p.m., Sunday when the
ferry is in port; $2, under 16 free.

### Where to Stay and Eat in Wrangell

**Diamond C Cafe**, 223 Front Street (at Thunderbird Hotel), 874-
3677. Family menu; daily breakfast and lunch.

**Stikine Inn**, 1 block from ferry terminal, 874-3388. Motel, restaurant,
chamber of commerce, Stickeen Wilderness Adventures, on the water,
rooms range from $70 to $100.

**Thunderbird Hotel**, 223 Front Street, 874-3322. Basic motel.

**Wrangell Hostel** (First Presbyterian Church), 220 Church Street,
2 blocks from the ferry, 874-3534. Only hostel in Wrangell. $10.

## PETERSBURG

*Location/Climate: 120 miles south of Juneau, 120 miles north of
Ketchikan. 106"/yr. precip., 27°F–56°F.*
*Population: 3,350 (10.4 percent native).*
*Travel Attractions: Access to Petersburg Creek–Duncan Salt Chuck
Wilderness, road access on Mitkof Highway (AK 7) to Forest Service
roads (logging) and kayak put-ins, Wrangell Narrows ferry route.*
*Getting There: Scheduled ferry from Juneau, Ketchikan, and other
points; scheduled air service from Juneau and Ketchikan.*
*Information: Chamber of Commerce, P.O. Box 649, Petersburg, AK
99833, 772-3646, chamber@petersburg.org, www.petersburg.org.*

A working town, Petersburg is rich in Norwegian heritage. It is
named after Peter Buschmann, who arrived in Alaska from Norway

Paul Otteson

*Working the waters near Petersburg*

with his family in 1891, settling finally at the northern end of the Wrangell Narrows in 1897. Others followed him to this new home that must have reminded many of the fjord lands of coastal Norway. The town is at the northern tip of Mitkof Island, most of which is part of the Tongass National Forest. Scandinavian heritage is visible in the style and manner of the community and embodied by the 1912 **Sons of Norway Hall** on Nordic Drive.

Today Petersburg is a fishing and lumbering town. The harbor is home to Alaska's largest halibut fishing fleet and four seafood processing plants that handle over 113 million pounds of fish and shellfish annually. Eagles are commonly seen in town and along the Wrangell Narrows, and active nesting sites are accessible by road.

An extensive network of Forest Service roads built for timber harvesting reaches most areas of Mitkof Island. Most can be accessed via the 34-mile **Mitkof Highway** (AK 7), which runs south from Petersburg along the eastern shore of the Wrangell Narrows, then eastward to Blaquiere Point at the island's southeastern tip. Vehicle travelers and cyclists may enjoy utilizing the extensive road network for exploration. A map of Petersburg, available

through the chamber of commerce, offers information on view-points, trailheads, fishing, picnicking, and other opportunities found on or near the roads.

Access to the trails, cabins, and watercraft routes of Petersburg Creek–Duncan Salt Chuck Wilderness involves a short crossing from town to Kupreanoff Island. Inquire at the ferry terminal or small-boat harbor regarding cheap shuttles.

Kayakers planning to explore the Stikine River and south end of the Stikine-Leconte Wilderness can put-in at Blaquiere Point for best access. Horn Cliffs, Leconte Bay, Leconte Glacier, and the northern end of the wilderness area can be accessed via Frederick Sound right from Petersburg. See the appendix for outfitters, rentals, and drop-offs.

## Things to See and Do in Petersburg
**Clausen Memorial Museum**—Step in if only to see the world's largest king salmon, estimated at 126.5 pounds, and the world's largest chum salmon, which weighs about 36 pounds. Local heritage items are on display. Second and Fram Streets, 772-3598. Open daily in the summer, 10 a.m. to 4:30 p.m. (may be closed Sundays).

## Where to Stay in Petersburg
**Harbor Day Bed-and-Breakfast**, 404 Noseeum Street, 772-3971. Two rooms in home with shared bath, good town access.

**Ohmer Creek National Forest Campground**, Mitkof Highway (AK 7), 22 miles south of town. Nice sites, near Blind Slough and access to the south coast.

**Tides Inn**, First and Dolphin Streets, 772-4288, fax 772-4286. Motel, cable TV, kitchenettes, continental breakfast, downtown, rooms are $70 to $85 a night.

## Where to Eat in Petersburg
**Helse Cafe**, Sing Lee Alley and Goja Street, 772-3444. Health food and deli offerings, lunch only.

**Pellerito's Pizzeria**, Nordic Avenue (Mitkof Highway), 772-3727. Across from the ferry terminal.

## STIKINE-LECONTE WILDERNESS

*Location/Size:* At the mouth of the Stikine River, northeast of Wrangell and east of Petersburg; 448,926 acres.

*Main Activities:* Kayaking, canoeing, rafting, powerboating, wilderness exploration, mountaineering.

*Gateway Towns/Getting There:* Wrangell and Petersburg/scheduled ferry service from Ketchikan and Juneau; regular small-plane air service. Park access via personal watercraft from Wrangell, Petersburg, British Columbia; rafting via water drop-off or British Columbia; foot access via drop-offs.

*Facilities, Camping, Lodging:* Hot-springs tubs and short access trail. Several reservable backcountry cabins, a few free shelters, primitive camping only.

*Headquarters and Information:* Petersburg Ranger District, Tongass National Forest, 12 N. Nordic Dr., Petersburg, AK 99833, 772-3871.

LeConte Bay to the north and the Stikine River to the south are the two main areas of attraction in the wilderness. Wrangell is a good base for exploring the wide flats of the Stikine River mouth and accessing the lower channels, but Petersburg is a better overall base for developing loop routes and avoiding the winds north of Wrangell.

After 300 miles in Canada, the **Stikine River** finishes its long run with a 30-mile segment in Alaska, dissipating into the ocean via many channels across expansive tidal flats. Long-distance river runners begin journeys at Telegraph Creek, 70 road miles from Dease Lake, British Columbia, or perhaps even further upstream from the Cassiar Highway. Others use air drop-offs, or paddle upstream from Wrangell or the end of the Mitkof Highway (AK 7) from Petersburg. About 20 miles upstream, the all-too-popular **Chief Shakes Hot Springs** offers wooden tubs to soakers, often those who've arrived via powerboat with no shortage of cheap beer. The springs are about 3 miles upriver from the mouth of Shakes Slough, which provides access to a lovely, steep-walled bay at the foot of Shakes Glacier. There are several reservable cabins along the Stikine.

To the north, LeConte Bay opens into Frederick Sound southeast of Petersburg, allowing water access to the southernmost tidewater glacier in the state, **LeConte Glacier.** The glacier is long and sinuous, blending into vast icefields among the high, sharp peaks of the Coast Range. Icebergs often litter the bay, deterring powerboaters when they are at their thickest.

Good kayak and canoe loop routes are possible by linking Blaquiere Point at the end of the Mitkof Highway (AK 7) with the town of Petersburg by water. The National Forest Service has a number of recommended routes, but the best dips into the Stikine Valley and LeConte Bay, offering a good, several-day journey. Flightseeing and glacier drop-offs are possible. See the appendix for outfitters and rental agencies.

## ADMIRALTY ISLAND NATIONAL MONUMENT

*Location/Size: Between Stephen's Passage and the Chatham Strait south of Juneau. 955,921 acres.*

*Main Activities: Bear viewing, wilderness exploration, coastal kayaking, freshwater canoeing and kayaking, fishing.*

*Gateway Towns/Getting There: Juneau/scheduled ferry or air from several points; Angoon/scheduled ferry from Juneau or Sitka, charter air, and boat; Kake/scheduled ferry from Juneau, charter air, and boat. Monument access by kayak, tour or charter boats, and floatplane; limited foot access from Angoon.*

*Facilities, Camping, Lodging: No facilities. Numerous backcountry cabins available (see headquarters for contact), primitive camping with some designated sites and shelters. Some private lodging at Angoon and Funter Bay.*

*Headquarters and Information: Headquarters, 8461 Old Dairy Road, Juneau, AK 99801 (10 miles north of town), 586-8790; Forest Service Information Center, 101 Egan Drive, Juneau, AK 99801, 586-8751, www.fs.fed.us/r10/chatham/anm.*

Ninety percent of the thickly forested and rugged Admiralty Island is preserved in this 956,000-acre monument south of Juneau. All but two small sections of the monument are designated as the **Kootznoowoo Wilderness**—one in the north where a road enters the Green Creek watershed, another surrounding the tiny village of Angoon on the island's west coast. The Kootznoowoo offers great opportunities for recreation and wilderness adventure, with two options that stand out from the rest.

### Pack Creek

The most famous place to view some of Admiralty Island's 1,500 brown bears is at Pack Creek on the west shore of Seymour Canal. Here, about

50 square miles of the Kootznoowoo Wilderness are closed to hunting and bears are easily viewed along three separate streams and the associated tide flats: Pack Creek, Swan Cove, and Windfall Harbor. The **Stan Price State Wildlife Sanctuary,** named for the pioneering researcher who studied area bears, gives special status to submerged and tidal lands near the mouth of Pack Creek. Price's cabin still stands, though it is closed to visitors. A 1-mile trail leads to a bear observatory along Pack Creek, open from 9 a.m. to 9 p.m. A couple of other observation points have been designated by the Forest Service.

You must obtain a $50 permit to visit Pack Creek. Contact the Forest Service Information Center for a permit application. On guided trips, permits are included in the price. Access is generally from Juneau via canoe, kayak, floatplane, or charter boat. All camping is a mile offshore on Windfall Island, so you will need a personal watercraft for site access. See the appendix for outfitters.

### Cross-Admiralty Canoe Route

Canoers and stillwater kayakers can enjoy the finest freshwater route in the Southeast on this series of lakes, deep bays, and portage trails. The route connects Angoon on the island's west side with Mole Harbor on the Seymour Canal. Canoe rental is possible in Angoon (see appendix). Six backcountry cabins are available for rent and several open shelters are found at other key locations. The route is over 40 miles in length and takes four to six days to complete.

Easy access is available via a scheduled ferry to Angoon, floatplane or boat charter from Juneau, or by continuing the trip to include kayaking to or from Juneau (inquire about the portage from Oliver Inlet to the Seymour Canal). Get detailed information from the Forest Service Information Center or Admiralty National Monument Headquarters. They have a list of approved outfitters as well as information on hazards.

Independent explorations of Admiralty Island are possible via sea kayak, floatplane drop-off, and off-trail exploration. Scheduled ferry service can take you to gateway towns including Juneau, Angoon, and Kake. Prepare for wet, rain-forest conditions and expect bears.

### JUNEAU

*Location/Climate: 560 air miles east-southeast of Anchorage on the continental mainland side of the Inside Passage. 92"/yr. precip. (downtown),*

*54"/yr. precip. (airport, 10 miles north of downtown), 101"/yr. snowfall,
20°F–65°F.*

**Population:** *29,755 (12.9 percent native, mainly Tlingit).*

**Travel Attractions:** *Mendenhall Glacier, Mount Roberts Tramway,
city walking tour, Alaska State Museum, tours and backcountry access
for Tracy Arm, Admiralty Island, Glacier Bay.*

**Getting There:** *Alaska Marine Highway System from Prince Rupert,
Haines, and Sitka; scheduled air service from Anchorage and Seattle.*

**Information:** *Davis Log Cabin Visitor Information Center, 134 Third
Street, Juneau, AK 99801, 586-2201, (888) 581-2201, jcvb@
ptialaska.net, www.juneau.com.*

America's most beautiful capital city is also its least recognizable. No
capitol dome graces the meager skyline. No sprawling commons surround a stately government complex. Instead, a capitol that looks like an
old bank is crowded among similarly inauspicious structures on a narrow backstreet of this small and wonderful town. In addition to being a
compact city, easy to tour on foot in an afternoon, Juneau is the main
gateway for backcountry activities in the northern panhandle.

Long a fishing camp for Tlingit Indians, Juneau came into existence in 1880 when Joe Juneau and Richard Harris discovered gold
in Gold Creek. The town became the Alaska state capital in 1906.
Mining declined in the 1930s and all but ended when the Alaska-
Juneau Gold Mine closed in 1944. With new technologies available,
mining is beginning again with as many as three major operations to
be underway by the turn of the century.

Today Juneau is the chief city of the Southeast, a major regional
transportation hub, and a destination for nearly a million visitors annually. Travelers arrive by plane, ferry, or cruise ship to enjoy a walking
tour of historic and government sites, the shops and lanes of downtown, a tram ride up Mount Roberts, and the excellent exhibits of the
state museum. The city has every modern convenience, including
scores of restaurants, lodging options, and minor attractions. Mendenhall Glacier—the only glacier in the Southeast where close road access
is possible—is the most popular destination for short excursions.

## Mendenhall Glacier

Located about 11 miles north of downtown, the Mendenhall
Glacier is Juneau's premier attraction. Unless you're spending time
with some wilder glaciers elsewhere, the Mendenhall is well worth a

visit. The glacier ends at Mendenhall Lake, about 3 miles from the coast. The visitor center is at the lake's west end and features a viewing platform and naturalist-led activities. Below the lake is suburban Juneau. Capital Transit's Mendenhall Valley buses (#3 and #4) run hourly from downtown to a spot 1- to 1.5 miles from the visitor center ($1.25, 789-6901). Various companies operating on or near the cruise dock offer tours (see appendix).

Paul Otteson

*Juneau*

If you're driving, take the Glacier Highway north from town and turn right on Mendenhall Loop Road. Follow the signs for the visitor center and eastside trails. Continue on the Loop Road to reach Montana Creek Road, the Mendenhall Lake Campground, and the westside trailhead. All trailheads can be reached with a 1- to 1.5-mile walk from a city bus stop (ask the driver).

## Hiking Trails near Juneau

Road access to Douglas Island and 45 miles of coastline makes it easy to get to several short but excellent hiking routes, including the following:

**Amalga Trail** (Eagle Glacier, 5½ miles, 200' gain)—The trailhead is north of Juneau at Mile 28.4 of the Glacier Highway. This easy hike passes beaver ponds on the way to great views of Eagle Glacier. RT—all day.

**East Glacier Loop** (3½ miles, 400' gain)—One of the two main Mendenhall Glacier routes, this easy trail begins at the visitor center. Take Mendenhall Loop Road. Glacier views and wildlife. Loop—2–3 hrs.

**Mount Juneau Trail** (4 miles including 1 mile on Perseverance, 2,900' gain)—Head north from the junction, 1 mile up the Perseverance Trail. This steep, difficult trail climbs to the summit

of Mount Juneau, which presides over the city. Certain sections require care, especially in the early summer when an ice axe may be handy. Stellar views! RT—all day (because you won't want to come down).

**Mount Roberts Trail** (4½ miles, 3,500' gain)—The first 2½ miles and 2,500 feet are via a steep but well-used route, from the upper end of 6th Street to a view, memorial cross, and tram station. The route continues a half mile to **Gastineau Peak** (3,666'), then 1½ additional miles to the high ridge of **Mount Roberts** (3,819'), about 4½ miles from town. For a shorter hike to the heights, use the Mount Roberts Tram to gain the early elevation and hike from there. RT—half day (with tram leg).

**Perseverance Trail** (3 miles, 700' gain)—From downtown Juneau, take Gold Street to Basin Street and follow it to its end. This easy trail climbs gently to the site of old Perseverance Mine. Views, wildlife, and mining ruins. RT—3–4 hrs.

Two miles in, the Perseverance links up with the **Granite Creek Trail** (1½ miles, 1,200' gain plus Perseverance gain), a more difficult route that climbs to an old mining area in Granite Creek basin. RT—3–4 hrs.

**Sheep Creek Trail** (6 miles, 900' gain)—The route follows Sheep Creek Valley from the parking area and trailhead, 8 miles south of Juneau on Thane Road. Views and several mining sites. RT—all day.

**West Glacier Trail** (3.4 miles, 1,300' gain)—Take Mendenhall Loop Road to Montana Creek Road. Follow signs to campground and trailhead. More difficult but beautiful trail with outstanding glacier, valley, and icefall views. RT—5–6 hrs.

## Other Things to See and Do in Juneau

**Alaskan Brewing Company**—Brewery tours are offered, followed by beer sampling. 5429 Shaune Drive, 780-5866. Open May–September Tuesday–Saturday; rest of year Thursday–Saturday; tours every half hour.

**Alaska State Capitol**—Duck in for a peek and a self-guided walking tour if you wish, though don't expect much. A pamphlet points out architectural features, history, and artworks. Fourth Street between Seward and Main, open during government hours.

**Alaska State Museum**—A must-see in my book! As you might expect, it features permanent and rotating exhibits on the natural

# Excursions from Juneau

*Several flying services and tour/charter boat companies are based in or near town, equipment rental is easy, and a number of wilderness outfitters offer great packages (see appendix for listings). Use Juneau as a well-served gateway for trips to:*

**Tracy Arm** *(kayaking, boat tours)*

**Admiralty Island National Monument** *(bear viewing, backcountry lodging, long-distance canoeing)*

**Pack Creek Brown Bear Sanctuary** *(bear viewing)*

**Gustavus/Glacier Bay** *(glacier viewing, tours, kayaking, hiking)*

**Alsek River** *(rafting, kayaking, fishing)*

**Tatshenshini River** *(great rafting and kayaking)*

**Taku River and Inlet** *(backcountry lodging, kayaking, rafting)*

**Juneau Icefields** *(flightseeing, glacier landings)*

**Point Adolphus** *(whale-watching area)*

and human history of Alaska as well as displays of native arts. If it's wet outside, this is a great place to come in from the rain for an hour or two. 395 Whittier Street, 465-2901, www.educ.state.ak. us/lam/museum/asmhome.html. Open business hours daily mid-May–September; winter Tuesday–Saturday; $4.

**House of Wickersham**—At the age of 45, James Wickersham was the first white man to attempt the summit of Mount McKinley. He went on to become a Congressional delegate and district court judge, fighting along the way for the establishment of the Alaska Railroad and Mount McKinley National Park, as well as introducing the idea of Alaska statehood. His Victorian home (also home to other Alaska luminaries) is on the National Register of Historic Places. 213 7th Street, 586-9001. The house is open daily May 15–October 1.

**Juneau–Douglas City Museum**—Across Main Street from the capitol, you'll find this small museum of Juneau and local gold-mining history. Fourth and Main Streets, 586-3572. Open daily in summer; winter Friday–Saturday; $2.

**Last Chance Mining Museum**—Located at Jualapa Mine Camp National Historic District, this museum features mining-history items in an old compressor building. Mining ruins are found outside. Basin Road on Gold Creek, 586-5338. Open daily, morning and late afternoon, $3.

**Mount Roberts Tramway**—Climbing from the cruise-ship area at the south end of downtown, the tram takes tourists up 2,000 feet to the slopes of Mount Roberts. You can link up with the Mount Roberts Trail, for the walk down, or for a hike deeper into the hills to Gastineau Peak and the Mount Roberts summit (see Mount Roberts Trail above). South Franklin Street at cruise docks, 463-3412. Open daily during tourist season, 9 a.m. to 9 p.m., $16.

**Naa Kahidi Theater**—Essentially a native dance show for cruise tourists, Naa Kahidi is nonetheless worthwhile and true to form. Cultural Arts Park at cruise docks, 463-4844; check location or visitors bureau for performance times and admission.

**Saint Nicholas Orthodox Church**—Consecrated in 1894, this unique National Historic and Architectural Site was founded at the request of Tlingit Indians and Slavic immigrants, using Russian blueprints and furnishings. Inside, you can view various icons and liturgical items. Weekend services are held in English, Slavonic, and Tlingit Saturday at 6 p.m. and Sunday at 10 a.m. 326 5th Street. Open mid-May–September, daily 9 to 6, $1 donation.

## Where to Stay in Juneau

**Alaska Bed-and-Breakfast Association** (booking service for over 30 area B&Bs), 586-2959. Good central resource for B&Bs, tour bookings, and rental cars.

**The Alaskan Hotel and Bar**, 167 Franklin Street, (800) 327-9347, 586-1000. $60 (shared bath), $75 (private bath or studio). This oldest operating hotel in Juneau (1913) is listed on the National Register of Historic Places. It's charming, well-kept, reasonable, and right in town.

**Inn at the Waterfront**, 455 South Franklin Street, 586-2050. $60 and up (shared bath), $77 and up (private bath and suites). Historic hotel (once a brothel) with fine keeper and charming bar. Somewhat famous, but the remodeling cut some corners.

**Juneau International Hostel**, 614 Harris Street, Juneau, AK 99801, 586-9559. Beds range from $7 for members to $10 for non-members. Expect sex segregation and typical hostel rules.

**Taku Lodge**, head of Taku Inlet, 30 air miles from Juneau, 586-8258. The lodge caters to day-trippers and offers glacier and wildlife viewing, salmon-bake dining, and a chance to relax. Call for information on charter flights and packages. **BL**

### Where to Eat in Juneau
**Armadillo Tex-Mex Cafe**, 431 South Franklin Street, 586-1880. Tasty and friendly! A favorite of mine.

**Fiddlehead Restaurant and Bakery,** by the Alaska State Museum, 429 W. Willoughby Avenue, 586-3150.

**Hangar on the Wharf Pub & Grill**, 2 Marine Way, 586-5018. Juneau's best selection of microbrews on the waterfront.

**Heritage Coffee Company**, 174 South Franklin Street, 586-1087. Open until 11 p.m.; good coffee and conversation.

**Third Street Pizzeria**, 3rd and North Franklin Streets, 586-1087. Good stuff!

## TRACY ARM–FORDS TERROR WILDERNESS
*Location/Size: Between the Canada border and Endicott Arm, south of Juneau, contiguous with Chuck River Wilderness. 653,179 acres.*
*Main Activities: Kayaking, canoeing, tour boats, wilderness exploration, mountaineering.*
*Gateway Towns/Getting There: Juneau/scheduled air service from Seattle and Anchorage, scheduled ferry service from Ketchikan, Sitka, Haines, Skagway; regular small-plane air service from several points. Wilderness access via tour boat from Juneau, extended kayaking, air or water drop-offs.*
*Facilities, Camping, Lodging: No facilities. Primitive camping only.*
*Headquarters and Information: Forest Service Information Center, 101 Egan Drive, Juneau, AK 99801, 586-8751.*

This spectacular wilderness features numerous jagged peaks and glaciers, including three major tidewater glaciers, two meeting the waters of Tracy Arm and the third at the head of 30-mile-long Endicott Arm. Fords Terror is a narrow, sinuous, T-shaped channel reaching 7 miles into the high country from the northeast side of Endicott Arm. The Chuck River Wilderness is contiguous with Tracy Arm–Fords Terror on the west, completing protection of Endicott Arm from the divide down to the water.

Tracy Arm is well served by tour boats from Juneau. Sawyer Glacier and South Sawyer Glacier meet the water 3 miles apart on either side of a 6,000-foot spur of the Coast Range. Calving can be observed and bergs dot the waters. Endicott Arm has the advantage of being far from any town, offering relative solitude to long-distance kayakers with spectacular Coast Mountain scenery and the impressive Dawes Glacier. Access is almost exclusively by water, though air drop-offs and flightseeing are always possible.

## SITKA

*Location/Climate:* West coast of Baranof Island, 95 air miles south-southwest of Juneau. 94"/yr. precip., 23°F–61°F.

*Population:* 9,194 (20.9 percent native, including Tlingit, Aleut, Haida, and Eskimo).

*Travel Attractions:* Sitka National Historic Park, Sheldon Jackson Museum, Isabel Miller Museum, Castle Hill State Historic Site, Old Sitka State Historic Park, St. Michael's Cathedral, local hiking trails, Mount Edgecumbe, Sitka Sound kayaking, wilderness access.

*Getting There:* Scheduled air and ferry service from Juneau.

*Information:* Sitka Visitor Center, at cruise dock on Harbor Drive, Sitka, AK 99835; Sitka Visitors and Convention Bureau, P.O. Box 1226, Sitka, AK 99835, 747-5940, www.sitka.org.

When the first Russians arrived at the village of Shee-Atika in 1799, they found the Kiksadi clan of Tlingit Indians long established in the region. Together with Aleuts who were more slaves than allies, soldiers fighting for Alexander Baranov and the Russian-American Fur Trading Company drove the Tlingit from the area in 1804, established a stockade and settlement, and renamed the town "New Archangel." The town served as the capital of Russian America until Alaska was sold to the United States in 1867. Under the Rus-

Paul Otteson

*Sitka Harbor*

sians, Sitka grew with the wealth of the fur trade, then hung on through the decline of the otter by developing shipping, fishing, milling, and ice-export industries.

Today Sitka is a favorite destination in Southeast Alaska. The town has two institutions of higher education (University of Alaska Southeast–Sitka campus and Sheldon Jackson College), is rich in history, and is no longer home to a major pulp mill (closed several years ago). While a popular cruise-ship destination, Sitka feels far less touristy than Skagway or Juneau. In addition, its location on Baranof Island means that glacier-capped peaks and sheltered waters are close by.

Sitka is easily reached by scheduled air or ferry service from Juneau and other points. The airport is on Alice Island, also home to the small U of A campus and a short shuttle from town over the very visible bridge. The ferry terminal is 6 miles and a $5 shuttle from town on Halibut Point Road—though you can comfortably walk to the campground at Old Sitka from the ferry dock (1 mile). The road system on Baranof is very short, so it's not worth paying to bring a car over on the ferry unless it's part of a larger journey.

One marvelous feature of the Sitka area is the 3,200-foot, near-perfect volcanic cone of **Mount Edgecumbe**, 16 miles west of town across Sitka Sound on Kruzof Island. The 6-mile **Mount Edgecumbe Trail** climbs to the summit from the island's east shore, with a reservable cabin and additional shelter on the way. Two miles northeast of the peak is **Crater Ridge**, featuring a perfect, 600-foot-deep volcanic crater 1.5 miles in diameter.

Sitka offers numerous attractions, most of which are easily reached on foot from the town center. Check at the visitor center, where Harbor Drive swings by the cruise dock, for information on native dance performances in Centennial Hall.

## Hiking Trails near Sitka

Several good trails are accessible from Sitka; a couple begin right in town.

**Gavan Hill Trail** (6 miles, 3,100' gain)—From the end of Baranof Street in town, the trail climbs 4 miles through forest to the exposed ridge and summit of Gavan Hill (2,650'). From here it's a 2-mile ridgewalk to Harbor Mountain (3,160'). To make a loop, continue down the Harbor Mountain Trail to the end of Harbor Mountain Road and hope for a 10-mile ride back to town. Otherwise, RT—all day.

**Indian River Trail** (5.5 miles, 700' gain)—The trail begins left of the pumphouse and dam at the end of Indian River Road off of Sawmill Creek Road, just south of Sitka, about 1.3 miles from downtown. This easy route follows the river through rain forest to Indian River Falls. Rough access to the ridges above the watershed offers possible high-country routes with exposure and views. RT—all day.

**Mount Verstovia Trail** (2.5 miles, 3,300' gain)—From the trailhead on Sawmill Creek Road 2 miles south of town at Rookies Bar and Grill, this route switchbacks up to the ridge-end summit of Mount Verstovia, offering great views of town and Sitka Sound. It's possible to follow the ridge inland if desired. RT—half day.

## Things to See and Do in Sitka

**Alaska Raptor Rehabilitation Center**—A volunteer effort has made this the Southeast's premier raptor rescue center. Animals that cannot be released into the wild are on display to visitors. It's located on Sawmill Creek Road, just south of Indian River and the

Sitka National Cemetery. Open daily in summer; hours vary so call ahead, 747-8662.

**Castle Hill State Historic Site**—Climb the steps from Lincoln Street near the Sitka Hotel to reach this National Historical Landmark. Originally the site of a Tlingit settlement, the Russian-American Fur Trading Company built a castlelike edifice atop the hill for high officials. The structure burned in 1894. Castle Hill was the site of the official transfer of Alaska from Russia to the United States on October 18, 1867, as well as where the 49-star flag was first raised in an Alaskan statehood ceremony on July 4, 1959. The hill is now crowned with a small plaza surrounded by a low wall and guarded by historic Russian cannons.

**Isabel Miller Museum**—Home of the Sitka Historical Society, this museum covers all aspects of the town's history from Russian, Tlingit, and American perspectives. A favorite exhibit is the scale model of Sitka in 1867. Located in the Centennial Building by the cruise dock, 747-6455. Open May 15–October 1, daily 9 a.m. to 5 p.m.; winter Tuesday–Saturday; $1.

**Old Sitka Historical Site and State Park**—Located about 7 miles north of town on Halibut Point Road, this small park has nature trails, a boat launch, and a campground. The park is on the site of the original 1799 Russian settlement. After they were driven out by the native Tlingits, the Russians fought their way back in 1804 and established the town on the current site.

**Pioneers Home**—Another of Sitka's landmarks, this large retirement home at the north end of Lincoln Street is fronted by a wide plaza and Totem Square. It's worth a walk-through.

**Russian Cemetery, Princess Maksoutov Grave, and Russian Blockhouse**—Reached from Marine Street above Seward Street, these sites are a walk-and-look window into Sitka's Russian past. The princess was the wife of Sitka's second governor. Get a city map and guide from the visitor center to pinpoint locations and get historic details.

**Saint Michael's Russian Orthodox Church**—The centerpiece of Sitka and its chief identifying structure, St. Michael's and its onion-shaped domes is unmistakable. The original church, built in 1848, burned to the ground in 1966, though many artifacts were saved and installed in an exact replica constructed in the 1970s. Lincoln Street, 747-8120. Open summer, daily 11 a.m. to 3 p.m. or at other hours to accommodate cruise ships; $2 suggested donation.

**Sheldon Jackson Museum**—Located on the campus of Sheldon Jackson College, this excellent museum of native heritage artifacts was built in 1897 with funds raised and donated by the Reverend Dr. Sheldon Jackson, a Presbyterian missionary and the first General Agent of Education for Alaska. The octagonal structure is modeled after a Northwest Coast native community house. 104 College Drive, 747-8981. Open daily mid-May–mid-September 9 a.m. to 5 p.m.; winter Tuesday–Saturday.

**Sitka National Cemetery**—Established in 1867 as the first national cemetery west of the Mississippi. Sawmill Creek Road at Jeff Davis Street.

**Sitka Tribe of Alaska Community House**—Offers presentations of native songs and dances, as well as artwork. 200 Katlian Street, 747-7290. Stop at the gift ship for performance times.

## Where to Stay in Sitka

**Homestead Outfitters**, P.O. Box 691, Sitka, AK 99835, (800) 995-0461, 747-6765. Enjoy an affordable cabin stay on an island 10 minutes from Sitka Harbor. Cabins have kitchenettes, private baths, wood-fired saunas, and spacious decks. Lund and bareboat rentals available. Open May–September. $70.

**Sitka Hotel**, 118 Lincoln Street, 747-3288, sitkah@ptialaska.net. Nicely remodeled and well kept, this historic inn is a great choice. Rooms are $50 to $100.

**Sitka Youth Hostel** (Hostelling International), 303 Kimsham Street, P.O. Box 2645, Sitka, AK 99835, 747-8356. Beds are $9.

**Tongass National Forest Campgrounds:** Starrigavan—Old Sitka site, 7 miles north of town, Halibut Point Road, $8. Sawmill Creek—7 miles east of town, Sawmill Creek Road, no treated water, free.

**Westmark Shee Atika**, 330 Seward Street, 747-6241, $90 to $140. This is Sitka's hotel and the best place to get a shuttle to the ferry terminal. All the amenities.

## Where to Eat in Sitka

**The Backdoor Cafe/Old Harbor Books,** 201 Lincoln Street, 747-8808. An excellent bohemian retreat for book browsing, espresso drinks, and pastries.

**Ginny's Kitchen,** 236 Lincoln Street, 747-8028. Good soups and sandwiches, great pies and baked goods, espresso drinks.

**Highliner Coffee,** Seward Square Mall, across from the Westmark Hotel, 747-4924. Coffees, bagels, pastries, cookies, and more. Internet and e-mail access.

**Lane 7 Snack Bar,** 331 Lincoln Street (at the bowling alley). Burgers, fries, and breakfast. A favorite local place for good grub.

## SITKA NATIONAL HISTORIC PARK

*Location/Size: Main unit is at the end of Lincoln Street, ¼-mile east of downtown. Russian Bishop House is on Lincoln at Monastery Street, across from the cruise dock. Less than 40 acres.*
*Main Activities: Historic tours, totem poles, shoreline walks, visitor center.*
*Gateway Towns/Getting There: Sitka/scheduled air or ferry service. Park is accessible by a short walk from town center.*
*Facilities, Camping, Lodging: Visitor center at main unit, Russian House, totems, Tlingit fort, footpaths. No camping or back-country lodging.*
*Headquarters and Information: Headquarters, P.O. Box 738, 106 Metlakatla Street, Sitka, AK 99835, 747-6281, www.nps.gov/sitk; visitor center, end of Lincoln at park entrance.*

Established in 1910 as Alaska's first federally designated park, Sitka National Historic Park preserves key pieces of both Tlingit and Russian history and is Sitka's top travel attraction. The park was created to commemorate the 1804 Battle of Sitka, when the Kiksadi clan of Tlingit Indians repelled an attack by Russians and Aleuts. The main unit of the park includes the battleground, the site of the Kiksadi fort held during the siege, a number of wonderful totems, a fine forest walk, a salmon stream, and a good visitor center.

A smaller unit of the park preserves the marvelously restored **Russian Bishop's House,** home and offices for Bishop Ivan

Veniaminov, first Bishop of Sitka. Completed in 1842, the house served as the center of Russian ecclesiastical authority in a diocese that ranged from Fort Ross, California, to the Kamchatka Peninsula of Russia. The house is on Lincoln Street across from the boat harbor, 3 blocks from the park visitor center and across the street from the striking St. Peter's Episcopal Church.

## WEST CHICHAGOF–YAKOBI WILDERNESS

*Location/Size: Near western coast and mountains of Chichagof and Yakobi Islands, about 30 miles north of Sitka. 264,747 acres.*
*Main Activities: Fishing, kayaking, wilderness exploration, hot springs, backcountry stays.*
*Gateway Towns/Getting There: Sitka/scheduled air service from Juneau and other points; scheduled ferry service from Juneau and Ketchikan. Wilderness access via floatplane, charter boat, or sea kayak.*
*Facilities, Camping, Lodging: Maintained trails and hot-springs pools. Primitive camping, five reservable backcountry cabins.*
*Headquarters and Information: Sitka Ranger District, Tongass National Forest, 201 Kaitlian Street, Sitka, AK 99835, 747-4220.*

West Chichagof–Yakobi features a rugged coastline and a mountainous interior shaped by glaciers—though the highest peaks here rarely break 3,000 feet and do not have active glaciers. One of the best features of this wilderness is the excellent inside passage available to kayakers. The route covers about 30 air miles from the White Sulfur Hot Springs trailhead on Portlock Harbor, south to Slocum Arm. The water miles can vary depending on several factors, including how much you explore. Several trails, forest roads, and non-wilderness segments can be thrown into the mix, permitting extended journeys based in Sitka, Pelican, Angoon, or elsewhere.

### White Sulfur Hot Springs

Two deep, 104-degree, sheltered pools are located at the head of Bertha Bay on the Pacific coast of Chichagof Island, about 20 water miles from the town of Pelican. The springs are probably the most popular attraction in the wilderness; the backcountry cabin on site is often reserved well in advance. Floatplane access is generally unavailable, but a very expensive helicopter shuttle can be booked from Sitka. The best access is via ferry to Pelican and kayak or charter boat to the springs. A 6-mile trail links the kayak area around Portlock Harbor with the springs, allowing access without risking the open ocean. Contact Lisianski Wilderness Lodge in Pelican about possible drop off (see appendix).

## SOUTH BARANOF WILDERNESS
*Location: 319,568 acres at southern end of Baranof Island, south of Sitka.*
*Main Activities: Fishing, sea kayaking, wilderness exploration.*
*Gateway Towns/Getting There: Sitka/scheduled air service from Juneau and other points; scheduled ferry service from Juneau and Ketchikan. Park access via floatplane, charter boat, or sea kayak.*
*Facilities, Camping, Lodging: Short inter-lake trails access fishing and cabins. Primitive camping only, five reservable backcountry cabins on lakeshores.*
*Headquarters and Information: Sitka Ranger District, Tongass National Forest, 201 Kaitlian Street, Sitka, AK 99835, 747-4220.*

This wet and rugged wilderness features dozens of tight, twisting, glacier-carved valleys, numerous fjords and lakes, ragged peaks, a few small glaciers, and wild weather. Fierce storms pound the island's Pacific coast from September through December. Annual rainfall can exceed 200 inches. Intrepid sea kayakers can reach the north end of the wilderness from Sitka by using a combination of portages, lakes, and island-sheltered waters. If the weather cooperates, challenging open-water routes may also be possible, though south of Walker Channel the headlands are all severely exposed.

Floatplane access is the preferred method, with five reservable backcountry cabins on five different lakes in the southwestern part of the wilderness offering great bases for fishing, canoeing, kayaking, and attempts on ridges and summits. Contact outfitters in Sitka and the Sitka Ranger District office for recommended options (see above and appendix).

## HAINES
*Location/Climate: 80 miles north of Juneau on the Chilkat Peninsula at the head of Lynn Canal. Moderated maritime climate, 23°F–66°F.*
*Population: 1,394 (18.1 percent native, mainly Tlingit).*
*Travel Attractions: Fort Seward, Alaska Chilkat Bald Eagle Preserve,*

*local and regional arts center, Sheldon Museum, Mount Ripinski and other hikes, kayaking, tours and flightseeing, regional access.*
***Getting There:*** *Vehicle access via Haines Highway from Haines Junction, Yukon; scheduled ferry from Skagway or Juneau; scheduled small-plane air service from Juneau.*
***Information:*** *Haines Visitor Information Center, 122 2nd Avenue, Haines, AK 99827, (800) 458-3579, 766-2234, www.haines.ak.us.*

Most visitors to Haines are just passing through, arriving with their vehicles from Prince Rupert or Bellingham and heading inland on the Haines Highway (or vice versa). Built during World War II along the route of an old Klondike gold-rush toll road, the Haines Highway is the most direct of the two road routes from the Southeast to the rest of the state. Those who stay on the ferry to reach Skagway have another road option, though it is longer and no more scenic. Consider Haines as both a destination in its own right and as a transit alternative to historic but very touristy Skagway.

Haines is an excellent recreational gateway. Located on the Chilkat Peninsula where the Lynn Canal (longest fjord in the United States) splits in two, Haines is situated at a remarkable junction of valleys. Within 15 miles of town, six major watersheds branch off from Lynn Canal, reaching up toward the glaciers of the jagged divide that circles the head of the panhandle, roughly parallel to the U.S.-Canada border. Access to trailheads and raft, canoe, and kayak put-ins is good. In addition to the Haines Highway along the Chilkat River, minor roads lead south along the peninsula to Chilkat State Park and northward to the mouth of the Chilkoot River. Haines hosts several tour-boat, flightseeing, and charter companies.

## Things to See and Do in Haines

The town of Haines is given historic character by the marvelous old homes of Fort Seward. Cruise ships are infrequent visitors, which means that merchants move less junk while residents are more open and less jaded. Artists and craftspeople have made Haines a regional center of creativity. Best of all, perhaps, Haines is sheltered from the west winds by many mountains and receives about a third of the annual rainfall experienced in Sitka or Ketchikan.

**Alaska Indian Arts**—Native artisans can be observed making totems, masks, blankets, and jewelry at this nonprofit center in the old base hospital at Fort Seward. Head to the south side of the parade grounds, 766-2704, www.ravenswindow.com/aia.htm, open Monday through Saturday, 9 a.m. to 5 p.m.

**American Bald Eagle Foundation**—This nonprofit foundation was established in 1982 to study and protect the American bald eagle. There's an excellent wildlife museum, featuring dioramas that include most of Alaska's native species. It's on 2nd Avenue at the Haines Highway, halfway between town and Fort Seward, 766-3094, www. gauntletllc.com/abef; open in summer, Monday through Friday 9 a.m. to 10 p.m., Saturday and Sunday 9 a.m. to 6 p.m.; open Monday, Wednesday, and Friday afternoons in winter. Donation requested.

**Chilkat Center for the Arts**—Located in Fort Seward's old recreation hall a block south of the parade ground, this is home to the Chilkat Dancers, 766-2160, who perform throughout the summer. The center also hosts melodrama shows. Call the visitor center for information, (800) 458-3579, 766-2234, www.haines.ak.us.

**Fort Seward**—The stately, evenly spaced, uniformly designed structures of old Fort Seward surround a parade green and are unmistakable to those passing by on the ferry. The fort was built at the turn of the century as a military base to secure a region heated by gold fever. Located about half a mile south of downtown via 2nd Avenue, several structures of this designated national historic site are privately occupied today, but some are used in whole or part for lodging, food, or arts-and-crafts centers

**Sheldon Museum**—The chief downtown attraction, a library and exhibits, ". . . interpret the history and native culture of the local region while conveying unique local stories, tales and legends." It's just up from the shoreline at 11 Main Street, Haines, 766-2366, www.sheldonmuseum.org; open daily in summer, 1 p.m. to 5 p.m.; open shorter hours, Monday through Saturday in the off-season: $3.

## Alaska Chilkat Bald Eagle Preserve
For about two months starting in late September, tens of thousands of chum salmon return to area rivers to spawn and die.

Birds, bears, and wolves feed on the bounty; over 3,000 bald eagles at a time have been counted along the 5-mile stretch of the Chilkat River north of Haines during the feast. Road access to the preserve is excellent since the Haines Highway follows the lower Chilkat past prime viewing areas. Another unit of the preserve is north of town along the lower Chilkoot River.

Don't forget that eagles can be seen year-round throughout the Southeast, perching in the treetops, fishing or scavenging near harbors, and winging along the shore. Several hundred nesting sites are located in the region. Indeed, if the ferry hours are long and most of the tourists are snoozing in the recliners, step out on deck into the bracing wind and search for bright white heads atop the spruce and hemlock.

Remember that eagles should not be approached or disturbed in any way. Observers along the Chilkat and elsewhere should stay behind binoculars and telephoto lenses, well clear of feeding areas. Information on the preserve is available at the Alaska State Parks, Southeast Area office, 400 Willoughby, 4th floor, Juneau, AK 99801, 465-4563, www.dnr.state.ak.us/parks/units/eagleprv.htm.

## Where to Stay in Haines

**Alaska State Park Campgrounds—Portage Cove**, Beach Road, just south of Fort Seward. No vehicles. **Mosquito Lake**, Mile 27, Haines Highway. **Chilkoot Lake**, Lutak Road, 10 miles north of town, past ferry dock. **Chilkat State Park**, off Mud Bay Road, 7 miles south of Haines. Open mid-May–mid-October, $6–$10 per night.

**Bear Creek Camp and International Hostel**, Small Tracts Road, 766-2259. $8 (camping), $14 (dorm), $38 and up (family cabins). Showers, kitchen facilities, free ferry shuttle, tours, bike rental, laundry, store.

**Fort Seward Lodge**, Fort Seward, (800) 478-7772, 766-2009, fax 766-2006. $60–$70 (private bath), $45–$55 (shared), $75–$85 (kitchenette). Located in old Post Exchange, family owned, restaurant and saloon.

**Hotel Halsingland**, Fort Seward, (800) 542-6363, 766-2000. A fine hotel in an original Fort Seward Victorian. Rooms with bath start at $90, cheaper ones with shared bath start at $50.

*Skagway*

Paul Otteson

**A Sheltered Harbor Bed-and-Breakfast**, 57 Beach Road (below Fort Seward at Port Chilkoot dock), 766-2741. Waterfront location, breakfast, private baths, views, no pets, no smoking.

### Where to Eat in Haines
**Bamboo Room Restaurant/Pioneer Bar**, downtown Haines, restaurant, 766-2800; bar, 766-9901. Open year-round, daily 6 a.m.

**Chilkat Restaurant and Bakery**, 5th Avenue and Main Street, 766-2920. Open daily. Fresh baked goodies and a big, tasty menu.

**33 Mile Roadhouse**, Mile 33 Haines Highway, 767-5510. Open daily in summer. Food, gas, propane, dining, breakfast all day, big burgers, steaks. **RH**

## SKAGWAY
*Location/Climate: Northernmost end of the Lynn Canal, 95 air miles north of Juneau. 26"/yr. precip., 18°F–67°F.*

**Population:** *811 (5.5 percent native).*
**Travel Attractions:** *Klondike Gold Rush National Historic Park,*
*Chilkoot Trail, Dyea site, White Pass and Yukon Railroad excursions,*
*Historic District, various private museums and tourist attractions.*
**Getting There:** *Scheduled A.M.H.S. ferries from Haines, Juneau, and*
*points south; scheduled air service from Juneau, Haines, and Whitehorse,*
*Yukon; scheduled water taxi from Haines; vehicle access via the Klondike*
*Highway (AK 2) from the Alaska Highway; bus/rail from Whitehorse.*
**Information:** *Visitor Information Center in the Arctic Brotherhood*
*Hall, Broadway between 2nd and 3rd in the Historic District, 983-2855,*
*www.skagway.org.*

In 1897 thousands of gold seekers began arriving in the new towns
of Skagway and Dyea. They came from Seattle and other Pacific
ports, most having no idea that the majority of worthwhile Klondike
claims had been staked the year before. Early seekers found a Skagway that was no more than a lawless jumble of tents and shacks. By
the turn of the century, Dyea was fading fast, the White Pass and
Yukon Railroad was shuttling people inland, and Skagway was a
bustling, established town.

Situated at the head of the Inside Passage, Skagway is 600 miles
from Dawson City and the historic gold fields. Before the railroad was
completed, miners could choose between two 35-mile trails to reach
Bartlett Lake, the beginning of a long downriver passage to their goal.
The Chilkoot Trail from Dyea was the toughest on the miners. Pack
animals couldn't manage the high pass, forcing men to shuttle their
gear into Canada on repeated foot trips. Only at the end of 1897 were
trams completed to aid in the task. The other route was the White
Pass Trail out of Skagway. Over 3,000 pack animals, overloaded and
unsuited to the trail's rocky terrain, perished on this route.

The Canadian authorities, fearing a famine, demanded that miners
come equipped with enough food to last a year. It took an average of
three months for each of the 20,000 to 30,000 men to shuttle their gear
to the lakes. Crime and disease took a heavy toll on the American side
of the border. Though life was better ordered by the mounties in
Canada, most miners who reached Dawson were lucky if they found
jobs working the "diggins" for others. By the end of 1898, the lode was
failing and miners began to leave for home or newer strikes elsewhere.

Today Skagway is a tourist town catering to cruise-ship visitors
who come for the gold-rush history of Skagway's historic district,

excursions on the narrow-gauge White Pass and Yukon line, and the other attractions of the Klondike Gold Rush Historic Park. More adventurous travelers enjoy a four- to six-day hike over Chilkoot Pass on the Chilkoot Trail, certainly one of the best of Alaska's developed trails. There are also several good day hikes and overnight options out of the basin.

## Hiking Trails near Skagway
**Lower Dewey Lake Trail** (0.7 mile, 500' gain)—An easy trail, the Lower Dewey starts at the east end of 2nd Avenue and climbs to the north end of the lake. At the lake, head south along either shore to the **Sturgill's Landing Trail** (3.2 miles total from town, 1,000' gain mid-hike, no net gain) for moderate forest hiking and picnic/camping options on the shore of Taiya Inlet. From the north end of Lower Dewey Lake, a strenuous trail climbs to **Upper Dewey Lake** (3 miles total from town, 3,080' gain) and on to **Devil's Punchbowl** (4.2 miles total from town, 3,700'). A reservable Forest Service cabin is found at the upper lake and the views above treeline are stunning. RT—1.5 hours to all day.

**Icy Lake Trail** (2 miles, 1,000' gain)—An easy trail contours north from Lower Dewey Lake, or you can start directly from the east end of 2nd Avenue. Icy Lake is a good picnic spot; a mile beyond is pretty Upper Reid Falls. RT—half day from town.

**A.B. Mountain Trail** (4.8 miles, 5,000' gain)—Plan for a long, strenuous day to earn the stellar views from this ridge summit on the spur between the Taiya and Skagway Rivers. Some good views lower down. Cross the airstrip and footbridge at the west end of 1st Avenue. Trail follows ridgecrest from bend in Dyea Road. RT—8–10 hrs.

**Denver Glacier Trail** (3.5 miles and 1,200' gain from train drop-off)—Have the WP&Y train drop you at the trailhead before it crosses the East Fork of the Skagway River. A difficult and poor trail climbs above treeline to the glacier's moraine. Good high-basin exploring. RT—8–12 hrs.

**Laughlin Glacier Trail** (1.5 miles and 200' gain from train drop-off to cabin; 2 more miles and 1,900' gain to glacier)—Easy trail into wonderful cirque with hanging glaciers. Reservable cabin available (park visitor center in Skagway or Forest Service office in Juneau). Have train make flag stop at south side of Skagway River bridge. Stay overnight if possible. RT—6–10 hrs.

## Things to See and Do in Skagway

The old buildings and boardwalks of the Historic District are themselves the main attraction in touristy Skagway. Stop at both the Klondike Gold Rush National Historic Park visitor center at the train station and the Visitor Information Center in the **Arctic Brotherhood (A.B.) Hall**, both near 2nd and Broadway. Walking-tour informational pamphlets are free.

**Alaskan Wildlife Adventure and Museum**—This new museum features about 70 mounted Alaskan and Yukon animals, including moose, musk ox, bear, lynx, and Dall sheep. Located at 480 Spring Street, open daily in summer, 983-3600.

**Corrington Museum of Alaskan History**—Exhibits of Alaskan history and prehistory are featured, including original art and a collection of scrimshawed walrus tusks. Located at 5th and Broadway, open daily in the summer from 8 a.m. to 9 p.m.

**Gold Rush Cemetery**—Graves include that of Soapy Smith, the local crime boss during the first year of the gold rush. Located 1.5 miles north of the Historic District (take State Street north and follow signs). A short walk from the cemetery is **Reid Falls**, named for Frank Reid, the town hero who shot Soapy Smith and died from the wound he received at the time. Guide booklets to the cemetery can be purchased at the visitor center.

**Skagway Overlook**—Take State Street and the Klondike Highway out of town, then drive 2 miles up Dyea Road for a great view of Skagway and the harbor.

**City of Skagway Skagway Museum**—Located in the Arctic Brotherhood Hall, Broadway between 2nd and 3rd, though it may be moved back into old McCabe College. Features a collection of gold-rush and native Alaskan artifacts. Gold-rush centennial films are shown. Open daily in summer 9 a.m. to 5 p.m., 983-2420.

## KLONDIKE GOLD RUSH NATIONAL HISTORIC PARK

*Location/Size: Several small units in Skagway.*
*Main Activities: History appreciation, hiking, backpacking.*
*Gateway Towns/Getting There: Skagway/scheduled ferry service from Haines and points south; scheduled air service from Juneau, Haines, and Whitehorse; vehicle access via the Klondike Highway (AK 2) from the Alaska Highway; bus/train from Whitehorse.*
*Park access is on foot in downtown Skagway, via 9-mile road or boat*

*shuttle to Dyea and head of Chilkoot Trail, via White Pass and Yukon Railroad or Klondike Highway (AK 2) for views of White Pass (inaccessible on foot).*

**Facilities, Camping, Lodging:** *Visitor center, established trails, historic buildings and sites. Established campgrounds along Chilkoot Trail and at the Dyea site.*

**Headquarters and Information:** *Headquarters, P.O. Box 517, Skagway, AK 99840, 983-2921, www.nps.gov/klgo; visitor center and White Pass and Yukon Railroad Station, 2nd Avenue and Broadway.*

The main tourist attraction in Skagway is the downtown Historic District with its vintage buildings. For adventurous visitors, the Chilkoot Trail is the big draw. Both are a part of Klondike Gold Rush National Historic Park, as are the historic site of Dyea, much of the White Pass Trail route, and an area of Pioneer Square in Seattle. Gold-rush history dominates Skagway, and the park manages the best of it. Stop at the visitor center for a park map, displays, and information.

**Chilkoot Trail** (33 miles, 3,700' gain northbound, 1,200' gain southbound)—Perhaps the best developed of Alaska's relatively few long-distance trails, the route begins at the abandoned town of Dyea, a short drive or boat shuttle from Skagway. Climbing along the Taiya River to Chilkoot Pass, the trail crosses into Canada and continues through lake country to the train station at Lake Bennett. Northbound walkers enjoy the same experience the miners had on their first trip into Canada. Southbound walkers can enjoy a hike with less elevation gain.

At the north end of the Chilkoot, hikers can take a cutoff trail to the train tracks from Bare Loon Lake, then walk the tracks to the highway (5 miles). A daily train departs Lake Bennett for Skagway at 9 a.m., while a tour train that runs Thursday through Monday arrives in Lake Bennett from Skagway at noon, then returns at 1 p.m. (see White Pass & Yukon Route below). A water taxi shuttles travelers from the Lake Bennett station to Carcross, Yukon, (867) 667-1486.

There are established campgrounds every 3 or 4 miles along the route, as well as numerous historic sites and random artifacts from the gold-rush days. Stop at the park visitor center in Skagway for detailed information on conditions, Canadian customs, north-end transport, and easy-to-get permits. Through trail—3–4 days.

Paul Otteson

*White Pass and Yukon Route train*

## Where to Stay in Skagway

**Golden North Hotel**, P.O. Box 343, 3rd and Broadway, 983-2451. $45–$75 (some private bath, some shared). Skagway's oldest operating hotel, in the heart of the Historic District.

**Portland House**, 5th and State Street, 983-2493. $30–$45. Nine-room inn built in 1897, shared baths, restaurant, in Historic District.

**Skagway Home Hostel**, 3rd between State and Main, 983-2131. $15. Fifteen beds, curfew, shuttle, laundry, kitchen, common room.

**Westmark Inn**, 3rd and Spring Street, (800) 544-0970, 983-6000. Large, modern hotel. Alaska's nicest chain. Restaurants, free shuttle.

**Wind Valley Lodge**, Klondike Highway, half-mile north of Historic District, 983-2236. $62–$80, under 12 free. Nice motel, AAA, courtesy shuttle, restaurant.

### Where to Eat in Skagway

**Corner Cafe**, 4th and State Street, 983-2155. Breakfast and lunch. **Red Onion**, 2nd and Broadway, 983-2222. Pizzas, nachos, entertainment, and tourists.

**Sweet Tooth Cafe**, 3rd and Broadway, 983-2405. Real home cooking and ice cream.

## WHITE PASS AND YUKON ROUTE

Skagway's most popular single attraction for tourists is also of interest to backpackers and those traveling between the Southeast and the Yukon or Alaskan Interior. Completed in 1900, the narrow-

# Skagway Train Schedule

*Reservations for all trains are strongly advised! Call to confirm the current schedule, but it should look a lot like this:*

|  | Depart Skagway | Depart Whitehorse | Arrive Skagway | Arrive Whitehorse |
|---|---|---|---|---|
| A.M. summit | 8:30 a.m. | — | 11:30 a.m. | — |
| P.M. summit | 1:00 p.m. | — | 4:00 p.m. | — |
| Tue & Wed summit | 4:30 p.m. | — | 7:30 p.m. | — |
| *To Whitehorse | 12:40 p.m. | — | — | 6:00 p.m. |
| *To Skagway | — | 8:00 a.m. | noon | — |
| Thu–Mon Lake Bennett tour | 8:00 a.m. | — | 4:30 p.m. | — |

*Bus/train transfer in Fraser—10:20 a.m. southbound, 2:40 p.m. northbound.

gauge White Pass & Yukon Route replaced the trails as the main mode of transit for the first leg of the trip to the Klondike. Today the route's historic trains offer spectacular views, flag stops at trailheads, and a 5-times-weekly round-trip to Lake Bennett where the early miners finished walking and took to the water. It's also possible to link with a bus to Whitehorse.

Three trains operate regularly. One takes three-hour round trips to the summit of White Pass, two or three times daily. A second is based in Fraser, British Columbia, and serves the daily train/bus run between Skagway and Whitehorse. A third takes an all-day tour between Skagway and Lake Bennett. Chilkoot Trail hikers can catch Skagway-bound Fraser-based train at Lake Bennett at 9 a.m. Thursday through Monday. The Lake Bennett tour train arrives at the lake at around noon and departs for Skagway at 1 p.m. About six times a summer, a special train does the Lake Bennett tour, pulled by a Mikado-class 282 Baldwin steam engine. It's a must for rail buffs (call for schedule).

The station is at 2nd Avenue and Broadway, (800) 343-7373, 983-2217, www.whitepassrailroad.com. Summit trips are $80; the Lake Bennett tour goes for $120 (includes coffee, lunch, Lake Bennett guide), the Chilkoot Trail pick-up or drop-off for $65, and the special steam-engine tours for $160. Kids are half-price on all trips.

## GLACIER BAY NATIONAL PARK AND PRESERVE

*Location/Size:* Northwest of Gustavus, which is 45 miles northwest of Juneau. National park—3,225,284 acres (99 percent federal land); national preserve—57,884 acres (95 percent federal); designated wilderness—2,770,000 acres.

*Main Activities:* Glacier viewing, tours, kayaking, off-trail coastal and open-country hiking, wilderness exploration.

*Gateway Towns/Getting There:* Gustavus/scheduled air service from Juneau, Haines; charter and tour-package boat service from Juneau. Park access by charter boat or tour, floatplane or boat drop-off, or kayak from Gustavus and Bartlett Cove.

*Facilities, Camping, Lodging:* Visitor center, Glacier Lodge, and free campground at Bartlett Cove. Primitive camping only in backcountry.

*Headquarters and Information:* Headquarters, P.O Box 140, Gustavus, AK 99826, 697-2230, www.nps.gov/glba; visitor center above Glacier Bay Lodge at Bartlett Cove.

Superlatives usually accompany any discussion of Glacier Bay. Two hundred years ago, when Englishman George Vancouver explored the region, only a small indentation existed at what is now a deep inlet. Since then, Vancouver's "solid mountains of ice rising perpendicularly from the water's edge" have retreated almost 60 miles inland. The nearest tidewater glacier is 40 miles from the park center.

Several factors influence the retreat of the glaciers in Glacier Bay and throughout the state. Global warming may be a part of it, but changes in cloud cover, snowfall, and ocean currents can have a tremendous impact. Alaska's coastal glaciers thrive primarily because of high precipitation rather than low temperatures. It should be noted as well that both Johns Hopkins Glacier and the Grand Pacific Glacier began growing again after the 1920s (though others continue to retreat).

The fantastic retreat of Glacier Bay's glaciers actually offers the observant traveler a visible history of plant succession. Near the bay mouth, land has been exposed for 200 years, allowing soil to establish and host a succession of plants all the way up to mature stands of western hemlock and Sitka spruce. Traveling inward, exposure time decreases until you near the margins of the existing glaciers and find plant communities in their infancy. The actual picture is somewhat complex but, with a little research, is easily observed.

The great majority of the 350,000 annual park visitors arrive on one of the many cruise ships permitted to enter the bay each summer. Almost all ships take the same route, cruising up the West Arm to the ice, then cruising out again. Non-cruisers commonly arrive in Gustavus by air, staying in town or shuttling to Bartlett Cove to camp or stay at Glacier Bay Lodge, the only park hotel. Smaller tour boats operate from both Gustavus and Bartlett Cove to shuttle visitors to the glaciers.

Both kayaking and hiking are great activities to pursue in the park, though access to drop-off and pick-up points can be expensive. Kayakers can enjoy solitude in the several bays and inlets that are designated wilderness. Most are accessed via the East Arm. Part-time wilderness status is designated for other areas (call for schedule). Hikers can follow good routes along the beaches, across meadows, along low ridges, and on the barren areas of recent deglaciation. Permits, detailed information, and a complete list of tour and shuttle providers are available through the park headquarters and visitor center (see the appendix for recommended providers).

Bartlett Cove is the park center, offering a campground, Glacier Bay Lodge, visitor center, boat dock, information station, and headquarters building. It also has two short trails: **Bartlett River Trail** (2 miles) and **Forest Loop Trail** (1.5 miles).

The **Bartlett Lake Trail** (4.5 miles) passes through temperate rain forest from the Gustavus Road trailhead near the headquarters to Bartlett Lake. **RT**—7–9 hrs.

## GUSTAVUS

*Location/Climate:* 50 miles northwest of Juneau. 26°F–63°F.
*Population:* 328 (4 percent native).
*Travel Attractions:* Gateway to Glacier Bay National Park and Preserve, tours, rentals.

*Getting There: Scheduled air service and water-taxi service from Juneau and Haines.*
*Information: Gustavus Visitors Association, P.O. Box 167, Gustavus, AK 99826, 697-2285.*

Not much of a town at all, Gustavus' homes and businesses are scattered on about 40 square miles of private land along the roads between the airport and Bartlett Cove. Virtually all travelers to Gustavus come because it is the gateway to Glacier Bay National Park. Several good food and lodging options are found near town. Most lodging operators are also involved in the tour, outfitting, and rental business. Consider booking short visits and tours directly through one of them.

## Where to Stay and Eat in Gustavus

**Glacier Bay Country Inn**, 697-2288, $195 per person (single), $161 per person (double), $410 for Glacier Bay Tour, whale-watching, and meals. A beautiful, full-service inn.

**Gustavus Inn At Glacier Bay**, 697-2254. $135 per person. Meals, shuttles, bikes, and fishing poles included. Lovely inn in large, restored 1928 home.

**A Puffin's Bed-and-Breakfast Lodge**, 697-2260, $90 (private bath). Five nice cabins, three with bath. Free shuttle to transport. Package deals with tours offered.

**TRI Bed-and-Breakfast**, 697-2425, $90 and up (breakfast, bikes included). Cabins with ensuite bath, packages offered, kayak rentals, tours.

## Tatshenshini and Alsek River Running

Some of the best paddling in the north can be enjoyed on the Alsek River and it's major tributary, the Tatshenshini River. The Tatshenshini parallels the Haines Highway in the Yukon before swinging south at Dalton Post. Many put-in at Dalton Post for a week-long (or more), 140-mile trip to Dry Bay on the Alaskan coast. An early Class III-IV canyon run gives way to Class II waters through Tatshenshini-Alsek Wilderness Park in British Columbia.

Haines Junction is the put-in for the Alsek and the 172-mile trip to Dry Bay. The river flows for many miles through Yukon's Kluane

National Park. About halfway down is the unrunnable Turnback Canyon where a glacier pinches the channel too close for comfort. There is no walking portage so guided trips use a helicopter shuttle to close the gap. Independent paddlers must make similar arrangements.

Below the confluence of the rivers, the route crosses into the spectacular western tip of Glacier Bay National Park and on to the take-out at Dry Bay. A highlight is a close encounter with Alsek Glacier where it calves bergs into the lake below. A permit is required for the Glacier Bay segment and Dry Bay arrivals, and since Dry Bay is about the only place to link up with your charter air shuttle, you'll want to get a permit. Getting a permit is easy enough, though you'll probably need to be flexible about the dates. Apply well in advance if you aren't working through a guide company. Call the 24-hour information line for up-to-date permit-availability info, 784-3370. Contact the park service's Yakutat District Office to speak with human experts, 784-3295. Several outfitters and guide companies support trips on the Tatshen-shini and Alsek (see Appendix). Dry Bay has limited lodging.

## YAKUTAT

***Location/Climate:*** *Base of St. Elias Mountains on the Gulf of Alaska, 210 miles northwest of Juneau. Heavy precip., 17°F–60°F.*
***Population:*** *801 (55.1 percent native, mainly Tlingit and Eyak).*
***Travel Attractions:*** *Recreational fishing, sea kayaking, access to Russell Fiord Wilderness, access to Wrangell–St. Elias National Park, glacier viewing.*
***Getting There:*** *Scheduled air service from Juneau and Anchorage; air-taxi and charter plane, monthly A.H.M.S. ferry.*
***Information:*** *City and borough offices, P.O. Box 160, Yakutat, AK 99689, 784-3323; Tongass National Forest/Yakutat Ranger Station, P.O. Box 327, Yakutat, AK 99689; 784-3359, www.fs.fed.us/r10/tongass/districts/yakutat/yakutat.html.*

The word "Yakutat" means "the place where the canoes rest." Eyak Indians, driven from the Copper River delta by Tlingits, were probably the original settlers. The Russian-American Company built a fort here in 1805, though it was later destroyed by Tlingits fighting for access to traditional fishing grounds. Beginning in the mid-1880s, gold mining, fishing, and timber harvesting entered the economic picture. Later,

World War II troops came and went, leaving a military airstrip for civilian use. Fishing and fish processing employ most workers today.

Adventurers can use Yakutat as a base for exploring the Russell Fiord Wilderness, the St. Elias Mountains, and the southeast corner of Wrangell–St. Elias National Park and Preserve. Several Forest Service cabins are scattered in the "Yakutat Foreland"—the lowland strip between the mountains and the sea. Fishing the Situk River, glacier hiking, and sea kayaking are all excellent possibilities.

Several tidewater glaciers meet Disenchantment Bay and Nunatak Fiord in Russell Fiord Wilderness. The edge of Malaspina Glacier is 20 miles from town, across Yakutat Bay. In general, Russell Fiord and Icy Bay (up the coast) offer the best chances for truly wild access to amazing, glacier-fed fjords. If you can afford the flights, consider investigating further. Service providers are listed in the appendix.

### Where to Stay and Eat in Yakutat
**Glacier Bear Lodge**, P.O. Box 303, Yakutat, AK 99689, 784-3202, www.glacierbearlodge.com. Rooms are $90 and up. **BL**

## RUSSELL FIORD WILDERNESS
*Location/Size: North of Yakutat, arms of Yakutat Bay, at the feet of the St. Elias Mountains, 349,000 acres.*
*Main Activities: Sea kayaking, wilderness camping, mountaineering, glacier access.*
*Gateway Towns/Getting There: Yakutat/scheduled regular and small-plane air service from Anchorage and Juneau monthly A.M.H.S. ferry. Wilderness access by air and boat drop-offs, extended sea kayaking, 1-mile trail from road-accessed trailhead.*
*Facilities, Camping, Lodging: No facilities. One Forest Service cabin at Situk Lake, one near wilderness boundary at Harlequin Lake. Primitive camping.*
*Headquarters and Information: Tongass National Forest, Yakutat Ranger Station, P.O. Box 327, Yakutat, AK 99689, 784-3359, www.fs.fed.us/r10/tongass/districts/yakutat/yakutat.html.*

Wrangell–St. Elias National Park, the Yukon's Kluane National Park, British Columbia's Tatshenshini-Alsek Wilderness Park, and the Russell Fiord Wilderness of the Tongass National Forest meet at the most fantastic wilderness "four corners" on the planet, intersecting at the summit of Mount Jette in the St. Elias Range. The fifth corner is a de facto wilderness sliver of the Tongass that includes massive icefields and glaciers.

Pristine and little-visited, Russell Fiord Wilderness protects the narrow, 30-mile-long Russell Fiord, and the 15-mile-long Nunatak Fiord, which branches off to the east. The peaks of the St. Elias Range tower over the water. Russell Fiord opens into Disenchantment Bay right at huge Hubbard Glacier. A road from Yakutat provides access to a 1-mile portage to a good kayak put-in at the southern tip of Russell Fiord, as well as to Harlequin Lake in the southern tip of the wilderness. **Alaska Discovery, Inc.,** leads several kayak trips annually (see appendix). Reservable lakeside Forest Service cabins are available at Harlequin Lake and at Situk Lake not far from the fjord. There are great hiking possibilities on beaches and along recently glaciated valleys.

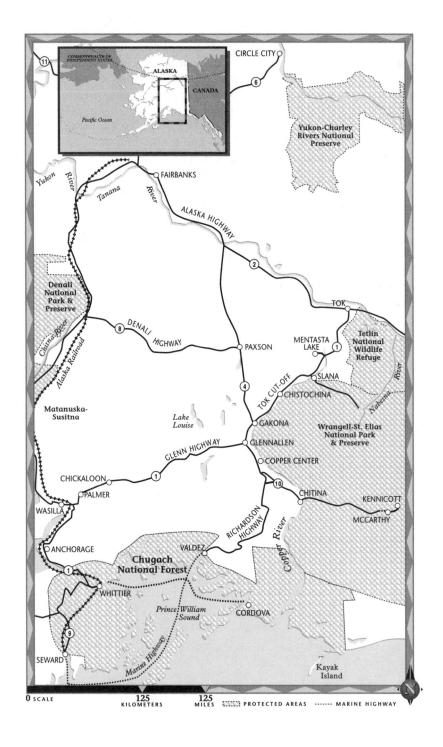

# SOUTHCENTRAL MOUNTAINS & PRINCE WILLIAM SOUND

## 8

Spreading south of the Alaska Range, west of the Canadian border, and east of the MatSu valleys, this varied region features easy access to great destinations. The mountain-ringed Copper River Basin, Wrangell–St. Elias National Park and Preserve, and the coastal delights of Prince William Sound are the main areas of visitor activity. Vehicle travelers are well served by a five-legged road system roughly centered in Glenallen. Regular A.M.H.S. ferries ply the waters of Prince William Sound, connecting to highways at Valdez and Whittier, with Cordova, Seward, and the Southwest as possible extensions.

## THE COPPER RIVER VALLEY

The Copper River gathers the waters of the Talkeetna, Alaska, Chugach, and Wrangell Mountains before cutting its deep path through the Chugach Mountains to the Pacific. Much higher in elevation than the MatSu basin to the west, the Copper Valley does not support agriculture. Residents are few and towns small, but the area's attractions and accessibility by road make it a popular destination for hunters, fishers, and outdoor adventurers.

Ahtna Athabascans lived in the basin for hundreds of years before explorers and trappers arrived in the 1800s, followed soon

Paul Otteson

*The Copper River delta*

thereafter by miners. Most prospectors saught gold, but it was copper mining in the Wrangells that had the greatest impact on the region. The establishment of the Kennecott Mine north of McCarthy led to road and railroad building. An important early trade and transport route from Valdez to Fairbanks followed the path of what is today the Richardson Highway. Several Copper River basin communities began as roadhouse and supply locations for both the mine and the overland route. Today the Trans-Alaska Pipeline parallels the Richardson, adding oil-service jobs and industry to the corridor.

Visitors usually reach the basin by road via one of four mountain passes, reinforcing its isolated image. Much of the region is forested with white and black spruce, while stands of aspen trees turn brilliant yellow and orange in the fall. In upland and boggy areas, the forest thins, yielding to expansive areas of brush, muskeg, and wetlands. Towns are small and services spread out. The climate is more like that of the Interior than the coast, with extreme temperatures and light precipitation. The high peaks of the Wrangells dominate the landscape and include **Mount Wrangell** (14,163'), the largest active volcano in the United States; **Mount Blackburn** (16,390'); **Mount Sanford** (16,237'); and **Mount Drum** (12,010').

Many Copper River basin listings are found in the milepost guides for three main highway segments: the Glenn Highway, Tok Cutoff (part of the Glenn), and the southern half of the Richardson. The milepost listings for the northern half of the Richardson are found in chapter 12.

## Floating the Copper

The Slana River bridge near Slana at the head of the Nabesna Road is a recognized put-in for long-distance float trips on the Copper River. The river parallels highways as far as Chitina, then cuts through the Chugach Mountains along the historic, abandoned rail line from Kennicott to Cordova. The take-out is the Million Dollar Bridge near Childs Glacier, 245 miles from Slana. Several shorter routes are possible because of generally easy land access. Class II to IV whitewater stretches are found along the way. To experience the most scenically rugged portion of the route, start in Chitina.

Towns on the highway near the Copper include Slana, Gakona, Gulkana, Glenallen, Copper Center, and Chitina. A few outfitters and riverboat services operate along the route (see appendix). Consult the rangers of Wrangell–St. Elias National Park and Preserve when planning, as most of the route is within the park boundary (much of it *is* the boundary).

## GLENALLEN
*Location/Climate:* On the Glenn Highway near the Copper River. 9"/yr. precip., 39"/yr. snowfall, -74°F–96°F.
**Population:** 493 (6.7 percent native, mainly Ahtna Athabascan).
**Travel Attractions:** Crossroads gateway for various points.
**Getting There:** Vehicle access via the Glenn Highway from Anchorage or Tok or via the Richardson Highway from Valdez or Fairbanks; charter air.
**Information:** Copper River Valley Visitor Center, P.O. Box 469, junction of Glenn Highway and Richardson Highway, Glenallen, 822-5555, www.alaskaoutdoors.com/copper, chamber@alaska.net.

Though it's not saying much, Glenallen is the chief town in the region. Essentially a crossroads for the Richardson and Glenn Highways, Glenallen offers a full range of highway and travel services, but little else. One spot worth a stop is the **Copper River Valley Visitor Center** at the northwest corner of the highway junction. There is plenty of info, some displayed items, and a helpful staffer who will happily paint you a picture of local life.

### Where to Stay and Eat in Glenallen
**Caribou Hotel**, Mile 187 Glenn Highway, (800) 478-3302 (AK only), 822-3302, $130 and up, $10–$15 less in winter. The hotel features modern rooms, a gift shop, and the Caribou Cafe.

**Copper Basin Travel** (reservation service), 822-5445. Lodging and recreation reservations for Copper Valley, Valdez, and Cordova.

**Dry Creek State Recreation Site Campground,** 5 miles north of Glenallen along Richardson Highway (AK 4). Basic sites in a forested setting.

## TOK CUTOFF (AK 1/GLENN HIGHWAY)— GAKONA JUNCTION TO TOK

*Road Conditions and Attractions—125 miles. Good, paved road open year-round with some tight turns, narrow lanes, and steep grades. Views across Copper River to Wrangell Mountains, Alaska Range scenery, wildlife.*

Known as the Tok Cutoff because Tok is where travelers can turn from the Alaska Highway to head for Anchorage, this 125-mile segment of the Glenn Highway connects the Tanana River valley of the Interior with the Copper River basin. The road follows a beautiful route through winding high valleys of the Alaska Range, crossing a low divide near Mentasta Lake. There are few specific attractions for the visitor beyond the road itself, which is enough. The mileposts for the Tok Cutoff start from zero near Gakona at the junction with the Richardson Highway and count up to Tok. Allow about three hours with no long stops.

**Gakona Junction Village** (Mile 0), junction of Tok Cutoff and Richardson Highway, Gakona, (888) 462-3221, 822-3664. New duplex cabins go for $100. Gas station and convenience store. **RH**

**Gakona Lodge and Trading Post** (Mile 2), Gakona, 822-3482. Historic Eagle Trail roadhouse dates to 1905. Motel rooms go for $50–70. Carriage House Restaurant and Trappers Den bar. **RH**

**Riverview Bed and Breakfast** (Mile 3), Gakona, 822-3321. Nice log home overlooking Copper River, full breakfast, smoke free, $65 and up.

**Chistochina Trading Post** (Mile 32), 822-3366. Rooms, cabins, restaurant, campground, gas, gifts, airstrip. Rustic, typical roadhouse. Rooms are $65, cabins $60–$80. **RH**

**Chistochina Road** (Mile 32.9)—Most residents of **Chistochina** (population 58, 62 percent native) are Athabascan Indians, living

126

largely traditional subsistence lives. Their homes are located at the confluence of the Chistochina and Copper Rivers.

**Nabesna Road Junction** (Mile 59.8)—Turn here to drive the Nabesna Road (see Wrangell–St. Elias National Park and Preserve, below) into Wrangell–St. Elias National Park and Preserve. The settlement of **Slana** (population 61) stretches along the first 2.5 miles of the Nabesna Road where the Slana River meets the Copper. Town residents are mainly homesteaders who received 5-acre parcels of BLM land to build on before the remaining land in the area was incorporated into Wrangell–St. Elias National Park and Preserve. Many have been embroiled in disputes with the park service about land use ever since—as roadside signs attest. It is worth being especially sensitive to the rights of private landholders in the park and preserve boundaries. Slana has a general store, a bed-and-breakfast, an art gallery, canoe rental, and the Wrangell–St. Elias National Park and Preserve ranger district office. It is also a put-in point for long-distance floats on the Copper River.

**Duffy's Roadhouse** (Mile 62.7), Slana, 822-3888, 822-3133. Restaurant, gas, store. Inexpensive rustic room available. **RH**

**Porcupine Creek State Recreation Area** (Mile 64.2)—Twelve campsites ($8) are available at this 240-acre wayside where Porcupine Creek meets the Slana River. Fishing and hiking are options.

**Mentasta Lodge** (Mile 78.1), Gakona, 291-2324. Cafe, motel, gas, showers, Laundromat, overnight parking. Rooms are $50. **RH**

**Mentasta Summit** (Mile 79.4, 2,434' elevation)—North of Slana the Tok Cutoff follows the valley of the Slana River as it winds around several 5,000- to 6,000-foot peaks. The road opens into a wide basin before crossing this low divide and heading down the Station Creek valley and into the Interior. Look for Dall sheep on the slopes.

**Mentasta Lake Junction** (Mile 81)—A road leads west to fishing spots at Mentasta Lake and the native village of the same name (population 115, 73 percent native). There are no public facilities at the lake.

**Eagle Trail State Recreation Area** (Mile 109.3)—About 15 miles south of Tok, this 640-acre recreation site is located along the original trail from Eagle to Valdez, the length of which is followed today by the Tok Cutoff and Taylor Highway. You can hike along a segment of the original trail. Forty campsites available.

The **Clearwater Creek Trail** (10 miles, 1,200' gain) follows the valley of Clearwater Creek northeast to a high, exposed valley with possible ridge walks. **RT**—2–3 days.

**Tok** (Mile 125)—See chapter 14.


# GLENN HIGHWAY (AK 1)/PALMER TO GLENALLEN
*Road Conditions and Attractions*—155 miles. Good paved road with some tight turns and steep grades, open year-round. Talkeetna and Chugach mountain scenery, Matanuska Glacier, Sheep Mountain, Copper River basin with views of the Wrangell Mountains.

The Palmer-Glenallen segment of the Glenn Highway links Anchorage and the MatSu region to the Richardson Highway. It follows the course of the Matanuska River up between the Talkeetna and Chugach Mountains, then spills down into the broad Copper River basin. Several attractions are worth a stop, while a number of settlements, roadhouses, and state recreation area campgrounds accommodate the traveler. The highway actually begins in Anchorage.

Allot three to four hours with no long stops to complete this segment. Matanuska Glacier and Sheep Mountain are highlights, as are certain scenic areas near the divide and the long-distance views of the Copper River basin and Wrangell Mountains to the east.

**George Parks Highway Junction** (Mile 35.3)—The George Parks Highway (AK 3) heads west and north toward Denali and Fairbanks, while the Glenn continues south, 35 miles to Anchorage.

**Palmer** (Mile 42)—See chapter 9.

**Hatcher Pass Road Junction** (Mile 49.5)—Turn north for Hatcher Pass and Independence Mine State Historic Park. (See chapter 9).

**Musk Ox Farm Road** (Mile 50.1)—See Palmer in chapter 9.

**Moose Creek State Recreation Area** (Mile 54.6)—Twelve campsites, $10.

**Sutton** (Mile 61)—On its way to becoming a satellite of the larger MatSu residential area, Sutton (population 328, 6 percent native) was established in 1918 as a station on the Matanuska Branch of the Alaska Railroad. There are a variety of services.

**Alpine Historical Park** (Mile 61.6)—This outdoor museum features area heritage items and the ruins of the Alpine Coal Washery, 745-7000. Donations are accepted.

**King Mountain State Recreation Site** (Mile 76.1)—Nice campground on the banks of the Matanuska River with 22 sites for $10 each.

**Chickaloon** (Mile 76.3)—Located at the confluence of the Chickaloon and Matanuska Rivers, Chickaloon (population 200, 6.2 percent native) established around 1916 as the terminus of the Matanuska branch of the Alaska Railroad. Local retail and highway services occupy most residents. The community is fiercely independent regarding subsistence and sovereignty issues, issuing its own driver's licenses and vehicle registration tags. Though there are few natives, it is a recognized native village with an established council, corporation, and land claims. Be considerate of private property rights when exploring any trails or side roads in the area.

**Chickaloon Bed and Breakfast** (Mile 76.5), 4 miles from General Store, Chickaloon, 745-1155, $85–$105. Large, private, quiet cottage with sundeck and mountain view.

**Bonnie Lake State Recreation Site** (Mile 83.2)—Turn up a short gravel road to reach eight free campsites.

**Long Lake State Recreation Site** (Mile 85.3)—Nine free campsites near the lake. Matanuska River access, great canyon scenery.

**Matanuska Glacier** (approximately Mile 91 to Mile 114)—Along this main route to Anchorage, no glacier comes closer to the highway than the Matanuska Glacier, source of the Matanuska River. The debris-covered tongue of the glacier can be seen below the road to the south, 2 miles away. There are several good viewpoints, including the official one at Mile 101. Private land, including the Glacier Park Resort, surrounds the glacier. For a fee you can drive to the terminal moraine and hike up to the ice. Easier, free access to near-the-highway glaciers can be found on the roads to McCarthy (Kennicott Glacier), Valdez (Worthington Glacier), and Seward (Exit Glacier), though the cross-valley view of the Matanuska, with the jagged Chugach Mountains in the background, is worth a long look and a photo.

**Matanuska Glacier State Recreation Site** (Mile 101)—Twelve campsites, $10 each. Short trails and excellent views of the glacier.

**Glacier Park Resort** (Mile 102), Glenn Highway, Palmer, 745-2534. Owns land at terminus of glacier. Snacks and $50 rooms. It costs $6.50 per person to drive to the glacier.

**Tundra Rose Bed-and-Breakfast** (Mile 109.5), Glenn Highway (base of Sheep Mountain), Palmer, (800) 315-5865 (AK only), 745-5865. $90 double, $10 each additional guest. Closest B&B to Matanuska Glacier; Dall sheep–viewing access.

**Sheep Mountain** (approximately Mile 108 to Mile 118)—The mountain north of this stretch of road is a well-known area for Dall sheep sightings.

**Sheep Mountain Lodge** (Mile 113.5), Glenn Highway (base of Sheep Mountain), Palmer, 745-5121. $125 cabins (private bath), $50 for four-person "dorm" room (shared bath). Well-run rustic log lodge and cabins, dining room, bar, rafting, hiking trails, wildlife viewing.

**Tahneta Pass** (Mile 122, 3,000' elevation)—Another high point on the Glenn, the divide here is between two branches of the Matanuska watershed. Two high-country lakes are near the road—Leila and Tahneta.

**Eureka Lodge** (Mile 128), Glenn Highway, Glenallen, 822-3808. Opened 1936, first roadhouse on the Glenn. All services. Rooms $55 and up. **RH**

**Eureka Summit** (Mile 129.3, 3,222' elevation)—This is the divide between the Copper River basin and the Matanuska watershed, and the highest point on the Glenn Highway. There are good views of surrounding mountains.

**Little Nelchina State Recreation Site** (Mile 137.6)—Eleven free campsites, but no treated water source.

**Lake Louise Road Junction** (Mile 159.8)—**Lake Louise** offers fishing, hunting, and boating as well as year-round lodging and flightseeing opportunities. From the junction, a 20-mile gravel road leads to the lake where you'll find four lodges (see appendix) and the **Lake Louise State Recreation Area** and campground. Canoeing, hiking, birding, and wildlife observation are options in the summer. Cross-country skiers can keep the snowmobilers company in the cold months. For information on Lake Louise lodging and outfitters, contact the Greater Copper Valley Chamber of Commerce, P.O. Box 469, Glenallen, 822-5555, www.alaskaoutdoors.com/Copper; or just stop in at the visitor center in Glenallen.

**Ranch House Lodge** (Mile 173), Glenn Highway, Glenallen, 822-3882. Rustic log lodge, bar, restaurant, cabins. Rooms are $50.

**Tolsona Creek State Recreation Area** (Mile 173)—Camping, fishing, creek access.

**Glenallen** (Mile 189)—Junction with the Richardson Highway (see Glenallen, above).

## SOUTH RICHARDSON HIGHWAY (AK 4)— VALDEZ TO GLENALLEN

*Road Conditions and Attractions—115 miles. Good, paved road open year-round with some tight turns and narrow lanes in the mountains. Mountain scenery, Worthington Glacier, Keystone Canyon, Copper Center.*

This first third of the Richardson begins in Valdez, climbs quickly to Thompson Pass in the Chugach Mountains, then drops gradually into the Copper River basin before reaching Glenallen and the

south junction with the Glenn Highway. The drive takes about three hours at an easy pace with no stops.

**Old Valdez** (Mile 0)—The official beginning of the Richardson is at the site of the original settlement of Valdez before the 1964 quake prompted its relocation.

**Keystone Canyon** (approximately Mile 13 to Mile 16)—Stop for views of waterfalls and signs of the old trail. River runners enjoy the canyon.

**Blueberry Lake State Recreation Site** (Mile 24.1)—Very nice campground with $10 sites.

**Thompson Pass** (Mile 26, 2,678' elevation)—The highway crosses into the Copper River watershed, dropping down first along the Tsina River, then the Tiekel, Little Tonsina, and Tonsina Rivers. Reaching the basin, the route starts gradually uphill again as you parallel the Copper north to Glenallen.

**Worthington Glacier State Recreation Site** (Mile 28.7)—This is about the closest you can get by road to a glacier in the state. Park the car, check out the displays, and take a walk—but remember that proximity to the highway does not mean that crevasses are any less dangerous or ice any less slippery.

**Little Tonsina State Recreation Site** (Mile 65.1)—Typical small campground with river access. Sites are $6.

**Bernard Creek Trailhead** (Mile 78.9)—From here, the **Bernard Creek Trail** (15-plus miles, 1,600' gain) heads southeast along Bernard Creek and the former route of a telegraph line, and up into Kimball Pass with views and the possibility for further climbs. The BLM recommends this packed dirt route for mountain bikers. **RT** (mountain bike)—all day.

**Squirrel Creek State Recreation Site** (Mile 79.6)—Campsites on the bank of the creek are $10. A store is next door.

**Edgerton Highway Junction** (Mile 82.6)—Turn here to reach

Chitina, McCarthy, Kennicott, and the heart of Wrangell–St. Elias
National Park and Preserve. Pleasant **Pippin Lake** is across the road.

**Edgerton Highway Cutoff** (Mile 91.1)—If you're coming from
the north and heading to Wrangell–St. Elias, take this 8-mile
gravel cutoff—the Old Edgerton Highway—to hook up with the
Edgerton.

**Copper Center Loop** (Mile 100.2 and Mile 106)—Don't miss this
little detour onto a short loop of the Old Richardson Highway. The
headquarters and visitor center for Wrangell–St. Elias National
Park and Preserve is on the old road (See Copper Center, below).

**Klutina Lake Trailhead** (Mile 101.5)—The Klutina Lake Trail
(25 miles, 600' gain) is an old, rough road suitable for mountain
bikes. The route follows the Klutina River through mainly forested
country southwest to Klutina Lake. Consult with BLM officials or
the Wrangell–St. Elias ranger in Copper Center. **RT** (mountain
bike)—2 days.

**Glenallen** (Mile 115)—See above.

## COPPER CENTER
*Location/Climate:* Miles 101–105 Richardson Highway, on Copper
River. 9"/yr. precip., 39"/yr. snowfall, -74°F–96°F.
*Population:* 494 (34.5 percent native, mainly Athabascan).
*Travel Attractions:* Copper River access, Wrangell–St. Elias
National Park and Preserve access and information.
*Getting There:* Vehicle access via the Richardson Highway (AK 4);
regular and charter small-plane air service.
*Information:* Wrangell–St. Elias National Park and Preserve Head-
quarters, P.O. Box 439, Mile 105.5 Richardson Highway, Copper Cen-
ter, 822-5234, www.nps.gov/wrst/.

A long-time fishing camp for the Ahtna Athabascan Indians, the
native village eventually grew into a "tent city" for miners taking the
Eagle Trail from Valdez to the Yukon River and on to the Klondike.
Soon thereafter, travelers shifted their attentions to Fairbanks and
other gold fields. Ringwald Blix built a roadhouse here in 1896 and

Paul Otteson

*Old service station across from Copper Center Lodge*

Copper Center quickly became an important trade and supply center for the region. In 1932 the original roadhouse was replaced by the **Copper Center Lodge**, which still operates today and is one of the best lodging/dining places in the state.

To visit Copper Center, detour from the new Richardson Highway bypass at Mile 100.2 or 106. Services are along this stretch, as is the headquarters for Wrangell–St. Elias National Park and Preserve. The lodge and oldest settled area are found along Copper Loop Road, which loops east from the Old Richardson Highway and back again.

See heritage exhibits at the **Ashby Museum** located within the lodge, open Monday through Saturday, 1 p.m. to 5 p.m. Close by is the **Chapel on the Hill,** built by Vince Joy and army volunteers in 1942, now featuring slide presentations. Call 822-3291 for information. Other historic buildings are scattered throughout the area, though they're generally on private land and not open to the public. River guides operate out of Copper Center; the town is one of several put-in sites for Copper River floats.

## Where to Stay and Eat in Copper Center

**Copper Center Lodge**, Drawer J, Mile 101 Richardson Highway (on Loop Road—Old Richardson Highway), 822-3245. $95 single/double (private bath), $85 single/double (shared bath) summer. A classic, historic Alaska roadhouse inn. Wonderfully kept with an attention to detail. Perhaps the best place on the Copper River. Fine restaurant. **RH**


## EDGERTON HIGHWAY (AK 10)

*Road Conditions and Attractions—32 miles. Good, paved road, open year-round. Views of the Wrangells, Copper River valley, Liberty Falls.*

This 32-mile route links Mile 82.6 of the Richardson Highway with Chitina and access to the McCarthy Road. An 8-mile gravel cutoff from Kenny Lake to Mile 91.1 of the Richardson saves time for those coming from or heading to Glenallen. At Mile 23.7 is the **Liberty Falls State Recreation Site**, offering camping and easy access to noisy Liberty Falls.


## CHITINA

*Location/Climate:* 66 miles northeast of Valdez at the confluence of the Chitina and Copper Rivers. 12"/yr. precip., -58°F–91°F.
*Population:* 64 (47 percent native, mainly Ahtna Athabascan).
*Travel Attractions:* River access, Wrangell–St. Elias National Park and Preserve access.
*Getting There:* Vehicle access via Edgerton Highway (AK 10) from Richardson Highway (AK 4); charter air.
*Information:* Ranger Station, Wrangell–St. Elias National Park and Preserve, Chitina, AK 99566, 823-2205, www.nps.gov/wrst.

Long an important settlement of Ahtna Athabaskans, Chitina is located on the west shore of the Copper River across from the confluence of the Copper and Chitina Rivers. With the construction of the railroad to serve the Kennicott mining region to the east, Chitina attracted non-native settlers and began to boom. Early travelers and settlers who arrived in Cordova via steamship could travel by train to Chitina, then on to Interior mining areas and towns by stagecoach, dogsled, or horse. The town faded with the closing of

the mine and the end of rail service, but enjoys limited revitalization as a gateway to Wrangell–St. Elias National Park and Preserve.

Visit the **Chitina Ranger Station**, located in the original home of the Ed S. Orr Stage Co., which served travelers after the turn of the century. Park and town information is available here. Ask here or elsewhere about informal lakeside camping near town. Before traveling on to McCarthy, gas up and check your spare.

### Where to Stay and Eat in Chitina
**Chitina Motel**, 823-2211. Basic rooms are $60. Inquire at the grocery.

**It'll Do Cafe**, Main Street, 823-2244. Open daily. It'll do nicely.

## WRANGELL–ST. ELIAS NATIONAL PARK AND PRESERVE

*Location/Size:* *210 road miles from Anchorage; bounded by Copper River, Gulf of Alaska, and Canadian border. National park—8.3 million acres; national preserve—4.8 million acres; designated wilderness—8.2 million acres. In southeast corner of Alaska "mainland."*

*Main Activities:* *Historic mine site, backpacking, mountaineering, hiking, river running, wilderness exploration, sea kayaking, cross-country skiing.*

*Gateway Towns/Getting There:* *Chitina/vehicle access via Edgerton Highway (AK 10) from Richardson Highway (AK 4); McCarthy/vehicle access via McCarthy Road from Chitina, charter air access; Yakutat/scheduled air service from Anchorage, other points; Slana/vehicle access via Tok Cutoff (AK 1). Park access: vehicle access via Nabesna Road from Tok Cutoff (AK 1), or McCarthy Road from Edgerton Highway (AK 10) via Richardson Highway (AK 4); charter air drop-offs from Gulkana, McCarthy, Cordova, Yakutat, Valdez; foot access from several points including Nabesna, McCarthy Road, Kennicott.*

*Facilities, Camping, Lodging:* *No facilities. Primitive camping. Lodging on private land within park including Nabesna, Kennicott, McCarthy.*

*Headquarters and Information:* *Headquarters, P.O. Box 439, Mile 105.5 Richardson Highway, Copper Center, 822-5234, www.nps.gov/wrst/. Nabesna Ranger Station, 822-5238; Chitina Ranger Station, 823-2205; Yakutat Ranger Station, 784-3295.*

The Chitina River flows westward to the Copper from near the Yukon border, draining the meltwater from the Chitina, Logan, and several other glaciers, and separating the Wrangell Mountains from the St. Elias Mountains. Both ranges are heavily glaciated and feature magnificent peaks, including Mount St. Elias, second tallest in the United States at 18,008 feet; and Mount Wrangell, tallest active volcano in the United States at 14,163 feet. Wrangell–St. Elias National Park and Preserve encompasses the Wrangells, the Chitina valley, and much of the St. Elias Mountains. The park is America's largest— more than twice the size of Denali National Park and Preserve.

Wrangell–St. Elias is contiguous with Kluane National Park in the Yukon, Tatshenshini-Alsek Wilderness Park in British Columbia, and Glacier Bay National Park and Preserve. Together, they secure a 24-million-acre wilderness in perpetuity—an area about the size of New Hampshire, Vermont, Massachusetts, and Connecticut combined. The four parks collectively have been designated a World Heritage Site.

## THE MCCARTHY ROAD

***Road Conditions and Attractions***—*60 miles. Very rough gravel road on old rail bed, but drivable by regular vehicles; open year-round. Chitina valley views, historic rail route with bridges and artifacts, Kennicott Glacier terminus.*

Most visitors come to the park via the Chitina valley and the town of McCarthy. From the Edgerton Highway (AK 10) and the town of Chitina, the McCarthy Road follows the original railroad bed of the Copper River & Northwest Railroad that ran from Cordova to the Kennicott River. The road can be exceedingly rough and should be driven at modest speeds—especially if you have any doubts about your dental work. Numerous parcels of private property are found along the road and should be respected.

At Mile 13.5 an access road on the left passes through some private property to the trailheads for the **Dixie Pass Trail**, **Kotsina Trail**, and **Nugget Creek Trail**—starting points for extended backpack treks and mountaineering in the Wrangells. Consult the ranger in Chitina about routes and conditions.

The McCarthy Road features some historic rail bridges, including the narrow, 390-foot-high, 525-foot-long **Kuskulana River**

*Hand-drawn cable car crossing the Kennicott River*

Paul Otteson

**Bridge**, which passes over the water at Mile 16. Watch for clandestine bungy jumpers (inquire quietly in Chitina and McCarthy if you're interested in buying a leap). Viewpoints along the way are good for driving breaks and cleaning up the shards of any fine china you were carrying.

At Mile 58.2 the road ends at the source of the short Kennicott River and the foot of Kennicott Glacier, the ice of which is invisible under thick moraine. There is awkward, free parking, but it's worth it to pay the small fee required to park in the private gravel lot by the river. Inquire about nearby camping possibilities.

To reach McCarthy, Kennicott, and beyond, visitors once had to haul themselves over the Kennicott River in a two-person hanging basket. A footbridge now makes the crossing easier if a lot less exciting. If the chance exists, take the hand-hauled basket across to see what it's been like for McCarthy residents for so many years. All supplies either came this way or by plane during the summer months. See McCarthy and Kennicott, below, for more information on park access.

No other access routes to Wrangell–St. Elias are as simple as the McCarthy Road, nor do they offer similar services. North and east of Chitina, there are no bridges over the Copper River, which serves as the park boundary for many miles. Other than the Nabesna Road (see below), access requires air drop-offs, long treks in difficult terrain, coastal boat drop-offs, or extended kayaking.

## NABESNA ROAD

The gravel, 46-mile-long **Nabesna Road** enters Wrangell–St. Elias National Park and Preserve from the north, beginning at the town of Slana where the Nabesna Road meets the Tok Cutoff (Glenn Highway, AK 1). Park information is available at the Slana Ranger Station at Mile 0.2 of Nabesna Road. The road provides access to the headwaters areas of both the Tanana and Nabesna Rivers and to possible pathless wilderness routes into the mountains. Hunters and fishers are the most frequent users of the road.

For much of its length, Nabesna Road follows the boundary between national park and national preserve. On the preserve side, sport hunting and trapping are allowed, while in the park, only subsistence hunting by local residents is permitted. At Mile 29.4 and Mile 31.2 the road crosses streams that can challenge non–four-wheel-drive vehicles during times of heavy runoff. Elsewhere the road is easy for most vehicles, though long RVs and fifth wheels are not recommended. Several private properties are located along the road, including a fishing lodge near its end.

## ICY BAY

The outer half of **Icy Bay** separates two coastal parcels of native corporation land, while its inner reaches cut a fantastic four-fingered hand into the heart of the St. Elias Mountains. Less than 20 miles separate the tidewater at the foot of Tyndall Glacier from the summit of Mount St. Elias, the second tallest peak in the United States after Denali. Along with Tyndall, the Yahtse and Guyot Glaciers account for almost all of the coastline of aptly named Icy Bay. This is an adventure kayaker's paradise.

Access is via a landing strip at the west entrance to the bay. Beyond the eastern shore are the wide moraines of the terminus of the Malaspina Glacier, the largest in the nation. There are no services or lodging options; consult your outfitter or pilot about timing, supply needs, and pick-up options (see appendix).

## MCCARTHY AND KENNICOTT

*Location/Climate: McCarthy is 60 miles east of Chitina in the heart of Wrangell–St. Elias National Park and Preserve. 12"/yr. precip., 52"/yr. snowfall, -58°F–91°F.*
*Population: 31 (4 percent native).*
*Travel Attractions: Historic buildings and setting, Kennecott Mine ruins, Kennicott and Root Glacier access, Wrangell–St. Elias National Park and Preserve access, running the Chitina River.*
*Getting There: Vehicle access from Valdez, Glenallen via Richardson Highway (AK 4), Edgerton Highway (AK 10), and McCarthy Road; regular and small-plane charter service.*

*Information:* *Wrangell–St. Elias National Park and Preserve Head-*
*quarters, P.O. Box 439, Mile 105.5 Richardson Highway, Copper Cen-*
*ter, 822-5234, www.nps.gov/wrst/. Chitina Ranger Station, 823-2205.*

The settlement of Kennicott grew from its mining-camp beginnings
in 1908 until it featured not only the massive mine buildings, but
homes, a school, gym, tennis court, and a silent movie theater. By
1911 the Copper River & Northwestern Railway was completed and
trains began hauling copper ore down the Chitina and Copper
Rivers to Cordova.

Since drinking and gambling were forbidden in company-owned
Kennicott, McCarthy was developed 5 miles to the south along
the margin of the Kennicott Glacier. As Kennicott's alter ego,
McCarthy hosted saloons and a red-light district, as well as stores,
hotels, restaurants, and a newspaper. The area population reached
about 800, but both towns were abandoned in 1938 when the mine
closed, having extracted $200 million worth of ore from the hills.
The National Trust for Historic Places identifies the area's structures as among the nation's most endangered. Steps to preserve
them are underway.

Today the rekindled village of McCarthy is a great place to stroll,
shop, sup, and stay. Visitors arrive by air or via the McCarthy Road
and foot bridge (see McCarthy Road, above). Ask around about the
shuttle vans that take you up the road from McCarthy along the east
side of Kennicott Glacier to the buildings and ruins of the Kennecott
Mine. The mine area offers great views, glacier access, and good hiking. The wonderful Kennicott Glacier Lodge serves travelers at the
mine site, though most services are in McCarthy.

From Kennicott, an old road-turned-trail follows the east margin of Kennicott Glacier and Root Glacier into the hills. Glacier-
based ventures into the high peaks often begin here, as do less-
ambitious backpacking trips. Hiking a few miles in from the mine to
find a spot for rough camping is a good idea. Be careful when walking on Kennicott or Root Glacier, and follow all bear advice religiously. Steep trails also climb up behind the mining buildings to
the sites of old shafts and service structures.

## Where to Stay and Eat in McCarthy and Kennicott
**Historic Kennicott Bed-and-Breakfast**, #14 Silk Stocking Row,
Kennicott, 554-4469. Small B&B in old mine house, $120 for two.

**Kennicott Glacier Lodge**, Kennicott, (800) 582-5128, 258-2350, $120 single, $170 double, add about $40 per person for meals, McCarthy shuttle and mine-ruins tour included. The only lodge/ restaurant at the old Kennecott Mine site, renovated historic building, great view, fantastic location, restaurant; can't be beat! **BL**

**McCarthy Lodge: Ma Johnson Hotel & Restaurant/Saloon**, McCarthy, 554-4402. Historic rooms with modern shared baths at the hotel. Rooms are $95 and up. "Beer, Bull & Grub" at the restaurant/saloon.

## PRINCE WILLIAM SOUND
## CHUGACH NATIONAL FOREST
*Location/Size: Eastern Kenai Peninsula and Prince William Sound. 5.6 million acres.*
*Main Activities: Wilderness exploration, hiking, fishing, sea kayaking, river running, mountaineering, backcountry stays, wildlife observation, glacier viewing.*
*Gateway Towns/Getting There: Portage, Whittier/scheduled ferry service to Whittier from Valdez and Homer, vehicle access to Portage via Seward Highway, Alaska Railroad shuttle or new road link from Portage to Whittier; Valdez/vehicle access via Richardson Highway, scheduled ferry from Whittier and Seward, scheduled air from Anchorage and other points; Cordova/scheduled ferry from Valdez, scheduled air from Anchorage; Seward/vehicle access via Seward Highway, scheduled ferry from Valdez and Homer, scheduled air service from Anchorage. Park access: road and trail access in eastern Kenai Peninsula, sea-kayak and tour-boat access in Prince William Sound, road and trail access from Cordova, river access in Copper River valley and delta, floatplane and glacier landings elsewhere.*
*Facilities, Camping, Lodging: Beggich Boggs Visitor Center at Portage Glacier, Turnagain Pass Winter Sports Area south of Portage on the Seward Highway (ski area). Several campgrounds are located along the Seward and Sterling Highways on the Kenai Peninsula; one is found east of Cordova on Alaganik Slough. All other camping is primitive. There are 41 Forest Service cabins and all are reservable; the Kenai Peninsula has 19, Prince William Sound has 15, and the Cordova area has 7. Cabins are $25 to $40 per night. Reservations can be made in*

*person only at the ranger district offices, and in person or by mail at*
*the Alaska Public Lands Information Center (see below).*
**Headquarters and Information:** *Glacier Ranger District, 783-*
*3242; Cordova Ranger District, 424-7661; Seward Ranger District,*
*224-3374; Alaska Public Lands Information Center, 605 West 4th*
*Avenue, Suite 105, Anchorage, 271-2599; Chugach National Forest*
*Supervisor, Anchorage, 271-2500.*

This mountain-wrapped, island-rich bay on the northern edge of the
Gulf of Alaska is famous as a beautiful travel destination, as an area
rich in fish and wildlife, and as the victim of a drunken tanker captain. Long one of Alaska's three premier coastal tour regions, Prince
William Sound was thrust into national awareness in 1989 when the
*Exxon Valdez* leaked 258,000 barrels of oil—about 20 percent of its
cargo—into the water.

The oil spill was not the first cataclysm to strike the region. In
1964, Valdez and Cordova were both severely damaged by a great
earthquake and the ensuing tsunamis. Cordova had to move and
rebuild its harbor, while the entire town of Valdez was relocated to
new ground. While the region has seen it all, it remains one of the
most beautiful areas of the state, well salted with some amazing and
very human stories of trial and triumph.

The A.M.H.S. ferries are a good way to experience the sound. If
you're traveling by car, consider driving to Valdez, then continuing
by ferry to Whittier, where you can take the short rail shuttle or new
road link to Portage and the Seward Highway (Portage to Valdez
works just as well). Kowtowing to the greed of the cruise lines, the
state no longer allows the ferry to enter Columbia Bay for a decent
look at Columbia Glacier. Other ferry routes incorporate Cordova,
which has regular air connections to Anchorage and elsewhere. Taking a vehicle to Cordova is an expensive luxury since the road system is so short, though having one available to explore the Copper
River Delta at your own pace is nice. Rentals are available (see
appendix).

A general map of Alaska will show virtually all of Prince William
Sound and the surrounding mountains encompassed by the
Chugach National Forest. In reality, there are large parcels of native
corporation lands, particularly between Cordova and Valdez, in the
lower Copper River valley, and on the southeastern projection of the
Kenai Peninsula. The casual visitor may see the corporation land

clear-cuts and think the U.S. Forest Service has lost its mind, which is not the case (in Alaska at least). In spite of these glaring exceptions, public holdings are vast, and the Chugach is easily America's second-largest national forest.

The Chugach does not yet feature any Congressionally designated wilderness or monument areas, though study areas exist. The western end of the national forest is laced by the highways, trails, streams, and long lakes of the Kenai Peninsula, and is a well-used recreation paradise that enjoys de facto protection. High-country areas are extremely rugged and largely covered in ice, again affording de facto protection. Management of the harvestable, lowland spruce-hemlock forests on the coastlands and islands of Prince William Sound so far errs on the side of preservation.

Visitors to the Chugach can enjoy recreational opportunities that parallel the landforms. The Kenai Peninsula offers camping and wildlife viewing, lake fishing and canoeing, great long-distance and day-hike options, and easy glacier access (see chapter 10). Prince William Sound offers outstanding kayaking, as well as glacier- and wildlife-viewing boat tours out of Whittier and Valdez. Fishing charters are also popular. Roadside glacier and wildlife tours of the Copper River Delta are based in Cordova. Bush planes can drop you in the high country for cabin stays, mountaineering, and fishing.

## Things to See Around Prince William Sound

**College Fiord**—Northeast of Whittier, Port Wells (an ocean passage) leads deep into the Chugach Mountains, branching into College Fiord and **Harriman Fiord**. Scores of small glaciers cut down the slopes, and a dozen or so, including larger tidewater glaciers like Yale and Harvard, reach the sea. Tour boats tend to be few and small—ideal if you're a kayaker.

It's about 50 miles from Whittier to the head of College Fiord and 45 miles to the head of Harriman Fiord. Both fjords are spectacular. For a shorter trip, consider Blackstone Bay and **Blackstone Glacier**, about 22 water miles south of Whittier. Outfitters in Anchorage and Whittier can support your trip (see appendix).

**Columbia Glacier**—The most popular tour out of Valdez is a trip to Columbia Glacier, one of Alaska's most spectacular tidewater glaciers and one of the largest on the continent. The A.M.H.S. ferry no longer detours into Columbia Bay so you'll need an alternative if you want a look. The face of the glacier reaches 300 feet in height, though it has receded significantly, making it more difficult to observe calving. Icebergs move about the bay at the whim of wind and current, often preventing the close approach of large boats, but small tour-boat captains thread their way up close—as do kayakers. The glacier is 35 water miles from Valdez. Drop-off charters and rentals are available in town (see appendix).

**Kayak Island**—Seventy water miles west of Cordova, this remote island was the first spot on the Northwest Coast of North America to be visited by Europeans. George William Steller arrived at the island aboard the Russian packet boat *St. Peter* and sent men ashore on July 17, 1741. His journal documents the entire journey. He replenished his ship's freshwater supply then sailed back home.

Kayak Island offers the chance for a truly remote wilderness experience. The island is 22 miles long, 1.5 miles wide, and free of Forest Service facilities. Brown bear make the only paths (which should not be used by people), though beach areas and ridgecrests are open to walking. The Coast Guard lighthouse at Kayak's rugged southwest tip is listed on the National Register of Historic Places and is now uninhabited. Access is by charter plane, floatplane, helicopter, or boat from Cordova. For information, contact the Cordova Ranger District office (see details above).

## Copper River Delta/Cordova-Area Hiking

The third main unit of the Chugach after Kenai and Prince William Sound is the Copper River delta region east of Cordova. Hundreds of square miles of wetlands dominate a 60-mile-long swath of coastline from Point Whitshed, near Cordova, to Cape Suckling, near the terminus of massive Bering Glacier. The Copper and other rivers drain into marshlands, ponds, braided streams, sloughs, shallows, tidal flats, and sandbars, creating an outstanding habitat. The value of these wetlands to regional fisheries cannot be overstated.

The Copper River Highway (AK 10) provides access from Cordova to the western wetlands and up into the Copper Valley, while various trails offer limited access to the surrounding areas. The highway follows the path of the railroad that carried ore trains from the Kennecott Mine to Cordova between 1908 and 1936. At Mile 48, the road effectively ends at the **Million Dollar Bridge**, built to allow the railroad to avoid both Childs and Miles Glaciers, which meet the river on opposite sides. Twenty years after the last train rolled, the bridge was opened as a highway bridge. A section of the bridge collapsed in the 1964 earthquake, ending its use for a time. In the mid-1970s the placement of a temporary connector made the bridge usable again, but 1995 flood damage closed it once more. Van tours from Cordova run out to the bridge and include wildlife and glacier viewing (see appendix). Exploration by canoe and kayak is possible from several put-ins along the road.

A number of short hiking trails are accessible from the Copper Highway and the road system around Cordova. For detailed information on additional hiking trails, visit the Chugach National Forest office in Cordova (see Chugach National Forest details above). These include:

**Child's Glacier Trail** (1.2 miles)—This easy gravel trail follows the Copper River from the end of the Million Dollar Bridge to a viewing platform directly across the river from the 300-foot face of Child's Glacier. If you're down at the riverside, watch for waves created by calving bergs across the way. **RT**—2 hrs.

**Crater Lake Trail** (2.4 miles)—From Cordova, follow Power Creek Road 1.5 miles along the north shore of Eyak Lake to just past the airstrip. Head north at the trailhead up a steep contour through spruce-hemlock forest with Mount Eyak on your left and views of the delta on your right. Enjoy the lake at trail's end or continue on the exposed ridge 5.5 miles north, until the difficult, cairn-marked route drops into Power Creek Valley and joins the Power Creek Trail (12-mile total loop). **RT** to Crater Lake—4–5 hrs.; entire Power Creek loop—all day.

**McKinley Lake Trail** (2.4 miles)/**Pipeline Lakes Trail** (3.2 miles to McKinley Lake)—Start at Mile 21.4 of the Copper River Highway for the Pipeline Lakes option, mile 21.6 for the direct route. These easy trails are basically fishing-access routes, but lead to two reservable backcountry cabins, the McKinley Lake Cabin (best location) and the McKinley Trail Cabin (100 yards from the road). For reservation information, see Chugach National Forest details above.

**Muskeg Meander Ski Trail** (3.1 miles)—From the trailhead at Mile 18.6 of the Copper River Highway, the trail climbs gradually through muskegs and forest patches to a high point that affords views of the delta. Winter use only. **RT**—4 hrs.

**Power Creek Trail** (4.2 miles)—Follow Power Creek Road to its end, 7 miles from Cordova along the north shore of Eyak Lake. The moderate trail continues upvalley to the reservable Power Creek

╓─────────────────────────────────────╖

# Recreational Gold Panning

*In several areas throughout the state, visitors are permitted
to pan or sluice for gold. Small suction dredges may also be
used in some locations. However, sluicing, dredging, and
even panning can contribute to the siltation of streams, the
lowering of oxygen levels, and the disruption of spawning
gravels, representing a small but acute assault on local
habitat. There are many opportunities to pan for gold in
the state. This guide doesn't identify them.*

╙─────────────────────────────────────╜

Cabin. This lovely valley is surrounded by 4,000-foot glacier-capped
peaks. It's possible to return via Crater Lake (see above). **RT—6–8 hrs.**

**Saddlebag Glacier Trail** (3 miles)—Good for hiking, mountain biking (because it's relatively dry), and skiing, this easy trail
heads north from Mile 25 of the Copper River Highway. Look for
mountain goats as you enjoy the splendid glacier viewing at Saddlebag Lake at trail's end. **RT—4–5 hrs.**

## CORDOVA

***Location/Climate:*** *On Prince William Sound, 140 air miles east-
southeast of Anchorage. 151"/yr. precip., 80"/yr. snowfall, 17°F–63°F.*
***Population:*** *2,568 (12–20 percent native).*
***Travel Attractions:*** *Access to Prince William Sound, Kayak Island,
Copper River delta, Million Dollar Bridge, and Child's Glacier; Chugach
National Forest; kayaking, hiking, and fishing.*
***Getting There:*** *Scheduled ferry service from Valdez and Whittier;
scheduled air service from Anchorage.*
***Information:*** *Chamber of Commerce, P.O. Box 99, Cordova, 424-
7260, www.ptialaska.net/~cchamber.*

Definitely off the beaten path, Cordova is inaccessible by road (for
now), unvisited by cruise ships, at the end of the ferry line, and

somewhat expensive to reach by air. Commercial fishing and fish processing dominate the economy, with a big dose of timber harvesting and government work thrown in. The travelers who do visit tend to be independents or small groups, since there is little for large groups to do and no good way for them to get there.

Like almost all coastal towns, Cordova outfitters and charter companies support fishing, wildlife viewing, river running, and coastal touring itineraries (see appendix). Of particular note are the van tours that travel 48 miles out to the Million Dollar Bridge and back, stopping for views of wetland wildlife, eagles, mountains, and the glaciers at the end of the road.

A van shuttle to town meets every plane and ferry, but consider walking into town instead. The coast road north of town along Orca Inlet is also pleasant for a walk. Beyond the ferry dock you'll find "Hippie Cove," where several low-budget residents live in vans, trailers, and tents. Most hiking access requires a hitch or a shuttle, though Mount Eyak, Crater Lake, and Power Creek are close enough to walk. Strolling the pleasant town center and meeting local folks is a great way to spend a day.

## Things to See and Do in Cordova

**Cordova Historical Museum**—Located with the visitor center at 1st and Browning, this museum features cultural artifacts of the Chugach, Eyak, and Tlingit peoples, including a three-hole baidarka and a dug-out canoe. Centennial Building, 622 1st Street, 424-6665, open Monday–Saturday in summer, Tuesday–Saturday in winter.

**Mount Eyak Skiing/Chairlift Rides**—For a great view, ride to the summit of Mount Eyak. With a moderate scramble down the north side of the peak, you can reach Emerald Lake and good hiking options (see Copper River Delta/Cordova–Area Hiking, above). Winter visitors can enjoy the slopes. Walk up Browning Street, take a left on 4th, a right on Council, then a left on 6th to the ski area. In summer, call for lift-operation information, 424-7766.

## Where to Stay in Cordova

**Cordova Rose Lodge**, 1315 Whitshed Road (half a mile from town past camper park), 424-ROSE. My favorite place—a restored barge (on land) and cottage, $50 and up.

**The Reluctant Fisherman**, 407 Railroad Avenue (on water at

small boat harbor), (800) 770-3272 or 424-3272. $85–$135 (in
season), $60–$75 (winter). Closest thing to a luxury hotel; restaurant
and bar with view; car rentals $60–$75 per day, unlimited mileage.

## Where to Eat in Cordova

**Baja Taco**, New Harbor (in lot below Railroad at Nicholoff), 424-
5599. Outdoor seating. Great Mexican when the weather is good!

**Cookhouse Cafe**, Cannery Row (follow 1st west and north for half a
mile to cannery and piers), 424-5926. Open May–September, 5:30
a.m. to close. Hearty worker fare, pancakes, Sunday brunch.

**The Killer Whale**, P.O. Box 769, 1st Street, 424-7733. Great place
teamed with a bookshop. Omelets, deli fare, soups, and salads.


## VALDEZ

*Location/Climate: North shore of Port Valdez in Prince William
Sound, 120 air miles and 305 road miles from Anchorage. 60"/yr.
precip., 300"/yr. snowfall, 18°F–63°F.*
*Population: 4,469 (5.9 percent native).*
*Travel Attractions: Crooked Creek salmon run.*
*Getting There: Vehicle access via Richardson Highway (AK 4) from
Glenallen, Anchorage, Fairbanks; scheduled ferry service from Whittier,
Cordova, Seward; scheduled air service from Anchorage, Fairbanks.*
*Information: Visitor Information Center, P.O. Box 1603, 200 Chenega
Street, Valdez, (800) 770-5954 or 835-4636, www.valdezalaska.org.*

The town of Valdez was established in the winter of 1897–98 as the
beginning point of the All American Route to the Interior gold
fields. It continues to be important as the northernmost ice-free
port on the continent. Once situated on the geologically unstable
flats at the head of Port Valdez, the town was virtually destroyed in
the 1964 earthquake, then reestablished on safe ground 4 miles to
the west.

Valdez is the terminus for the Trans-Alaska Pipeline. A "tank
farm" and tanker port are located on the south side of Port
Valdez—the very port from which the town's namesake tanker, the
*Exxon Valdez*, departed the night it ran aground in Prince William
Sound. Valdez became the center for the clean-up effort, though the

oil slicks never reached the town's shores. Today many residents work in pipeline- and oil shipping–related jobs.

Though Valdez doesn't have the charm or easy pace of Cordova, its setting is among the most spectacular of any town in the state. The shops and restaurants on Harbor Plaza beside the small boat harbor make for pleasant browsing with a working, marine ambiance. Though the Alyeska pipeline, tank farm, and tanker terminal may not be attractive to some, they offer a vivid contrast to the mountains and sea.

Valdez is an excellent base for several types of adventures. With kayak segments of less than 10 miles each, Valdez can be connected with Shoup Bay State Marine Park, Sawmill Bay State Marine Park, Jack Bay State Marine Park, and a Chugach National Forest cabin at the head of Jack Bay. Outfitters offer rafting trips through Keystone Canyon east of town. Wilderness access to the high country and glaciers of non-designated state and BLM lands is possible from the Richardson Highway. Flight-seeing over the ice and peaks of the Chugach is offered from the Valdez airport. Tour companies provide fishing and Columbia Glacier excursions, while charter boats can drop you and your kayak or backpack just about anywhere you want (see the appendix for listings).

## Things to See and Do in Valdez
**Alyeska Marine Terminal**—This facility receives up to 75,000 barrels of oil per hour through the pipeline. It stores the oil in huge tanks, then loads it onto the 70 tankers that use the port each month. Call 835-2686 for information about the $15 tour.

**Crooked Creek Salmon Viewpoint**—About a mile east of town on the Richardson Highway, the mouth of Crooked Creek meets **Duck Flats** and Port Valdez. A parking area, information site, and viewing platform have been set up to facilitate viewing of spawning salmon as they crowd the creek mouth. A bike path also reaches the site from the top of Meals Avenue.

**Valdez Museum and Historic Archive**—Located 3 blocks from the boat harbor and ferry dock where Tatilek Avenue meets Egan Drive, the museum has Valdez-area heritage exhibits. Highlights include a restored steam fire engine, as well as a log cabin, lighthouse, photographs, and audio-visual programs. P.O. Box 397, 217 Egan, Valdez, 835-2764, www.alaska.net/~vldzmuse.

## Where to Stay in Valdez

**Keystone Hotel**, 401 Egan Drive, (888) 835-0665 or 835-3851. $85–$115. Open May–September. Nicely remodeled, full amenities, near ferry and town.

**Totem Inn**, 100 Egan Drive, 835-4443. $104 and up, 30 percent less in winter. High-grade motel, good family-style **Totem Inn Restaurant**.

**Harbor Reservations**, 201 N. Harbor Drive, (800) 830-4302, is a good one-stop source for information and reservations for about 20 Valdez-area bed-and-breakfasts. Using a reservation service is a real time saver if you're arriving on short notice.

**Tsaina Lodge**, Mile 35 Richardson Highway, 835-3500. Nice accommodations, fantastic **Tsaina Lodge Restaurant**, and glacier views. The Tsaina is the home of the World Extreme Skiing Championships. $95 and up in summer, $160 and up in winter. **RH**

**Valdez Bear Paw Camper Park**, North Harbor Drive at Meals Avenue, Seward, 835-2530. Tentsites $15–$17, hook-ups $20–$22. Right at small boat harbor in town, good place to stay if you need to make an early-morning ferry.

## Where to Eat in Valdez

**Chinook Books & Coffee**, 126 Pioneer Drive, 835-4222. A bookstore and gift shop adjoins this relaxing breakfast/lunch spot.

**Fu Kung**, 207 Kobuk Street, 835-5255. Big Chinese menu. Tasty and pricey.

**Mike's Palace**, 201 North Harbor Drive, 835-2365. Open 11 a.m.–11 p.m. Try their famous lasagna and halibut.

## WHITTIER

*Location/Climate:* West side of Prince William Sound at the head of the Kenai Peninsula, 50 miles southeast of Anchorage. 66"/yr. precip., 80"/yr. snowfall, 17°F–63°F.
*Population:* 284 (12.3 percent native).

***Travel Attractions:*** *Ferry link, Prince William Sound tours and access, Blackstone Glacier, kayaking, remote stays, Chugach National Forest access.*
***Getting There:*** *Vehicle and foot access via Alaska Railroad shuttle and new road from Portage; scheduled ferry service from Valdez and Seward.*
***Information:*** *Visitor information available during business hours, 472-2379, www.alaskaone.com/whittier.*

Isolated and small, yet still accessible to those with thin wallets, Whittier has a slightly colorful reputation as a home to those who don't wish to be found. It's situated at one end of a portage route once used by the Chugach Indians of Prince William Sound for accessing fishing areas on Turnagain Arm. The town was created during World War II, serving as the main Alaskan debarkation point for troops and materiel after the railroad spur was completed in 1943. This ice-free, strategically located port stayed busy until it was closed in 1960. The town's population subsequently dropped from 1,200 to 284, giving it the distinctly eerie feel of a ghost town.

The most visible legacies of the military era are the Begich Towers, a 14-story high-rise; and the Buckner building, long known as a "city under one roof," having held 1,000 apartments, a bowling alley, hospital, theater, library, shops, gymnasium, and pool. The Buckner building is abandoned, though the Begich Towers and the Whittier Manor, a large structure built in the 1950s for civilian workers, now host the condominium homes of many Whittier residents. The accommodations, both past and present, are thoroughly un-Alaskan. Indeed, if it were not for Whittier's marvelous location and key transportation links, the "town" itself would be a must-miss for most travelers.

Whittier's boat harbor and dockside businesses form the heart of the tourist part of town. Cruise ships stopped coming to avoid a head tax and because of limited dock facilities, but may return with the opening of the new road. Ferry passengers generally use Whittier as a transfer point for the Kenai Peninsula, Anchorage, or the Interior. The small harbor shelters many vessels owned by Anchorage residents and charter companies. Almost everyone who arrives in town quickly finds a way out again—as perhaps you should.

On the other hand, Whittier's old military ambiance is intriguing in its own right. Certainly the people of Whittier are friendly and the immediate surrounds of the town are quite beautiful. Whittier makes an awkward postcard, but with glaciers, waterfalls, bird

Paul Otteson

*Ferry off-loading in Whittier*

rookeries, fjords, and peaks a walk or paddle away, how bad could a bit of ugliness be?

## Train and Ferry Connections/The New Road

Independent travelers typically arrive or leave Whittier via one of six daily train shuttles to or from Portage (four on Wednesday and Thursday), connecting with the once- or twice-daily arrival of an A.M.H.S ferry (see Ferry Travel, chapter 6). Plans are in the works to build a short road and to open the train tunnel to vehicles at certain hours of the day. For current information on the train schedule and rates, or the road schedule and tolls, call the Alaska Railroad at (800) 544-0552 or 265-2494.

## Things to See and Do in and Around Whittier

Moderate and inexpensive natural-destination options around town include the following:

**Portage Pass Trail** (2 miles, 700' gain)—The best views of Portage Glacier are found at the end of this easy route. Take West

Camp Road (the only road) west from town and past Army Bunker Road to the trail. The path crosses the stream then contours up and around the southern slopes of Maynard Mountain. You'll soon reach a small lake and pass with splendid views of Portage Glacier and Portage Lake. The old portage route once crossed the glacier, which has now receded beyond usability. To reach Portage and the road to Anchorage, you'll need to take a more adventurous route. **RT**—3–4 hrs.

Other short hikes include a scramble up to the falls on Whittier Creek and beyond to **Whittier Glacier** (rough path along creek above Begich Towers), or an easy walk to the picnic area at the **Salmon Run** (up Cove Creek Road beyond the Buckner building). Consider a walk down the road around the head of the canal for town views and a look at the tank farm and mill ruins.

**Passage Canal**—Rent a kayak at Prince William Sound Kayak Center (see appendix) and explore the local waters. Across Passage Canal from town is a frantic kittiwake rookery and a splendid waterfall. A shifting panorama of peaks and glaciers accompanies you through the sheltered waters. Decision Point State Marine Park, Entry Cove State Marine Park, and Surprise Cove State Marine Park campsites are about 8, 10 and 12 miles from town, respectively. Longer trip options include Blackstone Glacier and College Fiord (see Chugach National Forest, above).

## Where to Stay and Eat in Whittier

**Anchor Inn**, Whittier Street at Depot, 472-2354. A dive of a motel—a last resort. Bar, grocery, coin-operated laundry, $70.

**Captain Ron's Berth & Biscuit** (hostel), 235-4368 (winter phone/fax in Homer), 472-2393 (summer). Good budget lodging choice. Call for information.

**Irma's Outpost**, Harbor Triangle, 472-2461. Delicatessen, pastries, orders to go.

**Whittier Public Campground**, Glacier Street on Whittier Creek (above town). $5 per site. Convenient, cheap, not bad.

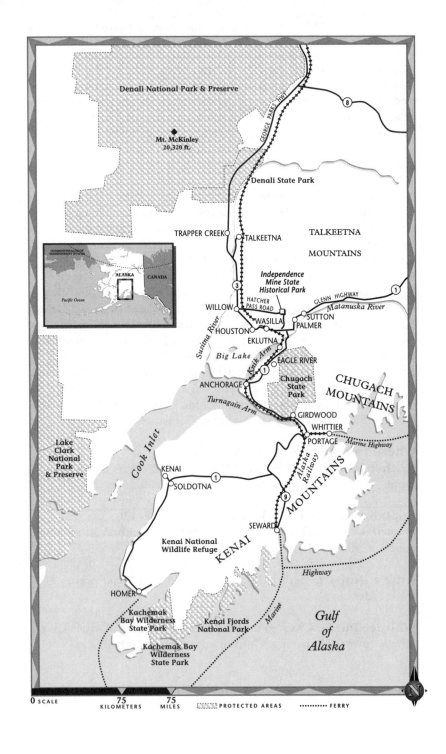

# 9
# ANCHORAGE, MATSU, AND COOK INLET

Well over half of all Alaskans live on or near the eastern shore of Cook Inlet—most in metropolitan Anchorage. The word "metropolitan" may seem an unlikely choice to describe anything in the 49th state, but the visitor will soon see the truth of it. Suburban features from strip malls to traffic jams are yours to enjoy. Fortunately, development is limited in scope and you are never more than a few minutes away from hikes, views, and solitude.

Anchorage occupies the tip of a peninsula set between two branches of Cook Inlet—Knik Arm to the north and Turnagain Arm to the south. The Chugach Mountains dominate the peninsula and are preserved almost entirely in Chugach State Park and Chugach National Forest. The mountains rise directly from the north shores of Turnagain Arm, while Knik Arm has gentler shores and hosts the bedroom communities of Eagle River, Peters Creek, and Birchwood.

Northeast of Anchorage is "MatSu" (Matanuska-Susitna), Alaska's fastest growing region. MatSu spreads east of the Susitna River, south of the Talkeetna Mountains, and north of Knik Arm, and includes the towns of Wasilla and Palmer. The Matanuska River flows into Knik Arm from the east, while the Susitna River watershed drains much of the central Alaska Range into Cook Inlet. The Glenn Highway follows the Matanuska River east through the towns of Palmer and Sutton, while the George Parks

Highway heads west through Wasilla, then north along the Susitna and on to Denali and Fairbanks.

Area development is limited by the rugged Chugach and Talkeetna Mountains—much of which is public land—and by the broad, forested flats of the Susitna basin with its huge expanses of wetlands. Further north and east, the land rises and the climate is less hospitable. In some respects, Anchorage is already nearing capacity, its neighborhoods bordering the margins of parklands, the shores of Cook Inlet, and the military bases to the north. Managing future growth will be a challenge.

No roads access the region west of the Susitna River and Cook Inlet, where the Alaska Range collides with the volcano-strewn Aleutian Range. This land features a jumble of fantastically ragged peaks and long, U-shaped valleys, many of which are protected in Lake Clark National Park and Preserve. Visitors to the area enjoy some of the wildest adventures the state has to offer. Access is difficult or expensive, and gateway towns are small and remote.

It is perhaps strange that Cook Inlet offers such a schizophrenic window on Alaska—to the east, traffic and tract homes; to the west, trackless tranquillity. If you want to get out of Anchorage to find some splendid natural destinations, you don't have to go too far.

## ANCHORAGE

*Location/Climate:* Head of Cook Inlet in Southcentral Alaska. 16"/yr. precipitation, 69"/yr. snowfall, 8°F–65°F.
*Population:* 257,780 (6.4 percent native).
*Travel Attractions:* Access to entire state, center of information and public lands administration, Chugach State Park, Tony Knowles Coastal Trail, ski basins, zoo, museums, arts options, tourist attractions.
*Getting There:* Scheduled air service from Seattle and many other points, including direct service to and from many Alaska towns; scheduled rail service from Seward and Fairbanks; scheduled bus and shuttle-van service from many points; vehicle access from Kenai Peninsula via Seward Highway (AK 1), from Fairbanks via George Parks Highway (AK 3), and from Tok and the Alaska Highway via Glenn Highway (AK 1).
*Information:* Anchorage Convention and Visitors Bureau, 1600 A Street, Suite 200, Anchorage, AK 99501, www.anchorage.net; "Log Cabin" Visitor Information Center, 4th Avenue at F Street, Anchorage, AK 99501, 276-4118 for information by phone, (800) 478-1255 for a printed visitors guide. Various public lands information outlets.

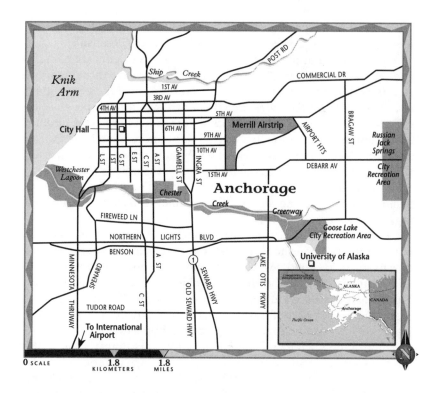

Anchorage is Alaska's version of "Everycity"—strip malls and chain stores, steel and glass office towers, fast-food joints, tract homes, and six-plex apartments. All are tied together with a thick flow of— prepare yourself—traffic! It can be a rude shock to someone who has spent two weeks with only the sounds of wind and water in their ears. Still, 250,000 people are only 250,000 people; 20 minutes and a little luck will take you from one end of Anchorage to the other. The city center still has that "Nebraska county seat" feel to it—all you have to do to see the edge of downtown is peer up a side street.

Situated on the shores of Cook Inlet with the mountains of the Alaska and Aleutian Ranges visible across the water, Anchorage enjoys a marvelous setting. On clear summer days, Denali can be seen 140 miles away, small but presidential on the horizon. To the east, the city is backed by the western end of the Chugach Mountains and the huge Chugach State Park. Around the bend south of

157

town, the highway follows Turnagain Arm 40 miles to Alyeska Ski Resort, then on to Portage Glacier and the Kenai Peninsula.

Recreational opportunities for Anchorage residents are plentiful and outstanding. Over 120 miles of bike trails weave throughout the city, including dedicated non-motorized routes like the very popular, 10-mile **Tony Knowles Coastal Path**. Mountain bike and hiking trails are found in Chugach State Park. There are great birding opportunities along protected coastal flats and tide lands. Urban parks and lakes offer easy sites for walking, jogging, canoeing, and relaxing. Rock climbers frequent a couple of locations along the Seward Highway (AK 1) just south of town. The Alaska classics of fishing and flightseeing are readily available, while winter brings skiing, skating, snowmobiling, and dog mushing.

In town there are arts facilities, hotels and restaurants, nightlife opportunities, coffeeshops, bookstores, and sights to see. There are dozens of parks, good golf courses, and a fine zoo where Alaskan and exotic wildlife can be viewed up close. Merrill Field and Lake Hood Seaplane Base are bustling hubs of the small-plane activity that is such a big part of intrastate transport. Anchorage is a major interstate and international transportation hub as well.

Stop at the Anchorage Convention and Visitors Bureau's **Log Cabin Visitor Center** on 4th Avenue at F Street. Although it's oriented toward directing tourists to commercial enterprises, the staff possess a wealth of information. The center (274-3531) is open 7:30 a.m. to 7 p.m. in summer, 8 a.m. to 6 p.m. in May and September, and 9 a.m. to 4 p.m. the rest of the year. Anchorage has the **People Mover**, a fair bus system that you can use to get around town (343-6543 for information).

A number of valuable offices are accessible by foot, bus, taxi, or car. Start with a phone search to make sure you find the correct bureaucratic maze. Addresses are listed in the relevant sections below and in the appendix.

## Things to See and Do in Anchorage

**Alaska Aviation Heritage Museum**—Twenty-one vintage aircraft are on display and a 60-seat theater offers a short film. You can watch takeoffs and landings at the adjacent Lake Hood Seaplane Base, located on the south shore of Lake Hood. Take International Airport Road west to Aircraft Drive. Open May 15–September 15 from 9 a.m. to 6 p.m. daily, Tuesday–Saturday 10 a.m. to 4 p.m., 248-5325, www.alaska.net/~aahm.

# Valuable Resources

**Alaska Department of Fish and Game, 349-4687**
**Alaska Marine Highway System, 272-4482**
**Alaska Public Lands Information Center, 271-2737**
**Alaska Railroad, 265-2494**
**Alaska State Division of Tourism, 465-2010**
**Anchorage Chamber of Commerce, 272-2401**
**Anchorage Parks and Recreation, 343-4484**
**Better Business Bureau, 562-0704**
**Chugach National Forest, 271-2500**
**Chugach State Park, 345-5014**
**United States Customs Service, 248-3373**

**Alaska Botanical Gardens**—Still under development, the gardens feature native Alaskan plant species. Interpretive signs can be followed through the two existing gardens, or you can take a guided tour. Take Tudor Road east and turn right on Campbell Airstrip Road. Park in the Benny Benson School lot. 265-3165. Open 9 a.m. to 9 p.m. daily.

**Alaska Experience Center**—An IMAX theater with a 3-story curved screen is the main attraction and one of my favorite visitor spots in Anchorage. Regular showings of 40 minute-long *Alaska the Greatland* are featured, along with other films. With IMAX, you feel as if you're part of the action. Since the "action" is often a swooping plane flight through wild terrain, you might start feeling a little queasy. If that happens, just close your eyes. It's a great way to spend an hour on a rainy afternoon.

Also at the center is the Alaska Earthquake Exhibit, which features displays, murals, a movie, and a floor that shakes you in your seat. The center is at 705 West 6th Avenue, Anchorage, 276-3730, www.alaska.net/~alaskaxp, open daily 9 a.m. to 9 p.m. in summer, 11 a.m. to 7 p.m. in spring and fall, noon to 6 in winter. Admission is $7 for the theater, $4 for the earthquake exhibit, or $10 for both.

**Alaska Public Lands Information Center**—One of three such centers in the state, this is your one-stop site for information on all of Alaska's parks, preserves, refuges, and undesignated public lands. Exhibits, videos, a theater, and a bookstore are part of the center. Call or stop in for a schedule of programs, films, and slide shows. Old Federal Building, 4th Avenue and F Street, 271-2737, open daily in summer, Monday–Friday the rest of the year.

**Alaska Zoo**—This is almost certainly the only place you'll find an elephant in Alaska. The zoo specializes in native species but throws in a few curve balls for the entertainment of all. Many of the individual animals were rescued and unable to be reintroduced to the wild. Take O'Malley Road east from the Seward Highway (AK 1) or from the Old Seward Highway near the south end of town. Open 9 a.m. to 6 p.m. daily in summer, 10 a.m. to 5 p.m. Wednesday– Monday October–April, 346-3242, www.goworldnet.com/akzoo.htm.

**Anchorage Museum of History and Art**—This outstanding museum is one of Alaska's finest and an architectural jewel as well. A fine permanent art collection is on the main floor. Upstairs is the large Alaska Gallery, featuring an excellent collection of artifacts and diora-

*Anchorage, on the Cook Inlet, sits along the Chugach Mountains.*

Anchorage Convention and Visitors Bureau

mas related to the state's native and settlement history. Twenty touring exhibits come through annually, native dance performances are presented daily, and the Children's Gallery has hands-on opportunities for young ones. There's also a pleasant cafe and museum shop. 121 West 7th Avenue, 343-4326. Open 9 a.m. to 6 p.m. daily mid-May–mid-September, closed Mondays in winter.

**Earthquake Park**—When the Good Friday earthquake struck in 1964, a huge section of land on the coast southwest of downtown subsided dramatically, destroying 75 homes. The remaining landscape—a series of broken ridges and troughs barely above sea level—was preserved as a legacy of the event. An interpretive display tells the story and short trails offer access to coastal views.

Unfortunately (perhaps), trees have grown up to cover the area, making the patterns of destruction invisible to the casual observer. The park now resembles little more than a ragged hunk of undeveloped coastline. Take Northern Lights Boulevard west, past Wisconsin Street. The park is between the road and Cook Inlet.

**Imaginarium**—A nice science discovery museum for kids of all ages. Lots of hands-on exhibits and activities (Marine Life Touch Tank, Polar Bear Lair, Physics of Toys, and Bubbles are a few). 725 West 5th Avenue, 276-3179. Open daily 10 a.m. to 6 p.m., $5.

**Oscar Anderson House**—This is the only one of the city's few historic homes that functions as a museum. It was the first wood frame house in Anchorage, built in 1915 by Swedish immigrant Oscar Anderson. 420 M Street, 274-2336. Open mid-May–September, daily noon–4 p.m., $2.

**Resolution Park and Captain Cook Monument**—Captain James Cook, explorer of the inlet that bears his name, is immortalized in this small park overlooking the water. Take a look on your downtown walkabout. 3rd Avenue and L Street.

**Wolf Song of Alaska**—Part gift shop, part wolf exhibit, Wolf Song is a nonprofit organization "dedicated to promoting an understanding of the wolf through educational programs, research, and increased public awareness." Stop in if you're downtown. 6th and C Street, 346-3073.

## Where to Stay in Anchorage

Anchorage has several chain accommodations, including Best Western, Super 8, Holiday Inn, Ramada, Comfort, Executive Suites, and Quality Inn, all with 800 numbers. There are numerous

independents as well. Call or stop at the visitor center for help in getting your chosen location and price.

**AAA B&B Reservations** (reservation service), Anchorage, 346-2533. Also Aurora Winds B&B.

**Adventure Alaska Bed and Breakfast Reservations**, 6740 Lawlor Circle, 243-0265, www.alaska.net/~alaskabb. Central reservations for B&Bs in Anchorage, Homer, Seward, Kenai, and Denali. Outfitting and tours, too.

**Anchorage Hilton**, 500 West 3rd Avenue, (800) HILTONS, 265-7152, 272-7411. Mid-May–September $195–$215, winter $150–$170. The works. Even if you're not staying, enjoy the view at the **Top of the World Restaurant** and bar on the top floor.

**Anchorage Youth Hostel**, 700 H Street, 276-3635. $16 members, $19 non-members. 95 beds, closed noon to 5 p.m., downtown, midnight curfew, reservations advised.

**Centennial Park Campground**, take Boundary Road east from Muldoon Road, just south of Glenn Highway, 333-9711. $13 sites, RVs okay, free showers.

**Copper Whale Inn**, 440 L Street, 258-7999. $100 and up in summer, $55 and up in winter. Great downtown location overlooking Cook Inlet. Very nice.

**Hotel Captain Cook**, 4th and K Street, (800) 843-1950, 276-6000. $230–$240 summer, $130–$140 winter. The other fine downtown luxury hotel, with a nice rooftop bar and restaurant with a view.

### Where to Eat in Anchorage
**Elevation 92**, 3rd Avenue and L Street, 279-1578. Enjoy fine seafood dining with Cook Inlet views 92 feet above sea level.

**F Street Station**, 325 F Street, Anchorage, 272-5196. Upscale pub grub.

**Glacier Brew House**, 735 West 5th Avenue, 274-2739. A new and popular brew pub with good food.

**Humpys Great Alaskan Alehouse**, 610 West 6th Avenue, 276-2337. Tasty food and more than 40 microbrews on tap.

**Phyllis's Cafe and Salmon Bake**, 436 D Street, 273-6656. Open daily 8 a.m. to midnight. Indoor/outdoor seating, big menu, touristy, fun.

**Sea Galley & Pepper Mill Restaurant**, 4101 Credit Union Drive, 563-3520 (Sea Galley), 561-0800 (Pepper Mill), fax 563-6382. Opens at 11 a.m. for lunch and dinner. Popular and huge place for big and tasty meals. Seafood, steaks, prime rib, pastas.

**Simon & Seafort's Saloon and Grill**, 420 L Street, 274-3502. Enjoy Cook Inlet views and fine dining downtown.

**V.I.P. Restaurant**, 555 West Northern Lights Boulevard, 279-8514, 279-7549. Could be the best Korean food in town. Chinese cuisine served as well.

## CHUGACH STATE PARK
*Location/Size: At west end of Chugach Mountains, adjacent to Anchorage. 495,204 acres.*
*Main Activities: Hiking, fishing, kayaking, wildlife observation, short hikes and jogging, camping, cross-country skiing, mountaineering.*
*Gateway Towns/Getting There: Anchorage/scheduled air service from Seattle, Fairbanks, and many other points; vehicle access via Glenn Highway (AK 1) and Seward Highway (AK 2) from Kenai Peninsula, Canada, and the Interior. Park access: vehicle parking with trailheads at Crow Creek Canyon via Girdwood; Bird Creek, Indian Creek, and Falls Creek, all along Turnagain Arm; Ship Creek via Ski Bowl Road and Arctic Valley Ski Area; Peters Creek and Eklutna Lake from the Glenn Highway; and Pioneer Ridge from the Knik River Road. In southeast Anchorage, several trails can be reached from Rabbit Creek Road, Hillside Drive, and Hilltop Ski Area.*
*Facilities, Camping, Lodging: Visitor center, parking lots, access roads, dump station, picnic sites, and viewpoints all around the park perimeter, at campgrounds, and along the highway. Eklutna Lake Campground, Mile 10 Eklutna Lake Road; Eagle River Campground, take Hiland Road toward mountains from Mile 12 of Glenn Highway*

*(AK 1); Bird Creek Campground, Mile 101 Seward Highway. Primitive camping in park interior, a few designated sites. No backcountry lodging.* **Headquarters and Information:** *Visitor Center, Mile 12 Eagle River Road, 694-2108, open daily in summer 10 a.m. to 5 p.m.; Chugach State Park Headquarters, Mile 115 Seward Highway (AK 1), 345-5014; Eklutna Ranger Station, Mile 10 Eklutna Lake Road, 688-0908.*

While several American cities are backed by mountain wilderness parks, Anchorage tops them all. At nearly half a million acres, Chugach State Park is the third-largest state park in the United States—there's plenty of room for solitude. The east-central section of the park is crowned with an almost continuous layer of glaciers, while to the west and north long valleys drain northwestward into Cook Inlet. The towns of Eklutna, Peters Creek, and Eagle River are at the mouths of three such valleys, while Ship Creek and several smaller streams flow through greater Anchorage.

Eagle River Road follows the Eagle River a dozen miles into the mountains, providing access to a popular river run. Intermediate or advanced canoeists, kayakers, and rafters can enjoy Class I to Class III waters. The best put-ins are at Mile 7.5 and Mile 9 of the road. See the appendix for outfitters.

Virtually every watershed draining the park has vehicle access and trailheads. Thirty trails are identified by the park service, including six open to mountain biking. Most are short hikes up into closed valleys, though they allow access to high ridges and peaks. Several short spurs and loops climb up from the foothills neighborhoods above Anchorage. With so many options, it pays to stop for information at the **Eagle River Visitor Center** at Mile 12 of Eagle River Road, the **Chugach State Park Headquarters** at Mile 115 of the Seward Highway, or the **Eklutna Ranger Station** at Mile 10 of Eklutna Lake Road (see details above).

## Chugach State Park Trails

The routes listed below include all designated through trails, most longer trails, and a few shorter spurs. For details on the shorter trails from the Anchorage foothills, stop in at park headquarters.

**Arctic to Indian Trail** (22 miles, 2,100' and 1,000' gains northbound, 1,000' gain southbound)—This rugged route starts at Arctic Valley Ski Basin at the end of Ski Bowl Road near Fort Richardson, drops 1,000 feet into the Ship Creek valley, and follows the creek south until the trail disappears in open terrain. From here, you may have a difficult, muddy slog up to 2,100-foot Indian Pass before dropping down Indian Creek on the **Indian Valley Trail** to the trailhead at Mile 102 of the Seward Highway (AK 1). Day hiking to the pass from the south end is a good option (6 miles to pass, 2,100' gain). Through route—2–3 days.

**Bird Creek Trail** (15 miles, 2,500'-plus gain)—Begins at Mile 100.5 of Seward Highway just west of Bird House Bar and follows Bird Creek up to treeline in a high basin. The first 5.5 miles are an old road open to ATVs and bikes. The rest is unmaintained and sometimes overgrown. Cirque and ridge options are possible among 5,000- to 6,000-foot peaks with small glaciers. **RT**—2–4 days.

**Bird Ridge Trail** (1.5 miles, 2,500' gain)—At Mile 102.1 of the Seward Highway, you'll find the trailhead for a route that climbs quickly up Bird Ridge, unlike its near neighbor to the east, the Bird Creek Trail, which follows the valley. For a moderate to steep, early season, fast climb to great views, this is a fine choice. The trail ends at the ridgecrest, inviting further exploration. **RT**—3–4 hrs.

**Eklutna Lake Recreation Area and Trailhead** (various options)—Take the 10-mile Eklutna Lake Road from the Eklutna exit of the Glenn Highway to the recreation area, a designated portion of Chugach State Park which features a good campground near the foot of this long, lovely lake. There are several trail options:

The **Eklutna Lakeside Trail** (13 miles, 300' gain) follows the east lakeshore to campsites 2.5 miles beyond the lake's head at the valley fork, then continues through a deep, narrow valley called the Mitre to the tip of Eklutna Glacier. It is open to bikes and ATVs (Sunday–Wednesday only). The **Bold Ridge Trail** (3-plus miles, 2,500'-plus gain) climbs steeply from Mile 5 of the Lakeside Trail, accessing a high ridge below Bold Peak (7,522'). Good possibilities for further explorations. **RT**—half day from Lakeside Trail. The **East Fork Trail** (3-plus miles, 300'-plus gain) heads from the campsites at the head of the lake up a deep valley to the east, offering access to higher ridges and glaciers. **RT**—half day. The **Twin Peaks Trail** (3.2-plus miles, 1,500' gain) climbs immediately, sometimes steeply, from the campground to high tundra with great lake views. Further exploration is possible. Watch for Dall sheep. **RT**—half day.

**Falls Creek Trail** (1.5-plus miles, 1,500'-plus gain)—Officially ending at treeline, this steep climb can be continued another couple of miles through open tundra into a high cirque. Hikers are rewarded with high-country scenery and outstanding views. Dall sheep may be sighted. The trailhead is at Mile 105.7 of the Seward Highway. **RT**—half day.

**Glen Alps Trailhead** (several options)—From New Seward Highway, take O'Malley Road east about 4 miles to Hillside Drive, turn south 1 mile to Upper Huffman Road, then east again for less than a mile to Toilsome Hill Drive. Follow Toilsome Hill Drive as it winds up to the trailhead. Four trails begin here:

**Anchorage Overlook Trail** (¼ mile, 50' gain)—An easy paved and gravel stroll to an overlook deck with stunning Anchorage and sunset views. Wheelchair accessible. **RT**—½–1 hr. **Flattop Mountain Trail** (1.5 miles, 1,300' gain)—The most popular—and occasionally deadly—climb in Alaska. Some steep scrambling; watch for rocks dislodged by hikers above you. **RT**—2–3 hrs. **Powerline Trail** (11-plus miles, 1,300' gain southbound, 2,000' gain northbound)—This trail gradually climbs South Fork valley, crosses over a high pass, then drops steeply to merge with the Indian Creek Trail near its Seward Highway trailhead. Good access to high peaks and small lakes, recommended for mountain bikes. Through route—1–2 days. **Middle Fork Loop (to Williwaw Lakes)** (3.5 miles to Williwaw Lakes Trail junction, minimal gain to junction)—Take the Powerline Trail ¾ mile to Middle Fork Loop Trail, follow Middle Fork Loop Trail about 2 miles to Williwaw Lakes Trail (see below). **RT** to junction—half day; to lakes—1–2 days.

**Historic Iditarod (Crow Pass) Trail** (26 miles, 2,500' gain northbound, 3,500' gain southbound)—This generally good route follows Eagle River from the park visitor center, climbs gradually to 3,883-foot Crow Pass, then drops down Crow Creek to the trailhead at the end of Crow Creek Road north of Girdwood. Great views, mining ruins, and a couple of unbridged streams to cross. Good day hikes from either end. Through trail—3–5 days.

**McHugh Lake Trail** (7 miles, 2,750' gain)—This moderate route climbs from McHugh Creek Picnic Area at Mile 111.8 of the Seward Highway. Hike northwest on Turnagain Arm Trail for half a mile to a junction, then up to the lakes basin, high peaks, and possible through route to Powerline Trail over Ptarmigan Pass. **RT**—all day.

**Prospect Heights Trailhead** (several options)—From New Seward Highway, take O'Malley Road east about 4 miles to end of road, swing left onto Hillside Drive, then right up Upper O'Malley

Road about ½ mile to fork. Bear left up Prospect Drive to trail-head. Three trails begin here:

**Middle Fork/Williwaw Lakes Trail** (7-plus miles, 1,600'-plus gain)—Follow Near Point Trail 1.3 miles to junction. The route follows Middle Fork Trail then Williwaw Lakes Trail to small lakes in a high cirque with steep faces. The Middle Fork Trail continues about 2 miles to a junction with the Powerline Trail (see above). **RT**—1–2 days.

**Near Point Trail** (4 miles, 1,900' gain)—First 3 miles are easier and open to bikes. Last mile climbs to Near Point and great views. **RT**—half day.

**Wolverine Trail** (5.5 miles, 3,400' gain)—Take Near Point Trail 2 miles to junction. Follow easy to moderate route to summit of Wolverine Peak (4,400') for great views. **RT**—all day.

**South Fork Valley Trail** (6 miles, 400' gain)—Follow Hiland Road from Mile 11.6 of the Glenn Highway near Eagle Creek. From Mile 7.5 of Hiland, follow the signs for half a mile to the trailhead. This easy route follows an open valley among high peaks to beautiful lakes, and includes boardwalk segments for crossing wet areas. **RT**—all day.

**Turnagain Arm Trail** (9.4 miles, 750' gain) The trail begins at the Potter Section House Historic Site and Chugach State Park headquarters at Mile 115.3 of the Seward Highway. The path follows an old rail construction support route, paralleling the highway and tracks southeast along Turnagain Arm. The views are splendid, the separation from vehicle traffic is sufficient, and the trail is open early in the season. The route can be shortened or extended in various ways. Look for Dall sheep. Through trail—all day.

## SEWARD HIGHWAY (AK 9)—PORTAGE TO ANCHORAGE

*Road Conditions and Attractions—45 miles. Good, paved route, often slowed by traffic, some dangerous curves and drivers, some narrow lanes. Potter Marsh, Turnagain Arm bore tides, beluga whale sighting, Dall sheep viewing, Chugach State Park trailheads, Girdwood, Alyeska Ski Resort, Portage Glacier.*

The Seward Highway hugs the steep north shore of Turnagain Arm between Anchorage and Portage, then heads south onto the Kenai Peninsula. On summer weekends, this two-lane road can be bumper to bumper with Anchorage-area residents heading to

# Turnagain Arm

The western end of the Chugach Mountains splits Cook Inlet into two shallow arms, both of which are largely unnavigable and heavily silted. The southern of the two is Turnagain Arm, named by Captain Cook, who quickly discovered the shallow inlet was a poor choice for a vessel with deep draft. After turning into the arm, he turned again to get out.

Turnagain Arm is famous for a tidal phenomenon known as a bore tide, bore wave, or tidal bore. When the incoming tide hits the shallow, narrowing channel, it often forms a churning wave front or short series of waves that speed inward from 10 to 15 mph over the flats. Usually only a foot or two in height, the bore wave can reach 6 feet during spring tides. Only the foolish wander onto the sucking tidal flats to look for clams or adventure.

Check the tide tables for Anchorage. The bore wave should pass by viewpoints along the Seward Highway and Turnagain Arm according to the following schedule (allow 30 minutes on either side of suggested time). Remember that the phenomenon fluctuates and is sometimes largely absent:

| Viewpoint | Time after Low Tide in Anchorage |
|---|---|
| Beluga Point | 1 hour, 15 minutes |
| Indian Point | 1 hour, 30 minutes |
| Bird Point | 2 hours, 15 minutes |
| Girdwood | 3 hours |
| Peterson Creek | 3 hours, 45 minutes |
| 20-mile Creek | 4 hours |

favorite Kenai fishing spots and vacation cabins. The road has a well-earned reputation for accidents. If you are unlucky enough to be trapped in a long line behind a trundling RV, you'll understand the frustration that drives people to recklessness. Fortunately, interesting diversions allow you to break the 70-mile Anchorage–Portage stretch into endurable segments.

Mileposts are listed in reverse since most travelers make their stops heading south from Anchorage.

**Anchorage** (Mile 127 to Mile 118)—See Anchorage, above.

**Potter Marsh** (Mile 117.4)—The boardwalks of Potter Marsh provide easy access to excellent bird habitat and a busy salmon stream. Located east of the road where the Seward Highway meets Turnagain Arm just south of Anchorage, it's a popular stop for families and for anyone with some spare time. The marsh is part of the **Anchorage Coastal Wildlife Refuge**, which encompasses coastal wetlands and a large tidal-flats area southwest of the city. For information, visit www.dnr.state.ak.us/parks/asp/relasite.htm.

**Potter Section House State Historic Site** (Mile 115.3)—Just south of Anchorage along the Seward Highway is the site of Potter, an original camptown for those who constructed the Alaska Railroad. The headquarters of Chugach State Park are here: open daily in summer, Monday–Friday in winter, 8 a.m. to 4:30 p.m., 345-5014. The park encompasses much of the coast between here and Girdwood. The 9.4-mile Turnagain Arm Trail, also known as the Old Johnson Trail, begins here. See Chugach State Park Trails, above.

**McHugh Creek State Wayside** (Mile 111.8)—A picnic area with access to the creek and the Turnagain Arm Trail.

**Beluga Point** (Mile 110.3)—This is a good spot to stop for a binocular scan of the waters of Cook Inlet. You may see a pod of white beluga whales or, perhaps, a bore tide. A display offers information on both.

**Falls Creek Trailhead** (Mile 105.7)—See Chugach State Park Trails, above.

**Bird Ridge Trailhead** (Mile 102.1)—See Chugach State Park Trails, above.

*Dall Sheep, Turnagain Arm*

**Bird Creek State Recreation Site** (Mile 101.2)—Fishing, camping, and creek and trail access. Sites are $10 and fill up early on summer weekends.

**Girdwood and Alyeska Junction** (Mile 90)—Turn here for access to Girdwood, the ski basin, Alyeska Tram, Crow Creek Canyon, and the Iditarod National Historic Trail. See Girdwood, below, and Chugach State Park Trails, above.

**Alaska Railroad–Whittier Shuttle** (Mile 80)—If operations are the same when you arrive, this is where you put your vehicle on a flatcar for the short train ride to Whittier and the Prince William Sound ferries. Foot passengers are carried as well. Contact the Alaska Railroad for information (see chapter 6 or appendix).

**Big Game Alaska** (Mile 79)—This small wild game park is basically a drive-through native-species zoo with a gift shop—though it may be of more interest than Portage Glacier to those short on time (see Portage Glacier, below). While not exactly an animal rescue center, the park is home to several injured or abandoned animals. You aren't likely to get a better look at musk ox, caribou, Sitka black-tailed deer, elk, moose, bison, or bald eagles. Mile 79 Seward Highway, Portage Glacier, 783-2025, open daily June–August 9:30 a.m. to 7:30 p.m. and September–May 11:30 to dusk. $5.

**Portage Glacier Road** (Mile 78.9)—Turn here for Portage Glacier (see below).

## GIRDWOOD AND ALYESKA

*Location/Climate:* Girdwood is 30 miles east-southeast of Anchorage on Turnagain Arm. See Hope (chapter 10) for climate info.

**Population:** *Several hundred, variable.*

**Travel Attractions:** *Alyeska Ski Resort, access to Chugach National Forest and Chugach State Park via Crow Creek Road, access to Portage Glacier, several hiking trails, bike route, cross-country skiing, summer tram rides.*

**Getting There:** *Vehicle access via Seward Highway (AK 1) from Anchorage, Kenai Peninsula; charter small-plane air service; possible rail to Portage with shuttle to Girdwood.*

**Information:** *Chugach National Forest Office, P.O. Box 129, Alyeska Access Road (just north of railroad crossing), Girdwood, AK 99587; check with ski resorts, area businesses, or Alyeska Prince Hotel (see below).*

Girdwood is a classic ski village. Small clusters of chalets, cabins, and condos are concentrated near the base of Mount Alyeska and the **Alyeska Ski Resort**, while others are scattered through the rest of Glacier Creek and Crow Creek valleys. The new Alyeska Prince Hotel, the queen of Alaskan resorts, is a large ski hotel that probably could have used another million for exterior architecture. It is, however, luxurious in that ski-boots-and-kids-welcome sort of way.

The funky, tiny town of Girdwood is home both summer and winter to friendly, active people who spend a lot of time with the wind in their hair.

## Things to See and Do in Girdwood

**Alyeska Tramway**—Girdwood's big attraction is a gondola ride to the 2,300-foot level of Mount Alyeska. Here you'll find ski runs or hiking trails, depending on the time of year, and the **Seven Glaciers Restaurant**—a great place to enjoy a drink or a meal with a marvelous view. (For a quick, less-pricey bite, the **Glacier Express** has some tasty goodies.) Though you can basically be sure of a ride within a half hour during the day throughout the summer, call for specific hours of operation. Things change depending on the season and the tram maintenance schedule. The station and ticket windows are behind the Alyeska Prince Hotel—you'll have to walk a ways from the hotel parking areas or wait a bit for the shuttle bus. 1000 Arlberg Avenue, (800) 880-3880, 754-1111, www.alyeskaresort.com. $16.

**Crow Creek Road and Mine**—North of Girdwood, Crow Creek Road follows the path of the original Iditarod Trail, a winter route which ran from Seward to Nome. The road climbs 7 miles into a narrow valley to the head of **Crow Creek Trail**, which climbs 3 steep miles to a mining ruin and reservable Forest Service cabin. The longer route continues north to Eagle River (see Historic Iditarod Trail in Chugach State Park Trails, above).

Three miles up Crow Creek Road from its junction with Alyeska Access Road, the century-old **Crow Creek Mine National Historic Site** features eight original buildings, a gift shop, and campground. 278-8060, open May 15–September 15 daily 11:30 a.m. to dusk. $50.

**Hiking Trails**—Several short and easy trails suitable for day hikes are found in the valley around town. Great views and fun scrambles can be enjoyed from the tram station at 2,300 feet. For a map of possibilities inquire at the Forest Service office, Monarch Mine Road, just north of rail crossing, 783-3242.

### Where to Stay in Girdwood
**Alyeska Home Hostel**, Alpina Road, 783-2099. Rustic and small, $10 members and $13 non-members.

**Alyeska Prince Hotel**, 1000 Arlberg Avenue, (800) 880-3880, 754-1111. $125–$1,500. At the foot of the Alyeska Tram and ski slopes, this is Alaska's top resort hotel.

### Where to Eat in Girdwood
**Alpine Diner and Bakery**, Girdwood Station Mall, Mile 90 Seward Highway, 783-2550. Open daily 7 a.m. to 10 p.m. Italian dishes, burgers, sandwiches, baked goods, espresso drinks.

**The Bake Shop**, Alyeska Ski Resort, 783-2831. Open daily, 7 a.m. to 7 p.m. (until 8 p.m. Saturday). Breakfast, soup, pizza, sandwiches.

## PORTAGE GLACIER RECREATION AREA (CHUGACH NATIONAL FOREST)
*Location/Size: 8,600 acres within Chugach National Forest, located in the Portage Valley at head of Turnagain Arm, 50 miles from Anchorage.*
*Main Activities: Glacier viewing, camping, nature hikes.*
*Gateway Towns/Getting There: Girdwood/vehicle access from Anchorage and Kenai Peninsula via Seward Highway (AK 1). Recreation-area access by short paved road to visitor center and boat dock; boat tours of*

*lake and glacier; Byron Glacier Trail (1 mile), Willawaw Trail (½ mile),*
*Moraine Trail (¼ mile).*
**Facilities, Camping, Lodging:** *Begich, Boggs Visitor Center;*
*Portage Glacier Lodge (private—food and gifts); Willawaw Salmon*
*Viewing Facility; Portage Glacier Tour (private—Gray Line of Alaska,*
*277-5581, $21). Williwaw Campground and Black Bear Campground,*
*both about 1½ miles west of the visitor center.*
**Headquarters and Information:** *Glacier Ranger District, Chugach*
*National Forest, P.O. Box 129, Monarch Mine Road, Girdwood, AK*
*99587; 783-3242, Begich, Boggs Visitor Center, Portage Lake, 783-2326.*

Alaska's single most popular visitor attraction is Portage Glacier in
Portage Valley. The sight is famous in part because of the glacier,
lake, and beautiful setting—but also because there are established
visitor facilities at the end of a nice, paved road just a short detour
from the state's main tourist route. Those of you who are visiting
the glaciers of Kenai Fjords, Prince William Sound, or Glacier Bay
might choose to skip Portage for more time elsewhere.

R. Hood/Alaska Tourism Marketing Council

*Portage Lake at the foot of Portage Glacier*

In 1893 the glacier deposited the rocks of what is now the terminal moraine at the foot of Portage Lake. Since then the ice has receded 3 miles up and around a bend in the valley. Boat tours of the berg-dotted lake and glacier are available 2 miles beyond the center on the lake's south shore. Though the glacier is not among the most spectacular, it has a decent vertical face and calves small bergs on occasion. Gray Line operates the $25, naturalist-led boat trip to the face, which is the only way for the non-hiker to get a good look, 277-5581.

The best features of Portage are the easy nature paths and the **Begich, Boggs Visitor Center** at the foot of the lake. Ranger-guided nature hikes are pleasant, informative, and frequent in season. The valley also has 50 campsites at two good campgrounds, three smaller glaciers, and three short trails.

## KNIK ARM

A single map spread in the 150-page *Alaska Atlas and Gazetteer* shows Knik Arm of Cook Inlet, the mouths of the Susitna, Matanuska, and Knik Rivers, and the communities of Anchorage, Palmer, and Wasilla—the hub of "human Alaska." About 300,000 people live within 10 miles of its shores, yet Knik Arm provides habitat aplenty for area wildlife and is hardly an urban slough. The region is as scenic as many others in the state, offering a variety of attractions for the visitor.

Three state refuges protect much of the expansive waterfowl habitat on the north shore of the arm. **Susitna Flats State Game Refuge** (300,800 acres) is the largest, encompassing much of the land at the mouth of this many-channeled river. **Goose Bay State Game Refuge** (10,880 acres) south of Big Lake is popular with hunters because of easy access. Of most interest to travelers is **Palmer Hay Flats State Game Refuge** (26,048 acres) because of its location at the head of Knik Arm. The Glenn Highway passes through the refuge, offering good photo and birding opportunities. Use caution when stopping on the highway shoulder.

## THE GLENN HIGHWAY (AK 1)— ANCHORAGE TO PARKS HIGHWAY JUNCTION

*Road Conditions and Attractions—35 miles. Multilane freeway and four-lane paved road, open year-round, occasional thick traffic. Chugach State Park access, Eklutna Village, Knik Arm wetlands.*

This short segment of the Glenn Highway runs northeast out of Anchorage between the Chugach Mountains and Knik Arm. It's a speedy freeway for much of its length and a busy four-lane for the rest. Since this is the only road route into Anchorage from the north and east, traffic can be thick—especially during commute hours.

**Anchorage** (Mile 0–Mile 6)—See Anchorage, above. Note that the Glenn splits into a pair of one-way city streets in Anchorage, 5th Street and 6th Street. The heart of downtown is from C Street to I Street between 6th and 3rd. If you're racing into town from the north, just stay on the Glenn and you'll end up in the heart of the city.

**Arctic Valley Road and Fort Richardson** (Mile 6.1 northbound exit, Mile 7.5 southbound exit)—Fort Richardson Military Reservation —a piece of property as big as Anchorage itself—is to the north. To the south, the steep, winding, and lovely Arctic Valley Road leads to Ski Bowl Road, Arctic Valley Ski Area, and trailheads.

**Hiland Road Exit** (Mile 11.6)—Go 1.5 miles to reach the very popular **Eagle River Campground**, 58 sites, $15, day use $3, 345-5014 for information. Access to Eagle River and South Fork trails can be found along the road.

**Eagle River and Old Glenn Highway** (Mile 13.4)—The town of **Eagle River** (area population approximately 18,000) is largely a bedroom community and the chief suburb of Anchorage. It was homesteaded after World War II and continues to grow rapidly. Eagle River Road is an access route for Chugach State Park and the kayak runs of the upper Eagle River (turn right just south of the highway). There are numerous services, most along the Old Glenn Highway which parallels the new route for about 10 miles. For information, call 694-4702, or stop at the **Visitor Information Office**, 11401 Old Glenn Highway in Eagle River.

The **Southcentral Alaska Museum of Natural History** offers wildlife dioramas, extensive fossil and mineral collections, other exhibits, and a gift shop. 11723 Old Glenn Highway, Parkgate Building (across from McDonalds), Eagle River.

**North Eagle Access Road** (Mile 17.2)—If traveling toward Anchorage, turn here for the Old Glenn Highway and access to Eagle River.

**Peters Creek** (Mile 21.5)—Access to the Old Glenn Highway and Peters Creek Trail (see Chugach State Park Trails, above).

**Thunderbird Falls and Eklutna Road (northbound access)** (Mile 25.3)—Exit here and drive ⅓ mile to reach the **Thunderbird Falls Trail** (1 mile, small gain), which leads to a pretty falls with some dangerous cliffs. The road continues to a junction with Eklutna Road and access to Eklutna Lake State Recreation Site (see Chugach State Park Trails, above).

**Eklutna Village and Eklutna Road (southbound access)** (Mile 26.3)—Exit here to reach Eklutna Village (north of the highway, see below), as well as Eklutna Road and access to Eklutna Lake State Recreation Site (see Chugach State Park Trails, above).

**Old Glenn Highway** (Mile 29.6)—The flats between the Matanuska and Knik deltas host lowland forest, modest farms, and several small lakes and wetlands. Firmer soils gradually give way to wet meadows, channel isles, tidal wetlands, and the tidal flats of the arm itself. For a swing through the dryer end of the lowlands and a look at Knik River, take Old Glenn Highway into Palmer (19 miles).

From its junction with the Old Glenn Highway just south of the bridge, **Knik River Road** follows the Knik River inland. The Pioneer Ridge trailhead is about 3 miles up the road (see Palmer-Area Trails, below). The foot of Knik Glacier can be glimpsed with a little effort, or by heading upriver via powerboat.

**George Parks Highway Junction** (Mile 35.3)—Turn east here to stay on the Glenn for Palmer, the Matanuska valley, the Copper River basin, and beyond. Head west if you are going to Wasilla, Denali, or Fairbanks.

## EKLUTNA

For a short but rewarding detour from the Glenn Highway, take the Eklutna exit and follow the signs to Eklutna Village, just north of the road between Peters Creek and the Knik River. Eklutna has been continuously occupied by Dena'ina (or Tanaina) Athabascan Indians since 1650. The town is located at the junction of several traditional Indian trails, including the Iditarod. Russian trappers and mission-aries arrived in the late eighteenth century.

Today, **Eklutna Village Historical Park** is operated by the village corporation, Eklutna Inc. The Eklutna Village Heritage House offers local arts-and-crafts items for sale and provides access to outdoor exhibits for a small fee. Outside is the small **Saint Nicholas Russian Orthodox Church**, the oldest standing structure in the Anchorage area. It was originally built in the 1830s and refurbished in the 1970s. Nearby are several colorful Spirit Houses—elaborately decorated "houses" placed by the Dena'ina over the graves of relatives. For information, contact: Eklutna Village Historical Park, 688-6026. Admission is $3.50.

Anchorage Convention and Visitors Bureau

*Eklutna Village Historical Park*

# MatSu

The lowland region north of Knik Arm and the Chugach Mountains is dominated by the Matanuska and Susitna Rivers, which flow into Cook Inlet. The region is commonly called Matsu. Surrounded by the Chugach, Talkeetna, and Alaska Ranges, MatSu is home to the rapidly growing town of Wasilla, and the center of the state's tiny agricultural region, Palmer. Both towns are surrounded by private parcels, homesteads, small farms, vacation cabins, and numerous minor roads.

## PALMER

*Location/Climate:* On Glenn Highway and Matanuska River, 42
miles northeast of Anchorage. 16.5"/yr. precip., 6°F–67°F.
*Population:* 4,141 (7.7 percent native).
*Travel Attractions:* Access to Talkeetna Mountains and Matanuska
River, musk ox farm, regional agriculture, charming town.
*Getting There:* Vehicle access via Glenn Highway (AK 1).
*Information:* Visitor Center (Chamber of Commerce), P.O. Box 45,
723 South Valley Way (downtown by tracks), 745-2880, www.akcache.
com/Alaska/Palmer, open May–September daily 8 a.m. to 7 p.m.;
MatSu Visitors Center, Mile 35.5 Parks Highway, Palmer, AK 99645,
746-5000, www.alaskavisit.com.

"Did I fall asleep and wake up in Iowa?" is a common flash in the
minds of those entering Palmer. But then, upon looking up to see
the surrounding mountains, the illusion is instantly quashed.
Located near the mouth of the Matanuska River where it flows into
Knik Arm, Palmer is one of Alaska's more established and steady
towns—a notable contrast to the scattered, exploding strip of
Wasilla. The area was settled by homesteaders early in the century,
but got its biggest boost in 1935 when 200 families arrived to popu-
late the Matanuska Valley Colony—a farm settlement program
designed by the Federal Emergency Relief Administration as part of
the New Deal. Settlers were largely of Scandinavian descent, coming from failed farms in the northern Midwest. The descendants of
those who succeeded here still live in the area.

A small but vital agricultural region, the lower Matanuska Valley is wide and flat, the soil rich, and the weather moderate. Much
of the famous giant Alaskan produce is grown here, thanks to the
months of unending daylight. It's a fine town for a look about—
there are bikes on loan for free at the visitor center. Drop in at the
**Alaska State Fairgrounds** to see the fair (last week in August
through Labor Day), or walk through **Colony Village**—a collection
of historic structures, 2075 Glenn Highway, (800) 850-3247, 745-
4827, www.akstatefair.org. Get a walking-tour pamphlet for the
town at the visitor center.

### Things to See and Do in Palmer

**Musk Ox Farm** (private nonprofit corporation)—Qiviut is the soft fur from the underside of a musk ox that's used in the creation of traditional textile products. The captive herd at the farm is both the source of qiviut for subsistence thread makers and of breeding stock for the reintroduction of musk ox to various parts of the state. Once hunted virtually to extinction, stable wild herds are now established on Nunivak Island, the Arctic Coast, and the North Slope. Mile 50.1, Glenn Highway, 745-4151, www.muskoxfarm.org; open Mother's Day–September daily 10 a.m. to 6 p.m.; tours every half hour, $8.

**Williams' Reindeer Farm**—Over 300 reindeer roam this farm at the base of Bodenburg Butte, between the Matanuska and Knik Rivers south of Palmer. Guided tours, feeding, and petting. Mile 12 Old Glenn Highway, 745-4000, www.corecom.net/~reindeer; open June, July, and August daily; small admission fee.

## Palmer-Area Trails

Several established trails are found in the Talkeetna and Chugach Mountains around the head of Knik Arm. They include:

**Crevasse Moraine Trail System** (7 total miles, less possible, no significant elevation gain)—Several trail loops interconnect in a variety of ways. Good for running, hiking, and cross-country skiing. Trails wind through moraine deposits. From Mile 2 of Palmer-Wasilla Highway, take Loma Prieta Drive to end. **RT**—½–2 hrs.

**Lazy Mountain Trail** (3 miles, 3,000' gain)—Begins at **Lazy Mountain Recreation Area,** then climbs to the summit of Lazy Mountain, with great views of Sutton, the Matanuska valley, and Knik Arm. Take Old Glenn Highway (Arctic Avenue in Palmer) from Mile 42 of Glenn Highway, cross the river, turn left on Clark-Wolverine Road, and turn right on Huntley. **RT**—5–7 hrs.

**Matanuska Peak Trail** (7-plus miles, 5,600' gain)—Trail contours up around drainage of McRoberts Creek, crossing several small streams, then climbs up exposed ridge to stellar views from the 6,117-foot summit. Take Old Glenn Highway (Arctic Avenue in Palmer) from Mile 42 of Glenn Highway, cross the river to mile 15.5, turn east on Smith Road, and drive to its end and the trailhead. **RT**—all day (start early, check weather, be prepared).

**Pioneer Ridge–Knik River Trail** (6 miles, 5,200' gain)—Take the Glenn Highway to the Old Glenn Highway 4 miles east of Eklutna. From Old Glenn Highway, turn up Knik River Road and continue 3.6 miles to the trailhead. Trail climbs through cleared alder and spruce to

high exposed ridge. Fantastic views of Chugach Mountains and Knik Valley. **RT**—all day (start early, check weather, be prepared).

### Where to Stay in Palmer
**Colony Inn**, 325 Elmwood Street, (800) 478-ROOM (AK only), 745-3330. The Colony Inn is a former teachers' dorm for the Matanuska Valley Colony. Rooms are $80–$100; there's a small café.

**Fairview Motel and Restaurant**, P.O. Box 745, Mile 40.5 Glenn Highway, 745-1505. $50–$65 summer, $45–$60 winter. Basic motel with regular live local bands in the bar.

**Valley Hotel**, 606 S. Alaska Street, 99645, 745-3330, (800) 478-7666 (AK only), rooms are $55–$75. **Roundhouse Cafe** inside.

### Where to Eat in Palmer
**Mary's Fish and Burgers**, 535 W. Evergreen Avenue, 745-0190. Tasty and familiar American cuisine.

**Peking Garden**, 775 W. Evergreen, 746-5757. The Peking Garden offers a taste of distant lands.

**Vagabond Blues Coffee House**, 642 S. Alaska Street, South Valley Way, 745-2233. For a fresh cup of the hot stuff or lunch.

## WASILLA
*Location/Climate: On Parks Highway, 43 miles north of Anchorage. 17"/yr. precip., 4°F–68°F.*
*Population: 4,635 (5.3 percent native)*
*Travel Attractions: Access to recreation areas, museums, services.*
*Getting There: Vehicle access via Parks Highway (AK 3) from Fairbanks and Denali, or via Glenn Highway (AK 1) from Palmer and Anchorage.*
*Information: MatSu Visitors Center, Mile 35.5 Parks Highway, Palmer, AK 99645, 746-5000, www.alaskavisit.com; Dorothy G. Page Museum and Visitors Center, 323 Main Street, Wasilla, AK 99654, 373-9071.*

Named after a Dena'ina chief, Wasilla was established in 1917 where the new Alaska Railroad crossed the old Carle Trail. It served as a supply town and the "gateway to the Willow Creek Mining District." Wasilla has grown from a wide spot in the road along the Parks Highway into a very wide spot in the road along the Parks Highway. As you drive through, you'll keep waiting to arrive, only to find after a few miles that you're headed out of town.

Wasilla is representative of a common lifestyle in Alaska. Many state residents prefer to live in relative independence on fairly large plots of land. There are no building codes, property taxes, or zoning in most towns. Development reflects this, appearing random and centerless. Small roads lead away from larger ones, with long drives heading off into the trees, ending at cedar chalets, cabins surrounded by junk, or neat mobile homes. This residential style surrounds the more compact offerings of Wasilla proper.

Numerous lakes in the area host vacation cabins, parks, and lodges. While the Matanuska valley is well drained and suited for farms, the Susitna valley is an extension of the wider Cook Inlet basin, featuring broad, boggy flats and lakes. As the nearest place to Anchorage with a concentration of lake and river recreation—and lots of land available—Alaska-style development here is rapid. For a time, Wasilla was the fastest-growing city of its size in the nation.

## Things to See and Do near Wasilla

There are a variety of interesting and not-so-interesting travel attractions in and around Wasilla. They include:

**Big Lake**—The waters, town, and recreational areas of Big Lake mainly attract vacationers, boaters, and fishers. To get there, take the Big Lake Road turnoff from the George Parks Highway about 7 miles west of town. The **Big Lake North State Recreation Site** (S.R.S.) and **Big Lake South State Recreation Site** both have campgrounds and lake access. Nearby, **Rocky Lake State Recreation Site** also offers camping. The **Alaska State Fish Hatchery** beyond Rocky Lake offers free tours. Services are available on Big Lake Road. A few lodges operate along the lakeshore. For information, contact the Big Lake Chamber of Commerce, P.O. Box 520067, Big Lake, AK 99652, 892-6109.

A huge fire consumed thousands of acres of spruce forest and destroyed several structures around Big Lake in 1996. The fire scars are visible along area backroads.

**Iditarod Trail Dogsled Race Headquarters**—You can check out displays of race history in the museum, talk with a musher, and see sled dogs. Mile 2.2 Knik Road (south from Wasilla), 376-5155, www.iditarod.com. Open daily 8 a.m. to 7 p.m., summer 8 a.m. to 5 p.m. Free.

**Knik Museum and Mushers Hall of Fame**—Housed in a restored turn-of-the-century building, the museum features artifacts and archives of Knik—a gold-rush village on Cook Inlet from 1898 to 1916. The Hall of Fame features musher portraits, equipment, and race-history exhibits. Mile 13.9 Knik Road, 376-7755. The museum and Hall of Fame are open June 1–August 31 Wednesday–Sunday noon to 6 p.m., $2.

**Museum of Alaska Transportation and Industry**—Trains, planes, automobiles, and various transportation memorabilia are on display in the hall and on the grounds. There are some real delights for buffs and families. Take West Neuser Drive from Mile 47 of the Parks Highway (AK 2), 3800 West Neuser Drive, Wasilla, www.alaska.net/~rmorris/mati4.htm. Open May–September daily (closed Sunday and Monday in winter).

**Old Wasilla**—Several historic buildings are preserved in **Town Site Park**, located behind the **Dorothy G. Page Museum and Visitors Center** (323 Main Street, 373-9071, open daily in summer). The museum has area heritage displays and provides tourist information. A farmer's market is held in the park every summer Wednesday from 4 to 7 p.m.

## Where to Stay in Wasilla
**B&B Association of Alaska: MatSu Chapter** (reservation service), (800) 401-7444, 376-4461, www.alaska.net/~akhosts. Represents more than 30 area bed-and-breakfasts, plus cabins, host homes, suites, and apartments.

**Lake Lucille Inn (Best Western)**, 1300 West Lake Lucille Drive, (800) 528-1234, 373-1776. Nice lakeside inn. Rooms are $95–$125.

**Roadside Inn**, Mile 49.5 Parks Highway, 373-4646. Basic, includes a restaurant, $45 and up.

**Wasilla Backpackers**, 3950 Carefree Drive, Wasilla, 357-3699,

www.AlaskaOne.com/akhostel, travel@wasillabackpackers.com. A
clean home hostel located on 3 wooded acres. Beds are $22, one
private room is available for $60, tenting sites for $15 per person.
Laundry, internet, bike rentals.

**Windbreak**, Mile 40.5 Parks Highway, 376-4109. Basic rooms,
café, $65 and up.

### Where to Eat around Wasilla
Fast-food joints abound, but you might try:

**The Deli Restaurant & Bakery**, 185 East Parks Highway, 376-2914.
Breakfast, deli sandwiches, Italian dishes; open Monday–Saturday.

**Cheppo's Fiesta Restaurant**, 731 West Parks Highway,
373-5656. Decent Mexican fare right on the highway.

## HATCHER PASS
Most Alaska roads seem to cross over mountain passes reluctantly;
Hatcher Pass Road seems to do it just for fun. Originally built as an
access road to the mines in the Talkeetna Mountains, the road now
offers travelers a route through high peaks and history. If you are
driving and have four extra hours to spend on your way from Cook
Inlet to Denali, opt for this wonderful alternative route. The crisp
air and views at the top of the 3,886-foot pass are splendid.

Most of the Talkeetna Mountains are state-owned land, and
much of it is managed by the Department of Natural Resources
(see appendix for contact information) in the Hatcher Pass Management Area. Along with thousands of undesignated acres, the
area includes Independence Mine State Historic Park, **Summit
Lake State Recreation Site**, and the proposed Hatcher Pass
Ski Area. Also found in the area are the headwaters of the Little
Susitna River, protected as the **Little Susitna Recreation
River**—one of six designated state recreation rivers in the Susitna
watershed.

Quick visits to Hatcher Pass can include a drive with views,
mining history, wildlife observation, and short roadside hikes.
Experienced river runners can match their kayaking skills to the
Class V whitewater of the "Little Su." ( See appendix for outfit-

ters.) Downhill and cross-country skiing are possibilities. Excellent longer trails and ridge routes allow access to the high country.

Hatcher Pass is reached from Wasilla on Wasilla-Fishhook Road, from the Glenn Highway north of Palmer on Palmer-Fishhook Road, and from Willow on Willow-Fishhook Road. The pass is about 30 miles from Willow and about 20 miles from Palmer. Much of the road is gravel. It's narrow and often slippery up high, with tight turns, steep grades, and limited maintenance (not recommended for RVs or the timid).

## Trails near Hatcher Pass

Trails near Hatcher Pass include:

**Gold Mint Trail** (7-plus miles, 1,000-plus-foot gain)—The trailhead is located where the road takes a sharp turn near Motherlode Lodge. The route follows the west bank of the Little Susitna River and climbs gradually through open country. The first miles are along the original trail to Lonesome Mine. The valley steepens into a cirque rimmed by small glaciers, including Mint Glacier below Montana Peak. Enjoy a relatively easy walk, valley views, isolation, and primitive camping. **RT**—all day.

**Reed Lakes Trail** (3-plus miles, 1,600' gain)—Follow Archangel Road from Hatcher Pass Road to the Reed Lakes Trail trailhead. The trail follows Reed Creek as it winds into a high cirque with two small lakes. Primitive camping, beautiful alpine scenery. **RT**—5–7 hrs.

## INDEPENDENCE MINE STATE HISTORIC PARK

*Location/Size: On Hatcher Pass Road between Palmer and Willow in the Talkeetna Mountains, 18 miles from Palmer, 32 miles from Willow. 271 acres.*

*Main Activities: Mining history, high-country access.*

*Gateway Towns/Getting There: Palmer/vehicle access via Glenn Highway (AK 1); Willow/vehicle access via Parks Highway.*

*Park Access: Vehicle access via Hatcher Pass Road to parking lot; foot access through mining ruins.*

*Facilities, Camping, Lodging: Visitor center, historic buildings, roads and paths. No camping or lodging.*

*Headquarters and Information: DNR Public Information Center, 3601 C Street, Suite 200, Anchorage, AK 99503, 269-8400;*

*Matanuska-Susitna Area Office, 745-3975; Park Visitor Center, park entrance, 745-2827, www.dnr.state.ak.us/parks/units/indmine.htm.*
The first gold claim along Willow Creek was staked by Robert Lee Hatcher in 1906. Placer deposits in the creek hinted at lodes in the Talkeetna Mountains and it wasn't long before big companies got involved in hard-rock mining around Hatcher Pass. In the peak year of 1941, the Alaska-Pacific Consolidated Mining Company (largest in the area) had 83 claims and produced almost 35,000 ounces of gold. Profits fell after World War II and, in 1951, the mines closed. In 1974, Independence Mine was listed on the National Register of Historic Places, leading to the creation of the state historic park in 1980.

A number of historic buildings, machinery, shafts, tailings, and ruins are protected within the small park. More are scattered throughout the larger mining district. Make a stop at the visitor center near the park entrance for information and a walking-tour pamphlet. From there, you can explore the 271 acres via roads and footpaths.

The visitor center is open daily in summer, 11 a.m. to 7 p.m. Guided tours are offered at 1:30 and 3:30 p.m. daily, with an additional 4:30 p.m. tour on weekends.

## LAKE CLARK NATIONAL PARK AND PRESERVE

*Location/Size: Encompasses northern end of the Aleutian Range and western end of the Alaska Range, and includes a coastal segment of Cook Inlet, west of Anchorage and the Kenai Peninsula. National park— 2.6 million acres; national preserve—1.4 million acres; wilderness— 2.4 million acres.*

*Main Activities: Backpacking, mountaineering, river running, fishing, backcountry-lodge stays (outside park boundaries).*

*Gateway Towns/Getting There: Anchorage, Homer, Kenai/vehicle access via Glenn, Seward, and Sterling Highways; regular air service; scheduled ferry to Homer. Port Alsworth/regular small-plane air service, charter air. Park access by charter air drop-off or via canoe or kayak on Lake Clark from Port Alsworth; possible foot access from Iliamna Lake and Cook Inlet.*

*Facilities, Camping, Lodging: No facilities. Primitive camping only; lodging on private land on Lake Clark. See Alaska's Lake Clark Inn, below.*

*Headquarters and Information: Headquarters, 4230 University*

## Russian and Native Names

*The spelling of certain names and words varies from source to source, with no arbiter in sight. Alexandr Baranov and Alexander Baranof are certainly the same person. If you visit an Inupiaq village, then an Inupiat village, you haven't crossed any Eskimo cultural lines. I try to be consistent, but when relying on a direct source, I yield to their choice of spellings. The differences are always small enough to make safe intuitive judgments that the two versions refer to the same person, people, place, or thing.*

*Drive, Suite 311, Anchorage, AK 99508, 271-3751; Field Headquarters, Port Alsworth, AK 99653, 781-2218, www.nps.gov/lacl.*

Home to two impressive volcanoes, beautiful lakes, and the glacier-shredded Chigmit and Neacola Mountains, Lake Clark National Park and Preserve is a wilderness jewel. Located at the junction of the Alaska and Aleutian Ranges, the park and preserve encompass about 4 million acres of a much larger mountain wilderness. There are no roads in the park and only one 3-mile-long trail, which accesses Tanalian Falls from the remote park headquarters at Port Alsworth on Lake Clark.

Two spectacular volcanoes are located in the park. **Redoubt Volcano** (10,197') erupted in 1989, sending ash miles into the atmosphere, showering cinders on areas downwind, and halting air traffic over a large region. Though it hasn't erupted recently, beautiful **Iliamna Volcano** (10,016') sleeps uneasily and the steam from its peak is thick at times. If you should happen to fly from Anchorage to Dutch Harbor or elsewhere in the Southwest on a clear day, your aerial views of these snow-covered mountains and the glaciers they launch will be long remembered.

The majority of visitors to Lake Clark National Park and Preserve fly from Anchorage, Kenai, or Homer directly to a chosen backcountry drop-off point. Facilities exist at **Port Alsworth,** including accommodations, a designated camping area, and a small park visitor center. Other facilities are found on the shores of Cook Inlet and in **Iliamna** (population 99, 66 percent native) on huge **Iliamna Lake,** which sprawls across state, private, native corporation, and BLM holdings between Lake Clark National Park and Preserve and Katmai National Park and Preserve.

Canoeing and kayaking are possible on Lake Clark and other lakes within the park. **Tlikakila River,** a designated National Wild River, is one of several within the park suitable for float trips. The best backpacking access is via high-country drop-offs since many of the long glacial valleys are thickly forested and low in elevation. Glacier walkers, mountaineers, and rock climbers have a paradise of offerings, though routes jump from basic to extreme very quickly with little middle ground. Consult outfitters, guides, and flying services (see appendix).

Remember, Lake Clark is a wild park. All backcountry users should be self-sufficient. Backcountry lodging is available at **Alaska's Lake Clark Inn** (on Lake Clark within preserve; great view), 1 Lang Road, Port Alsworth, AK 99653, 781-2224, 781-2252. The very accommodating owner/pilot will take you flightseeing or to fishing spots.

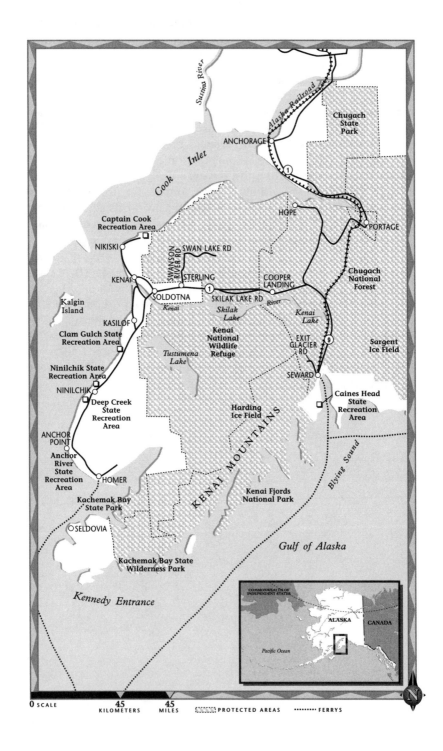

# 10

# THE KENAI PENINSULA

The Kenai Peninsula is Alaska's vacationland, offering trail-laced mountains to the east, freshwater sports and coastal access to the west, and fjords and glaciers to the south. Visitor facilities are more developed and familiar here than anywhere else in the state.

The two most popular destinations for out-of-state visitors are the towns of Homer and Seward. Homer is famous for halibut fishing, ferry trips to the villages of Halibut Cove and Seldovia, and the famous Homer Spit. Seward is the primary launching point for tour-boat visits to the calving glaciers and beautiful inlets of Kenai Fjords National Park. Opt for Seward if time is tight and it's got to be one or the other. The road route is shorter, with mountain scenery and trailheads, access to Exit Glacier, and a Kenai Fjords boat tour at the end. It's also accessible by rail from Anchorage.

## KENAI NATIONAL WILDLIFE REFUGE AND CHUGACH NATIONAL FOREST (KENAI UNIT)

*Location/Size: Refuge is 1.97 million acres (1.4 million acres of designated wilderness); Kenai National Wildlife Refuge encompasses much of the central and northern Kenai Peninsula.*

 ALASKA

**Main Activities:** *Fishing, hunting, canoeing, hiking, camping, boating, wilderness exploration.*
**Gateway Towns/Getting There:** *Sterling, Cooper Landing/vehicle access via Seward Highway (AK 1); Hope/vehicle access via Hope Highway from Seward Highway; Kenai, Soldotna/vehicle access via Seward Highway (AK 1), scheduled air service from Anchorage. Refuge access by vehicle through center of refuge via Seward Highway (AK 1) and via roads; canoe and kayak access to lakes and established canoe routes; foot access via several trails from Hope and the Seward Highway.*
**Facilities, Camping, Lodging:** *200 miles of trails, two established canoe routes, numerous campgrounds. Many established campgrounds and campsites along the trails and roads. Private lodges and bed-and-breakfasts are numerous on private lands adjacent to refuge lands.*
**Headquarters and Information:** *Refuge Manager, P.O. Box 2139, Soldotna, AK 99669, 262-7021, www.r7.fws.gov/nwr/kenai/kennwr.html, r7kenwr@mail.fws.gov (type "Attention Refuge Manager" in subject line).*

Much of the northern and western lowland areas of the Kenai Peninsula are within Kenai National Wildlife Refuge. The **Kenai Wilderness** unit of the refuge and the western reaches of the Chugach National Forest protect wild lowland areas and the Kenai Mountains. The Kenai River and others are exceedingly popular with salmon fishers, while hikers and backpackers enjoy good trail access to high open country, ridges, and summits. Numerous opportunities are available for users of personal watercraft such as innertubes to powerboats. Later in the year, moose hunters eagerly pursue their allotted quarry.

The **Kenai River Special Management Area**—administered by the Division of Parks and Outdoor Recreation of the Alaska Department of Natural Resources—includes the entire Kenai River corridor, plus Kenai Lake and Skilak Lake. Access, camping, and boating rules are covered in the management plan. The only area devoted strictly to non-motorized watercraft is a 10-mile stretch from the confluence of the Kenai and Russian Rivers to Skilak Lake. This route is served by rafting companies and includes a 2.5-mile Class III and Class IV stretch through Kenai River Canyon. Expect motorized boats elsewhere on the river throughout the summer.

Good long-distance trails access the refuge and national forest lands, including some that end a comfortable hitch or second-car ride from where they begin (van or bus shuttles may be possible; see appendix).

## Resurrection Trail System

Several trails form a network in the mountains west of the Seward Highway, offering a possible through route from Hope to Seward with shorter options along the way. Be careful when inquiring about trails since there is some confusion as to the names. Resurrection Creek flows north from Resurrection Pass to Hope, while the Resurrection River flows south to Seward from the Russian Lakes area. The three main trail segments are the Resurrection Pass Trail, linking Hope and the Sterling Highway; the Russian Lakes Trail, from the Sterling Highway south to the Russian Lake basin; and the Resurrection River Trail, continuing southeast to Seward.

## Kenai National Wildlife Refuge/
## Chugach National Forest Trails

In addition to the trails described here, other fishing-access trails are described in the milepost guides for the Seward and Sterling Highways. Consult forest and refuge information sources for details.

**Crescent Lake Route** (19 miles total, 1,200' gain)—Three trails link up for an easy and beautiful route with two reservable Forest Service cabins and several good campsites along the way. The route can be linked with the Johnson Pass Trail for a total hike of 42 miles. (Through route—2–3 days.) The **Crescent Creek Trail** (6.4 miles, 1,000' gain) climbs gradually east then south from Mile 45 of the Sterling Highway along Crescent Creek. (**RT**—long day.) The path becomes the **Crescent Lake Trail** (9 miles, 200' gain) and contours above the curving south shore of the lake, first heading southeast, then east, then northeast to the head of the lake. (Through trail—all day.) Here, it becomes the **Carter Lake Trail** (3.3 miles, 1,000' gain), dropping past Carter Lake to Mile 33.1 of the Seward Highway. (**RT**—half day.)

**Devils Pass Trail** (10 miles, 1,400' gain)—From mile 20.5 of the Resurrection Pass Trail, the trail climbs east 2 miles above a feeder of Juneau Creek into Devils Pass, then drops southeast along Devils Creek to Mile 39.4 of the Seward Highway. Through trail—all day.

**Fuller Lakes & Skyline Trails** (13 miles, 2,400' gain)— Both trails are in the Kenai Wilderness of Kenai National Wildlife Refuge. Through route—1–2 days. The **Fuller Lakes Trail** (3 miles, 1,400' gain) climbs from Mile 57.1 of the Sterling Highway

to Lower and Upper Fuller Lakes, two popular fishing spots.
**RT**—half day. From the upper lake, the **Skyline Trail** (10 miles,
1,000' westward gain, 2,400' eastward gain) cuts west and winds up
to the crest of the Mystery Hills. It then follows the curving ridgeline past easy summits before dropping down to the highway. Outstanding views! **RT**—2 days.

**Johnson Pass Trail** (23 miles, 1,000' gain)—This route connects Mile 32.6 and Mile 63.7 of the Seward Highway. Johnson
Pass separates Johnson Creek to the south from Bench Creek to the
north. The trail follows both streams closely. There's good high-
country access to cirques, small glaciers, ridges, and 4,000-foot
summits. The route can be linked with the Crescent Lake Route
(see above) for a total hike of 42 miles. Through trail—2–3 days.

**Resurrection Pass Trail** (35.2 miles, 2,400' gain)—The north
trailhead of this maintained route is 5 miles south of Hope at the
end of Resurrection Creek Road. The trail gradually climbs through
Resurrection Creek Valley, up into Resurrection (Mile 20.5), then
down Juneau Creek to the highway near Cooper Landing. Six
reservable Forest Service cabins are on or near the route. Brown
bear sightings are not uncommon (nor are sightings of other hikers).
Through trail—3–4 days.

**Resurrection River Trail** (17.8 miles, 900' gain)—The southern trailhead is on Exit Glacier Road north of Seward where the
road heads west up Exit Creek and away from the Resurrection
River. The route follows a forested valley between glacier-capped
ridges and offers scrambling climbs to high cirques. Two reservable
Forest Service cabins are located at about midpoint. The trail meets
the Russian Lakes Trail about 15 miles from the Sterling Highway,
enabling a 33-mile extended route. Through trail—2 days.

**Russian Lakes Trail** (21.5 miles, 800' gain between Sterling
Highway and pass)—This trail climbs 3 miles from the Russian
Lakes Campground at Mile 52 of the Sterling Highway to Lower
Russian Lake, then 8 miles more to Upper Russian Lake. The route
begins in a narrow, swampy valley, then reaches a wide, forested
upland. Three reservable Forest Service cabins are located between
the two lakes. Swinging east, the route crosses an easy, open divide,
then drops to Cooper and Kenai Lakes, both of which offer road
access to the highway via the Snug Harbor Road. The route can be
linked with the Resurrection River Trail (see above) for a 33-mile
route. Through trail—2 days.

**Summit Creek Trail** (8.4 miles, 2,600' gain westbound, 1,500' eastbound)—This rough alternate route forks off from Devils Pass Trail at the junction with Resurrection Pass Trail, angling up the north side of the spur while Devils Pass Trail stays to the south. The trail climbs to 4,000 feet (splendid views and summit access), crosses two small divides, and drops down Summit Creek to the Seward Highway pass, 1.5 miles south of Upper Summit Lake. There may be snow on the trail into the summer. Through trail—all day.

### Swan Lake and Swanson River Canoe Trails
A unit of the Kenai Wilderness protects two of Alaska's best established canoe routes. From the town of Sterling on the Sterling Highway, the Swanson River Road heads north about 15 miles through forested, lake-dotted flats. Three campgrounds and the Swanson River Oil Field are found near the junction with Swan Lake Road. Turn east on Swan Lake Road. The 80-mile, 40-lake **Swanson River Route** is to the north, while the 60-mile, 30-lake **Swan Lake Route** is south of the road. Roadside put-ins and parking are marked. Outfitters offer guided trips, rentals, and shuttles (see appendix).

**Kenai Backcountry Lodge,** south shore of Skilak Lake, P.O. Box 389, Girdwood, AK 99587 (mailing address), (800) 334-8730. Cabin tent stays start at $250 to $300 per person, per night; log cabins are $25 more. Cost includes transportation to and from Kenai, all meals, guided activities, and programs. Stays of three or more nights include a free raft trip. **BL**

## SEWARD HIGHWAY (AK 1/AK 9)— SEWARD TO PORTAGE
***Conditions and Attractions:*** *80 miles. Paved road, open year-round. Mountain scenery, numerous trailheads, fishing and winter-sports options, wildlife observation; access to Kenai Lake, Exit Glacier, and Seward.*

After threading the shoreline of Turnagain Arm to Portage, the Seward Highway heads south onto the Kenai Peninsula, passing through long glacier-carved valleys on its way to road's end at Seward. The route features the splendid scenery of the Kenai Mountains, beautiful lakes, five easy passes, glacier access, and many recre-

ational opportunities. Allow about two hours with no stops for the 80-mile drive. The mileposts are listed in descending order since most travelers will travel the Seward first from north to south.

**Portage Glacier** (Mile 78.9)—See chapter 9.

**Turnagain Pass** (Mile 68.5, 988' elevation)—The road crosses out of the Ingram Creek valley and into the Granite Creek valley, descending for a time before heading up again at the junction with the Hope Highway. At the pass is **Turnagain Pass Recreation Area**, a popular winter-sports zone. Snowmobilers head out west of the road while cross-country skiers own the east.

**Johnson Pass North Trailhead** (Mile 63.7)—See Kenai National Wildlife Refuge/Chugach National Forest Trails, above.

**Granite Creek National Forest Campground** (Mile 63)—Good creekside sites for $6, fishing, trail access.

**Hope Highway Junction** (Mile 56.7)—Turn north here to reach the historic mining town of Hope, the north end of the Resurrection Trail system, and the Gull Rock Trail along Turnagain Arm (see Hope, below; and Kenai National Wildlife Refuge/Chugach National Forest Trails, above).

**Summit Lakes** (Mile 47.2 and Mile 45.5)—These lovely lakes offer good spots for a photograph. Just above Upper Summit Lake, the road crosses another divide and drops into the Quartz Creek valley and the Kenai River watershed. Between the two lakes, you'll find:
    **Summit Lake Lodge** (Mile 45.8), Mile 45.5 Seward Highway, Cooper Landing, 595-1520. Good restaurant, bar, and rustic rooms. **RH**

**Devils Pass Trailhead** (Mile 39.4)—This route climbs steeply to the west to link up with the Resurrection Trail (see Kenai National Wildlife Refuge/Chugach National Forest Trails, above).

**Sterling Highway Junctions** (Mile 37.7 and Mile 37)—Turn here if you're heading for the Kenai River, Kenai National Wildlife Refuge, Kenai, Homer, or the Southwest.

**Carter Lake Trailhead** (Mile 33.1)—From this point, you can take the Carter Lake Trail (3 miles, 1,000' gain) up to Carter Lake for fishing and views. The trail becomes the Crescent Creek Trail, part of an excellent long-distance hiking route (see Kenai National Wildlife Refuge and Chugach National Forest Trails, above).

**Johnson Pass South Trailhead** (Mile 32.6)—See Kenai National Wildlife Refuge and Chugach National Forest Trails, above.

**Spruce Moose Bed-and-Breakfast** (Mile 30.1), Moose Pass, 288-3667. Two nice chalet homes. Great for families or groups. $120 and up, open year-round, hot tubs in winter.

**Trail Lake Lodge** (Mile 29.5), Moose Pass, 288-3101. Restaurant, bar, motel. Rooms $90–$100.

**Moose Pass** (Mile 29.4)—This little settlement on Upper Trail Lake (population 119, 11 percent native) began as a camp for the builders of the Alaska Railroad, which parallels the road from here to Seward. North of town, the rail line follows the original Iditarod Trail route to Portage. The actual pass is a narrow strip at the south end of Upper Trail Lake. Another low divide lies between the west end of the lake and the Sterling Highway junction. Moose Pass has food, gas, and lodging options.

**Trail River National Forest Campground** (Mile 24.2)—$6 campsites and access to the shores of Kenai Lake. East of the road, the **Falls Creek Trail** (3.2 miles, 1,000' gain) climbs into a steep valley past mining claims. It is officially 3.2 miles, but the valley continues to climb fairly gently at trail's end and it's tempting to keep going. About 9 miles in from the highway, it reaches a high saddle, 4,000-foot peaks, and glacier access. Conditions may be difficult. **RT**—half–all day (or more).

**Ptarmigan Creek Trailhead and Campground** (Mile 23.1)—There's a 16-site campground east of the road here. Sites are $6. The Ptarmigan Creek Trail (9 miles, 200' gain) reaches Ptarmigan Lake in 4 miles, then follows the narrow lake's northern shore. **RT**—half–all day. **Primrose Creek Trailhead and National Forest Campground** (Mile 17)—Turn west 1 mile through area homes to reach $6 sites

overlooking Kenai Lake. From the campground, the **Primrose Creek Trail** (5-plus miles, 1,500' gain) follows Primrose Creek above treeline to Lost Lake. From the west end of the lake, there is access to the gentle high basins of this small massif. The trail continues along the east lakeshore and becomes the Lost Lake Trail, which continues south to the trailhead near Seward. The two trails combined are about 16 miles long. **RT**—all day.

**Grayling Lake Trailhead** (Mile 13.3)—The Grayling Lake Trail (1.6 miles, 200' gain) climbs up to Grayling Lake, a small fishing lake in thick forest. There's also access to Meridian and Leech Lakes. **RT**—3–4 hrs.

**Exit Glacier Road** (Mile 3.7)—Turn here to reach Exit Glacier and the Harding Icefield Trail (see below). There's also access to the Resurrection River Trailhead, the south end of the Resurrection Trail System (see Kenai National Wildlife Refuge and Chugach National Forest Trails, above).

**Seward** (Mile 0)—See below.


## HOPE
*Location/Climate:* South shore of Turnagain Arm of Cook Inlet, at the top of the Kenai Peninsula. 20"/yr. precip., 14°F–60°F.
*Population:* 170 (3.1 percent native).
*Travel Attractions:* Historic mining community.
*Getting There:* Vehicle access via Hope Highway from the Seward Highway (AK 1).
*Information:* Inquire locally, www.advenalaska.com/hope.

Like so many Alaskan towns, Hope grew from gold. Prospectors were at work here as early as 1889, a decade before the Klondike and Nome strikes. Hope was named arbitrarily when early residents decided to honor the youngest arrivee on the next boat to land—one Fred Hope. The town population reached 3,000, but as the gold supply ran out the town declined and never recovered.

Today, 200 people live in the area, including a number of independent prospectors who still work claims. Visits to local gold and jewelry shops offer the chance to talk with folks about the mining life.

Located at the mouth of Resurrection Creek on Turnagain Arm, Hope is reached via the Hope Highway, which intersects the Seward Highway about 20 miles from town. It's a great place to escape the Kenai summer crowds to enjoy a bit of quiet history and charm. The general store has been serving customers since 1896 and several other vintage buildings still stand. You can walk to the old townsite and grab a bite at the local cafe.

Hope offers access to the north end of the Resurrection Pass Trail (see Kenai National Wildlife Refuge and Chugach National Forest Trails, above). A couple of smaller local trails also offer good hiking options. One of the best is the **Gull Rock Trail** (4.5 miles). From the trailhead at the end of the loop in Porcupine Campground (end of Hope Highway), the trail follows the shores of Turnagain Arm west to Gull Rock. There are good views across the inlet, as well as a chance to see the Turnagain Arm tidal bore (see Turnagain Arm, above). **RT**—6–8 hrs.

## Where to Stay and Eat in Hope
**Bear Creek Lodge**, Hope Highway, 782-3141. $80 summer, $50 winter. Very nice cabins in quiet wooded setting on Bear Creek.

*Long-abandoned miner's cabin near Hope*

**Coeur D'Alene Campground**, Chugach National Forest, Palmer Creek Road (12 miles from Hope Highway). Nice valley, near mine sites.

**Discovery Cafe**, Mile 16.5 Hope Highway, 782-3282. "Where the Gold Miners Meet"—if it's rebuilt after burning in 1999.

**Henry's One Stop**, Hope Highway, 782-3222. $50 double, $16.50 RV site. Laundry, showers, groceries, propane, rooms, trailer hookups and discharge. No credit cards.

**Porcupine Campground**, Chugach National Forest, Hope Highway (end). Good sites, trailheads.

**Seaview Cafe and Motel**, Main and B Streets, 782-3364. Turn-of-the-century building. Bar, motel, gift shop.

## SEWARD

*Location/Climate:* *128 road miles south of Anchorage at head of Resurrection Bay on southeast coast of Kenai Peninsula. 66"/yr. precip., 80"/yr. snowfall, 17°F–63°F.*
*Population:* *3,034 (15.2 percent native, mainly Tanaina).*
*Travel Attractions:* *Gateway to Kenai Fjords National Park, tours, rentals, outfitters, charming town.*
*Getting There:* *Vehicle access via Seward Highway (AK 9 and AK 1); scheduled ferry service from Homer, Valdez; regular air service from Anchorage and other points.*
*Information:* *Chamber of Commerce, P.O. Box 749, Seward, AK 99664; Visitor Center, 2001 Seward Highway, 224-8051, www.seward.net/chamber, open daily Memorial Day–Labor Day, weekdays otherwise; Information Cache, 3rd and Jefferson (in railcar), www.kenaipeninsula.com/Seward.html.*

Seward is the only town on the south coast of the Kenai Peninsula. As a port, it serves commercial, recreational, and fishing boats, as well as ferry and cruise ships. The town is known as a base for boat tours into Kenai Fjords National Park, but is also a travel destination in its own right, offering shops, accommodations, beach strolling, parks, and restaurants. There are great opportunities for kayaking, fishing, and hiking in the area. Exit Glacier is nearby.

Seward was founded in 1902 by surveyors for the Alaska Railroad, though it didn't become established until the actual construction occurred between 1915 and 1923. It was named for U.S. Secretary of State William Seward—the man who secured Alaska from the Russians and whose name suddenly seemed worth honoring after the discovery of gold. It has been an important shipping center ever since and played a vital role as a supply center during World War II. Tsunamis from the 1964 earthquake wrecked terminal facilities and killed several residents.

The setting for Seward is the mountain-rimmed, wildlife-rich **Resurrection Bay**, named by Alexander Baranof in 1791 when he saught shelter here during a storm on the Russian Sunday of the Resurrection. The bay is strategically located as an ice-free, deepwater port. Otters, whales, and seals are frequently seen in the foreground as fishing vessels, tour boats, cargo ships, or ferries pass behind.

In addition to Caines Head State Park (see Coastal Trail, below), five undeveloped state marine parks (S.M.P.) are located on either side of the Resurrection Peninsula, which bounds the bay to the east. **Thumb Cove S.M.P.** is directly across from Caines Head, below Porcupine Glacier; **Sandspit Point S.M.P.** and **Sunny Cove S.M.P.** are on Fox Island at the bay's head; and **Driftwood Bay S.M.P.** and **Safety Cove S.M.P.** are on Day Harbor on the east side of the peninsula. All the parks are accessible only by water, offer no designated camping or other facilities, and are used primarily as fishing anchorages or kayak destinations.

Though it can be crowded with cruise tourists (count the moored ships as you arrive in town and multiply by 1,000), Seward is an active and historical town and is definitely worth a walkabout. Kenai Fjords tour-boat activity and the associated tourist commerce is centered at the small boat harbor, half a mile north of downtown. The visitor center, museum, ferry terminal, and many businesses are found on or near the south end of Third Avenue (Seward Highway), Seward's main street. Ballaine Boulevard follows the water past a pleasant town campground. The easy **Two Lakes Trail** makes a nice ½-mile loop, starting a block north of A Street from 1st Avenue and returning to 2nd Avenue north of Van Buren.

## Things to See and Do in Seward

**Alaska SeaLife Center**—This outstanding and brand new facility is ". . . dedicated to understanding and maintaining the integrity of

the marine ecosystem of Alaska through research, rehabilitation, and public education." Most of the $50 million spent to build it came from the *Exxon Valdez* oil-spill settlement. Steller sea lions, harbor seals, marine birds, and fish are exhibited. 301 Railway Avenue, (800) 224-2525, 224-6300, www.alaskasealife.org, open daily in summer 8 a.m. to 8 p.m., winter 10 a.m. to 5 p.m. Admission is $12.50 (less for kids).

**Coastal Trail** (4.5 miles, no gain)—Follow the coast road from the south end of town to Lowell Point. From here, the trail follows the coast to a good campsite and access to the World War II bunkers of

**Caines Head State Park.** Stretches of the route can only be covered at low tide—plan to start the hike about two to 2½ hours before the scheduled low tide if you want to do it as a day hike. Watch for otters, seals, and eagles—and consider the advantages of kayaking the same coastal stretch. **RT**—all day.

**Iditarod National Historic Trail**—Though the Iditarod dogsled race goes only from Anchorage to Nome, the original route taken by hopeful gold seekers began in Seward. The trail is marked from the ferry terminal and follows the road through town to Nash Road before it becomes a true trail. The route parallels Sawmill Creek, the train tracks, and the Seward Highway north. There are better hikes.

**Kenai Fjords National Park Visitor Center**—If time permits, stop here before you take your boat tour or head off for a kayak or backpack drop-off. It's located in the small boat harbor. 1212 4th Avenue, 224-3374, www.nps.gov/kefj; open daily Memorial Day–Labor Day, weekdays in the winter.

**Mount Marathon Trail** (2 miles, 3,000' gain)—This route is the scene of the annual July 4th Mount Marathon Race, in which kamikaze racers struggle to a high spur on the mountain's flank then hurtle pell-mell down the gravely slope to the finish—bruised and battered, but hopefully conscious. You can take the same route from the trailhead at the end of Lowell Street (Jefferson Street) near the water tanks. Great views! **RT**—4–6 hours.

**Seward Museum**—Local heritage displays cover the 1964 earthquake, Seward history, and native culture. The museum is operated by the Resurrection Bay Historical Society, Jefferson and 3rd, 224-3902; open May–mid-October daily 9 a.m. to 5 p.m., call for winter hours. Admission is $2.

## Where to Stay in Seward
**Automated Visitor Help Line Reservation Service**, (800) 844-2424, 224-2424. An awkward series of automated cues leads to detailed information on many options and instant connection to the one you choose. Have 10 minutes available.

**Hotel Seward** (Best Western), 221 5th Avenue, (800) 528-1234 or (800) 478-4050 (AK only), 224-2378. $150 and up. Nicest hotel in Seward. Near ferry dock.

**Moby Dick Hostel**, 432 Third Avenue, 224-7072. Great location right in town. Beds are $16.50.

**Van Gilder Hotel**, 308 Adams Street, (800) 204-6835, 224-3079. $95–$120 with private bath, $75 with shared bath. National Historic Site. Open May 15–October 1.

## Where to Eat in Seward
**Harbor Dinner Club**, 220 5th Avenue, 224-3012. Seafood, steaks, prime rib, and great clam chowder.

**Peking Restaurant**, 338 4th Avenue, 224-5444. Open until 10 p.m. Tasty Chinese.

**Ray's**, Seward Boat Harbor, 224-5606. Seafood, cocktails, nice harbor view.

**Resurrect Art Coffee House Gallery**, 320 3rd Avenue (an old church), 224-7161. For a shot of art with your coffee and snacks, this is the place.

## KENAI FJORDS NATIONAL PARK
*Location/Size: South coast of the Kenai Peninsula, stretching southwest of Seward. 669,000 acres.*

**Main Activities:** *Boat tours, glacier flightseeing, sea kayaking, hiking, backcountry-cabin stays.*

**Gateway Towns/Getting There:** *Seward/vehicle access from Anchorage via Seward Highway (AK 1, AK 9), scheduled air service from Anchorage, scheduled ferry service from Valdez and Kodiak; Homer/vehicle access from Anchorage via Seward Highway and Sterling Highway (AK 1), scheduled air service from Anchorage, scheduled ferry service from Kodiak and Valdez. Park access: tour-boat access from Seward; flightseeing and charter air access from Seward and Homer; foot and ski access via Harding Icefield Trail at Exit Glacier; sea kayak access via drop-offs from Seward and possibly from Rocky Bay via Seldovia.*

**Facilities, Camping, Lodging:** *Visitor information, nature trail, and Harding Icefield Trail at Exit Glacier; visitor center in Seward. Reservable backcountry cabins, primitive camping only.*

**Headquarters and Information:** *Headquarters, P.O. Box 1727, Seward, Alaska 99664, 224-3175, www.nps.gov/kefj; Visitor Center, 1212 4th Avenue. Open Memorial Day–Labor Day daily 8 a.m. to 7 p.m., 8 a.m. to 5 p.m. weekdays in winter.*

The majority of the visitors to Kenai Fjords National Park experience this magnificent preserve via a half-day boat tour from Seward. Every morning and afternoon, boats head out through Resurrection Bay, around Aialik Cape, and into Aialik Bay. Some duck into Holgate Arm to watch Holgate Glacier calve cascades of ice into the sea. On longer trips, the boats circle the seal-basking sites and bird rookeries of the small islands off the point. It's about as touristy as Alaska gets, but it's a wonderful trip. If your time is limited, this option should be near the top of your list. See the appendix for tour-boat listings and reserve in advance for high season.

Ah, but there is so much more! The park is named for the fjords, bays, and many small inlets that line the southeast coast of the Kenai Peninsula, most of which rarely receive a tour-boat visit. Inland, the contiguous wilderness lands of Kenai Fjords National Park, Kachemak Bay State Wilderness Park, and the Kenai National Wildlife Refuge preserve most of the Kenai Mountains west of Seward. De facto wilderness preserves in the Chugach National Forest continue the protected lands to Prince William Sound and beyond.

Much of the Kenai Mountains are covered with ice. The road to Seward passes between two major icefields, the **Harding Icefield** in Kenai Fjords National Park to the west, and the **Sargent Icefield** in Chugach National Forest to the east. Several tidewater glaciers flow from 700-square-mile Harding Icefield, meeting the sea in Aialik Bay, Northwestern Fjord, and McCarty Fjord. Sea kayaking any of these fjords on multiday trips provides access to seals, sea lions, otters, eagles, berg paddling, glacier walks, remote camping, and solitude. Outfitters and flying services in Seward and Homer can set you up (see appendix), while road-based put-ins are possible via Seldovia or Seward. Exposed headlands make long-distance trips challenging for novices. Inquire with the Park Service about backcountry cabins with coastal access.

Flightseeing over the icefields is a great option if you're short of time. The stark images of barren summits rising from a sea of snow and ice are windows back into the ice ages. Weather sometimes complicates such opportunities. Flightseeing companies operate from Homer and Seward (see appendix).

## Exit Glacier

One of the best road-accessible glaciers in the state, Exit Glacier is easily reached by car or tour from Seward. About 2 miles long with a drop of 2,700 feet, the glacier is just one tiny finger of the vast Harding Icefield. The 9-mile Exit Glacier Road (closed in winter) heads northeast from Mile 3.7 of the Seward Highway, offering many glacier views as it follows the Resurrection River. Where Exit Creek meets the Resurrection, the road turns toward the glacier and enters Kenai Fjords National Park. From the ranger station and visitor center there are short and easy paths to the ice.

The best option at the site is the steep, rugged, and often slippery **Harding Icefield Trail** (3.5-plus miles, 2,500'-plus gain)—the park's only trail. The route follows the glacier flank right up to the icefield, offering views that get bigger the higher you go. You can walk, ski, or

Paul Otteson

*Exit Glacier*

snowshoe on the icefield—or perhaps begin your 40-mile ski to Tustamena Lake and a floatplane pick-up. Check at the ranger station about trail conditions since snow can clog the upper reaches well into summer. **RT**—half–all day.

## STERLING HIGHWAY (AK 1)

***Road Conditions and Attractions***—*140 miles. Good, paved road open year-round. Kenai River watershed access, Kenai Mountain trailheads, Ninilchik, Homer, access to Kenai and coast.*

While the Seward Highway primarily features mountains, glaciers, and hiking, the Sterling is the road through fishing heaven. During the summer, and especially in June, campgrounds and accommodations along the Kenai River and other streams and lakes are jammed on weekends with salmon-fishing residents. Visit Kenai midweek or in the shoulder season—unless you wish to fish.

Dropping quickly from the highway junction to the foot of Kenai Lake, the Sterling parallels the Kenai River all the way to the coast. Numerous campgrounds and river-access points line the route. At the town of Sterling, the road leaves the Kenai National Wildlife Refuge and enters the vacationland sprawl of the northwest Kenai coast. In Soldotna, the road heads southwest, regaining some charm as it reaches the Cook Inlet coast. Passing by historic Ninilchik, it swings east to Homer and road's end.

Milepost locations for the numerous campgrounds and recreation sites along this route are listed separately at the end of this section.

**Seward Highway Junction** (Mile 37.7)—The Sterling Highway mileposts reflect the distance to Seward.

**Crescent Creek Trailhead** (Mile 45)—See Kenai National Wildlife Refuge/Chugach National Forest Trails, above.

**Kenai Princess Lodge** (Mile 47.7)—Cooper Landing, (800) 426-0500, 595-1425. $230–$250 mid-June–August, $130–$150 shoulder seasons. Rustic luxury-tour hotel, all rooms overlook the Kenai River and mountains beyond, all amenities.

**Snug Harbor Road Junction** (Mile 47.9)—This 12-mile road follows the west shore of Kenai Lake, providing access to Cooper Lake and Russian Lakes Trail as well as to lakeside fishing sites. (See Kenai National Wildlife Refuge/Chugach National Forest Trails, above, for details).

**Cooper Landing** (Mile 48.4)—Businesses actually stretch for a couple of miles along this segment of road. Many residents of the largely non-native settlement of Cooper Landing (population 283, 1.2 percent native) work in fishing, tour, and travel services. Complete highway services are available.

**Russian Lakes Trailhead** (Mile 52.6)—See Kenai National Wildlife Refuge/Chugach National Forest Trails, above.

**Resurrection Pass Trailhead** (Mile 53.2)—See Kenai National Wildlife Refuge/Chugach National Forest Trails, above.

**Chugach National Forest/Kenai National Wildlife Refuge Boundary** (Mile 54.7)—The highway enters the refuge here, trading the mountains for the lowlands at about the same time.

**Fuller Lakes Trailhead** (Mile 57.1)—See Kenai National Wildlife Refuge/Chugach National Forest Trails, above.

**Skilak Lake Loop Road East Junction** (Mile 58)—This 19-mile loop provides access to Skilak Lake and several campgrounds, and links up with the Sterling further west. There's also a **U.S. Fish and Wildlife Service information cabin** here with data on regional public lands and opportunities.

**Skyline Trailhead** (Mile 61.4)—See Kenai National Wildlife Refuge/Chugach National Forest Trails, above.

**Seven Lakes Trailhead** (Mile 70.4)—The Seven Lakes Trail (6 miles, no gain) crosses forested and sometimes boggy flats between the Sterling Highway and Skilak Lake Road. As the name indicates, it passes seven lakes along the way. Through trail—half day.

**Skilak Lake Loop Road West Junction** (Mile 75.2)—Turn here for Skilak Lake and several campgrounds.

**Kenai National Wildlife Refuge Boundary** (Mile 76)—It will quickly be clear that you're out of the protected area.

**Sterling** (Mile 81)—From here through Soldotna and beyond is a human-habitation zone (see Northwest Kenai, below, for details).

**Swanson River Road Junction** (Mile 83.4)—Head north for access to several lakes and the put-ins for outstanding long-distance canoe routes (see Swan Lake and Swanson River Canoe Trails, above, for details).

**Kenai Spur Highway Junction** (Mile 94.2)—Turn here to reach Kenai, Nikiski, and Captain Cook State Recreation Area.

**Soldotna** (Mile 95)—Plenty of services here. See Northwest Kenai.

**Kalifornsky Beach Road/Funny River Road Junction** (Mile 96.1)—Turn west on Kalifornsky Beach Road, then take first right for the Soldotna Historical Society Museum and Visitor Information Center. Continue west for coastal access. Turn east on Funny River Road, then take first right for Kenai National Wildlife Refuge Visitor Center. Continue east for the Soldotna airport and access to south bank of Kenai River.

**Kenai National Wildlife Refuge Visitor Center** (Mile 97.9)— Turn east on Ski Hill Road to reach the center.

**Kasilof and Kalifornsky Beach Road South Junction** (Mile 108.8)—Coastal access, alternate route to Soldotna. See Northwest Kenai, below, for Kasilof information.

**Cohoe Loop Road North Junction** (Mile 111)—Coastal access (see Sterling Highway Public Campgrounds and Northwest Kenai, below, for information on Cohoe and Crooked Creek State Recreation Area).

**Cohoe Loop Road South Junction** (Mile 114.3)—See Mile 111.

**Clam Gulch** (Mile 118.2)—The settlement of Clam Gulch (population 94, 12.7 percent native) is more location than town.

**Ninilchik Village Access** (Mile 135.1)—Turn west here to reach the historic village (see below).

**Happy Valley** (Mile 143.8)—This is actually the point where the Sterling crosses Happy Valley Creek, but the surrounding residences comprise the unincorporated settlement of Happy Valley (population 388, 6.1 percent native).

**Anchor Point** (Mile 156.7)—Just north of town, you'll pass the westernmost point of the North American highway network. Anchor Point (population 1,137, 3.7 percent native) is largely a residential satellite of Homer. Services are available.

**Homer** (Mile 172.8)—See below.

**Homer Spit End** (Mile 179.5)—Here, in the heart of Kachemak Bay, is road's end. Stop in at the Land's End Resort or the Salty Dawg Saloon for a well-earned refreshment.

## Sterling Highway Public Campgrounds and Recreation Sites

Virtually all of the following campgrounds are on a lake or river, have potable water and restrooms, and are open to tents and small RVs. They are used primarily by fishers, boaters, canoeists, other watersports enthusiasts, and hunters—though travelers of every sort are welcome. Call 235-7024 (Homer office) or 262-5581 (Soldotna office) for state park information.

   **Stern Lake National Forest Campground** (Mile 37.4)— 25 sites, $6.
   **Quartz Lake National Forest Campground** (Mile 45)— 31 sites, $6.
   **Crescent Creek National Forest Campground** (Mile 45)— Nine sites, $6, 3 miles down Quartz Creek Road from Mile 45.
   **Cooper Creek National Forest Campground** (Mile 50.5)— 26 sites, $6.

**Russian River National Forest Campground** (Mile 52.6)—84 sites, $10, 2 miles down road from Mile 52.6.

**Skilak Lake Loop Road East Junction** (Mile 58)—This 19-mile gravel road passes several campgrounds: **Jim's Land Campground** (0.2 mile on Skilak Road)—five sites; **Hidden Lake Campground** (0.5 mile on Skilak Road)—44 sites, $6; **Upper Skilak Lake Campground** (8.5 miles on Skilak Road)—26 sites, $10, take spur road 2 miles along Ohmer Lake; **Lower Skilak Lake Campground** (13.8 miles on Skilak Road)—14 sites.

**Kelly and Peterson Lakes Turnoff** (Mile 68.3)—Two three-site camp areas.

**Watson Lake Campground** (Mile 71.3)—Three sites.

**Skilak Lake Loop Road West Junction** (Mile 75.2)—See East Junction listings, above.

**Bing's Landing State Recreation Site** (Mile 80.3)—Turn here to reach riverside sites, $8.

**Isaak Walton State Recreation Site** (Mile 82)—25 riverside sites, $10.

**Scout Lake State Recreation Site and Morgan Lake State Recreation Site** (Mile 84.9)—Turn here to reach campgrounds via Scout Lake Loop Road, 64 total sites, $8 to $10.

**Centennial Park Campground** (Mile 96.1)—Turn west 0.1 mile, 126 sites.

**Kasilof River State Recreation Site** (Mile 109.4)—16 sites, $8.

**Johnson Lake State Recreation Area** (Mile 110)—Go east and turn right at T to reach 50 sites, $10. Continue on Tustamena Lake Road 6 miles to **Tustamena Lake Campground**—10 sites.

**Crooked Creek State Recreation Site** (Mile 111)—Go 2 miles west to campground.

**Clam Gulch State Recreation Area** (Mile 117.4)—116 sites, $8.

**Ninilchik State Recreation Area** (Mile 134.5)—Three small campgrounds located in the immediate vicinity, 43 sites, $10.

**Deep Creek State Recreation Area** (Mile 137.3)—$10 sites.

**Stariski State Recreation Site** (Mile 151.9)—13 sites, $10.

**Anchor River State Recreation Area** (Mile 156.9)—Turn on Old Seward Highway and turn again to reach six campgrounds along Beach Access Road.

**Anchor River State Recreation Site** (Mile 162)—Nine sites.

▲ Flowers bloom next to the mountains near Skagway. (Paul E. Otteson)

▲ Brown bear with salmon (Paul E. Otteson)

▼ The road through Hatcher Pass near Palmer (Paul E. Otteson)

▲ A Dall ram relaxes in Denali National Park. (Paul E. Otteson)

▼ The Petersburg waterfront in Southeast Alaska (Paul E. Otteson)

▲ Landings on Ruth Glacier allow passengers to explore the icy wilderness.
(Paul E. Otteson)

▼ An A.M.H.S. ferry noses into the bergs of Columbia Glacier.
(Paul E. Otteson)

▲ Smoldering Mt. Iliamna and Tuxedni Glacier near Cook Inlet (Paul E. Otteson)

▲ Glacier ice cave (©Mark Newman/Photo Network)

▼ Russian Orthodox Church, Ninilchik (Paul E. Otteson)

▼ Kayaking near Kachemak Bay (©Mark Newman/Photo Network)

▲ Blueberries, ripe and ready to munch (Paul E. Otteson)

▼ A small settlement near False Pass in the Aleutians (Paul E. Otteson)

▲ View from the Taylor Highway between Tok and Eagle (Paul E. Otteson)

Kennecott Mine and
▼ Wrangell Mountains (Paul E. Otteson)

▼ Cycling to the Arctic (Paul E. Otteson)

## NORTHWEST KENAI

The lower Kenai River flows through one of Alaska's fastest-growing regions. History, oil, salmon, and federal public land boundaries have shaped regional growth, producing a T-shaped area of development. The cross of the "T" fronts the shores of Cook Inlet while the post extends inland from Soldotna to Sterling. Where you don't find wetlands and oilfields, you'll find wandering small roads leading to homes, cabins, tiny lakes, campsites, fishing access, and scores of small lodges and B&Bs.

The great majority of visitors come to the area to fish for salmon. During the peak of the king salmon run in June, campgrounds are packed and rooms are difficult to find. There is little to attract the non-fishing visitor to the area, though there are historic sites, coastal access points, and two excellent canoe trails. Unless you're after salmon or have another specific reason to visit, "passing through" should describe your time here.

**Sterling** (population 4,949, 2.1 percent native) is located along the Sterling Highway near the east end of the tongue of non-federal land that pierces Kenai National Wildlife Refuge. Many roadside businesses serve travelers and act as a supply base for the surrounding vacation cabins, homes, and fishing areas. The access road for the Swan Lake Canoe Trail and Swanson River Canoe Trail heads north from town—outfitter and rental businesses operate along the highway near the junction (see appendix).

As you travel west from Sterling to Soldotna, you'll pass a long stretch of roadside businesses, homes, and minor road junctions. When the buildings start to jam together, you've reached Soldotna (see below). From Soldotna, the Kenai Spur Highway heads northwest from the Sterling Highway to the coast and the town of Kenai (see below)—the area's original Russian settlement.

The highway continues north of Kenai, becoming North Kenai Road and following the shores of Cook Inlet to **Nikiski** (population 3,087, 6.1 percent native). There are several refineries, oil extraction operations, and other related companies in the area. Timbering, commercial and sport fishing, government jobs, retail, and tourist services round out the economic picture. I've never met anyone who said, "I'm going to Nikiski for the weekend." Enjoy the views across Cook Inlet.

Beyond Nikiski, the North Kenai Road continues past **Bernice**

**Lake State Recreation Area** and through lake and lowland forest country to road's end and **Captain Cook State Recreation Area**. Both recreation areas have campgrounds—Captain Cook offers access to the coast.

South of Soldotna, things thin out a bit as you head toward the Kasilof, Cohoe, and Clam Gulch area. **Kasilof** (population 497, 2.9 percent native) is located where the Kenaitze Indians established an agricultural and fishing village around a Russian stockade built in 1786 by the Lebedef-Lastochkin Company. Excavations in 1937 uncovered 31 well-preserved houses from the original settlement. Today Kasilof is the center of a vacation, fishing, and homestead area and offers highway and travel services at roadside businesses. **Cohoe** (population 583, 1.8 percent native) is basically a residential area scattered near Cohoe Road, which loops from the Sterling Highway toward the coast and Cape Kasilof, then south along Cook Inlet and back to the highway.

The coastline from Cape Kasilof south to Happy Valley is protected in the **Clam Gulch State Critical Habitat Area**, famous as razor clam habitat but strictly managed with regards to harvesting. For information on clamming, call the Alaska Department of Fish and Game (see appendix).

## SOLDOTNA

*Location/Climate: Northwest Kenai Peninsula at junction of Sterling Highway (AK 1) and Kenai Spur Highway. 17.4" /yr. precip., 6°F–66°F.*
*Population: 3,990 (4.5 percent native).*
*Travel Attractions: Fishing access, museum, Kenai National Wildlife Refuge Visitor Center.*
*Getting There: Vehicle access via Sterling Highway (AK 1), scheduled air service to Kenai.*
*Information: Kenai Peninsula Visitor Center, Mile 96 Sterling Highway, Soldotna, AK 99669, 262-1337, www.soldotnachamber.com, open mid-May–mid-September daily 9 a.m. to 7 p.m.*

Like Wasilla to the north, this wide spot in the road just keeps getting wider. Located at the junction of the Sterling Highway and the Kenai Spur Highway—the heart of this buildable region—Soldotna is right up there in rate of growth. Many in the area work in the oil business or for the government, though the town's biggest role is as a base for vacationers who seek the not-very-elusive salmon. There are *many* motels and B&Bs in the area. For comprehensive town and accommodation information, head to the visitor center (see above).

The **Soldotna Historical Society Museum** offers wildlife exhibits and a historic log village. It's on Centennial Park Road off of Kalifornsky Beach Road, just west of Mile 96.1 Sterling Highway. 262-1337, open summers Tuesday–Saturday 10 a.m. to 4 p.m., Sunday noon to 4 p.m.

Another worthy stop is the **Kenai National Wildlife Refuge Visitor Center**. Turn east at Mile 96.1 Seward Highway onto Funny River Road, then right to the top of Ski Hill Road; or turn east directly onto Ski Hill Road at Mile 97.9 Sterling Highway. Information, exhibits, and presentations are excellent. 262-7021, www.r7.fws.gov/nwr/Kenai/Kennwr.html. Open Monday–Friday 8 a.m. to 4:30 p.m., weekends 10 a.m. to 6 p.m.

A trip down **Kalifornsky Beach Road** can be an interesting detour for connecting Soldotna or Kenai with Kasilof and the continuation of AK 1 south to Homer. The road runs straight for about 10 miles along a sandy bar backed by wide marshlands. Gas wells share the marsh with waterbirds, while the open sandbar offers views of Cook Inlet, the volcanoes across the water, and, possibly, beluga whales. From the Sterling Highway, turn toward the coast just south of the Kenai River bridge, bear right before the airstrip, then loop north and west to the coast.

## Where to Stay and Eat in Soldotna

**Accommodations on the Kenai** (reservation service), 262-2139. B&Bs, lodges, cabins, charters.

**Best Western King Salmon**, 35546 Kenai Spur Highway, 262-5857. Good motel, restaurant, $120–$160.

**Hogg Heaven Cafe**, 44715 Sterling Highway, 262-4584. This may be Soldotna's best breakfast place.

**Kenai River Lodge**, Kenai River Bridge, 262-4292. On the river, nice views. Rooms $60–$110.

**Sal's Klondike Diner**, 44619 Sterling Highway, 262-2220. A good 24-hour joint with typical diner fare.

**Soldotna Inn**, 35041 Kenai Spur Highway, 262-9169. Nice motel with rooms from $85–$105. Mykel's Restaurant is a good family choice.

**Through the Seasons Restaurant**, 43960 Sterling Highway, 262-5006. Lunch and dinner. Very nice.

# KENAI

*Location/Climate: 155 road miles southwest of Anchorage (70 air miles) on the Cook Inlet coast of Kenai Peninsula. 20"/yr. precip., 0°F–65°F.*
*Population: 7,006 (8.5 percent native).*
*Travel Attractions: Russian history, Kenai River fishing.*
*Getting There: Vehicle access via Kenai Spur Highway from Soldotna and Sterling Highway (AK 1), scheduled air service from Anchorage and other points.*
*Information: Kenai Visitor and Cultural Center, 11471 Kenai Spur Highway, Kenai, AK 99611, 283-1991, www.visitkenai.com. Open daily in summer 9 a.m. to 8 p.m., 11 a.m. to 7 p.m. on weekends. Open winter Monday–Friday 9 a.m. to 5 p.m., Saturday 10 a.m. to 4 p.m.*

Paul Otteson

*St. Nicholas Chapel in Kenai*

Russian fur traders established the town of Kenai in the summer of 1791, 13 years after Captain Cook sailed up Cook Inlet in a failed search for the northwest passage to the Atlantic. The Dena'ina Indian village of Skitok (shki-TUK) had existed for years at the site where the Kenai River meets the sea. The town quickly became a regional center of trade for Russians and Indians, and for the U.S. military after the purchase of Alaska in 1867. Fishing and fish processing became the main industries, complemented by oil-related commerce after the 1957 discovery of oil near the Swanson River and subsequent Cook Inlet finds.

Just east of town, the Beaver Loop Road (Bridge Access Road) provides access to the **Kenai River Flats**. The road meets the Kenai Spur Highway at Mile 6.4 and Mile 10.5. Waterfowl, including Siberian snow geese, are migratory visitors. A state recreation site provides boardwalk access to good viewing spots and a riverside campground.

The excellent and relatively new **Kenai Bicentennial Visitors and Cultural Center** is on Main Street south of the Kenai Spur Highway. Regional heritage exhibits and movies offer great background on area culture. It's right on the way to the main historic attractions and is worth a stop.

All of Kenai's historic sites are concentrated near the bluffs above the shores of Cook Inlet and can be visited in an hour or two. The main attraction is the **Holy Assumption of the Virgin Mary Orthodox Church**, first built in 1849, then replaced with the present structure in 1895. The onion-shaped domes are striking. Across the green from the church sits **Saint Nicholas Chapel**, built in 1906 where church leaders were buried. Just up the street is the site of **Fort Kenay**, including a reconstructed barracks building. The fort was built in 1869 to secure the area after it was purchased from the Russians, though it was garrisoned for less than two years. To reach all of these sites, turn southwest on Main Street from the Kenai Spur Highway, drive past the visitor center, then turn right on Overland Avenue.

From Overland Avenue and Fort Kenay, Mission Road follows the bluff edge east to a couple of good overlooks. Bluff erosion had limited vehicle access to one section when I was last there, making it perfect for a 1-block walk and a long look. You may see white beluga whales in Cook Inlet.

### Where to Stay and Eat in Kenai
**Beaver Creek Cabin Rentals**, 283-4262. $100–$150 per cabin. On the water. Stay for any length of time.

**Katmai Hotel**, 10800 Kenai Spur Highway (at Main Street), 283-6101. Basic motel with $40–$90 rooms and Rick's Sourdough Cafe.

**Kenai Kings Inn**, P.O. Box 850, 10352 Kenai Spur Highway, 283-6060. Rooms from $60–$100. Don Again's Restaurant is on site.

**Little Ski-Mo Burger-N-Brew**, Kenai Spur Highway, Kenai, 283-4463. This place is known for their big burger menu. Mmmm.

**Paradiso's**, Kenai Spur Road (1 block east of visitor center), 283-2222. Good but pricey Greek, Mexican, and Italian.


## NINILCHIK

*Location/Climate: 40 road miles north of Homer on Cook Inlet. 24"/yr. precip., 14°F–60°F.*
*Population: 597 (19.5 percent native, mainly Tanaina).*
*Travel Attractions: Historic Russian Orthodox church, charming town, beach access, fishing, clamming.*
*Getting There: Vehicle access via the Sterling Highway (AK 1).*
*Information: Chamber of Commerce, P.O. Box 39164, Ninilchik, AK 99639, 567-3571, www.recworld.com/ncoc; Historic Ninilchik Village Visitor Center, Mile 135.1 Sterling Highway, Old Village, Ninilchik, 567-3500.*


This small, oceanside village, whose name means "peaceful settlement by the river," began as a community for retired employees of the Russian-American Trading Company. Many were Russians who had married native Alaskan women and were unwilling to return to their homeland. Their descendants have lived here for at least 140 years. Today Ninilchik is little more than a stretch of roadside businesses surrounded by a scattering of homes, but a visit to the historic village at the river mouth is worth a short detour.

The homes and beachfront of Ninilchik are reached via a short road from Mile 135.1 of the Sterling Highway. The right fork of the access road leads to the village, the left to Ninilchik Beach Road and access to the beach and clamming area of **Ninilchik State Recreation Area**. The small harbor at the mouth of the Ninilchik River is open to Cook Inlet only at high tide. A couple of shops and a small B&B are located in the village, while an interesting Russian Orthodox church and cemetery sits on the northern bluff overlooking town. The church can be reached by a short path from below, or via Coal Road just north of town from Mile 134.7 of the Sterling Highway.

## Where to Stay and Eat in Ninilchik

**Beachcomber Motel,** Ninilchik Beach Road, 567-3417. $60 (single), $70 (double).

**The Eagle Watch Hostel,** Oilwell Road (3 miles east of town), 567-3905. $10 members, $15 non-members.

**Happy Wok Restaurant,** Sterling Highway, 567-1060. Good stir-fry offerings.

**Homestead House B&B,** 66670 Oilwell Road, (888) 697-3474, 567-3412. Rooms are $70 and up. Fishing packages offered.

## HOMER

*Location/Climate: On the north shore of Kachemak Bay, 125 air miles southwest of Anchorage. 24" /yr. precip., 14°F–60°F.*
*Population: 4,133 (3.6 percent native).*
*Travel Attractions: Access to Kachemak Bay and Kenai Fjords, ferry link, interesting town, Pratt Museum, Alaska Maritime National Wildlife Refuge visitor center.*
*Getting There: Vehicle access via Sterling Highway (AK 1) from Kenai, Anchorage; scheduled ferry service from Kodiak, Seward; scheduled air service from Anchorage.*
*Information: Homer Chamber of Commerce, 135 Sterling Highway, Homer, AK 99603, 235-7740, www.homeralaska.org.*

Homer has long been a favored destination for visitors to the peninsula. It represents the end of the road for the Sterling Highway (AK 1), though a lesser route (East End Road) continues eastward high above the north shore of Kachemak Bay. The A.M.H.S. ferry offers access to Seldovia, Kodiak, Seward, and points beyond, while Jakolof Ferry Service and other companies serve Kachemak Bay (see appendix).

Homer was named for Homer Pennock, a gold-seeking adventurer from New York who arrived with his compatriots in 1896. The town grew into importance as a safe harbor near the rich fisheries of Kachemak Bay and the lower Cook Inlet. The Sterling Highway reached Homer in the early 1950s, linking it to Anchorage and the rest of the peninsula. Pleasant Seldovia is just across Kachemak Bay, while Augustine and Iliamna Volcanoes are visible across Cook Inlet.

Homer is a busy commercial-fishing port and is famous world-wide as a center for halibut sport fishing. It's also a bit of an artists colony, adding an important ingredient to the town's blend of hard-edged fishers and builders, halibut-hungry recreators, car tourists, and backpacking explorers. Several galleries are found in or near town. Though Homer lacks a real town center that makes you want to park your car and walk, it's still a great place to spend some time.

Homer's most distinctive feature is the **Homer Spit**. In an age-long effort by nature to smooth the rough edges of the coastline, the currents of Cook Inlet created this sandy, 4.5-mile projection into Kachemak Bay. Early residents built a road and buildings along the spit, only to find that the sands tended to shift in response to storms, earthquakes, and time. The 1964 quake reduced its width by as much as two-thirds. Since then, efforts have been undertaken to stabilize the spit with rocks and breakwaters. Along Homer Spit Road you'll find charter companies, gift shops, fishing spots, marine businesses, lodgings, and camping areas, as well as the famous Land's End Resort and the infamous Salty Dawg Saloon. Most tours, fishing trips, and Kachemak Bay shuttles leave from the spit, as does the ferry.

## Things to See and Do in Homer
**Alaska Maritime National Wildlife Refuge Visitor Center**—
The vast Alaska Maritime National Wildlife Refuge encompasses hundreds of islands and thousands of square miles of ocean, making it virtually impossible to visit in any traditional way. The visitor center offers an overview of the preserve, as well as details on local activities.

Refuge rangers offer guided coastal walks many mornings at Bishop's Beach and Land's End. The walks examine bird or intertidal life. Visit the center or call about walk times: 451 Sterling Highway, Homer, 235-6961, 235-6546 (refuge manager), www.r7.fws.gov/nwr/akmnwr/akmnwr.html.

**Pratt Museum**—Operated by the Homer Society of Natural History, the museum includes living marine exhibits, the *Cultures of Kachemak Bay* exhibit, and a homestead cabin. An excellent exhibit on all aspects of the *Exxon Valdez* oil spill is found in the basement. Outside there's a small botanical garden and a nature trail. 3779 Bartlett Street, 235-8635, www.alaska.net/~pratt; open mid-May–mid-September daily 10 a.m. to 6 p.m. (Thursday–Saturday until 8 p.m.); winter hours Tuesday–Sunday noon to 5 p.m., closed in January; $4.

**Salty Dawg Saloon**—Built in 1897 as one of Homer's first cabins, half of the present-day saloon was once the town's first post office and, later, the railroad station, a grocery store, and a coal mining office. A second building, built in 1909, also served as a post office and grocery, as well as a schoolhouse and family home. The buildings were joined and made into a saloon in 1957, then moved to the present location after the 1964 earthquake.

Though the years have softened its edge, the Salty Dawg still lays claim to a surly reputation as a hangout for the rough and rowdy. Scuffle into the small, dark bar through the wood chips and smoke. Sit down at one of the thick-topped plank tables, knife-etched with initials from 10,000 nights of drinking. Order quietly and wonder if the ragged fisherman at the bar will sneer at your teal and purple GoreTex jacket. Enjoy.

Look for the fake lighthouse on the left side as you drive out.

## Where to Stay in Homer

**Bay View Inn**, Mile 170 Sterling Highway (800) 478-8485, 235-8485 (AK only). Great views, nice rooms, $80 and up in summer.

**Homer's Finest Bed and Breakfast Network** (reservation service), (800) 764-3211, 235-4983. Save yourself some legwork when looking for available rooms in area B&Bs.

**Land's End Resort**, 4786 Homer Spit Road, (800) 478-0400, 235-0400. $110–$160 May–September, $93–$123 winter. Famous hotel at the tip of Homer Spit. Nice rooms, restaurant, deck, great views across Kachemak Bay.

**Land's End RV Park**, 4786 Homer Spit Road, 235-0404. $14–$23. Near end of Homer Spit, best option for campers or RVs on spit.

**Ocean Shores Motel**, 3500 Crittendon, 235-7775. Basic rooms $95 and up in summer. Kitchenettes.

**Seaside Farm**, 58335 East End Road, 235-7850. Hostel $15 per person; tentsite $6; $55 and up for a cabin. A wonderful hostel with camping and a couple of rustic cabins on the shores of Kachemak Bay. Bring your own bedding (rental $3).

## Where to Eat in Homer
**Cafe Cups**, 168 W. Pioneer Drive, 235-8330. You'll know it when you see it. Open 7:30 a.m. to 10 p.m.

**Neon Coyote Cafe**, 435 Pioneer Avenue, 235-6226. Good prices and great food.

**Two Sisters Espresso and Bakery**, 106 W. Bunnell, 235-2280. Espresso, baked goods, art gallery, great place to muse.

## KACHEMAK BAY STATE PARK AND STATE WILDERNESS PARK
*Location/Size:* Southeast of Homer across Kachemak Bay. 328,290 acres within Chugach National Forest.
*Main Activities:* Wilderness exploration, hiking, boating, kayaking, fishing, camping, mountaineering.
*Gateway Towns/Getting There:* Homer/vehicle access via Seward Highway (AK 1), scheduled ferry from Kodiak and Seward, scheduled air service from Anchorage; Seldovia/scheduled and chartered water taxi service from Homer.
*Park Access:* Charter and tour boat from Seldovia and Homer; charter air service from Homer; kayak from Homer and Seldovia.
*Facilities, Camping, Lodging:* Ranger station at head of Halibut Cove. Six designated campgrounds in Halibut Cove area, most on the shores of the cove. One public-use cabin (contact headquarters for information, see above). Primitive camping elsewhere.
*Headquarters and Information:* Kenai Area South District Office, Mile 168.5, Seward Highway, Homer, 235-7024; Halibut Cove Ranger Station (summer only), 235-6999; Division of Parks and Outdoor Recreation (Kenai Area Office), 262-5581; Department of Natural Resources, Public Information Center, 3601 C Street, Suite 200, Anchorage, AK 99510-7001, 269-8400.

The Kenai Mountains stretch southwestward to the end of the Kenai Peninsula between Kachemak Bay and the Gulf of Alaska. The inner half of this non-federal land is preserved in Kachemak Bay State Park and Kachemak Bay State Wilderness Park. There is little distinction between the two parks (both are roadless), though unlike the wilderness park, the regular park encompasses several private parcels, most along the coast of Kachemak Bay.

The parks are a favorite destination of local residents. The most popular area is **Halibut Cove** (the cove, not the village), only about 8 water miles from the tip of Homer Spit. Halibut Cove offers the parks' only trails—basically a single winding 10-mile path that parallels the east shore of the cove and a series of small lakes to the south, and several short spur trails that lead to 2,000-foot peaks, ridges, lakes, and glacier views. There are five designated campsites on the cove and one on Leisure Lake, as well as several small private parcels and campsites. A summer-only ranger station is at the head of the cove, close to the area's one public cabin (call for information; see details below).

Outside of Halibut Cove, the park is undeveloped. Ridge walking and cross-glacier hikes are possible activities, as is sea kayaking in Kachemak Bay, Port Dick, and the Nuka Passage.

**Rocky River Road** crosses the peninsula along the park boundary, heading south from Seldovia. The road once provided access to the southwestern tip of the peninsula, including Rocky and Windy Bays and a trailhead at road's end that leads 4 miles to Port Chatham. It is now basically impassable due to washouts and downed bridges. All of the land along the road is state (non-park), native corporation, or private. Outfitters are mostly in Homer, though Seldovia has some offerings (see appendix).

## The Town of Halibut Cove

Located at the mouth of Halibut Cove on Ismailof Island, this little artists colony was once an important center for the thriving herring fishery of Kachemak Bay. About 80 people live here, and only around 10,000 guests are permitted to visit each summer. A few blocks of boardwalk host some galleries and the excellent Saltry Restaurant (296-2223). The Saltry's menu includes fresh and international specials, pasta, chowders, and fresh mussels. Breads are baked in-house, and salads come from local gardens. Reservations are recommended. For information on the village, call 235-7847.

The way to get to Halibut Cove from Homer is via "Danny J" Tours (reserve via Central Charters, 907/235-7847). A charming old fishing boat covers the 5 miles from the Homer Spit to Halibut Cove on two daily RT voyages throughout the summer—at noon for day trips with a 4 p.m. return, or at 5 p.m. for residents, Saltry diners, and overnight guests. Jakolof Ferry Service (see appendix) operates a daily boat from Jakolof Dock.

## SELDOVIA

*Location/Climate: On south shore of Kachemak Bay, Kenai Peninsula, 20 water miles from Homer. 35"/yr. precip., 12°F–48°F.*
*Population: 334 (15.2 percent native, mainly Tanaina Indian).*
*Travel Attractions: Charming town, access to Kachemak Bay State Park and State Wilderness Park, access to Kenai Fjords.*
*Getting There: Scheduled water taxi, ferry, or air service from Homer; air service from Anchorage; charter air or boat service.*
*Information: Chamber of Commerce, Drawer D, Seldovia, AK 99663, 234-7612, www.alaskaoutdoors.com/Seldovia.*

This charming town across Kachemak Bay from Homer is a nice choice for long stays or for overnight excursions. Long the site of a camp used by Eskimos, Athabascans, and Aleuts, the modern community was established in the 1870s when Russians began trapping and trading furs in the area. They built **Saint Nicholas Orthodox Church** in 1891. The church, which still stands today, is a fully restored highlight of the community and a designated National Historic Site. Scandinavians arrived for the herring boom in the 1920s and stayed on to harvest halibut, salmon, and crab. Residents built a boardwalk in 1931 to facilitate travel through town—hence Seldovia's identity as "the boardwalk town." Several buildings constructed on pilings complete the picturesque image.

The 1964 earthquake had a devastating effect on Seldovia. Coastlands sank as much as 4 feet, allowing tide waters to wash over the boardwalk and into buildings. The town was subsequently moved and then reconstructed in the same theme, though a portion of the original boardwalk may still be seen in the Seldovia Slough. Today the charm of the town is very much intact.

Seldovia is situated on small Seldovia Bay, a narrow intrusion into the southwestern extension of the Kenai Mountains. Indeed, 2,000- to 3,000-foot peaks rise all around, providing a marvelous backdrop. Kayaks and mountain bikes can be rented for explorations of the bay area. Several shops sell gifts and local arts, while the **Seldovia Native Association Museum** and office has heritage exhibits. A road heads

Paul Otteson

*Seldovia*

east then south across the peninsula through a low gap, allowing access to the south shore and open waters of the Kennedy Entrance. Almost all of the land served by the road is native corporation land. You should inquire before exploring.

## Where to Stay and Eat in Seldovia

**Buzz Coffeehouse/Cafe**, Main Street, across from Russian church, 234-7479. "Gourmet food with a local flavor," vegetarian dishes, espresso drinks, open 6 to 6 daily in summer.

**Mad Fish Restaurant**, Main Street at Fulmore, 234-7676. Enjoy local fresh seafood, burgers, steaks, wine, and beer. Open daily.

**Seldovia's Boardwalk Hotel**, Boardwalk, (800) 238-7862, 234-7816. Private baths, harbor view deck. One night with a nature cruise and round-trip air transportation is $130.

**Seldovia Rowing Club Bed & Breakfast**, Historic Boardwalk, 234-7614. Sunset view, big decks, homey suites, charming and friendly keeper. My favorite place in town!

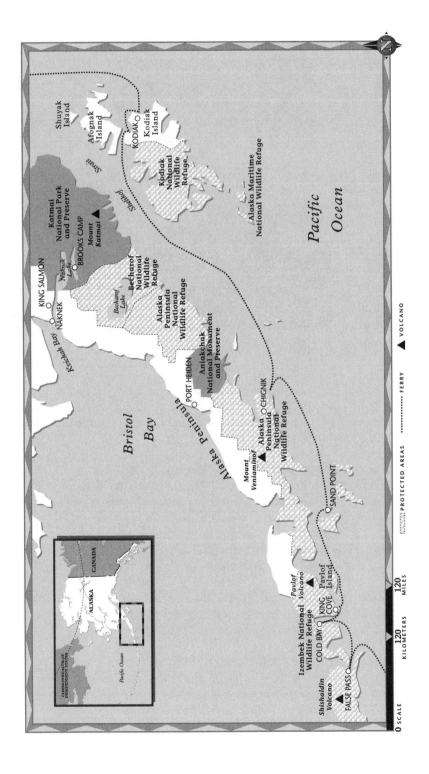

# KODIAK AND THE ALASKA PENINSULA

<figure>11</figure>

This magnificent region of rugged isles, wild coastlands, and glacier-capped volcanoes is famous primarily as the home of Alaska's huge brown bears. The browns are essentially grizzlies living the good life, growing larger than their inland cousins thanks to a steady summer diet of salmon. Though Kodiak Island is home to the largest of them, Katmai National Park is generally a better choice for bear observation. Hunters are allowed an annual quota of Kodiak bears, making the larger population more wary of humans. In the key viewing areas of Katmai and the adjacent McNeil River State Game Sanctuary, bears roam with little or no interest in human observers.

Bear-viewing trips are a mainstay of tour-service providers. You can choose from two basic approaches for a short-term, guaranteed look at brown bears. Reservations can be made for one of several destinations with a consistent summer presence of bears. The best and most popular are Brooks Camp and McNeil River—source of the most famous documentary video images. The second "guaranteed" choice is to take a bear-viewing flight with a flightseeing company that regularly monitors bear activity. Uyak Air and others fly from Kodiak to the hot spots for a couple hours of close-up viewing.

The town of Kodiak serves as the best gateway to Kodiak and Afognak Islands, as well as the south coast of Katmai and the Alaska Peninsula. To the north, Brooks Camp is an excellent base for bear observation, salmon fishing, and hiking access to the Katmai interior, including the Valley of Ten Thousand Smokes. To reach Brooks Camp, most fly from Anchorage to the town of King Salmon, then take a floatplane shuttle to Brooks. Together with nearby Naknek on Bristol Bay, King Salmon represents the largest settlement on the Alaska Peninsula and serves as a gateway to many remote fishing, hunting, and exploration destinations.

To the west, the peninsula gradually narrows before coming to an end at False Pass and the beginning of the Aleutian Islands. Throughout the peninsula, the south coast is mountainous and rugged, with steep, battered headlands and ragged bays backed by high ridges and volcanic cones. The north coast is much gentler, featuring thousands of lakes and ponds, sprawling boggy flats, and miles of beaches, bars, and tidal flats. Though the pattern is complicated, native lands are generally on the south coast, state lands on the north, and federal public lands along the peninsula's mountainous backbone. Settlement is so limited that it matters little—though if you plan to enter native lands it pays to inquire with native corporation offices about permissions. No permits are required in any of the public lands except McNeil River State Game Sanctuary (see below).

## Ferry Access

A few times every summer, the A.M.H.S. ferry *Tustamena* makes a run from Homer to Dutch Harbor–Unalaska and back, stopping at Kodiak and several coastal towns on the Alaska Peninsula and Aleutian Islands. The route is exposed to open ocean at many points so the journey can be rough, but if you're not daunted by challenges to the stomach, ferry travel in the Southwest offers a fantastic and comparatively inexpensive experience.

It is possible to create Southwestern journeys using the ferry for part or all of the transport. Perhaps you fly to Unalaska for an Aleutian trek, then ferry back to Kodiak for a stay before returning to Anchorage. You might take the outbound ferry as far as Cold Bay, enjoying two days of birding in Izembek National Wildlife Refuge before catching the *Tustamena* in King Cove on its return. The possibilities are many (contact A.M.H.S. for schedules; see chapter 6).

The towns below are served by the ferry or are useful as bases for exploring designated parks and refuges. For information on other settlements and their utility as bases for exploration, consult the Alaska

Department of Community and Regional Affairs, native corporation offices, and park and refuge offices—all listed in the appendix.

## KODIAK

*Location/Climate:* On the northeastern tip of Kodiak Island, 250 miles south-southwest of Anchorage. 74"/yr. precip., 14°F–76°F.
*Population:* 7,620 (12.7 percent native, mainly Sugpiaq Eskimo and Aleut). Kodiak Station Coast Guard Base hosts an additional 2,000 people, while 4,000 more live north of town around Monashka Bay.
*Travel Attractions:* Access to Kodiak National Wildlife Refuge, Katmai National Park and Preserve, and Afognak Island (Chugach National Forest); kayaking, flightseeing, bear viewing.
*Getting There:* Scheduled air service from Anchorage and Homer; scheduled ferry service from Homer and Seward.
*Information:* Chamber of Commerce, P.O. Box 1485, Kodiak, AK 99615, 486-5557; Convention and Visitors Bureau, 100 Marine Way, Kodiak, AK 99615, 486-4782, www.kodiak.org, kicub@ptialaska.net.

Before Russian explorers brought disease and conflict to Kodiak, the island may have been home to 20,000 Alutiiq (Sugpiak) Eskimos, whose ancestors had lived there for perhaps 9,500 years. Grigorii Shelikov established a non-native settlement for the Russians in 1784, just south of Old Harbor on Three Saints Bay. Alexander Baranof, commissioned to manage the Russian-American Company, was based at the settlement, but moved it to its present location after an earthquake and tidal wave devastated the original site in 1792. He named the new settlement "Pauloysk"—today it's called Kodiak. The town served as the capital of Russian Alaska for a decade.

With the purchase of Alaska by the United States, Kodiak's economy shifted from fur harvesting and whaling to salmon fishing. In 1912, Novarupta Volcano erupted across the strait, ejecting 6 cubic miles of debris into the atmosphere, blacking out the town for three days, and depositing a layer of ash as much as 2 feet deep over much of Kodiak Island. During World War II, the town became a major base for military operations, remnants of which can be visited at Fort Abercrombie and elsewhere. The 1964 quake severely damaged the Kodiak waterfront. Visitors can't miss the cannery made from a World War II liberty ship given to the town

Downtown Kodiak

Paul Otteson

to help reestablish commerce after the quake.

Commercial fishing, fish processing, and related services are still the mainstays of the Kodiak economy. The city also hosts hunters, sport fishers, and adventure travelers, though it is not a stop on the cruise circuit. Kodiak offers access to sea-kayak routes and small-plane access to bear-viewing areas, drop-offs, and backcountry lodges. With miles of barren ridges and empty bays to be found beyond the town, Kodiak Island hearkens to the stark beauty of the Aleutians more than to the forested isles of Prince William Sound or the Southeast.

Kodiak's short but helpful road system enables access to the coast and eastern valleys at several points. Multiday, ridgeline backpack routes can be devised that connect roads, allowing you to save money on flights. The relatively sheltered waters of Ugak Bay to the south and Kizhuyak Bay to the north are accessible by road for kayak put-ins. Consult outfitters, pilots, refuge managers, and topo maps when devising routes (see appendix).

## Kodiak-Area Attractions

Attractions in Kodiak include the following:

**Alutiiq Museum**—This new museum exists to preserve the language and culture of Kodiak's native peoples. Excellent touring exhibits are featured, and local archaeologists are on hand to answer questions. 215 Mission Road, 486-7004, www.ptialaska.net/~alutiiq2.

**Buskin River State Recreation Site**—This popular camping- and fishing-access park is geared to salmon seekers. It's located at the mouth of the Buskin River, within a mile of the airport. Take Rezanof Drive 4 miles south from downtown. Call the state parks office for details, 486-6339, www.ptialaska.net/~kodsp.

**Fort Abercrombie State Historic Site**—Here you'll find the remains of a World War II military installation and a rugged coastline with several trails. This popular site has a campground, group recreation site, and overflow parking for RV campers. It's located 4 miles north of downtown. A designated bike path covers the entire distance. Call the state parks office for details, 486-6339, www.ptialaska.net/~kodsp.

**Holy Resurrection Russian Orthodox Church**—Originally consecrated in 1794 and reconstructed for the fifth time in 1949, the church is a Kodiak landmark and the oldest orthodox parish in the state. A replica of the original church can be seen at the seminary on Mission Road near Island Bridge. Call for information on tours and services. 385 Kashavarof Street, Kodiak, 486-3854.

**Kodiak Baranov Museum**—Located in the Erskine House, a designated National Historic Landmark, the museum holds an interesting collection of Aleut, Koniag, Russian, and American artifacts. Built in 1808 as a secure magazine- and storehouse, the Erskine House is one of four original Russian structures remaining in the United States. 101 Marine Way, 486-5920. Open mid-May–Labor Day Monday–Friday 10 a.m. to 4 p.m., weekends noon to 4 p.m.; call for winter hours.

**Pasagshak State Recreation Site**—This small, riverside park with a campground is located 40 miles south of Kodiak and is a popular fishing spot. It's also a good kayak put-in for access to Ugak Bay and the Kodiak south coast. Take Rezanof Drive west out of town for 30 miles, then turn right on Pasagshak Road just past the Kalsin River and drive 9 miles. Contact the state park office for more information, 486-6339, www.ptialaska.net/~kodsp.

## Where to Stay in Kodiak

**Best Western Kodiak Inn**, 236 Rezanof West, (888) 563-4254, 486-5712. Expensive, but best place in town; restaurant, lounge, views. Tour-booking desk on site, friendly staff. Rooms $130–$200.

**Shahafka Cove Bed and Breakfast**, 1812 Mission Road, (888) 688-6565, 486-2409. Waterside with deck, near town center.

**Wintel's Bed and Breakfast**, 1723 Mission Road, 486-6935. On the water near shops and more. Rooms from $65–$100.

**Zachar Bay Lodge**, (800) 693-2333, 486-4120,

zbay@ptialaska.net. $375 per person (meals, guides), $1,700 for four nights (air shuttle, meals, guides). Located in an old salmon cannery; caters to hunters, fishers, and bear viewers. **BL**

### Where to Eat in Kodiak
**El Chicano**, 103 Center Avenue, 486-6116. Full Mexican menu, steaks, and burgers.

**Henry's Great Alaskan**, 512 Marine Way, 486-8844. Good food and camaraderie right across from the small boat harbor.

**Shire Bookstore**, 104 Center Avenue, 486-5001. Browse the shelves and have coffee and snacks. Open Monday–Saturday 9 a.m. to 5 p.m. (until 9 p.m. Friday), Sunday 1 to 5 p.m.

## KODIAK NATIONAL WILDLIFE REFUGE
*Location/Size: Kodiak Island and a portion of Afognak Island. 1.86 million acres (two-thirds of Kodiak Island, several native corporation and state land inclusions).*
*Main Activities: Fishing, hunting, bear viewing, backcountry lodging, hiking, backpacking, rafting, flightseeing, coastal exploring.*
*Gateway Towns/Getting There: Kodiak/scheduled air service from Anchorage, ferry service from Homer. Refuge access by charter air or boat from Kodiak; limited road access from Kodiak to eastern edge of the refuge.*
*Facilities, Camping, Lodging: No facilities. Primitive camping only (some well-used sites), several backcountry cabins are reservable through the headquarters. Private backcountry lodges operate adjacent to refuge lands.*
*Headquarters and Information: Refuge Manager, 1390 Buskin River Road, Kodiak, AK 99615, 487-2600, www.r7.fws.gov/nwr/kodiak/ kodnwr. html, r7kodwr@mail.fws.gov (type "Attention Refuge Manager" on subject line).*

About two-thirds of Kodiak Island, all of Uganil Island, and an additional 50,000 acres on Afognak and Ban Islands are encompassed in the Kodiak National Wildlife Refuge. Spruce forest covers much of Afognak and a number of coastal shores and valleys of northern and eastern Kodiak Island, but much of the refuge features a lush, dense cover of shrubs, tundra, and grass. The terrain consists of steep hills with 2,000- to 4,000-foot summits, tight valleys, and numerous

Paul Otteson

*Rugged Kodiak Island*

streams—though in the far southwest, bog lands and low, rolling, grassy hills predominate. The coastline is ragged with fjords and headlands while a few fair-sized lakes fill interior valleys.

The refuge was established in 1941 to protect the habitat of the Kodiak brown bear—largest of all bears and considered by some to be a genuine subspecies. Only five other mammals are native to the island (little brown bat, red fox, river otter, short-tailed weasel, and tundra vole), though introduced species, including black-tailed deer and beaver, thrive. As many as 2 million seabirds live along the coast.

Though hunting affects bear behavior, there are good viewing locations. Here as elsewhere, bears congregate in the summer along the salmon streams to feast. Ask the refuge manager about the **O'Malley Lake** viewing lottery. Fishing is also popular in the refuge, as are the nine reservable Fish and Wildlife Service cabins, four on southwestern lakes and five on the north coast.

Most access is via floatplane shuttle or drop-off from Kodiak. Hiking is difficult in forest and brush, easier on ridgecrests and high slopes. There are good options for extended ridge routes. Coastal explorations by sea kayak are possible, though headlands

are exposed in many areas. The **Karluk River** is a popular float with access from Karluk Lake, and is only a 4-mile portage from Larsen Bay. Air taxis serve drop-offs and the tiny town of Karluk.

## AFOGNAK, RASPBERRY, AND SHUYAK ISLANDS

These northern neighbors of Kodiak have no towns or regular transport access. They have more forest cover than their largely barren neighbor—though much of Afognak's has been logged by the native corporation that owns the land. Herds of Roosevelt elk roam on Afognak and Raspberry Islands, a non-native wild species.

The ragged, bay-riddled coastlines of the islands offer wonderful challenges for sea kayakers. The western coasts offer high cliffs and exposed headlands, while in the north, a portion of Kodiak National Wildlife Refuge and **Shuyak Island State Park** protect an intricate network of small islands and reefs. Four public-use cabins are available in the state park. At the eastern tip of Afognak Island, **Afognak Island State Park** offers primitive hiking, coastal access, and one public-use cabin. For information on either state park, contact Alaska State Parks, SR Box 3800, Kodiak, AK 99615, 486-6339. See the appendix for outfitters and flying services.

## KATMAI NATIONAL PARK AND PRESERVE

*Location/Size: National park, 3,716,000 acres (96 percent federal); national preserve, 374,000 acres (100 percent federal); designated wilderness, 3,473,000 acres. At the head of the Alaska Peninsula, 250 miles southwest of Anchorage, 100 miles northeast of Kodiak.*

*Main Activities: Bear viewing, fishing, canoeing, kayaking, volcanic sightseeing, backpacking, backcountry lodging, mountaineering, sea kayaking.*

*Gateway Towns/Getting There: King Salmon/scheduled air service from Anchorage; Kodiak/scheduled air service from Anchorage, scheduled ferry service from Homer and Seward; Homer/vehicle access via Sterling Highway (AK 9), scheduled air service from Anchorage, regular ferry service from Seward. Park access: floatplane to Brooks Camp and other lakes and sheltered coastal waters; by water to Brooks Camp via Naknek Lake; charter air service to drop-offs from Homer, Kodiak, and Anchorage; road access from Brooks Camp to Valley of Ten Thousand Smokes.*

*Facilities, Camping, Lodging: Bear-viewing platforms at Brooks Camp. Road from Brooks Camp to Valley of Ten Thousand Smokes,*

*short trails at Brooks Camp and Valley of Ten Thousand Smokes. Brooks Camp Campground, Brooks Camp Lodge, other park lodges, private lodges on private land inclusions, primitive camping elsewhere.*
**Headquarters and Information:** *Headquarters, P.O. Box 7, #1 King Salmon Mall, King Salmon, AK 99613, 246-3305, www.nps.gov/ katm; Kodiak Ranger Station, 486-6730.*

Katmai is perhaps the most fantastic of America's national parks, offering a combination of vast wilderness, active volcanoes, and the best bear viewing on the planet. The park is a haven for red-salmon fishers. Several large lakes offer routes for stillwater explorers, including the combined 100-mile length of Grosvenor, Naknek, and Brooks Lakes, linked by two short portages. Good hiking routes can be developed using the open lunar landscape of the Valley of Ten Thousand Smokes. The **Alagnik Wild River** and other river-running options are served by guides and outfitters in King Salmon. Mountaineers will gain rewards of volcanic proportions by attacking summits via glacier or ridge.

The brown bears of Katmai and nearby McNeil River are fast exceeding those of Kodiak in fame. Kodiak bears grow larger than their mainland kin, but the Katmai bears are impressive enough and easier to view. Most have known an extended period free from the threat of hunting and are not the least bit skittish over the presence of suitably respectful humans. Bears gather about key stretches of spawning streams in groups large and small to feast on the doomed fish, caring little for clicking cameras or the angler casting a line 100 yards upstream.

Of the 400 or so major volcanic eruptions that have been recorded in historic times around the Pacific's "Ring of Fire," an amazing 10 percent have been in Alaska. Most of those have occurred in the Aleutian Mountains of the Alaska Peninsula—Katmai is home to 15 of the state's 70 active volcanoes. The last major eruption was in June of 1912 when Novarupta Volcano blew, providing the impetus for the creation of Katmai National Monument—core of the current park. Several of Katmai's volcanoes emit occasional plumes of steam. Mount Trident has erupted four times in recent decades, most recently in 1968. Trident and Novarupta both appear to share a magma source with Mount Katmai, the splendid namesake of the park with a gorgeous crater lake.

The park concessionaire is Brooks Lodge, a division of Katmai Land, Inc. They operate Brooks Lodge at Brooks Camp ($320 for a

room, up to four people), Grosvenor Lake Lodge, Kulik Lodge on
Novianuk Lake, and two smaller facilities. For reservations, call
(800) 544-0551. Reservations for the 60-site campground at Brooks
Camp are necessary and can be made through Biospherics at (800)
365-2267; sites are $5. Primitive camping is permitted anywhere in
the park and preserve, except on private inclusions and within 5
miles of short, critical stretches of bear habitat near Brooks Camp.

Katmai is contiguous with Becharof National Wildlife Refuge
to the southwest and the McNeil River State Game Sanctuary.
Together, they offer one of the longest continuous stretches of undeveloped shoreline on the Pacific Coast. Visitors typically take a floatplane shuttle from King Salmon to Brooks Camp (see appendix).
Kodiak and Homer are the best gateways for shuttles and flightseeing
to the Katmai coast. There are no food or supply sources in the park
other than the beds and prepared meals offered at the lodges.

## Brooks Camp

This small national park enclave is the heart of Katmai and the base
of operations for most visitors. Brooks Camp is situated where
Brooks Lake drains into Naknek Lake via the short Brooks River.
Salmon struggle from one lake to the other via the cascading waters
of Brooks Falls. Fishers work the Naknek lakeshore and Brooks
River—as do numerous brown bears. Designated spots for optimal
bear viewing assist photographers. Rangers insist that all viewers and
fishers follow carefully crafted guidelines for behavior around the
bears (resulting in an outstanding safety record).

Unlike McNeil River, the number of visitors here is limited only
by the capacity of the air-taxi services (this may soon change),
though both the Brooks Lodge and Brooks Camp Campground
require reservations. You may be able to time your visit to enjoy
Brooks Camp bear viewing without actually having to stay there.
Backcountry explorers can spend part of the day at Brooks, then take
a shuttle to camp at the Valley of Ten Thousand Smokes (see
below). Water travelers and hikers can head down the lakeshores for
lonely campsites away from the action. Air taxis and outfitters serving
Brooks Camp are listed in the appendix.

## Valley of Ten Thousand Smokes

When Novarupta Volcano erupted in 1912, it spewed huge amounts of
volcanic ash over the landscape, affecting the atmosphere over the

entire Northern Hemisphere. Ash clouds caused blackout conditions in Kodiak, while damaging acidic rain fell as far away as Vancouver, British Columbia. Nearly a billion tons of ash, pumice, and debris settled over the upper Ukak River watershed, covering more than 40 square miles with a layer as deep as 200 meters. Shortly after the eruption, thousands of vents and fumaroles sent steam plumes into the air as seeping waters met the hot debris, earning the region its name.

Since then, the ash has cooled and settled, ending almost all steam activity and compressing the ash into a loose sedimentary rock called tuff. The feeders of the Ukak have cut deep, steep-walled canyons into the soft tuff, beginning the relatively rapid erosive process that will disperse the great ash field in a geologic eyeblink. Explorers can easily choose routes across the relatively unvegetated surface of the region, though venturing close to cliff edges and attempting certain stream crossings is foolish because of the loose rock.

Brooks Lodge operates a shuttle bus on the 23-mile road between Brooks Camp and the valley: $42 one-way, $79 round trip, (800) 544-0551 for information; reservations recommended. A trail leads down to

*Kodiak small boat harbor*

233

the valley from the viewpoint at the end of the road from Brooks Camp, but no developed routes into the park interior exist.

## MCNEIL RIVER STATE GAME SANCTUARY

*Location/Size:* Above Kamishak Bay on Cook Inlet, 200 miles southwest of Anchorage. 83,840 acres.

**Main Activities:** Bear observation.

**Gateway Towns/Getting There:** *Anchorage/scheduled air service, vehicle access via Seward Highway and Glenn Highway (AK 1); Kenai/scheduled air service, vehicle access via Sterling Highway (AK 1); Homer/scheduled air service, scheduled ferry from Seward and Kodiak, vehicle access via Sterling Highway (AK 1). Sanctuary access: limited access via lottery, charter plane to Kamishak Bay, hike to falls.*

**Facilities, Camping, Lodging:** *Trail to designated bear observation area. Designated primitive camping area.*

**Headquarters and Information:** *Alaska Department of Fish and Game, Division of Wildlife Conservation, 333 Raspberry Road, Anchorage, AK 99518, 267-2182 (applications), 344-0541, www.state.ak.us/local/akpages/FISHGAME/adfghome.htm.*

The greatest seasonal concentration of brown bears in the world is found along the McNeil River, which flows from high cirques and glaciers in Katmai National Park into McNeil Cove of Kamishak Bay. Upon recognition of its status, the state created a contiguous sanctuary from the national park wilderness boundary to the sea. Hunting and fishing are banned in the refuge, and only 200 to 300 visitors per year are permitted.

Entry to the sanctuary is by lottery selection from all applications received. Applicants must obtain an application via a written or phone request to the Alaska Department of Fish and Game, Division of Wildlife Conservation, 333 Raspberry Road, Anchorage, AK 99502. Call 267-2182 for an application, 267-2137 or 267-2344 for information. More information is available online at the Alaska Department of Fish and Game website: www.state.ak.us/adfg/wildlife/region2/refuge 2/mr-home.

Submit the application and a nonrefundable $25 fee before March 1. Non-Alaskan lottery winners must pay an additional $250 fee, while runners-up must pay $100 to hold a place on the stand-by list. Alaska residents pay half as much for both. Visitors must cover all transport costs and supply their own food, camping gear, and waders for stream crossings. From the camping area, a ranger takes small groups of visitors on a two-hour hike to an open gravel viewing pad by the falls where as many as 100 bears may gather at one time.

There are many other places to see bears, but McNeil River is an archetype for all the rest. You've certainly seen McNeil bears in photos and documentaries. Consider trying to visit the source.

## BECHAROF NATIONAL WILDLIFE REFUGE

*Location/Size:* West of Katmai National Park on the south coast of the Alaska Peninsula. 1.2 million acres (400,000 acres wilderness).
*Main Activities:* Fishing, hunting.
*Gateway Towns/Getting There:* King Salmon/scheduled air service from Anchorage. Refuge access: floatplane and charter air from King Salmon; water access from Ugashik and Egegik; south coast access via Shelikof Strait with oil camp trail leading to lake from Portage Bay.
*Facilities, Camping, Lodging:* No facilities. Primitive camping only.
*Headquarters and Information:* Refuge Manager, P.O. Box 277, King Salmon, AK 99613, 246-3339, www.r7.fws.gov/nwr/bec/becnwr, r7apbnwr@mail.fws.gov (type "Attention Refuge Manager" on subject line).

Becharof Lake, Alaska's second largest, covers about 25 percent of the refuge and is surrounded by low rolling hills, tundra wetlands, and volcanic peaks. Trees are found only in the southern coastal area, while to the north, tundra and brushy scrub dominate. The refuge is contiguous with Katmai National Park to the east and Alaska Peninsula Wildlife Refuge to the west. Huge numbers of salmon spawn in the refuge streams and rich wildlife populations are present, including brown bears and a caribou herd. It is a popular destination for hunters and fishers, generally to the exclusion of eco-travelers.

With Katmai on one side, Aniakchak Crater on the other, and Kodiak across the state, Becharof gets lost in the shuffle. Stillwater canoeing is possible on the lake, while river running is an option to the north on the Egegik and King Salmon Rivers. Contact the refuge manager for ideas on other explorations.

## ANIAKCHAK NATIONAL MONUMENT AND PRESERVE

*Location/Size:* On the Alaska Peninsula, 20 miles east of Port Heiden. Monument, 117,176 acres; preserve, 465,603 acres (97 percent federal).

*Main Activities:* Wilderness exploration, hiking, backpacking, kayaking.
*Gateway Towns/Getting There:* Port Heiden and King
Salmon/scheduled air service from Anchorage. Monument access by float-
plane to Surprise Lake, foot access through caldera, kayak access to
Pacific via Aniakchak River.
*Facilities, Camping, Lodging:* No facilities. Primitive camping only.
*Headquarters and Information:* Headquarters, P.O. Box 7, King
Salmon, AK 99613, 246-3305, www.nps.gov/ania.

Aniakchak Caldera is one of the planet's finest examples of a dry caldera. Six miles in diameter, 2,000 feet deep, and covering about 10
square miles, its features include lava flows, cinder cones, and explosion
pits. The larger caldera was formed thousands of years ago in a massive
eruption that ejected an estimated 15 cubic miles of debris. Many
smaller eruptions from vents and cones have followed, the last in 1931.

**Surprise Lake** on the eastern side of the caldera is the source of
the **Aniakchak River,** a designated National Wild River that offers
kayakers a spectacular trip to the sea on Class I–IV waters. The river
cuts a 1,500-foot gash in the side of the caldera where it spills out to
the southeast, heading for Aniakchak Bay and the Pacific. Floatplane
shuttles to the lake are possible from King Salmon and Port Heiden
(see appendix), both of which have regular air service from Anchorage.

Walking explorers can use the same shuttle services to reach the
caldera and explore its wonders. There are no services or facilities—
visitors must be self-reliant. Weather permitting, there are outstanding
views of the Alaska Peninsula, Bristol Bay, and the Pacific from the
caldera rim and the 4,400-foot summit of **Vent Cone.**

## CHIGNIK (CHIGNIK BAY)

*Location/Climate:* 260 miles west-southwest of Kodiak, 450 miles
southwest of Anchorage, on Pacific coast of Alaska Peninsula. 127"/yr.
precip., 58"/yr. snowfall, 21°F–60°F.
*Population:* 141 (45.2 percent native, Aleut and Eskimo).
*Travel Attractions:* Ferry link, access to Alaska Peninsula National
Wildlife Refuge and Aniakchak Crater National Park.
*Getting There:* Scheduled air service from King Salmon, scheduled
ferry service from Homer and Kodiak.
*Information:* Chignik Bay Village Council, 749-2282,
www.alaska.net/~bbha/chignik_bay.html.

This small town about 260 miles southwest of Kodiak more than triples in population during fish-harvesting season. It's a possible base for explorations of the Alaska Peninsula Wildlife Refuge, Mount Veniaminof Volcano, the forested land around Chignik Lake (eastern limit of forest on the peninsula), and coastal islands. The sheltered waters of Chignik Bay offer kayaking possibilities. There are few travel-related services other than scheduled small-plane air service and a ferry link. Two old canneries built in the 1800s are worth a look.

### Where to Stay and Eat in Chignik
**Aleutian Dragon Fisheries Guest House**, 749-2282 (city number for information).

**Grandma's Kitchen**, 749-2282.

## ALASKA PENINSULA NATIONAL WILDLIFE REFUGE
*Location/Size: South coast of the outer Alaska Peninsula between Becharof Lake and False Pass. 3.5 million acres.*
*Main Activities: Wilderness exploration, wildlife viewing, backpacking, fishing, mountaineering, kayaking.*
*Gateway Towns/Getting There: King Cove and Chignik/scheduled ferry service from Kodiak and Unalaska; Port Heiden/scheduled air service from Anchorage, charter air service. Park access: coastal access via charter boat, kayak; floatplane and charter air service from gateways, Kodiak, and King Salmon.*
*Facilities, Camping, Lodging: No facilities. Primitive camping only.*
*Headquarters and Information: Refuge Manager, P.O. Box 277, King Salmon, AK 99613, 246-3339, www.r7.fws.gov/nwr/ap/apnwr.html, r7apbnwr@mail.fws.gov (type "Attention Refuge Manager" on subject line).*

The refuge encompasses much of the mountains and Pacific coast of the Alaska Peninsula. Contiguous with Becharof National Wildlife Refuge to the east and Izembek National Wildlife Refuge to the west, the volcanoes and other peaks of the Aleutian Range dominate the scape. The Pacific coast is lined with ragged bays and headlands, some of which are sheltered by island groups offshore. There are numerous native and village corporation lands within the refuge boundaries, though Chignik, Chignik Lake, and Chignik Lagoon comprise the only populated area of consequence (see above).

West of Chignik on the Pacific coast, the village of **Perryville** (population 104, 94 percent Aleut) is a possible base for climbing **Mount Veniaminof** volcano, though there are no travel services and much of the population leaves during the summer for fishing-related jobs elsewhere. The base of the glacier-draped cone is a dozen miles from town. Perryville was established in 1912 when Mount Katmai erupted and destroyed the towns of Katmai and Douglas. Displaced residents, many of whom survived because they were out fishing when the eruption occurred, were relocated to their new home aboard the ship *Manning*, piloted by Captain Perry, for whom the village is named.

The refuge hosts abundant wildlife including moose, caribou, wolves, brown bears, and wolverines. Large populations of sea lions, seals, and migratory whales inhabit the waters and shores. Sea otters on the Pacific side of the peninsula number at least 30,000, having recovered from near extinction a century ago. The refuge provides valuable habitat for a variety of migratory birds.

Big-game hunting is a primary activity in the refuge, especially for caribou and brown bear. Fishing for king and silver salmon, arctic char, lake trout, northern pike, and record-setting grayling is similarly popular. Mountaineering, wilderness exploration, sea kayaking, and birding are still uncommon, offering the chance for truly unique and wild adventures.

## SAND POINT

*Location/Climate: 570 air miles from Anchorage, on Popof Island, off the Pacific coast of the Alaska Peninsula. 33"/yr. precip., 52"/yr. snowfall, -9°F–76°F.*
*Population: 989 (49.3 percent native, mainly Aleut).*
*Travel Attractions: Ferry link, access to Shumagin Islands of Alaska Maritime National Wildlife Refuge and to Alaska Peninsula National Wildlife Refuge.*
*Getting There: Scheduled air service from Anchorage, scheduled ferry service from Homer and Kodiak.*
*Information: City Office, 383-2696.*

Located on Humboldt Harbor on Popof Island, Sand Point was founded in 1898 by a San Francisco fishing company as a trading post and cod-fishing center. Scandinavian fishermen and Aleuts were early residents. The town served briefly as a repair and supply center for regional gold mining, but before and since it has been dominated by fishing. Today it is home to the largest fleet on the peninsula. A large transient population arrives to work seasonally in the canneries. The 1933 **St. Nicholas Chapel**, a Russian Orthodox church, is listed on the National Register of Historic Places.

Adventurers can use Sand Point for access to the Shumagin Islands and south coast of the Alaska Peninsula. There are no outfitters on the island, but small-boat charter is possible for drop-offs.

### Where to Stay and Eat in Sand Point
**Anchor Inn Motel**, 383-3272. $85 rooms, the only place in town.

## KING COVE
*Location/Climate: 18 miles from Cold Bay, 625 miles southwest of Anchorage on Pacific coast of Alaska Peninsula. 33"/yr. precip., 52"/yr. snowfall, -9°F–76°F.*
*Population: 879 (39.2 percent Aleut).*
*Travel Attractions: Ferry link, access to Alaska Peninsula National Wildlife Refuge.*
*Getting There: Scheduled air service from Anchorage, charter air, scheduled ferry service from Homer and Kodiak.*
*Information: City Office, P.O. Box 37, King Cove, AK 99612, 497-2340, www.ilovealaska.com/alaska/kingcove.*

Scandinavians and Aleuts were early settlers of King Cove, established as a salmon-canning town in the early 1900s. The Peter Pan fish-processing facility is the main employer and one of the largest operations under one roof in the state.

The 7,028-foot summit of **Pavlof Volcano** is 30 air miles from town. Overland access to the east unit of Izembek National Wildlife Refuge is possible in the treeless terrain, though shrub and tundra don't invite easy passage and you should consult the village corporation office about native land restrictions. Sea kayaking is a better option in the partially sheltered passage and bay waters. There are no outfitters in town, though charters and rentals may be available.

### Where to Stay and Eat in King Cove
**Fleet's Inn**, 497-2312. The main place in town. Rooms are $75–$105.

## COLD BAY

*Location/Climate:* 18 miles from King Cove, 634 miles southwest of
Anchorage, on Cold Bay of the Alaska Peninsula. 36"/yr. precip.,
61"/yr. snowfall, 25°F–60°F.
*Population:* 220 (5.4 percent native).
*Travel Attractions:* Ferry link, air-transit hub, access to Izembek
National Wildlife Refuge, birding, fishing.
*Getting There:* Scheduled air service from various points; scheduled
ferry service from Homer and Kodiak.
*Information:* City Office, 532-2401.

Archaeological findings dating to the last ice age indicate that the
site of Cold Bay was once a large Aleut settlement. Wildlife harvesters used the bay throughout the nineteenth century, though
they did not settle here. The town was effectively established in
World War II with the construction of Fort Randall, a strategic air
base. Most military structures have been removed, though the scars
to land and tundra will be visible for decades. The 10,000-foot run-
way remains, however, and the town has an important role in air
transport. Fishing-fleet support and air services are the biggest
employers.

Cold Bay is the best gateway to the Izembek National Wildlife
Refuge—particularly the Izembek Lagoon Unit, which hosts millions of migratory birds. The old military road system and the sheltered waters of the bay and lagoon enable excellent access to several
areas (see Izembek National Wildlife Refuge).

### Where to Stay and Eat in Cold Bay
**Pavlov Services**, 532-2437. Hotel and restaurant.

## IZEMBEK NATIONAL WILDLIFE REFUGE

*Location/Size:* On the tip of Alaska Peninsula and Unimak Island. Of
the nearly 3,000,000 acres, 1,200,000 acres of designated wilderness
administered by the Izembek manager are in the Alaska Maritime
N.W.R. and Alaska Peninsula N.W.R.
*Main Activities:* Birding, sea kayaking, mountaineering, wilderness
exploration.
*Gateway Towns/Getting There:* Cold Bay/scheduled air service
from Anchorage, scheduled ferry service from Kodiak and Unalaska;

*False Pass and King Cove/scheduled ferry service from Kodiak and Unalaska, regular small-plane air service from Cold Bay and Unalaska. Park access: vehicle access via roads from Cold Bay; water access via charter boat, personal watercraft.*
**Facilities, Camping, Lodging:** *Short road system, offices in Cold Bay. Primitive camping only.*
**Headquarters and Information:** *Refuge Manager, P.O. Box 127, Cold Bay, AK 99571, 532-2445, www.r7.fws.gov/nwr/izembek/ iznwr.html, r7izemwr@mail.fws.gov (type "Attention Refuge Manager" on subject line).*

At the end of the Alaska Peninsula, Izembek National Wildlife Refuge is bounded by volcanic peaks and includes rolling tundra uplands, coastal barrier islands, and the rich habitat of **Izembek Lagoon.** Three separate units are administered together in the modern refuge—the result of a recent reorganization of refuge lands.

The **Pavlof Unit** (1,447,264 acres of wilderness) features volcanic peaks including **Pavlof Volcano** and Pacific shoreline at the tip of the Alaska Peninsula. Pavlof is one of the most recently active volcanoes in the state and was sending up huge amounts of ash and steam through late 1996 and into 1997. Check with the refuge manager about the peak's current status. Access is from Cold Bay or King Cove via charter boat, air, or kayak.

The **Unimak Island Unit** (1,008,697 acres, 910,000 acres of wilderness) encompasses virtually all of Unimak Island (easternmost of the Aleutians) including very active **Shishaldin Volcano** and other volcanic peaks. False Pass, at the east end of the island, is 22 miles from Shishaldin's summit and is accessible by ferry.

The **Izembek Unit** (417,533 acres, 300,000 acres of wilderness) includes the Izembek Lagoon and the surrounding low hills. The lagoon is rich in eelgrass and serves as a vital migratory stopover for thousands of Canada and emperor geese, other waterfowl, and the world's entire population of black brandt (a small coastal goose). Most birds arrive in one of two waves, the first in late August and early September, the second in November—including sea ducks and Steller's eiders. The lagoon attracts both birders and waterfowl hunters. Federal lands are contiguous with the **Izembek State Game Refuge** (181,440 acres), which completes protection of the lagoon. Forty miles of old military roads around Cold Bay allow limited access to the lagoon and the western end of the Pavlof Unit.

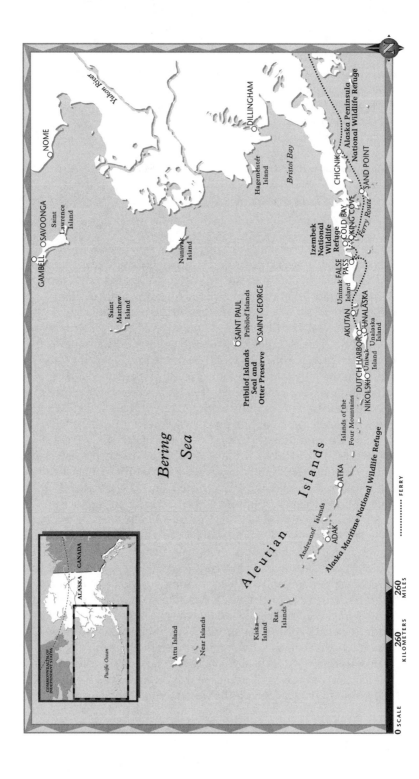

# ALEUTIANS AND BERING SEA ISLANDS

**12**

Few residents or visitors venture out beyond the Kenai Peninsula. Fewer still travel west of Kodiak Island and the Alaska Peninsula. Those who do are in for a special treat—the chance to experience rugged, barren lands exposed to the full brunt of Pacific Ocean weather. Though it rains more in the Southeast and gets much colder inland, the Aleutians offer the wildest of conditions.

Fifty-seven volcanoes are found throughout the islands, many of them active and 13 over 5,000 feet in elevation. The Alaska Volcano Observatory monitors conditions throughout the southwest (great website at www.avo.alaska.edu). The islands are really the peaks of a submerged mountain chain, a continuation of the Alaska Range and the Aleutian Range of the Alaska Peninsula.

The Aleutians experience a cool, moderated maritime climate with little variation between average high and low temperatures. Drizzly, misty conditions are common as wet clouds blow through on a collision course with the mainland. Perhaps the most dominating feature is the wind. It can seem to blow continuously, often with fast moving storms, squalls, rainbows, and sunsets along for the ride.

The islands and their surrounding waters feature an abundance of wildlife. Numerous seabird rookeries are found on isolated cliffs and islets. Sea lions and harbor seals gather on isolated beaches and tidal zone rocks. Sea otters are relatively abundant, particularly from Adak to Kiska, and whales and porpoises are common. The islands were originally free of mammals, but reindeer, caribou, and arctic fox have been introduced in some locations and thrive on the abundant food supply—as do some sheep and cattle. A grassland and tundra mix of grasses, sedges, lichens, mosses, and heath covers the islands. There are no trees to be found.

Of the 20,000 or so Aleuts who once lived throughout the chain, fewer than 1,000 survived the violence, slavery, and disease brought by the Russians. Today, Aleut settlements exist only on Atka, Umnak, Unalaska, Akutan, and Unimak Islands. These, along with the military and Coast Guard bases on Shemya, Adak, and Attu, are the only established settlements on the hundreds of Aleutian Islands.

*The M/V* Tustamena *in port*

## ALASKA MARITIME NATIONAL WILDLIFE REFUGE

*Location/Size: Aleutian Islands, Bering Sea Islands, and other coastal islands. 2.64 million acres.*

*Main Activities: Birding, wilderness exploration, backpacking, sea kayaking, flightseeing, ferry cruising.*

*Gateway Towns/Getting There: Several Aleutian Islands towns/scheduled ferry service to False Pass, Akutan, and Unalaska; scheduled air service to Unalaska; regular small-plane air service to Saint Paul, Akutan, Nikolski, False Pass, and other points; charter air and floatplane. Park access: coastal access via sea kayak in sheltered coastal areas and island groups; hiking access via gateway towns and drop-offs; very limited road access on Unalaska, Umnak, Kiska, Attu, Adak, Amchitka, and others (access to certain islands and roads requires military permission).*

*Facilities, Camping, Lodging: No facilities. Primitive camping only.*

*Headquarters and Information: Refuge Manager, 2355
Kachemak Bay Drive, Suite 101, Homer, AK 99603-8021, 235-6546,
www.r7.fws.gov/nwr/akmnwr/akmnwr.html, r7aiuwr@fws.gov (type
"Attention Refuge Manager" on subject line); Aleutian Islands Unit,
P.O. Box 5251, Adak, AK 99546, 592-2406.*

Virtually all of the Aleutian Island chain west of Unimak Island
is encompassed by the Aleutian Unit of the Alaska Maritime
National Wildlife Refuge. Large inclusions of native and village
corporation lands are found near settlements, while the military
lands on Attu, Adak, and Shemya require permission to visit.
Many islands are further protected in the refuge's designated
**Aleutian Islands Wilderness.** Any who visit wilderness areas
will find steep, treeless ridges and slopes, wave-battered cliffs,
thousands of seabirds, colonies of marine mammals, volcanoes,
solitude, water, and wind.

The Alaska Maritime National Wildlife Refuge is literally for
the birds; over 10 million migratory and resident birds nest within
its bounds. Kiska hosts the world's largest colony of crested and
least auklets. Chagulak is the choice of almost a million northern
fulmars. Alaska's largest colony of tufted puffins—about 100,000
—nest on the small island of Kaligagan. Visitor and "accidental"
Asian species are commonly seen on some islands, including
whooper swans, tufted ducks, Siberian rubythroats, wood sand-
pipers, far eastern curlews, and common black-headed gulls.
Common land birds include the bald eagle, raven, rock ptarmigan,
peregrine falcon, snow bunting, song sparrow, Lapland longspur,
winter wren, and rosy finch. Numerous other species visit the
islands at various times of year.

Though the Aleutians and Bering Sea Islands are the best
known units, the refuge encompasses many other islands, isolated
coastal locations, and stretches of open ocean from the Chukchi
Sea to the far Southeast. A visitor center for the Aleutian Unit of
the refuge is found on Adak Island (check to see if it's still open).
A better source for most folks is the refuge manager's office in
Homer, or one of the four Alaska Public Lands Information
Centers (see details above and appendix). Just about anywhere
it makes sense to be protecting ocean-going birds and marine
mammals, there's probably a unit of the refuge or a similar state
preserve.

If you're considering sea-kayak or backpack explorations in the Alaska Maritime National Wildlife Refuge, discuss options with outfitters, pilots, and refuge officials. A number of critical habitat areas are closed to humans at key times or permanently. No visit should be taken lightly; be prepared for storms, chill, rain, and wind. Traveling the open sea in a large boat or ferry may challenge the stomach, but excursions in smaller craft can be positively dangerous.

## FALSE PASS

*Location/Climate:* On the east shore of Unimak Island just beyond the tip of the Alaska Peninsula, 646 air miles southwest of Anchorage. 33"/yr. precip., 56"/yr. snowfall, 11°F–55°F.
*Population:* 87 (76.5 percent Aleut).
*Travel Attractions:* Ferry link, Unimak Island access, Shishaldin Volcano.
*Getting There:* Scheduled and charter air service; scheduled ferry service from Homer and Kodiak.
*Information:* City Office, P.O. Box 50, False Pass, AK 99583, 548-2319, www.apicda.com/fp.html.

False Pass is indeed near a hoped-for passage between the Alaska Peninsula and the first of the Aleutian Islands, but the route has proven too shallow for larger vessels. The area was settled by a homesteader after the turn of the century and grew quickly with the establishment of a Peter Pan Seafoods cannery in 1917. The community is largely Aleut, populated by native families originally from Morzhovoi, Sanak Island, and Ikatan who came to work at the cannery. Fishing and fleet services occupy most residents.

The town is located at the eastern end of Unimak Island, first of the Aleutians and largely encompassed by the Unimak Wilderness of the Izembek National Wildlife Refuge (see Izembek National Wildlife Refuge, chapter 11). The icy, 8,025-foot summit of **Isanotski Peak** is 15 air miles from town, while further along the ridge, **Shishaldin Volcano** tops out at 9,372 feet. These are by far the tallest peaks in the Aleutians. Though offering little in the way of support, False Pass is the best base for exploring the wilderness or attempting a summit. Consult the Izembek Refuge Manager for information.

## Where to Stay and Eat in False Pass

**The Bunkhouse**, 548-2208. Rustic accommodation operated by Peter Pan Cannery. $115 for a room and three meals.

## AKUTAN

*Location/Climate: On Akutan Islands in the Aleutians, 35 miles east of Unalaska, 766 miles southwest of Anchorage. 27.5"/yr. precip., 22°F–55°F.*
*Population: 436 (13.6 percent Aleut).*
*Travel Attractions: Ferry link, access to Akutan Island and Akutan Volcano, hot springs.*
*Getting There: Scheduled ferry service from Homer and Kodiak; chartered boat, floatplane.*
*Information: Akutan Corporation Office, General Delivery, Akutan, AK 99503; 698-2206, www.apicda.com/akutan.html.*

The island and village of Akutan is a good choice for a total Aleutian experience. Established as a fur storage and trading post in 1878, fishing soon became the main industry. Akutan was the only whaling station in the Aleutians from 1912 until 1942. Residents were evacuated to Ketchikan during the war, but subsequently reestablished the community without the whaling. Today, it is a largely non-native fishing and fish-processing town with a small, traditional Aleut village.

There is no airstrip on the island so it must be reached by float-plane shuttle from Unalaska, or via the monthly summer visits of the ferry *Tustamena*. Sheltered kayak waters, compact island size, and the summit of 4,275-foot Akutan Volcano only 8 miles from town are attractions to the intrepid. Two hotels and a cafe serve mainly business visitors and temporary workers.

## Where to Stay and Eat in Akutan

**Bayview Plaza Hotel**, next door to the cafe, 698-2206 (corporation office). Two one-bedroom apartments and four smaller rooms.

**Grab A Dab Cafe**, 698-2206 (corporation office). Open Monday–Friday.

**Salmonberry Inn**, 698-2206 (corporation office). Apartment, bunk rooms,"for the budget minded."

## UNALASKA/DUTCH HARBOR

*Location/Climate:* Northeast end of Unalaska Island, 800 air miles
from Anchorage. 58"/yr. precip., 25°F–53°F.
*Population:* 4,083 (8.4 percent native).
*Travel Attractions:* Russian and native history, ferry terminus, access
to Aleutians and Alaska Maritime National Wildlife Refuge, Makushin
Volcano.
*Getting There:* Scheduled air service from Anchorage, scheduled ferry
service from Homer and Kodiak.
*Information:* Convention and Visitors Bureau, P.O. Box 545,
Unalaska, AK 99685, 581-2612, www.arctic.net/~updhcvb.

Unalaska on Unalaska Island is an established settlement and home
to most of the island's residents. The working port of Dutch Harbor
is on Amaknak Island, which is connected by a short bridge to
Unalaska. Whether arriving by air or ferry, you'll first set foot in
"Dutch"—the top fishing port in the nation. All parts of both towns
are within short walking distance.

More than 1,000 Aleuts lived in 24 settlements on Unalaska Island
when the Russians arrived in 1759. The town of Unalaska became a
Russian trading port in 1768—and also a base for enslaved Aleuts who
worked harvesting fur seals on the Pribilof Islands. The famous **Russian Orthodox Church of the Holy Ascension of Christ** was constructed in 1825 by founding priest, Ivan Veniaminov, who later helped
the Aleut people compose their first writing system. World War II put
the island on the map when the Japanese attacked Dutch Harbor by air.

Half of all fish harvested in Alaska are landed in Dutch Harbor—
$160 million worth annually. The port is within 50 miles of the "Great
Circle" shipping route between West Coast ports and the Pacific Rim.
Residents and seasonal workers are employed almost exclusively in fish
harvesting, fish processing, or fleet services. If you want a job that you'll
be reluctant to tell mom about, here's where to look.

Unalaska/Dutch Harbor is the most accessible destination in the
Aleutians. Daily air service is offered from Anchorage and other
points. Dutch Harbor is also the end of the line for the A.M.H.S
ferry *Tustamena*. There are plenty of travel services, including a luxury hotel that's one of the state's nicest. Wildlife tours take birders
and marine mammal watchers out and around through the sheltered
bays. Anglers come to try their luck in the rich halibut and salmon
fisheries from the decks of charter boats. Charter air and boat ser-

Paul Otteson

*Aleutians*

vices offer options for remote island drop-offs and pick-ups. Unalaska Island itself offers remote ridge walking, sea kayaking, and beach camping. The icy, 6,680-foot cone of **Makushin Volcano** is 20 miles from town.

## Things to See and Do in Unalaska/Dutch
Things to do in this area include:

**Bunker Hill Trail** (¾-mile, 421' gain)—Take Henry Swanson Drive south from the west end of the "Bridge to the Otherside" to the switchback road that leads to the summit ruin of a World War II emplacement. You can also cut up the slope on casual paths from Airport Beach Road. Great views! Round-trip—1–1.5 hrs.

**Holy Ascension Cathedral** (Russian Orthodox Church of the Holy Ascension of Christ)—Built in 1825 and fully restored in 1996, the Holy Ascension Cathedral is Unalaska's unmistakable centerpiece. It is the oldest Russian Orthodox cruciform-style church in North America and is a designated National Historical Landmark. Inside is a marvelous collection of Russian artifacts,

religious icons, and artwork. Check with the visitors bureau regarding hours and tours (see details above).

## Where to Stay and Eat in Unalaska/Dutch Harbor

**Elbow Room**, 2nd and Bayview, Unalaska, 581-1271, 581-1470, fax 581-3350. Open Monday–Saturday 11 a.m. to 3 a.m. *The* bar to meet people, good for job finding, live music, rough edges.

**Grand Aleutian Hotel**, Airport Beach Road, Dutch Harbor, (800) 891-1194, 581-3844. $135 and up. Full service, all amenities, plush, complimentary airport shuttle.

## ADAK

*Location/Climate:* *1,250 air miles from Anchorage; Adak Naval Air Station on Adak Island. 21"/yr. precip., 41"/yr. snowfall, 11°F–65°F.*
*Population:* *874 (1.2 percent native). Population was almost 5,000 before the Naval Air Station was scaled back.*
*Travel Attractions:* *Remote cabins (military), Aleutian Islands wilderness access.*
*Getting There:* *Military air with permission.*
*Information:* *Arctic National Wildlife Refuge Manager, 2355 Kachemak Bay Drive, Suite 101, Homer, AK 99603-8021, 235-6546, r7aiuwr@mail.fws.gov (type "Attention Refuge Manager" on subject line); Aleutian Islands Unit, P.O. Box 5251, Adak, AK 99546, 592-2406, www.r7.fws.gov/nwr/akmnwr/akmnwr.html.*

Adak was long an important naval base in the Pacific, but those days are gone. Adak Naval Air Station is now scheduled to be completely shut down and virtually all island residents are to be moved. It will be interesting to see how the facilities are used, if at all. The island has a small road system, 3,000-foot Mount Moffett, sheltered bay waters, a military-grade airstrip, and lots of empty buildings. The southern half of the island is part of the Aleutian Islands Wilderness. Several reservable public-use cabins are scattered throughout the wilderness, offering the chance for comfort in the wild.

If you have the unique opportunity to consider visiting Adak, consult the Refuge Manager of the Alaska Maritime National Wildlife Refuge to get current information.

## OTHER ALEUTIAN ISLANDS

Several other Aleutian Islands can be visited. In general, they have no tourist or travel facilities and must be reached by expensive flights on relatively small aircraft.

**Umnak**—This big island just west of Unalaska hosts the largely Aleut community of Nikolski (population 27, 87percent native). Domestic animals roam freely over much of the island, including about 7,000 sheep, 300 head of cattle, and 30 horses. The eastern end of the island is dominated by **Okmok Caldera**, wrapped near the coast by a small road system centered around Fort Glenn. The wide coastal lowlands on parts of Umnak are somewhat unusual for the Aleutians.

**Atka**—Rugged, narrow, and long, the western end of Atka Island and most of Amlia Island to the east are part of the Aleutian Islands Wilderness. The town of Atka (population 97, 90 percent Aleut) is situated near a neck of land that separates two sheltered bays. North of this neck, the island swells to about 15 miles in diameter to accommodate 4,760-foot **Mount Kliuchef** with its splendid crater lake, and 5,030-foot **Korovin Volcano,** which rises from the north crater rim. Air service is available twice weekly.

**Attu**—The one great battle on American soil during World War II took place on Attu. The battlefield is preserved today as a historic site, while nearby locations such as Navy Town and Massacre Bay speak to the military history of the place. The Coast Guard is now in charge of access, though it isn't difficult to visit if you can afford it. Attu is the last of the Aleutians, over 1,200 air miles west of Anchorage. The island is rugged, though it has no high peaks. A short road system at the island's east end connects Navy Town, the settlement of Attu, Casco Cove Coast Guard Station, and the Attu Battlefield.

## PRIBILOF ISLANDS

*Location/Climate: 750 miles west of Anchorage. Saint Paul 25"/yr. precip., 56"/yr. snowfall, 19°F–51°F. Saint George 23"/yr. precip., 57"/yr. snowfall, 24°F–52°F.*

*Population: Saint Paul 767 (66.1 percent native, mainly Aleut), Saint George 195 (94.9percent native, mainly Aleut).*

*Travel Attractions: Saint Paul, wildlife viewing (fur seals, sea birds). Saint George, very little.*

*Getting There: Scheduled air service from Anchorage.*
*Information: City of Saint Paul, P.O. Box 901, Saint Paul Island, AK*
*99660, 546-2331, www.seanet.com/~fowler/st_paul.htm. City of Saint*
*George, P.O. Box 929, Saint George Island, AK 99591, 859-2263.*

Two million seabirds summer on the islands of Saint Paul and Saint
George, most finding some cranny among the cliffs for nesting. Fur
seals also congregate here by the hundreds to bear their young.
Saint Paul Island is the slightly larger of the islands at 40 square
miles. Each island has one principle community that shares the
name of its island host.

The uninhabited Pribilofs were discovered in 1786 by the Russian explorer Gavrill Pribilof. He was looking for—and found—the
breeding grounds of the fur seal. The Russians subsequently
enslaved Aleuts from Siberia, Unalaska, and Atka, and took them to
the islands to harvest the seals. In 1870 the Alaska Commercial
Company took over seal harvesting from the departing Russians,
improving the conditions of the Aleuts somewhat by providing
housing, food, and medical care in exchange for work. Aleut settlements gained permanence, but the people suffered with the decline
of the seal harvest and were long considered wards of the state.
During World War II, most were interred with other Aleutian
natives at Funter Bay in the Southeast.

After the war, many returned, adopting a constitution and charter under the Indian Reorganization Act in 1950. Residents still
depend in part on subsistence harvesting of fur seals (now tightly
regulated) and domesticated reindeer. Since 1969, $28.5 million
has been provided to island residents—part in consideration for the
shabby treatment they received for so many years, and part to boost
development of economic alternatives to seal harvesting. Today the
town of Saint Paul hosts the largest community of Aleuts in the
world (about 500). Saint George is a much smaller town, but is
almost entirely Aleut. Both have expanded their economies to
include commercial fishing, fish processing, and tourism.

Most of the approximately 700 annual visitors to the Pribilofs
come on birding tours. About 225 bird species have been identified
here, including red-faced cormorant, oldsquaw, rock sandpiper, northern fulmar, parakeet, least and crested auklet, common and thick-
billed murre, black and red-legged kittiwake, and puffins. Arctic blue
fox, sea lions, whales, and reindeer may also be seen. Saint Paul is the

more popular destination of the two islands since it has visitor facilities. Reeve Aleutian Airways offers tours (see appendix).

## Where to Stay and Eat on Saint Paul Island
**King Eider Hotel**, Saint Paul, 546-2477.

**King Eider Restaurant**, Saint Paul, 546-2312.

## Where to Stay and Eat on Saint George Island
No facilities. St. George Panaq Corporation Hotel, Saint George, AK 99591; 859-2255. No restaurant or meal service is available.

## SAINT LAWRENCE ISLAND
This low, lake-riddled island in the Bering Sea has been inhabited by Eskimos intermittently for as long as 10,000 years. In the eighteenth and nineteenth centuries, the activity of the fur trade resulted in as many as 4,000 people living here in 35 villages. Famine struck in the 1880s, decimating the population; it has never returned to historic levels. In 1881, Teddy Roosevelt established Saint Lawrence Island as a reindeer reserve. To this day, limited harvesting of the partially domesticated, free-roaming reindeer is an important subsistence activity, particularly near Savoonga.

All of Saint Lawrence Island is village corporation land belonging to the island's inhabitants. The island is unusual in that residents elected to take complete control over their lands, rather than assuming only surface rights plus a cash settlement. The latter was the more common choice during the implementation of ANCSA, inviting some cynicism.

The towns of Gambell and Savoonga, both on the northwest shore of the island, have conomies based on the subsistence harvest of fish, marine mammals, and reindeer. Tourists come in very small numbers to observe bird concentrations, and to buy the excellent ivory carvings for which island artisans are famed. Access to both cities is via scheduled air service from Nome. There are no travel services or facilities in either town.

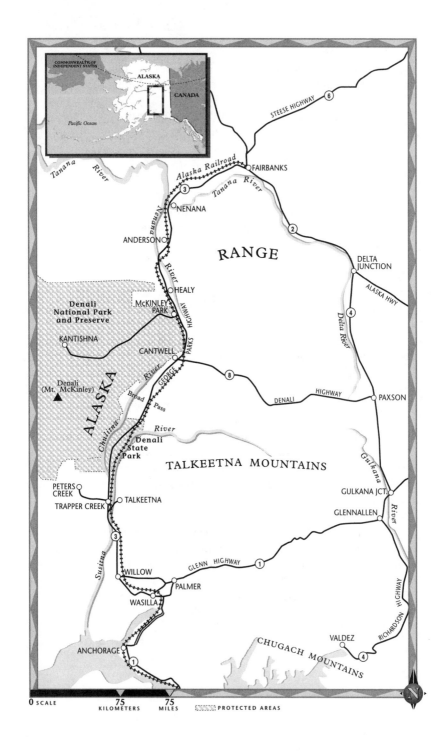

# 13

# DENALI AND THE ALASKA RANGE

Long before the mountain was dedicated to President McKinley after his assassination, the native people called North America's highest peak *Denali* (duh-NAH-lee), "the high one" or "the great one." At 20,320 feet, its elevation alone is impressive. What few visitors realize is that Denali is the largest continental mountain in the world—nowhere else on the planet can you see greater relief from base to summit (about 3.5 vertical miles) or a larger massif (a closely related grouping of peaks within a larger range). It is "the great one," indeed.

Denali rises from the heart of the impressive Alaska Range. More accessible by road than most others, the range is divided into thirds by two highways. The Parks Highway (AK 3) stretches from Palmer to Fairbanks, providing road access to Denali National Park; and the Richardson Highway (AK 4) parallels the Trans-Alaska Pipeline from Delta Junction to Valdez. Denali National Park and Preserve encompasses much of the western section of the range, the BLM administers most of the central section, and the eastern section includes large parcels of state and native lands. Most peaks of the Alaska Range are about 5,000 to 7,000 feet in elevation, but each of the three segments offers a set of lofty, glacier-crested summits visible for miles across the surrounding lowlands.

*Denali seen from Ruth Glacier*

Paul Otteson

There are numerous travel opportunities throughout the range. The 90-mile park road in Denali National Park and Preserve offers excellent access to hiking routes, wildlife observation, and mountain viewing—though it is closed to most private vehicles beyond Mile 15. The Richardson Highway crosses a higher pass and comes fairly close to a couple of glaciers. Best, perhaps, is the Denali Highway (AK 8)—a lonely gravel route from Cantwell to Paxson through the open high country south of the range.

Remote access to the Alaska Range is by small plane only. Pilots land on lakes, glaciers, gravel bars, and remote airstrips, shuttling people to backcountry lodges, recreational drop-offs, and mountaineering approaches. Flightseeing around any of the high-peak regions—particularly around the Denali massif—is one of the most memorable activities you might choose.

Many travelers simply enjoy their views of the Alaska Range as they race along the Alaska highways. Of those who opt for something more, the majority visit Denali National Park and Preserve, enjoying bus tours, hiking, and rafting close to the park entrance or along the park road. This is certainly the least expensive way to enjoy some of the best opportunities for wildlife and mountain viewing.

# GEORGE PARKS HIGHWAY (AK 3)— WASILLA TO FAIRBANKS

*Road Conditions and Attractions—320 miles. Good, paved road with some passing lanes; heavily traveled, areas of bad frost-heave damage and slumping, railroad crossings, open year-round. Access to Susitna River valley recreation, Hatcher Pass Road, Talkeetna, Denali Highway, Denali National Park and Preserve, Nenana, Fairbanks.*

The Parks Highway gets wilder in steps as it leaves the sprawl of Wasilla and curves north, following the Susitna River valley to the west and the Talkeetna Mountains to the east. Between Wasilla and Willow there is access to fishing lakes, lowland recreation areas, vacation cabins, homesteads, and scattered highway services. Beyond Talkeetna, the highway climbs gradually through increasingly scenic terrain, passing through Denali State Park and up into Broad Pass— one of the more lovely stretches of road anywhere. Views of Denali are possible from many points if the clouds lift.

Broad Pass separates the Chulitna and Nenana River basins and divides the Susitna and Yukon River watersheds. North of Cantwell the road descends the Nenana valley, sometimes through wide basins, often through narrow defiles. Moose can be seen near the river, and rafting parties are often seen in it. From Cantwell to the Alaska Range foothills at Healy, small inclusions of private lands host B&Bs, cabins, campgrounds, hotels, homes, airstrips, and businesses related to Denali National Park.

North of Healy the road follows the Nenana River through lowlands to its confluence with the Tanana in the town of Nenana, then traces a high ridgeline to the outskirts of Fairbanks.

**Glenn Highway Junction** (Mile 35)—The Parks Highway begins here. Mileposts reflect the distance to Anchorage.

**Wasilla** (Mile 42.2)—See Wasilla in chapter 9.

**Little Susitna River Campground** (Mile 57.3)—An 86-site developed campground operated by the City of Houston.

**Houston** (Mile 57.5)—One suspects that when Wasilla starts to look like metro-Anchorage, Houston (population 956, 3.6 percent native) will be the new Wasilla.

**Nancy Lake State Recreation Area** (Mile 67.2)—This 22,685-acre, multi-use state recreation area encompasses a region of forest-covered low hills interspersed with numerous lakes. A 6.5-mile road provides access to four trailheads, three put-ins, and a 98-site campground. Twelve rental cabins are scattered on the shores of four different lakes; two are on islands.

Of particular interest is the 8-mile chain of lakes in the **Lynx Lake Loop** canoe route. The route can be paddled in a day, though it makes a great overnight trip. With the long Alaska days, you can put-in in the late afternoon, paddle to a great campsite or cabin, and be back on the road by noon the next day. For a longer trip, put-in to the Little Susitna at Mile 57 of the Parks Highway. Take the marked portage to Skeetna Lake and follow the lake chain to the recreation area road. Contact the ranger, Mile 1.3, Nancy Lake Parkway, 495-6273, www.llbean.com/parksearch/parks/html/983lls.htm for information.

**Miners Last Stand Museum** (Mile 68.7)—You can't miss this thoroughly Alaskan-style combination of gift shop, museum, and theme attraction. The museum immortalizes Soapy Smith, who prospected at Hatcher Pass before heading to Skagway to enjoy a notorious final fling of ruthlessness. Open daily in summer, 495-6479, $3.

**Willow** (Mile 69)—This small settlement (population 368, 1.1 percent native) at Willow Lake near the junction of the Parks Highway and Hatcher Pass Road is essentially a roadside center for a larger homestead area. Travel services are spread out around Mile 69.

**Willow Trading Post Lodge** (Mile 69.5), Willow Station Road (turn east at Mile 69.5, turn left at post office after tracks), Willow, 495-6457. $70 double, $70–$80 cabin double, $50 cabin or room (shared bath). Good location, lots of character, cozy restaurant and bar, friendly hosts. **RH**

**Willow Creek State Recreation Area** (Mile 70.8)—Follow road 4 miles to $10 sites and creek access.

**Hatcher Pass Road Junction** (Mile 71.2)—Turn east here to reach Hatcher Pass and Independence Mine State Park (see chapter 9). The road climbs gradually along Willow Creek into the Talkeetna Mountains, passing small ranches, homes, and signs of mining activity.

**Lucky Husky Racing Kennel** (Mile 80)—Stop here for a look at the world of sled dogs and racing, and perhaps for a ride in a wheeled sled (or a real one in winter). Touristy but educational. Mile 80 Parks Highway, Willow, 495-6470, www.luckyhusky.com. Open May–September Wednesday–Saturday 9 a.m. to 5 p.m., by reservation at other times; tour $6, sled ride $24.

**Sheep Creek Lodge** (Mile 88.2), Willow, AK 99688, 495-6227. Impressive log lodge. Restaurant, camping, cabins for $30 and up. **RH**

**Montana Creek** (Mile 96.6)—Though not an incorporated town, the area was homesteaded in the 1950s and is now home to about 200 people.

**Talkeetna Road Junction** (98.7)—Turn east and head 15 miles down this spur road to reach Talkeetna (see below). Stop here at the **Talkeetna Visitor Information Center** for area info. Consider visiting Talkeetna and using one of the excellent air services for Denali area flightseeing.

One mile up Talkeetna Spur Road is **Mary Carey's Fiddlehead Fern Farm**, 733-2428. Not surprisingly, it's the only one of its kind in the world. Fiddleheads make a tasty, healthy Alaskan treat. Frozen, pickled, and fresh (in season) fiddleheads are on sale, as are plants and seeds. Read about Mary Carey below at the Mile 134.5 entry.

**Trapper Creek and Petersville Road Junction** (Mile 115)—The official population of Trapper Creek (population 304, 6.1 percent native) includes fewer than half of the area residents, many of whom homesteaded nearby and along Petersville Road. There are plenty of highway services.

**Denali State Park** (Mile 132 to Mile 169)—See below.

**Mary Carey and Mary's McKinley View Lodge** (Mile 134.5)— Mary Carey is an area legend. While a reporter, she explored the Mount McKinley region by air. She circled the world twice and

authored 10 books, mainly about Alaska and Texas. After home-steading here in 1962, she lived a rugged, isolated life while fighting for the development of the Parks Highway.

Though Mary Carey is no longer alive, her lodge is still in business on the only significant roadside private parcel within the bounds of Denali State Park. Some of the best southern views of Denali are available here.

**Mary's McKinley View Lodge**, George Parks Highway, Trapper Creek, 733-1555. Unbeatable views, $75 rooms, restaurant (open 8–8), keepers who know the area history.

**Denali Viewpoint** (Mile 135.2)—One of the best southern views of the mountain is found here, in part because the Denali State Park stretch of the Parks Highway is the closest highway approach to the summit—as close as the national park road.

**Troublesome Creek State Campground and Trailhead** (Mile 137.3)—The campground has 10 $6 sites near this lovely, clear stream. The Troublesome Creek Trail can also be accessed at Mile 137.6 (see Denali State Park, below, for details).

**Byers Lake State Campground** (Mile 147)—Black bears are common here. There is trail access around Byers Lake to the Troublesome Creek/Kesugi Ridge trail system. 66 sites, $12.

**Alaska Veterans Memorial** (Mile 147.2)—A nice location for a deserved monument.

**Denali View North State Campground** (Mile 162.5)—Twenty sites, short trail, and nice views.

**Little Coal Creek Trailhead** (Mile 163.8)—This is the north end of the state park trail system that includes **Troublesome Creek Trail, Kesugi Ridge Trail**, and **Byers Lake Trail** (see Denali State Park, below, for details).

**Hurricane Gulch** (Mile 174)—Stop at the south end of the bridge and find the unmarked trail on the east side of the road that leads along the gulch edge. The bridge is 550 feet above Hurricane Creek.

**The Igloo** (Mile 188.5)—You can't miss it, though you can easily live without it. Services here.

**Sourdough Paul's Bed and Breakfast** (Mile 193), Cantwell, 768-2020. Finnish sauna, full breakfast, Denali view, northern lights (winter).

**Broad Pass** (Mile 195 to Mile 210, 2,300' elevation)—This long, wide basin is largely unforested, affording marvelous views of the Alaska Range to the northwest, the Talkeetnas to the southeast, and "the great one"—if it's out. Watch for wildlife and photo ops.

**Cantwell** (Mile 209.9)—The little town of Cantwell (population 145, 22.4 percent native) sits at the north end of Broad Pass where the Nenana River curves north and cuts through the Alaska Range. Highway services are available around the intersection of the Parks and Denali Highways. The Cantwell Road heads west 2 miles to the actual settlement, located along the Alaska Railroad tracks. The annual Cantwell Music Festival, generally scheduled the first weekend after July 4, offers a small, enjoyable and very Alaskan weekend.

**Cantwell Lodge** (Mile 209.9), 768-2300, old-town Cantwell at train tracks (2 miles west of Mile 209.9), Cantwell. $75 and up. Roadhouse style in town, cafe, bar, liquor store, basic at best.

**Denali Highway Junction** (Mile 209.9)—Turn east to take the 136-mile route across the high country between the crests of the Alaska and Talkeetna Mountains. See Denali Highway, below, for details.

**Carlo Creek Lodge** (Mile 223.9), HC2 Box 1530, Healy 99743, 683-2576. Creekside cabins $75–$95, RV and tent sites $11 and up, store. Some very nice wooded sites.

**The Perch** (Mile 224), Healy, AK 99743, 683-2523. The closest thing to fine dining near Denali, serving breakfast, lunch, and dinner daily in summer. Cabins available year-round, $65–$95. Call for winter dining hours.

**Rick Swenson's Carlo Heights B&B** (Mile 224.1), 683-1615. Also a sled-dog school! Rick is an Iditarod champion.

**McKinley Village Resort** (Mile 231.1), 241 West Ship Creek Avenue, Anchorage, 99504, (800) 276-7234, 276-7234. One of Aramark's two big Denali resorts. Many bus tourists. Rooms $165–$200.

**Denali River Cabins** (Mile 231.1), (800) 230-7275, 683-2500. Cabins, lodge, and restaurant on the Nenana River. Crowded but nice, $150 and up.

**Denali National Park and Preserve Entrance** (Mile 237.3)— Turn west into the park. The visitor center, hotel, and entrance campgrounds are all within 3 miles (see below).

**McKinley Park** (Mile 238 to Mile 239)—See below.

**Healy** (Mile 248 to Mile 251)—See below.

**Anderson Road Junction: Clear and Anderson** (Mile 283.5)— **Anderson** (population 626, 3.7 percent native) is a small community situated on the banks of the Nenana River. Closer to the highway are the gates of the **Clear Missile Early Warning Station,** an active military installation. Both are reached by a westbound road that meets the Parks Highway at Mile 283.5. Clear is worth a peek at the gate, but that's all you'll get. Sleepy Anderson offers little more, except when the town comes alive the last weekend in July for the annual Anderson Bluegrass Festival. The large **Riverside Park,** where the festival is held, is good for picnicking and camping. Tent and RV sites are $10, $12 with hook-ups. P.O. Box 3100, Anderson, AK 99744, 582-2500.

**Nenana** (Mile 304.5)—See chapter 14.

**Monderosa** (Mile 308.9), Nenana, 832-5243. Known far and wide as the place to get delicious, big burgers and more.

**George Parks Monument** (344.2)—There's a viewpoint here as well.

**Ester Junction** (Mile 351.7)—See Fairbanks, chapter 14.

**Fairbanks City Limit** (Mile 356)—See chapter 14.

# TALKEETNA

*Location/Climate:* At confluence of Susitna, Chulitna, and Talkeetna Rivers, 80 air miles north of Anchorage. 4°F–68°F.
*Population:* 330 (1.6 percent native).
*Travel Attractions:* Base for Denali climbs, flightseeing, Denali-region drop-offs, rafting, charming town.
*Getting There:* Scheduled rail service from Anchorage and Fairbanks; vehicle access via George Parks Highway and Talkeetna Road.
*Information:* Talkeetna/Denali Visitor Center, Talkeetna Spur Road at Mile 99 Parks Highway (AK 2), Talkeetna, AK, (800) 660-2688, 733-2688, www.alaskan.com/talkeetnadenali, open 8 to 8 daily in summer.

Talkeetna is one of my favorite Alaskan destinations. Resist the urge to speed past the extra miles of the Talkeetna Spur Road on your way to Denali or Anchorage. Located at the confluence of three rivers—the Talkeetna, Chulitna, and Susitna—the town is the traditional base for mountaineering expeditions to the Denali massif. If you visit in May or June, you're likely to meet wild-eyed, sunburned climbers with stories to tell. It can be a bit awkward to elbow into the unique camaraderie of climbers, but they are, in my experience, universally nice folks.

Talkeetna is charming. Main Street features cafes, shops, and a handful of motels; B&Bs are scattered about, and a town campground is right on the river.

## Things to See and Do in Talkeetna

**Denali Flightseeing**—The trips offered by Talkeetna companies can't be beat. Four companies operate from the Talkeetna airport just south of town: **K2 Aviation, Doug Geeting Aviation, Hudson Air Service,** and **Talkeetna Air Taxi.** Each has offices at the airport, in town, or along the Talkeetna Spur Road (see appendix). Prices are usually based on a per-person rate for groups of a certain size. All are good.

**Museum of Northern Adventure**—An enjoyable mix of Alaskana can be found at this easy museum, located in the renovated, 70-year-old Alaska Railroad building. Check out the life-size wax dioramas. There's also a gift shop. Main Street, Talkeetna, 733-3999. Open in summer daily 11 a.m. to 7 p.m.; and in winter, afternoons and by request; $3.50.

**River Trip**—Whether by powerboat, raft, kayak, or canoe, the three-river junction at Talkeetna lends itself to some great trips (see the appendix for guides and outfitters).

**Talkeetna Historical Society Museum**—Don't miss the 144-square-foot scale model of the Denali massif or the climbing displays in the old railroad Section House. There is also an old one-room schoolhouse with heritage displays, and an early trapper's cabin. The museum is dedicated to bush-pilot legend Don Sheldon and mountaineer extraordinaire Ray Genet—both long-time Talkeetna residents. One block south of Main Street, just west of Talkeetna Spur Road (Airstrip Road), 733-2487. Open daily in summer 10 a.m. to 5 p.m., call in winter; $1.

## Where to Stay in Talkeetna
**Latitude 62°**, Mile 14 Talkeetna Spur Road, 733-2262. Motel, restaurant, bar. Rooms $50 and up.

**Swiss-Alaska Inn**, East Talkeetna (by boat launch, look for signs), 733-2424. $80–$110. A quiet motel with retaurant. Breakfast, lunch, and dinner.

**Talkeetna Motel**, P.O. Box 115, Talkeetna, AK 99676, 733-2323. Motel, restaurant, bar. Rooms $65–$100.

**Talkeetna Roadhouse**, Main Street, 733-1351. Rooms $50–$100, hostel bunks for $21. A Talkeetna fixture. Classic roadhouse and restaurant; homemade bread; good food, music, and company. **RH**

**Three Rivers Accommodations** (books several unhosted homes and cabins), Three Rivers Building, Main Street, 733-2741. Can match custom lodging to needs, interests, and budget.

## Where to Eat in Talkeetna
**The Deli**, Main Street. The only pizza in town—and it's good.

**Sparky's**, Main Street, 733-1414. Sandwiches, ice cream.

## Petersville Road
If you're ambitious, turn west at Mile 115 of the Parks Highway and head down Petersville Road to the mining area around Petersville, located in the foothills of the Alaska Range below Denali. The road winds through the forested, swampy flats of the Chulitna basin and is maintained as far as the Forks Roadhouse at Mile 18.7. Beyond

this point, four-wheel drive is generally recommended and the road is not plowed in winter. Homesteads and a few small subdivisions are found along the way.

If you can get in as far as the mines, you'll be a rugged hike away from the Kahlitna Glacier and the remote southern reaches of Denali National Park and Preserve. Inquire at the Talkeetna Visitor Information Center or in Trapper Creek about conditions and options. Respect all trespassing and private property signs in the mining area.

For food and lodging on the Petersville Road, try **Forks Roadhouse**, Mile 18.7 Petersville Road in Trapper Creek. This historic roadhouse offers a bar, meals, and lodging, 733-1851. Dorm bunks $25, rooms $45, cabins $60.

## DENALI STATE PARK

*Location/Size:* On either side of George Parks Highway (AK 3) north of Talkeetna, southeast of Denali National Park and Preserve. 325, 460 acres.
*Main Activities:* Fishing, hunting, backpacking, hiking, camping.
*Gateway Towns/Getting There:* Trapper Creek/vehicle access via Parks Highway (AK 3), small-plane air access. Park access by vehicle via George Parks Highway (AK 3); foot access via roadside trailheads.
*Facilities, Camping, Lodging:* Veterans Memorial, viewpoint. Three roadside campgrounds, primitive camping elsewhere.
*Headquarters and Information:* MatSu Area Office, HC 32 Box 6706, Wasilla, AK 99687, 745-3975, www.dnr.state.ak.us/parks/units/denali1.htm.

The views of Denali and the Alaska Range are of particular interest to travelers in Denali State Park. The long, low **Kesugi Ridge** separates the Parks Highway and the Chulitna valley to the west from the Susitna valley—path of the Alaska Railroad—to the east. A ridgetop trail is accessible from four trailheads along the road. There is also access to the old observation tower on Curry Ridge —once a popular train stop. The trail is about 42 miles long, a good four- to six-day backpack route.

The portion of the park west of the Chulitna is essentially a lowland extension of Denali National Park. Much of the area is boggy, cut by several streams and rivers, and is difficult to access directly. Beyond the flats, an arm of the park reaches westward into

the **Peters Hills,** a good destination for ridge walking, foothills access, and splendid views of the Denali massif. The hills are reached via Petersville Road (see above), though the road doesn't enter the park.

The Parks Highway follows the east bank of the Chulitna River through most of the state park, affording drivers and cyclists marvelous westward views of the Alaska Range and Denali. The best road viewpoint is near Mary Carey's McKinley View Lodge at Mile 135.2. If you opt to hike up to Kesugi Ridge, you'll earn the best view in the park.

## Trails in Denali State Park

The following trails are all interconnected. It is best to think of them as one long route with two cutoffs in the middle:

**Byers Lake Trail** (5-mile loop, no gain; 7 miles to ridge, 1,500' gain)—From the campground, the lake loop trail provides access to fishing spots. A spur climbs from the northeast end of the lake to a junction with the Kesugi Ridge Trail. Loop trail—3 hrs; **RT** to ridge—all day.

**Ermine Hill Trail** (about 5 miles, 1,000' gain)—This brand new trail will allow access to the ridge trail and to small Ermine Lake. Inquire for details. **RT**—unknown.

**Kesugi Ridge Trail** (23 miles, 1,200' drop and gain in gap)— This includes the length of trail from the north end of the ridge to the Byers Lake Trail junction. It links the top of the Coal Creek Trail with the Troublesome Creek Trail. Kesugi Ridge is largely tundra-covered, with a few easy summits and a broad, gentle crest. Outstanding views! Through trail—2–3 days (4–6 days for entire route).

**Little Coal Creek Trail** (4 miles to the ridge, 1,800' gain)— The trail climbs quickly to the crest of Kesugi Ridge and the Kesugi Ridge Trail above the north bank of Little Coal Creek. **RT** to ridge—5–7 hours.

**Troublesome Creek Trail** (15 miles, 2,000')—Named for the habits of the black bears along its length, this trail follows the stream closely for several miles before cutting up to the open, pond-dotted ridge top. At the junction with the Byers Lake Trail, the route becomes the Kesugi Ridge Trail. **RT**—2–3 days; through trail to Byers Lake trailhead—2 days; through trail to Little Coal Creek trailhead—4–6 days.

# DENALI NATIONAL PARK AND PRESERVE

*Location/Size:* Central Alaska in the heart of the Alaska Range. Park and preserve, 6 million acres; wilderness, 1.9 million acres.

*Main Activities:* Mountaineering, hiking, wildlife viewing, rafting, wilderness exploration, flightseeing, backcountry lodging, photography.

*Gateway Towns/Getting There:* Denali Park/vehicle access via George Parks Highway (AK 3), scheduled rail service, and regular small-plane air service from Anchorage and Fairbanks. Park access: vehicle access via Denali Park Road (first 15 miles without permit); shuttle and tour-bus access via Denali Park Road from Denali Park or visitor center; charter or air-taxi access to several points; foot access from air drops, Park Road, George Parks Highway, Healy, Cantwell, and Petersville Road.

*Facilities, Camping, Lodging:* Main visitor center, park hotel, headquarters, sled-dog kennel, Eielson visitor center, rest areas, viewpoints, short trail system, airstrips, rail station, stores and gas, post office, administration and maintenance, remote research and ranger stations. Roadside campgrounds with reservable sites, walk-in campground, concessionaire hotel, private lodgings in Kantishna, private rental cabin in Don Sheldon Amphitheater.

*Headquarters and Information:* Headquarters, P.O. Box 9, Mile 3 Denali Park Road, Denali Park, AK, 99755, 683-2294, www.nps.gov/dena; Visitor Center, Mile 1 Denali Park Road, 683-2290. Reservations, (800) 622-7275; park weather, (800) 472-0391.

The crown jewel of Alaskan parks is Denali. Hundreds of thousands of visitors come every year to observe wildlife and get close to "the great one." Prospector William Dickey named the peak Mount McKinley in honor of presidential nominee William McKinley, whose subsequent assassination gave the name staying power. The original park was created in 1917, the boundaries of which now demark the designated wilderness area within the larger park and preserve. The first park superintendent was Henry Karstens—an early Alaska pioneer and member of the first party to climb the true summit (south peak). About 3,000 climbers have since reached the summit. In 1980 the park was expanded through ANILCA and officially renamed.

The potential for experience here is huge: Perhaps you'll ride your bike over a rise on the park road and suddenly see an 800-pound grizzly dismembering a moose calf as the distraught mother moans from a hillock nearby. Perhaps you'll climb through the

drizzle to a ridgecrest, only to have the wind kick up, the clouds shred, a rainbow break over the tundra, and Denali suddenly appear from the swirling wrack like a god from the mists, knocking you to your seat and filling your eyes with tears.

Or maybe you'll ride for seven tedious hours on a bus with complaining tourists and a disinterested driver, seeing one bear a mile away through a tiny window blocked by clacking cameras and peering heads, with never a glimpse of the mountain. The potential for wonder is matched easily by the real chance of a bust. Nowhere in the state can you find a greater concentration of disappointed travelers than at Denali Park during a week of rain. Don't get caught in the trap of dependency and expectation!

It pays to treat the park as a mystery. If you are blessed by a view of the mountain in full sunshine regalia, that's wonderful. If you spot a trio of Dall sheep rams munching the grass as you round a rocky point, great. If a pack of wolves crosses the road as you watch from an overlook, outstanding. But if not, be ready to invent your own wonders from all of the amazing wildlands and wildlife that don't show up in tour-brochure photos. Get off the bus and into the hills. Let your independent spirit stand tall in the face of a tourist-shuffling routine that can smother and deflate.

The visitor center, Denali Park Hotel, Alaska Railroad Station, Riley Creek and Morino Campgrounds, park airstrip, gas station, store, restaurants, bar, and post office are all within walking distance of each other between Mile 0.2 and Mile 1.6 of Park Road—just in from Mile 237.3 of the Parks Highway. Park headquarters and the dog kennel are further up at Mile 3.5.

Free shuttle buses run very frequently between the national park center and the hotels in the tourist enclaves of McKinley Park and McKinley Village.

Paul Otteson

*A ridge above the Toklat*

## Rules, Regulations, and Reality

Denali is a park where the details of bureaucracy matter. Look among the following selections for issues that apply to you.

**Backcountry Camping Permits**—The area on either side of Denali Park Road is parceled out into "units" of 100 square miles or so, each of which can only be used by one or two small parties of backcountry campers on a given night. Permits are issued on a first come, first served basis, no more than one day in advance of your intended starting day (for example, Monday morning for a Tuesday first camping night).

You may find your hoped-for unit taken when your tur comes—even if you are the first in line. Your chosen unit may have been booked by someone who filed an itinerary a week earlier and will be hitting that unit on the sixth day of their trip—the same day you wanted it. Some units are closed due to wildlife activity. It pays to be very flexible about where you will camp and what route you'll take. As you might expect, certain units are more popular than others—the very ones you might want the most will generally be the hardest to get.

Permits are free for the asking and are obtained at the visitor center. Rangers will provide a bear-proof food container that should be used as instructed. You should easily get a $16 seat on a camper bus for the ride to your drop-off spot (see below). Those intending extended backcountry treks, mountain approaches, and range crossings where the availability of certain units is essential should consult the chief ranger at 683-2294.

**Camper or Backpacker Buses**—Some of the shuttle buses serving the park road are designated for those spending a night or more in a campground or the backcountry. Camper bus rides currently cost $16—about half the price of shuttle buses. The difference between the two is that the camper buses don't stop for viewing along the way, instead they take campers directly to their chosen drop-offs—though most camper-bus drivers won't pass up a good bear sighting. When you come out of the wilds, you can return to civilization on any shuttle.

Camper bus tickets are obtained when you get your backcountry permit or campground reservation, but no more than one day in advance.

**Campground Reservations**—Every campsite open to vehicles is available by reservation and all typically sell out for most of the

# Campsite Information

| | Park Rd. Milepost | Number Sites | Vehicles Allowed | Advance Reservations |
|---|---|---|---|---|
| Riley Creek | 0.5 | | 102 | Yes |
| | All Sites | | | |
| Morino | 1.5 (hike-in) | 60 | No | No |
| Savage River | 12 | 34 | Yes | All Sites |
| Sanctuary River | 22 | | 7 | No |
| | No | | | |
| Teklanika River | 29 | 50 | *Yes | All Sites |
| Igloo Creek | 34 | 7 | No | No |
| Wonder Lake | 85 | 28 | No | All Sites |

*Visitors staying at Teklanika are permitted to drive 14 miles past the road-closed point, but must book at least a three-day stay and cannot drive back out any more than once for every three days of that stay. Other campgrounds beyond Mile 15 must be reached by camper bus.

season. Reservations are not accepted within five days of intended campsite use. All remaining and non-vehicle campsites must be booked at the visitor center, no more than two days in advance. Call (800) 622-7275 or 272-7275 to reserve.

**Mountaineering Permits**—About 1,200 people try for the summit of Denali or take other major routes in the massif every year. Denali routes require registration and the purchase of a $150 permit. You must complete the process at least 60 days prior to your climb and file an itinerary with the ranger. If you are climbing with a guide, make sure they are taking care of this on your behalf. Contact the Talkeetna Mountaineering Center at 733-2231.

**Photography Permits**—Professional photographers are issued a limited number of permits allowing them to drive their vehicles the full length of the Park Road. Unambiguous credentials are required. Contact the chief ranger at 683-2294.

**Road Lottery**—Each fall, at the end of the tourist season but before Park Road closes, a few hundred lucky drivers get a permit to drive beyond the 15-mile limit and as far as they care to into the park. Permits are issued via lottery, the deadline for which is usually in August. Call the rangers at 683-2294 for details if you want to give it a shot.

**Shuttle Buses**—Since almost all private vehicles are forbidden past Mile 15 of the 91-mile Park Road, most visitors take a shuttle bus or tour into the park.

Denali buses are a grade above school buses and can be uncomfortable for anyone who is too tall or suffers from being cramped. They travel slowly, stopping for wildlife viewing—and with 30 or 40 pairs of high-riding eyes scanning the landscape, your chances of seeing moose and caribou are excellent. Bears are commonly seen, but one bus may see 20, the next two. Not rarely, the count is zero. Dall sheep are typically spotted at great distance. Wolves are a rare prize. You are not allowed to get off the bus to view wildlife when it is spotted near the road, but can get off at all other points and catch another bus going in either direction. Smart visitors get off and enjoy a day hike somewhere along the way. Make sure you know when the last inbound bus will pass your chosen pick-up point. Put goodies and fluids in your daypack since there are no refreshment options on the way.

Possibly 65 percent of shuttle bus seats are available for advance reservations at (800) 622-7275. Most sell out. Advance reservations are no longer taken within five days of intended use. Remaining seats are made available two days ahead of time (for example, Monday morning for a Wednesday shuttle ride), by phone and at the visitor center. Use the phone since getting to and from the visitor center and waiting in line there can take up a fair chunk of time.

Buses travel one of four varying distances up the park road and tickets are priced accordingly:

| Destination | Adult fare |
|---|---|
| Toklat/Polychrome | $12.50 |
| Eielson | $21 |
| Wonder Lake | $27 |
| Kantishna | $31 |

**Tour Buses**—These operate much like the shuttle buses with some key differences. Tour buses are more expensive, they depart from the hotels and not the visitor center, and they are narrated by a guide. You can choose from their Natural History Tour (half day, about $35) or Wildlife Tour (all day, about $65, includes box lunch), though both cover the same topics and look for wildlife. You cannot get off the buses at all except at designated rest areas. There's no day-hike option with these. Note that the Natural History Tour goes only a little farther up the road than private vehicles are permitted to go, making bear sightings unlikely. The Wildlife Tour goes only to Toklat River, 53 miles into the park, and does not reach Wonder Lake.

Aramark (Denali Park Resorts) runs the tours. Call (800) 276-7234 or 276-7234 for advance reservations. On the day of the tour, remaining tickets are available by calling the Denali Park Hotel at 683-2215. Be aware that many of the shuttle- and camper-bus drivers are quite informative and answer questions—narrative is not necessarily exclusive to tour buses. Let's face it, the tours are intended for those whose days of active exploration are behind them (or never arrived).

## The Denali Park Road

Whether by bus, bike, foot, or private vehicle, most visitors to Denali explore the park via Park Road. The 91-mile route follows a series of outwash lowlands, river valleys, and ridge flanks, paralleling the northern slopes of the Alaska Range south of a mixed set of hills, ridges, and low peaks. Campgrounds, rest areas, and designated viewpoints bead the park road from the park headquarters to road's end at Kantishna. Your park map will provide some details on mileage and highlights. The **Eielson Visitor Center** at Mile 66 offers water, restrooms, film, maps, information, and a good mountain viewpoint.

Wildlife of all sorts is commonly seen on the route, while mountain viewpoints are found in several spots. If touring by bus, the driver will have the latest information on wildlife activity while the collective eyes of the passengers guarantee good spotting. If driving or cycling, talk to rangers before hitting the road. Watch for the stopped buses and photographer caravans that indicate the presence of wildlife. Stop frequently and scan the land with binoculars. Look for grizzlies everywhere, but particularly around Sable Mountain, Sable Pass, and the Toklat River.

Endless day-hike possibilities exist along river bars, across open tundra, and up ridges—though areas are sometimes posted as closed due to wildlife-related considerations. While the only official trails are found near the park entrance, a few routes are commonly used and feature clear, beaten paths (Primrose Ridge is a nice route close to parking at Mile 15). The best access to good ridge walks is near Savage River, Polychrome Pass, and Toklat River, though nowhere are hills and low ridges far from the road.

The closest approach to the mountain is near the end of the road, above McKinley Bar and at the classically photogenic **Wonder Lake**. If the mountain is "out," you can enjoy some time in a living post-card, the lake at your feet and the great one in the background.

### Kantishna

At the very end of the park road is the old mining district of Kantishna. Several fine backcountry lodges are located on private land inclusions within the park boundary. Each offers accommodations to travelers desiring close access to Wonder Lake and Denali views, as well as opportunities for comfortable solitude. All are very expensive, though prices include round-trip ground transport (with sightseeing) to the town of McKinley Park, the Denali airstrip, or Alaska Railroad station. Meals are included, as is use of recreational equipment and optional guided activities.

**Camp Denali**, P.O. Box 67, Denali National Park, AK 99755, 683-2290. Three-night minimum, $975 per person (three nights). The nicest of the bunch though more rustic than partner North Face. Cabins on hill have best Denali views. Evening programs. **BL**

**Denali Backcountry Lodge**, P.O. Box 189, Denali Park, AK 99755, (800) 841-0692, 683-2594, winter 783-1342. $300 double, two-night minimum stay. Located in the valley along Moose Creek; hiking paths; nice cabins, though bunched together. **BL**

**North Face Lodge**, P.O. Box 67, Denali National Park, AK 99755, 683-2290. $325 per night with a two-might mimimun. Rustic plush, Denali views (lower than Camp Denali), partnered with Camp Denali, evening programs. **BL**

**Kantishna Roadhouse**, P.O. Box 81670, Fairbanks, AK 99708, (800) 942-7420, 479-2436. $280 per night, two-night minimum

Paul Otteson

*Camping above Ruth Glacier*

stay. On Moose Creek, features preserved original roadhouse, nice cabins, very nice lodge. **BL**

## Ruth Glacier

Planet Earth offers plenty of wonders to those who seek them, but a special few top the list as utterly extraordinary.

So it is with a trip by plane from Talkeetna, up the 25-mile length of **Ruth Glacier**, through the stunning **Great Gorge** with sheer walls rising 5,000 feet to ragged summits, and into the **Don Sheldon Amphitheater**—a 25-square-mile icefield fed by a half dozen glaciers. Conditions permitting, pilots will land in the amphitheater and let you step out and explore this utterly extraordinary place.

Better yet, stay in this wilderness of ice for a few days, as a camper or mountaineer, or in the reservable **Don Sheldon Mountain House** that's perched on a narrow ridge between glaciers. When the plane departs, this land of ice comes alive. Avalanches, small and large, tumble from the peaks. The sense of the gradual movement of the great glaciers is palpable, though impossible to observe. A hike onto the ice gives you a sense of scale, as well as access to the edge of crevasses that could easily swallow you.

Most of all, when the frequent fog and clouds clear for a time, the southern flank of Denali presides over all and you're closer than most people ever get.

The tiny, one-room Mountain House is reservable by calling Roberta Sheldon at Alaska Retreat (733-2414), but is often booked solid a year in advance. You must carry almost all supplies with you. Remember that there is always the risk that weather will keep the planes from flying and you'll lose your slot. On the other hand, you may get an extra day because your pick-up flight can't reach the landing zone. Spending a couple of days in the Don Sheldon Mountain House is my top choice in Alaska.

## Other Access

Besides the park road and the usual remote air drop-off possibilities, a couple of access options are worth noting. At Mile 251.1 of the Parks Highway, **Stampede Road** heads west through a thumb of non-park land, becoming decreasingly drivable until most vehicles must park about 8 miles in. The road/trail can be followed another 40 miles or so, as far as the Toklat River and beyond to the Stampede Landing Strip. Hiking is possible to the ridges north of Park Road, as well as through the valleys of the Savage, Teklanika, and Toklat Rivers. Few come this way.

Several points of access are possible along the Parks Highway, from Cantwell or Broad Pass into the valleys that drain the Alaska Range. A couple of old mining trails suggest the beginnings of possible routes, but all options involve raw exploration with no established trails or facilities. Similar rough routes can be devised via the **Dutch Hills** at the end of Petersville Road, including access to 45-mile-long Kahlitna Glacier and others that spill from the southern flank of the Denali massif. Respect all posted mining claims.

### Where to Stay and Eat in Denali

**Denali Park Hotel** (one of Aramark's three Denali Park Resorts hotels), Mile 1.5 Park Road, (800) 276-7234, 683-9214. Not a classic, Yellowstone-style park lodge. Okay rooms, snack bar, Spike Bar.

## MCKINLEY PARK (THE TOWN)

*Location/Climate:* On George Parks Highway 1 mile north of Denali National Park and Preserve entrance. 12"/yr. precip., -22°F–72°F.
*Population:* 200 (2.9 percent native), much larger in summer.
*Travel Attractions:* Access to Denali National Park and Preserve, rafting, hiking, flightseeing, tours, backcountry lodge access, travel services.
*Getting There:* Scheduled train service and van and bus shuttles from Anchorage and Fairbanks; vehicle access via George Parks Highway.
*Information:* Inquire with local businesses.

A mile north of the Denali National Park and Preserve entrance road is McKinley Park (sometimes called Denali Park)—the main area of services for park visitors. Big and small hotels, gift shops, and a few restaurants and stores are strung out along the road.

Buses of various sorts share parking space with RVs and smaller vehicles. Tourists, backpackers, and seasonal employees walk the road shoulders between sites. Nowhere in the state is there a more concentrated area of travel, tour, and seasonal employment activity.

The chief businesses of McKinley Park are certainly the **Lynx Creek Store**, mainly because it boasts the only gas pumps in town, and the wonderful **Lynx Creek Pub**, offering an outside deck, microbrews on tap, and unusually good pizza. It's a favorite hangout for seasonal workers, as well as for grubby mountaineers who want beer and pizza after an attempt on a frozen summit.

Bus and rail tourists arrive by the hundreds to stay in Aramark's **McKinley Chalets** or Princess Cruise Line's **Denali Princess Lodge**, both of which offer fine restaurants. RVers and car travelers fill the other lodges, cabins, B&Bs, and RV parks in July and August. Primitive, free camping options are accessible off the Parks Highway toward Healy to those with an experienced eye.

Several diversions are available, including half a dozen bars and restaurants, raft trips, helicopter flightseeing, occasional live music, primitive trails, and a 10-minute walk to wilderness. Most businesses can connect you with tours, lodging, shuttles, and advice. The **Northern Lights Photo Symphony** offers splendid multimedia presentations on the aurora borealis or Denali National Park, as well as a gift shop. It's across from McKinley Chalet Resort (683-4000, $7). The **Alaska Cabin Night Dinner Theater** offers two hokey melodrama shows a night with family-style meals at the McKinley Chalets (800-276-7234 or 276-7234, $40).

Note that McKinley Park closes up almost completely in the winter when it's home only to a skeleton hotel-maintenance staff. Cantwell and Healy are the closest year-round settlements.

## Where to Stay and Eat in McKinley Park

**Denali Crow's Nest**, above road on east side, Denali Park, 683-2723. $100–$150 cabins. Great views over Nenana River valley, **Overlook Bar & Grill**.

**Denali Princess Lodge**, Parks Highway, Denali Park, AK 99755, (800) 426-0500, rail tours 835-8907. Restaurant, bar. $140–$280 rooms.

**Lynx Creek Pub,** Parks Highway, Denali Park, 683-2547. Great pizza and brews, good Mexican food.

**McKinley Chalet Resort** (one of Aramark's three Denali Park Resorts), (800) 276-7234. Okay rooms $130–$200, restaurant.

**McKinley/Denali Salmon Bake,** Parks Highway, Denali Park, 683-2733. Typical salmon bake, paper plates, breakfasts. Tent-style cabins $70, regular cabins $110.

**Sourdough Cabins,** Parks Highway, Denali Park, (800) 354-6020, 683-2773. Nice cabins in the trees, not too close to each other, $90–$150.

## HEALY

*Location/Climate: On Nenana River, 11 miles north of Denali National Park and Preserve entrance on George Parks Highway. 12"/yr. precip., -22°F–72°F.*
*Population: 605 (1.4 percent native).*
*Travel Attractions: Alaska Range and Denali National Park and Preserve access, rafting, flightseeing.*
*Getting There: Vehicle access via George Parks Highway and bus and van shuttles; charter air.*
*Information: Inquire with local businesses, www.alaska.net/~denst1/ healy.chamber.html.*

You'd never know it by looking at it, but Healy is Alaska's wealthiest town and one of the richest in the country—the median household income is close to $60,000. This is due to the Usebelli Coal Mine, currently the only commercial coal mine in Alaska—though that could change since Alaska has huge coal reserves. Healy has gotten yet another boost with the construction of the $267 million state-of-the-art Healy Clean Coal Plant, completed in 1998. The Denali North Star Inn, located west of the road at Mile 248.8 of the Parks Highway, was moved in pieces to Healy from Prudhoe Bay, then rebuilt to house the construction crews.

Take the **Otto Lake Road** 1 mile west from Mile 247 of the Parks Highway to reach this small lake with camping, fishing, and swimming. There are also B&Bs, a youth hostel, foothills access, and a driving range. At Mile 248.8 of the Parks, **Healy Road** leads

east past the store and community center, and down to the rail tracks, airstrip, and Nenana River. Across the bridge is restricted access to the coal mine, but also the 8-mile **Sultrana Road**, which leads to mining ruins along Healy Creek, good free camping sites, and access to the forgotten Alaska Range east of Denali.

Healy offers all highway services, including car and tire repair, and is the main support town in the Denali region.

## Where to Stay and Eat in Healy

**Denali Dome Home Bed-and-Breakfast**, Healy Spur Road, 683-1239. Rooms are $90 and have private baths. Interesting geodesic structure, nicely kept and run.

**McKinley RV and Campground**, Mile 248.5 Parks Highway (AK 2), 683-2379. Sites are $18 (tents) and $29 (hookups). One of the nicer RV options around, with tentsites available.

**Stampede Lodge**, Mile 248.8 Parks Highway (AK 2), (800) 478-2370, 683-2242. Historic lodge and restaurant. Rooms $65–$90.

**Totem Inn**, Mile 248.7 George Parks Highway (AK 2), 683-2384. $60–$115 summer, $45–$90 winter, simpler rooms $40. Bar, restaurant, northern lights viewing dome (winter). The chief place in Healy for eating and meeting. **RH**

## DENALI HIGHWAY (AK 8)

*Road Conditions and Attractions—135 miles. Twenty-one miles at the east end are paved; the rest is graded gravel that can be rough, pot-holed, washboarded, muddy, or partially washed out in spots. Treeless high country with views, river and backcountry access, wildlife viewing, backcountry lodging, and solitude.*

Stretching 136 miles from Cantwell to Paxson, the mostly gravel Denali Highway crosses the wide, wild land south of the central Alaska Range. Before the Parks Highway was completed in 1971, all vehicle-dependent visitors to Denali came via the Richardson Highway to Paxson, across the Denali Highway to Cantwell, and up to the park entrance. Today this upcountry route is used by more-intrepid explorers, including hunters seeking backcountry access.

This is one of my favorite Alaskan roads. Three free BLM campgrounds and numerous roadside turnouts offer primitive bases from which to walk into the wild country with will, water, granola bars, compass, and map. The land is largely administered by the BLM and is open to unlimited exploration. There are several small trails leading off to lakes and fishing spots. Most of the route is between 3,000 and 4,000 feet in elevation. It pays to carry the *Alaska Atlas & Gazetteer* or other detailed maps since few of the many off-road options are marked along the highway.

The road is closed for much of the winter. Inquire about conditions before venturing forth, and make sure you are gassed up and supplied with emergency items—especially very early or late in the season.

**Paxson** (Mile 0)—See Richardson Highway, below.

**Tangle Lakes Archaeological District** (Mile 17 to Mile 35)— More than 400 archaeological sites have been identified within this 226,000-acre area, some with signs of human activity dating back 10,000 years. Restrictions are few within the district, though critical sites are off-limits to ATVs in the summer. For information, contact the BLM office in Glenallen (822-3217, see appendix).

**Tangle River Inn** (Mile 20), Paxson, 822-3970, 895-4022 (winter), $45 and up. Gas, cafe, motel, bar, showers, store, canoe rental, RV hook-ups. **RH**

**Tangle Lakes BLM Campground** (Mile 21.2), ¾ mile north of road on lakeshore. Access to **Delta River Canoe Trail** (see below).

**Tangle River BLM Campground** (Mile 21.7), access to **Upper Tangle Lakes Canoe Trail**.

**Tangle Lakes Lodge** (Mile 22), 822-4202. Good choice for birders. Cabins $65–$150. New restaurant. **BL**

**McLaren Summit** (Mile 35.2, 4,086' elevation)—This divide between the Delta and McLaren River valleys is also the divide between the Yukon and Cook Inlet watersheds.

**McLaren River Road** (Mile 43.3)—Mountain bikers can head

north (12 miles, 200' gain) to the terminus of McLaren Glacier, the closest glacier to the Denali Highway.

**Susitna River Bridge** (Mile 79.3)—Enjoy this one-lane, 1,000-foot bridge. The Susitna flows 260 miles from Susitna Glacier to Cook Inlet. River runners should inquire about Devils Canyon, which is downstream and generally considered unfloatable.

**Gracious House Lodge and Flying Service** (Mile 82), Cantwell, 333-3148, 822-7307. Cabins and motel ($110–$125), some private baths, bar, cafe, tentsites, "cash" gas, tire service. **BL**

**Brushkana River BLM Campground** (Mile 104.6)—Free camping with stream access.

**Nenana River Put-in** (Mile 117.7)—The highway passes very close to the Nenana River for a stretch, offering put-ins for trips that can utilize a variety of take-outs along the George Parks Highway as far as the Nenana-Tanana confluence in Nenana. From there, the Tanana flows to the Yukon, offering one last road's-end take-out at Manley Hot Springs before rolling on to the Bering Sea. Beyond McKinley Park there are Class V stretches unsuitable for canoes. Rentals are possible along the Parks Highway near Denali (see appendix).

**George Parks Highway Junction** (Mile 133.7)—The last two official miles of the Denali Highway lead into the village of Cantwell.

## NATIONAL WILD AND SCENIC RIVERS: DELTA AND GULKANA

True river-running adventure is available on routes that parallel the Richardson Highway, one draining north from the crest of the Alaska Range, the other south. Both the Delta and the Gulkana are administered by the BLM, though the Gulkana passes mainly through state, private, and native lands.

The **Delta River** route starts at the Tangle Lakes Campground at Mile 21.2 of the Denali Highway (AK 8), and flows 30 miles to the most commonly used take-out point at Mile 212.5 of the Richardson Highway. There is one portage around a waterfall and several stretches of Class II rapids; experienced canoeists can handle it if the water's not too high (or low). Scout all rapids before trying them! Adventurers can continue as far as they wish, taking the Delta to the Tanana at Delta Junction, then on to the Yukon and the Bering Sea. See you next month.

The main put-in for the **Gulkana River** is at the Paxson Lake BLM campground at Mile 175 of the Richardson Highway. This beautiful 10-mile lake drains into the main fork of the Gulkana. The first take-out at Sourdough Campground, Mile 147.6 of the Richardson, is about 50 miles from the put-ins.

Contact the BLM before taking either route to get the latest on permits and regulations, as well as current river information: Glenallen District Office, P.O. Box 147, Glenallen, AK 99588, 822-3217.

## CENTRAL RICHARDSON HIGHWAY (AK 4)— GLENALLEN TO DELTA JUNCTION

*Road Conditions and Attractions—150 miles. Good two-lane road with some tight turns, open year-round. Float access, glacier and lake views, historic trail route, Trans-Alaska Pipeline route, Delta Bison Range.*

The central segment of the Richardson offers beautiful scenery in the foothills and uplands of the Alaska Range. Most of the land is BLM-managed with large state and native corporation parcels. The Trans-Alaska Pipeline corridor parallels the highway. The road reaches 3,000 feet at Isabel Pass and is above treeline for many miles, offering great views. Several glaciers come fairly close to the road and are easily seen, though there is no official access beyond highway-turnout viewpoints. The Gulkana and Delta Rivers offer float possibilities (see above), while Alaska's only wild herd of bison may be seen near Delta Junction.

**Glenallen** (Mile 115)—See Glenallen, chapter 8.

**Dry Creek State Recreation Site** (Mile 118)—See Glenallen, chapter 8.

**Gulkana Road** (Mile 126.9)—Turn east here to enter the small, largely Ahtna Athabascan village of **Gulkana** (population 100, 59 percent native). The village was originally on the other side of Cop-

per River where once stood a store, roadhouse, and post office. Gulkana is one of the few largely native settlements close to a main highway. There are no businesses. The village is not oriented toward receiving visitors, but makes an interesting detour.

Gulkana, Gakona, and the road junction are located at the confluence of the Gulkana and Copper Rivers. Rafting the Gulkana is popular, in part due to easy put-ins and take-outs along the Richardson Highway (see the appendix for rafting outfitters).

**Gakona Junction and Tok Cutoff** (Mile 128.6)—See Tok Cutoff, chapter 8.

**Sourdough Creek BLM Campground** (Mile 147.6)—This is a standard take-out for a Gulkana River float that begins at Paxson or Tangle Lakes (see above). The site and several old outbuildings of the Sourdough Roadhouse are next to the creek, close to the old route of the Valdez Trail.

**Paxson Lake BLM Campground** (Mile 175)—Turn here and drive 1.5 miles to the campground. This is a good put-in for a 50-mile Gulkana River float to Sourdough (see above).

**Paxson and Denali Highway (AK 8) Junction** (Mile 185.5)—Here's where the Denali Highway (AK 8) meets the Richardson Highway (AK 4) and little else. Get some gas, grab a bite, stock up, and hit the road—make sure to do *all* of those things if you're taking the Denali Highway to Cantwell.

**Paxson Lodge** (Mile 185.5), Paxson, 822-3330. $60–$80. Rooms, cafe, bar, RV hook-ups, store, gas, airstrip, post office, gift shop, fishing licenses. **RH**

**Summit Lake** (Mile 192 to Mile 197)—This lovely lake sits near the divide between the Delta and Yukon watershed to the north and the Gulkana and Copper watershed to the south. A few B&Bs and a lodge are found near the lake.

**Isabel Pass** (Mile 197.6, 3,000')—It's all downhill from here.

**Fielding Lake State Recreation Site** (Mile 200.4)—Turn west and continue 1½ miles to reach campground with trails to the lake and good fishing.

**Black Rapids Glacier Viewpoint** (Mile 225.4)—To the west you can see the terminus of this 25-mile-long glacier that gathers many smaller glaciers on its way down from icy 12,000- and 13,000-foot summits. Now retreating, in the winter of 1936–37 the glacier "galloped" forward 3 miles, nearly reaching the road.

**Donnelly Creek State Recreation Site** (Mile 237.9)—Twelve $8 sites are located where Donnelly Creek meets the Delta River. Possible take-out for Delta River runs.

**Bison Viewpoint** (Mile 241.3)—There are no guarantees, but there's a fair chance you'll spot bison from wide-view turnouts between here and Delta Junction. (see chapter 14).

**Old Richardson Highway Loop** (Mile 247)—Reconnects with the new road at Mile 257.6. **Donnelly Dome** (3,910')divides the two routes. Access is uncertain; four-wheel drive may be needed.

**Meadows Road and Old Richardson Highway** (Mile 256.7)— Reconnects with new road at Mile 247. Four-wheel drive may be needed.

**Bison Viewpoint** (Mile 262.6)—This spot is one of several good points to browse with the binoculars.

**Delta Junction and Alaska Highway** (Mile 266)—Officially, the Richardson continues on to Fairbanks and the end of the Alaska Highway, but many consider the Delta Junction–Fairbanks stretch to be part of the Alaska Highway. See chapter 14 for Delta Junction and milepost information.

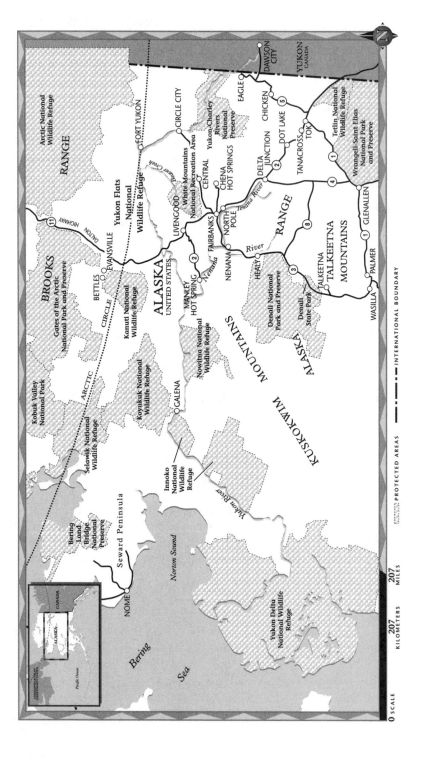

# THE INTERIOR: FAIRBANKS & THE YUKON VALLEY

## 14

The broad band of land north of the Alaska Range and south of the Brooks Range is known simply as "The Interior." The region features several chains of low mountains interspersed by miles of lowland forest and boggy flats. The spruce forest of the taiga predominates in all but the far west, though most of the land above 3,000 feet in elevation is treeless tundra (the treeline drops in elevation as you move north and west).

Most of the Interior is within the watershed of the mighty Yukon River, the fourth longest river on the continent. The Yukon originates in the Canadian coastal mountains, flowing northwest to Dawson City before entering Alaska on its long run to the Bering Sea. Three roads provide access to the Yukon: the Taylor Highway (AK 5) to Eagle in the east, the Steese Highway (AK 6) to Circle north of Fairbanks, and the Dalton Highway (AK 11), which is the only Alaskan road to bridge the river. Numerous small, mainly native settlements are found along the Yukon's shores, most largely dependent upon subsistence wildlife harvesting, native corporation income, and government jobs.

Fairbanks is the Interior's main city and the second largest in the state. Situated on the Tanana (TA-nuh-naw) River, it is a major center of commerce and the primary gateway to all of the Interior and Far North regions. Relatively few package tours visit

285

Fairbanks, but independent travelers benefit from the city's role as a major highway crossroads and air-transport hub.

Travel into the remote regions of the Interior can be expensive and challenging. While there are excellent options for birders, back-country lodges serve mainly hunters and fishers. Few backpackers tackle the challenges of trackless wetland and forest, though several villages and mining towns offer possible bases for ridge routes. More easily accessible recreational options include the Yukon-Charley National Preserve and Fortymile region for river running, the White Mountains for hiking, and the hot springs resorts near Fairbanks for soaking.

Scheduled flights, air drop-offs, or extended river travel are required to reach the Interior's small towns and huge wildlife refuges. Fairbanks or Anchorage are the best bases for such excursions, though Eagle, Circle, Tok, Delta Junction, and other towns offer possibilities. Suggestions are included in the following sections, while specific plans should be developed in consultation with outfitters, pilots, and refuge managers.

## ALASKA HIGHWAY AND RICHARDSON HIGHWAY (AK 2)—CANADA TO FAIRBANKS

*Road Conditions and Attractions*—*300 miles. Good paved road with some old grades and frost heaving, open year-round. Tetlin National Wildlife Refuge, Alaska Public Lands Information Center in Tok, Delta Junction Bison Range, Fairbanks, views of the Wrangells and the Alaska Range.*

Shortly after you enter the state via Port Alcan on the Alaska Highway, the wide basin of the Tanana River watershed opens before you. Enjoy the 100-mile roadside vista to the peaks of the Wrangell Mountains across a completely wild scape. Alaska knows how to say hello while revealing its utter lack of interest in your presence.

After meeting up with the Tanana near its headwaters, road and river stay together all the way to Fairbanks. The peaks of the Alaska Range rise to the south, sometimes at a distance, other times near at hand. The road is fast and easy, traffic is relatively thick, and services are plentiful. Tok and Delta Junction are good places to look for a motel, RV park, or car repair.

Officially, the Alaska Highway ends in Delta Junction where it meets the Richardson Highway. The Richardson follows one of

Alaska's earliest roads—a turn-of-the-century route linking the port of Valdez with the Tanana and Yukon Rivers and the Fairbanks mining country. At Delta Junction, the mileposts change to reflect the road switch. Most travelers fly along both roads en route to Denali or the coast—generally a good approach when time is tight.

**Port AlCan** (Mile 1,221.8)—The border and U.S. Customs station—always open.

**Tetlin National Wildlife Refuge** (Mile 1,221.8–Mile 1,284.2)—See below.

**Northway Junction** (Mile 1,264)—The dispersed community of Northway Junction (population 113, 70 percent native) is located around the highway's junction with Northway Road, which heads south through swamp and lake country to the settlement of **Northway** (population 133, 64 percent native). About 1.5 miles further on is the traditional Athabascan community of **Northway Village** (population 123, 95 percent native), where residents practice a largely subsistence lifestyle, harvesting fish and game from the Tetlin National Wildlife Refuge and native lands. Highway services are available at Northway Junction. Northway is centered around the regional airport.

Historically occupied by Athabascan Indians, Northway was a staging area for operations in World War II. Most employed residents work in transport services, fire fighting, and construction. A drive down the road for a look about the Tetlin flats and Northway Village is an interesting diversion.

**Tetlin Junction** (Mile 1,301.7)—There may be an operating roadhouse here when you arrive, or at least a gas station—though don't count on it. From here, the Taylor Highway heads north to Chicken and Eagle. You can also access the wonderful Top of the World Highway that follows the ridgetops to Dawson City (see Taylor Highway below).

**Tok River State Recreation Site** (Mile 1,309.2)—This small park offers camping, a boat launch, and a nature trail. Campsites are $8.

**Tok and Tok Cutoff Junction** (Mile 1,314.2)—Turn south here to follow the Tok Cutoff (see chapter 8) to the Copper River basin,

the Wrangells, Valdez, or Anchorage. Tok has every visitor service imaginable, but little more (see below).

**Tanacross Road Junction** (Mile 1,325.7)—Turn north for the 2-mile drive into the village of **Tanacross** (population 88, 94 percent native), home to many of the remaining Tanah or Tinneh Athabascan Indians. Across the Tanana River you can see the ruins of the old village that burned in 1979.

**Moon Lake State Recreation Site** (Mile 1,331.9)—Camping and swimming are options here. Sites are $8.

**Cathedral Bluffs** (Mile 1,335 to Mile 1,338)—The Tanana cuts a narrow path between the Alaska Range and hills of the Interior. Use the turnouts and enjoy the views. Beyond this point, much of the forestland to the north is part of the **Tanana Valley State Forest**, while to the south are the undesignated public lands of the Alaska Range. Several valleys and ridges offer pathless access to glaciers and high peaks.

Paul Otteson

*One of many gold dredges seen rusting throughout Alaska's Interior.*

288

**Dot Lake** (Mile 1,361.3)—Highway services are available here. Dot Lake (population 78, 54 percent Athabascan Indian) is the headquarters for the Dot Lake Native Corporation, which encompasses the native inclusions throughout the region.

**Dot Lake Lodge** (Mile 1,361.3), Dot Lake, 882-2691. Year-round camping, food, and gas. Sites $6–$14. **RH**

**Cherokee Lodge & RV Park** (Mile 1,412.5), Delta Junction, 895-4814. Restaurant open year-round 6 a.m.–10 p.m. A classic Alaskan roadhouse; stop if you need a break or a room. **RH**

**Delta Junction Bison Range** (Mile 1,392 to Mile 1,422)—Though bison were common in Alaska at the end of the last ice age, they later disappeared. A few were introduced to the area in 1927 and the herd grew to its current level of about 500 animals. About 90,000 acres south of the Alaska Highway were designated as a refuge in an effort to secure grazing range for the bison while keeping them out of the barley fields across the road. The results have been mixed—a bison that gets a whiff of barley is hard to discourage.

Use binoculars to look for bison along this stretch, as well as at viewing points between Delta Junction and Mile 240 of the Richardson Highway, 25 miles south of town. With the onset of winter, the bison concentrate in a smaller range and are easier to view. A limited number of hunting permits are sold each year.

**Delta Junction and Richardson Highway** (Mile 1,422 Alaska Highway, Mile 266 Richardson Highway)—Turn south here for access to the Denali Highway, the Wrangells, Valdez, and Anchorage (for town information, see Delta Junction, below). This is the official end of the Alaska Highway; the mileposts switch to indicate the distance to Valdez.

**Delta State Recreation Site** (Mile 267.1)—Campsites are $8. River access across the road.

**Big Delta State Historical Park** (Mile 275)—This is a great place to get a good dose of the Alaskan past. **Rika's Roadhouse** has served travelers along the Richardson route since 1910. Rika Wallen ran the roadhouse from 1917 until 1940, and lived there until her death in 1969. There are historic exhibits, a self-guided walking tour, a restaurant and gift shop, and a campground. Just up the road you can stop and inspect the **Trans-Alaska Pipeline Bridge** over the Tanana.

**Quartz Lake State Recreation Area** (Mile 277.7)—Turn northeast here and drive about 3 miles to reach Quartz Lake. Campsites are $8.

**Midway Lodge** (Mile 314.8), 11191 Richardson Highway, Salcha, 488-2939. Rooms $40–$55. Restaurant open daily 7 a.m. to 10 p.m. **RH**

**Harding Lake State Recreation Area** (Mile 321.5)—Turn east here and drive 1.5 miles to a lakeside campground. Sites are $8.

**Salcha River Lodge** (Mile 322.2), 9162 Richardson Highway, Salcha, 488-2233. All services. Rooms $50. Cafe open at 7 a.m. to 9 p.m. **RH**

**Salcha River State Recreation Site** (Mile 323.1)—Camping sites are $8.

**The Knotty Shop** (Mile 332.3)—If you see this gift shop and can drive by without a double take, you're really in a hurry. Stop and check out the spruce-gall animal sculptures out front and the Alaskana within. Mile 332.3 Richardson Highway, Salcha, AK 99714, 488-3014, open daily 9 a.m. to 8 p.m. in summer, 10 p.m. to 6 p.m. in winter (until 8 p.m. around Christmas).

**Eielson Air Force Base** (Mile 341)—Named for Carl Ben Eielson, famous explorer and bush pilot, the base was constructed in 1943 as part of the massive World War II build-up. Weekly tours are offered to groups, but most will have to be satisfied with distant views of expensive military aircraft. Call 377-3148 for information.

**Chena Lakes Recreation Area** (Mile 346.7)—Turn north here to reach a swimming beach and camping. $3 day use, $6 campsites.

**North Pole Visitor Center** (Mile 348.7)—Get the lowdown on the destination for all those letters to Santa. The village of **North Pole**

(population 1,649, 5.4 percent native) milks its name for all it's worth and in all the ways you might expect. If you're fatefully intrigued, go ahead and check out the schlock.

**Fort Wainwright Military Reservation** (Mile 358.6)—Entrance to the army base.

**Fairbanks** (Mile 360 and on)—See below.

## TETLIN NATIONAL WILDLIFE REFUGE

*Location/Size: Bounded on the east by the Canadian border; occupies a wedge of land between the Alaska Highway and Wrangell–St. Elias National Park and Preserve in the upper Tanana Valley. 730,000 acres.*
*Main Activities: Hunting, trapping, fishing, canoeing, photography.*
*Gateway Towns/Getting There: Northway and Northway Village (Nabesna Village)/vehicle access via Alaska Highway (AK 2) and Northway Road. Refuge access: north boundary road access via Alaska Highway, including short trails near High Cache and at Deadman Lake; limited road access via Northway Road; winter road access from Northway along Nabesna River; Chisana and Nabesna River access via drop-offs.*
*Facilities, Camping, Lodging: Information exhibits along Alaska Highway. Designated campgrounds along Alaska Highway at Deadman Lake and Yarger Lake. Roadhouses and lodging options along Alaska Highway and in Northway Village.*
*Headquarters and Information: Refuge Manager, P.O. Box 779, Tok, AK 99780, 883-5312, fax 883-5747, r7tenwr@mail.fws.gov (type "Attention Refuge Manager" on subject line); Visitor Center, Mile 1,229 Alaska Highway (near Canadian border).*

Those driving into Alaska from the Yukon via the Alaska Highway get one of the state's more inspiring roadside views when they look across the vast lowlands of Tetlin to the massive Wrangell Mountains. The view exists because the highway avoids the wet lowlands and hugs the hills that bound the valley of the Tanana and its feeders (Chisana and Nabesna) to the north. It begins to sink in that you have reached Alaska when you realize you could park the car and walk 200 miles to the sea without ever crossing a road, reaching a town, or seeing another living soul. Stop at the visitor center (Alaska Highway, Mile 1,229) for information and great views.

The Tetlin basin is largely sprawling spruce forest, interspersed with braided glacial rivers, willow-choked swamps, and lake-peppered flats. Nearly 150 species of birds nest here, while visiting sandhill cranes pass through in great numbers in the spring and fall. Bald eagles, arctic and common loons, osprey, trumpeter swans, and ptarmigan are commonly observed. Moose, black and grizzly bear, wolf, coyote, and red fox are among the mammalian residents.

Various points along the highway can be used for canoe put-ins to access the lower Chisina, upper **Tanana River**, and the maze of mosquito-swarmed lakes in between. The **Nabesna River** and **Chisana River** offer possible long-distance routes for personal watercraft. The small settlement at the end of the Nabesna Road in Wrangell–St. Elias National Preserve is 5 miles from the banks of the upper Nabesna River. Consult the refuge manager and area outfitters for trip ideas.

## TAYLOR HIGHWAY (AK 5)
*Road Conditions and Attractions—160 miles. Generally good, graded gravel, with tight turns, steep grades, and seasonally poor road conditions. Chicken, Fortymile River system, high ridges, Eagle, Yukon River, Yukon-Charley National Preserve.*

The Taylor is a hilly, winding, gravel route that can be dusty, muddy, washboarded, and potholed—though it's usually pretty good. The road was built between 1946 and 1953 to provide access to Eagle and the Yukon River. It is a road to river-runner's heaven, providing access to 600 miles of national wild and scenic rivers—392 in the BLM's Fortymile River system and 208 in Yukon-Charley National Preserve.

The Taylor is one of only two Alaska highways that closes in the winter. Maintenance ends in mid-October and the first snow of consequence closes the road until April. The **Top of the World Highway** to the border and Dawson City meets the Taylor at Mile 95.7. Both roads spend time on the ridgecrests, affording magnificent views.

**Tetlin Junction and Alaska Highway** (Mile 0 Taylor Highway, Mile 1,301.7 Alaska Highway)—The roadhouse here may be in operation. Get gas if you're low.

**Mount Fairplay Viewpoint** (Mile 35.1)—Views of the Alaska Range are possible. The land to the north is the Fortymile Mining

District, first worked in 1886. Signs of past and present mining is evident at many spots.

**West Fork BLM Campground** (Mile 49)—There are 25 camp-sites here, as well as the put-in for the West Fork of the Dennison Fork of the Fortymile River (see Fortymile, below).

**Mosquito Fork Access** (Mile 64.3)—Put in here to connect with the South Fork Fortymile route (see below).

**Chicken** (Mile 66)—This town (population 40 or so) began as a min-ing camp. It's rumored that early miners wanted to name their town "Ptarmigan," but couldn't spell it, so went with the simpler name. Sev-eral old structures are visible on private land near the road at about Mile 67. Today there's an airstrip to the east, while to the west is "Beautiful Downtown Chicken Alaska" (take a left at Mile 66.4), offering a cafe, bar, store, and gas. Fill up here if you're low. You can put-in at Mosquito Fork for the Fortymile route below the airstrip.

Paul Otteson

*Charming Chicken*

# Fortymile National Wild, Scenic, and Recreational Rivers

*The BLM administers much of the historic Fortymile mining region, threaded by the branches of the Fortymile River and its tributaries. About 392 water miles are protected by the wild (192 miles), scenic (208 miles), or recreational (10 miles) des-ignations, offering river runners a variety of options for trip length, scenery, and whitewater challenge. Two of the best routes are:*

*The **South Fork Fortymile River** route offers Class I–Class III waters and is accessible at several points from the Taylor High-way (see milepost listings). From the first put-in at Mile 49, dis-tances to roadside take-outs are about 25 miles to Mosquito Fork, 30 miles to South Fork Lodge near Chicken, 72 miles to Fortymile Bridge (Mile 112.6), and 165 miles to Eagle. There are other take-outs as well, though away from the road the river dips deeply into wild country. Mining activity is heavy in spots, particularly downstream of Chicken.*

*The **Middle Fork/North Fork Fortymile River** route is accessed by an air drop-off, often at the old mining camp of Joseph. Canyons and mining ruins are found along the 90-mile route to the first roadside take-out at Fortymile Bridge, as are rapids that can reach Class V. The North Fork meets the South several miles upstream of the road take-out at Fortymile Bridge (Mile 112.6 of the Taylor Highway).*

*An alternative or extension is to stay in or put-in at Fortymile Bridge for the loop through Canada to Eagle. It's a 100-mile, weeklong trip through varied country with canyons, the historic site of Fortymile town at the Yukon-Fortymile conflu-ence, and a wind-in-the-face final leg down the wide, silty Yukon to Eagle. Contact the BLM for information on all routes. The Tok office is the best choice, 883-5121.*

**BLM Chicken Field Office** (Mile 68.2)—Information is available here, as is the trailhead for the **Mosquito Fork Dredge Trail** (3 miles), which leads to an old mining dredge on the river. **RT**—3 hrs.

**South Fork Bridge** (Mile 75.3)—Access to South Fork Fortymile route.

**Walker Fork BLM Campground** (Mile 82.1)—16 sites.

**Jack Wade Number 1 Dredge** (Mile 86.1)—Enjoy this picturesque old gold dredge east of the road.

**Jack Wade Junction and Top of the World Highway** (Mile 95.7)—Head right along the ridge 11 miles to Canada and 68 more to the free Yukon ferry at Dawson City. The Top of the World Highway is a beautiful ridgetop gravel route with stellar views. The road is generally good but, like the Taylor, can be slippery, dusty, or rough. Stop at the **Boundary Inc.** roadhouse about halfway to the border for gas, food, lodging, gifts, or tire repair. The border stations are open May 15–September 15 9 a.m. to 8 p.m. (Alaska time).
Turn left at the junction to continue to Eagle.

**Fortymile River Bridge** (Mile 112.6)—Access to the South Fork Fortymile route—a week or so from here to Eagle.

**Lodge with gas** (Mile 125.4)—Next gas station is in Eagle, Chicken, or Boundary.

**Ridgecrest** (Mile 143.2)—Enjoy the wonderful views.

**Eagle** (Mile 160.3)—Turn left at 4th Street for Fort Egbert, campground, airstrip, and BLM field office. Continue to Yukon River for businesses and walkabout (see Eagle, below).

## EAGLE (CITY AND VILLAGE)
*Location/Climate: On Yukon River at end of Taylor Highway (AK 5). 12"/yr. precip., -60°F–85°F.*
*Population: 146 (3 percent native).*

*Travel Attractions: Yukon River access, tours, kayaking and canoeing, Yukon-Charley Rivers National Park headquarters and access, drop-offs, historic town.*
*Getting There: Vehicle access via Taylor Highway (closed in winter); charter air service.*
*Information: Eagle Historical Society, P.O. Box 23, Eagle, AK 99738, 547-2325; www.alaska.net/~eagleak; City Office, P.O. Box 1901, Eagle, AK 99738, 547-2282.*

Situated on a historically vital stretch of the Yukon River near the Canadian border, Eagle offers modern travelers that end-of-the-road feel. Just upriver from the main town—officially known as **Eagle City**—the native settlement of **Eagle Village** is home to about 30 people. Follow 1st Avenue upstream 2½ miles for a look.

Han Athabascan Indians were the original area residents when early trappers, miners, and traders arrived. To secure the Yukon River trade routes, the Hudson Bay Company established Fort Yukon in 1847 and Fort Reliance in 1874. Eagle Village and Johnny's Village just across the border were settled in the same period. Belle Isle Trading Post was built near Johnny's Village around 1880, but residents moved across the border, establishing Eagle at its present site in 1898.

**Fort Egbert** was built in Eagle in 1899 to secure the border during the Klondike Gold Rush, and as a vital link in the WAMCATS system (Washington-Alaska Military Cable and Telegraph System). One section of WAMCATS ran from Eagle to the Bering Sea, the other from Eagle to Fort Liscum near Valdez. The fort helped establish Eagle as a vital trade, supply, and customs center, though its importance faded with the easy gold. Today there is renewed gold extraction in the area.

Consider taking the walking tour offered by the **Eagle Historical Society** (B Street and 1st Avenue daily 10 a.m., $5). It leaves from the **Courthouse**, which was built (along with the jail) by the famous Judge James Wickersham in 1901. This tour takes in several excellent historic sites, including the **Northern Commercial Company** store and warehouse on Front Street and the 1899 **Custom House**—which, like the courthouse, offers local heritage exhibits. Old Fort Egbert is on the tour but can be visited independently. It's ¼ mile from the river where 4th Avenue meets Eagle's grass airstrip. The BLM maintains the remaining buildings and exhibits.

Drop in at the field office for the Yukon-Charley National Preserve for information on river trips. It's located at the lower end of the airstrip (follow 1st Avenue downriver).

## Where to Stay and Eat in Eagle
**BLM Campground**, out 4th, 1 mile west of town. Free. Primitive campground with wooded sites, free firewood, adjacent to historic cemetery, very nice.

**Eagle Trading Company**, Front Street (on river), 547-2220, fax 547-2202. $50–$60 rooms. Lodging, cafe, gas, groceries, repair, store, laundry, RV hook-ups. **RH**

**Falcon Inn Bed-and-Breakfast**, 220 Front Street, 547-2254, fax 547-2255. $65 and up. Nice and rustic.

# YUKON-CHARLEY RIVERS NATIONAL PRESERVE
*Location/Size:* 2.5 million acres (88 percent federal) straddling and to the south of the Yukon River between Eagle and Circle.
*Main Activities:* Rafting, kayaking, canoeing.
*Gateway Towns/Getting There:* Eagle and Circle/vehicle access to Eagle via the Taylor Highway (AK 10), to Circle via the Steese Highway (AK 6); charter air service; by boat via the Yukon River. Preserve access: direct float access from Eagle, air drop-off at several sites from Eagle, Tok, Delta Junction, Fairbanks, Central, and Circle.
*Facilities, Camping, Lodging:* No facilities. Two public-use cabins on the Yukon at Coal Creek and at Nation River. Primitive camping only.
*Headquarters and Information:* Headquarters, P.O. Box 74718, Fairbanks, AK 99707, 456-0593; Field Office, P.O. Box 64, Eagle, AK 99738, 547-2234.

About 115 miles of the 1,800-mile Yukon River is protected in this large preserve, as is the entire watershed of the Charley River, which flows into the Yukon from the south. All of the navigable portion of the 108-mile **Charley River** is designated as a National Wild River, as are four of its feeders: **Flat Creek, Bonanza Creek, Copper Creek**, and **Crescent Creek**—a total of 208 wild miles. While the Yukon is wide and clouded with glacial silt, the waters of the Charley are renowned for their clarity. Mining sites and artifacts are found in

Paul Otteson

*The wide Yukon River*

several places, as are peregrine falcon aeries. The preserve is contiguous with a unit of the Steese National Conservation Area to the west.

River running is the activity of choice in the preserve. With Eagle near the eastern edge of the preserve and Circle near the west, a relatively cheap, 158-mile, Class I trip down the Yukon is a manageable option. There are a few public-use cabins on the five-day route and many options for primitive camping. The Yukon is served by outfitters in Eagle who also offer shorter trips with air or powerboat links (see Appendix).

All routes in the Charley watershed require an air drop-off. Eagle is the closest source of shuttles. Tok and Delta Junction are within reason, but Fairbanks is much further. It is possible to drive to Central or Circle, fly to the drop-off, then float the nine-day route back to Circle (six days for the Charley, three for the Yukon). The river features Class I–Class III waters with occasional Class IV in the uplands during highwater periods. Consult the preserve rangers or outfitters for options.

## TOK

*Location/Climate: At junction of Alaska Highway (AK 2) and the Glenn Highway (Tok Cutoff, AK 1), in the Tanana River valley. -32°F–72°F.*

*Population:* 1,204 (12.5 percent native)
*Travel Attractions:* Travel services, access to Alaska Range, Tetlin National Wildlife Refuge.
*Getting There:* Vehicle access from Canada, Anchorage, and Fairbanks via Alaska and Glenn Highways; charter air service.
*Information:* Tok Mainstreet Visitors Center, P.O. Box 389, junction of Glenn Highway (AK 1) and Alaska Highway (AK 2), Tok, AK 99780; 883-5887, www.tokalaska.com; Alaska Public Lands Information Center, junction of Glenn Highway (AK 1) and Alaska Highway (AK 2), Tok, AK 99780, 883-5667, www.nps.gov/aplic.

As the driver's gateway to "mainland" Alaska, Tok is geared for travelers. Businesses stretch along the Alaska Highway (AK 2) and Tok Cutoff where the two highways meet near the Tanana River. Fittingly, the town originated as an Alaska Road Commission camp serving the construction of the Glenn and Alaska Highways during World War II. Tok serves as a trading center for the surrounding Athabaskan villages of Northway, Tetlin, Tanacross, Mentasta, Eagle, and Dot Lake. It is also known as a center for dog breeding, training, and mushing.

There are a few small-scale diversions for visitors, though gas, a meal, and a night's sleep are the main attractions. Two good visitor centers should not be missed, however. Both the **Mainstreet Visitor Center** and the **Alaska Public Lands Information Center** are excellent one-stop sources for travel and adventure information and reservations. Both are located at the highway junction and are open daily through the travel season.

### Where to Stay and Eat in Tok

**Fast Eddy's**, Mile 1,313 Alaska Highway, 883-4411. Open daily 6 a.m. to midnight. Pizza, sandwiches, burgers, steaks, seafood.

**Golden Bear Motel**, Mile 124.5 Tok Cutoff, 883-2561. Motel and camping. Rooms $50–$95, sites $15–$25.

**Loose Moose Espresso Cafe**, Alaska Highway (next to Valley Bakery), 883-5282. Friendly place with good coffee.

**Tok International Hostel (HIAYH)**, Pringle Drive, 883-3745. Ten miles west of town, 1 mile south of Mile 1,322.5 of the Alaska Highway, $10.

**Young's Motel**, Mile 1,313 Alaska Highway, 883-4411, fax 883-5023. $63–$68 summer. Basic motel, clean, satellite TV, phones.

## DELTA JUNCTION
*Location/Climate:* On Delta River at the junction of the Alaska Highway (AK 2) and the Richardson Highway (AK 4). 12"/yr. precip., -65°F–91°F.
*Population:* 828 (4.4 percent native).
*Travel Attractions:* Travel services, bison herd, Tanana River access.
*Getting There:* Vehicle access via Richardson and Alaska Highways; regular small-plane air and charter air service.
*Information:* Visitor Information Center, junction of Richardson and Alaska Highways, Delta Junction, AK 99737, 895-5068, www.akpub.com/akttt/delta.html.

The area around the confluence of the Delta and Tanana Rivers was first occupied in 1904 by the Army Signal Corps as the site of the McCarthy Telegraph Station. The telegraph line eventually ran from Chitina and Tonsina, up through Delta and Fairbanks, and across to Saint Michael on the Bering Sea. The settlement served as a road-construction camp in 1919 when work began to turn the Valdez, or All-America Trail, into the Richardson Highway. It came to be known as "Buffalo Center" because of the introduction of a bison herd to the region in 1927. Bison can be observed in the area, particularly in the fall and winter when they concentrate east of town in the Delta Junction Bison Range south of the Alaska Highway. The construction of the Alaska Highway, the establishment of Fort Greely, and the building of the Trans-Alaska Pipeline all contributed to area growth.

Delta Junction offers your first view of the Trans-Alaska Pipeline if you've come from Canada. For a good look, stop 10 miles up the Richardson toward Fairbanks where the pipeline crosses the Tanana.

All travel services are available in Delta Junction.

### Things to See and Do in Delta Junction
**Alaska Homestead and Historical Museum**—Homesteaders settled the area around Delta. A number of those settlers are today involved in farming barley. The museum features an operating

sawmill barn, corral, and salmon drying racks, as well as a home-steader's cabin and old equipment. There are also sled dogs and other animals. Dorshorst Road, south from Mile 1,415.4 Alaska Highway, 895-4627. Open May 30–September 15 9 a.m. to 7 p.m., free displays, tours $8.

## Where to Stay and Eat in Delta Junction

**Alaska 7 Motel**, Mile 270.3 Richardson Highway, 895-4848. $55–$60. Basic accommodations.

**AYH Youth Hostel**, Tanana Loop Extension from Tanana Loop Road, Mile 271.7 Richardson Highway, 895-5074. $5 beds.

**Kelly's Country Inn Motel**, Mile 270.3 Richardson Highway, 895-4667. $75. Basic.

**Pizza Bella**, downtown across from Visitor Center, 895-4841. Open daily 10 a.m. to midnight for pizza, pasta, and more.

**Victorian Inn Bed-and-Breakfast**, Mile 1,414.5 Alaska Highway, 895-4636. $65. Full breakfast, Victorian home.

## FAIRBANKS

*Location/Climate: At confluence of Tanana and Chena Rivers and junction of George Parks Highway (AK 3), Alaska Highway (AK 2), and northbound highways. 12"/yr. precip., -22°F–72°F.*
*Population: 32,655 (9.2 percent native).*
*Travel Attractions: Historic city, mining history, Trans-Alaska Pipeline exhibits, museums, Alaskaland theme park, hot springs, Tanana River, charter air center, travel services.*
*Getting There: Scheduled air service from Anchorage and other points; vehicle access via George Parks, Alaska, Elliot, Steese, and Dalton Highways.*
*Information: Fairbanks Visitors Bureau, 1st Avenue near Cushman (log cabin in park on south bank of Chena River), (800) 327-5774, 456-5774, www.explorefairbanks.com.*

It's not uncommon for the towns in Alaska to be relatively unattractive, particularly in the Interior and Far North where extreme winters

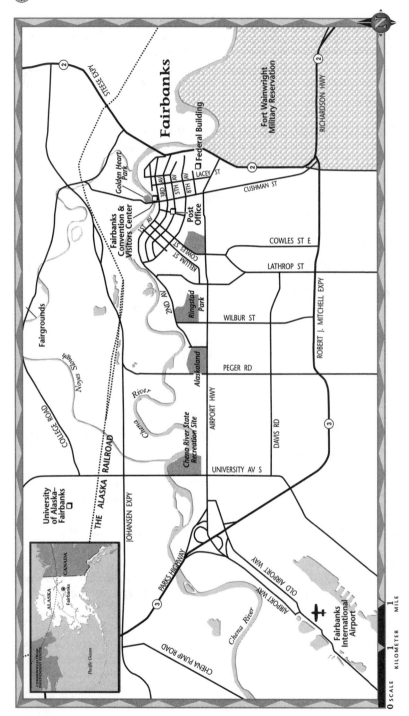

ALASKA

demand functional architecture and construction. Fairbanks is no exception—it isn't hard to see it as a small, ugly town grown big. But looks are not everything, and this vital, active, and rapidly growing city serves as a center for trade, transport, and culture for much of the state. The main campus of the University of Alaska is located here, while two busy military bases operate nearby.

The history of Fairbanks is awkward. In 1901, E. T. Barnette was on his way to establish a trading post at Tanacross, where the mining route from Valdez to Eagle crossed the Tanana River. Unfortunately, the sternwheeler *Lavelle Young* could not manage the shallow Tanana above its confluence with the Chena, so the captain put a disgruntled Barnette ashore and headed back downriver. Less than a year later, prospector Felix Pedro discovered gold in the area, instigating the "Pedro Dome Gold Rush" in 1902. Barnette saw his chance, set up shop, and became Fairbank's founding father. He convinced the miners to name the town after Charles Fairbanks, an Illinois senator who later served as Teddy Roosevelt's vice president. Barnette left his position in 1911, retiring to California. The bank went under a year later, swallowing the savings of hard-working miners and earning Barnette an evil reputation.

Miners were also frustrated by the fact that much of the region's gold was buried under thick layers of gravel and frozen mud, and was consequently difficult to extract by hand. It wasn't until the completion of the railroad in 1923 that companies began mining on a large scale, melting the frozen ground then dredging the placer layers to sluice out the gold. Despite these challenges, the town was soon established as a center of trade and government.

Modern Fairbanks is all things to the Interior and Far North, providing supplies, government, higher education, transport services, and more. The Parks, Richardson, and Steese Highways all reach the city, while the Elliott Highway, Dalton Highway, and Chena Hot Springs Road begin nearby. Fairbanks is a true crossroads—but let the roads tempt you, not the crossing. Stays should be short and oriented toward launching your next adventure.

Fairbanks visitors can lodge at one of the countless B&Bs, enjoying downtown history and nearby mining sites, trails, rivers, and hot springs. The **University of Fairbanks–Alaska** has several attractions, including the museum and Walk in the Woods described below (call the University Relations office for walking tours and information, 474-7581).

## Things to See and Do in Fairbanks

**Alaskaland**—It's hard to know quite what to make of this odd little theme park with its easy blend of historic buildings, museums, gift shops, eateries, and theaters. Yet this ultimate assemblage of Alaskana seems completely fitting and makes a good walkabout for an hour or two. Information is available at the gate and admission is free. Rides include an old carousel and the toy-sized **Crooked Creek and Whiskey Island Railroad** that makes 12-minute loops through the grounds. Check out the **SS *Nenana*,** the second-largest wooden vessel in existence and the largest sternwheeler ever built west of the Mississippi. It's permanently moored in a large pond. The **Pioneer Air Museum** features old aircraft and a history of Alaska's pilots (451-0037, $2). Besides several picnic areas and food stands, there is the **Alaska Salmon Bake,** offering a complete meal for $20 (open daily, 800-354-7274, 456-5960). Nearby is the **Palace Theater & Saloon** where the Golden Heart Revue offers happy melodrama to all comers nightly at 8:15, (800-354-7274, 452-7274, reservations recommended). Inquire about the 10 p.m. weekend show "for adults only." Check out the **Bear Art Gallery** for rotating exhibits with an Alaskan theme. It's upstairs in the civic center building, 456-6485.

Alaskaland is in full operation daily, Memorial Day through Labor Day, 11 a.m. to 9 p.m. It's open at any time for a walk and a look.

**Alaskan Tails of the Trail**—Musher and author Mary Shields will show you her dogs and describe the life of a musher. Personal, pleasant, and very informative. 7:30 p.m. $25. Call 457-1117 for reservations and information.

**Alaska Public Lands Information Center**—One of four in the state, this center is the best place to get information and advice on all of Alaska's public lands. There are informative displays as well. 250 Cushman Street, Suite 1A, 456-0527. Open daily 9 a.m. to 6 p.m., closed Sunday and Monday in winter.

**Chena Pump House National Historic Site**—Built to supply Chena River water to gold-dredging operations in the early 1930s, the building was remodeled to house a restaurant and saloon in 1978. It's a great place to dine surrounded by educational history.

Take Geist Road west from Parks Highway, then take first left and continue to Mile 1.3 of Chena Pump Road, 479-8452 (see Where to Eat, below).

**Historic Downtown**—Start at the **Visitor Information Center**, located in **Golden Heart Park** on the Chena River. They have complete information on downtown walkabouts and other sites. It's also pamphlet-central for food and lodging options—you can find and reserve your room or B&B here. 1st Avenue at Cushman, (800) 327-5774, 456-7774, 456-INFO (recorded event information). Open daily in summer, weekdays in winter. No public restrooms.

**Ester Gold Camp**—Eleven historic structures are preserved in this old mining camp turned tourist attraction. Turn in at Mile 351.7 Parks Highway to reach the hotel, buffet-style restaurant, the Malemute Saloon (where Robert Service composed several poems). Enjoy Alaskan ales while you take in a show that features comedy, music, poetry, and fun (performances daily in summer, Wednesday–Sunday at 7 p.m. and 9 p.m., Sunday–Tuesday at 9 only, $12). Nearby, the Firehouse Theater offers a 40-minute northern lights multimedia show (daily in summer, 6:45 p.m. and 9:45 p.m.; additional 6 p.m. show in July, $6). Call for complete information: 479-2500, www.ptialaska.net/~akttt/ester.html.

**Fairbanks Backroads**—A fairly extensive system of minor roads surrounds the city north of the Tanana River. Mining sites, views, trailheads, and rivers are interspersed with homes and other private acreage. Use your maps to explore. For ideas, consult with the happy experts downtown at the Visitor Information Center.

**Riverboat *Discovery***—For touristic history at its finest, ride the state's only operating sternwheel riverboat on a four-hour Chena and Tanana River trip. The boat stops at an Athabascan village site along the way. 1975 Discovery Drive, Fairbanks, AK 99709, 479-6673, fax 479-4613. Sailings daily in summer at 8:45 a.m. and 2 p.m., 6:30 p.m. cruises on selected evenings, $40, teens and military $37, children 3–12 $30. Call for reservations and directions.

**Tanana Valley Farmers Market**—See what area growers have to offer. From the Steese Highway or Johansen Expressway take

College Road west to the Tanana Valley Fairgrounds at Aurora Drive. Operates Wednesdays 11 a.m. to 6 p.m., Fridays 4 p.m. to 7 p.m., and Saturdays 10 a.m. to 5 p.m.

**University of Alaska Museum**—Easily Fairbanks' finest attraction, the museum features outstanding heritage exhibits in five galleries. Displays include totem poles, the Trans-Alaska Pipeline, and a 36,000-year-old steppe bison mummy, as well as numerous offerings on geology, natural history, native arts and cultures, and the northern lights. The state's largest gold display is also found here. From Airport Way, Geist Road, or College Road, take University Avenue north to the campus entrance and follow the signs (474-7505, www.uaf.edu/museum). Open June–August daily 9 a.m. to 7 p.m.; May and September daily 9 a.m. to 5 p.m.; October–April weekdays 9 a.m. to 5 p.m., weekends noon to 5 p.m. $5, $4.50 seniors, $3 age 12–17, under 12 free.

**Walk in the Woods**—This guided educational walk is an easy summer option with rich results. "Learn the northern niches of plants and wildlife . . . follow a quiet forest path and feel the spirit of the land." The two-hour tour starts in the U of A Botanical Garden at 2 p.m. Take Sheep Creek Road from Mile 355.8 of the Parks Highway and turn right on Tanana Loop Road to the barn and visitor center (457-1117, $20, kids $15).

### Where to Stay in Fairbanks
With the unbelievable number of B&Bs and other lodging options available in Fairbanks, it's highly recommended that you use a reservation service or stop at the downtown Visitor Information Center where Cushman meets the river. There are also a number of chain motels offering predictable facilities.

**All Seasons Inn**, 763 7th Avenue, Fairbanks, AK 99701, (888) 451-6649, $115–$125. Located right downtown, full breakfast provided.

**Bed-and-Breakfast Reservation Service**, P.O. Box 71131, (800) 770-8165, 479-8165, fax 474-8448. One hundred B&Bs, nine downtown guest rooms.

**Billie's Backpackers Hostel**, 2895 Mack Road, (800) 236-5350. $18, $10 tent space, $7 breakfast. Call for free shuttle from airport or train station; Denali/Anchorage van shuttle stops here.

**Captain Bartlett Inn**, 1411 Airport Way, (800) 478-7900, (800) 478-7900 (AK only). Motel with **Slough Foot Sue's Dining Hall** and the Dog Sled Saloon. Rooms $85–$130.

**Chena River State Recreation Site**, University Avenue (north of Airport Way). Nice $12 sites on or near the Chena River in town.

**Ester Gold Camp**, Ester, (800) 676-6925, 479-2500. Established in 1936, features Malemute Saloon and **Bunkhouse Buffet** for dinner. There are no phones or TVs in the $50–$80 rooms in this renovated bunkhouse.

**Fairbanks Association of Bed and Breakfasts**, P.O. Box 7334, Fairbanks, AK 99709-3334. You can write for a brochure on area B&Bs or visit their website at www.ptialaska.net/~fabb, which has web, e-mail, and reservation links to dozens of accommodations.

**Fairbanks Princess Hotel**, 4477 Pikes Landing Road, 455-4477, (800) 426-0500. Luxury option operated by Princess Cruises. Rooms are $200.

**Forget-Me-Not Lodge and Aurora Express**, 474-0949. Ten miles from town with views of the Tanana. Stay in an old railcar or the lodge. Rooms $80–$140, full breakfast included.

**Golden North Motel**, 4888 Old Airport Way, (800) 447-1910, 479-6201. $80 and up.

**Hotel Hotline** (reservation service), 1717 University Avenue, (800) 528-4916, 479-3650, fax 479-7951. Serves three fine hotels: **Sophie Station, Bridgewater Hotel,** and **Wedgewood Resort**. Rooms for all start in the $65 to $80 range and climb quickly to over $100.

**North Woods Lodge and International Hostel**, Chena Hills Drive (west of town, free transport), (800) 478-5305 (AK only),

479-5300. Rooms and cabins are $65 and up, hostel bunks $30, campsites $15.

**Seven Gables Inn**, 4312 Birch Lane, 479-0751. Rooms $50–$120. Huge, converted frat house on river. Atrium with waterfall. Excellent choice!

## Where to Eat Around Fairbanks

**Chena Pump House**, Mile 1.3 Chena Pump Road, 479-8452. Diner and saloon in a historic, riverside building. Take Geist west from the Parks Highway to Chena Pump Road.

**Gambardella's Pasta Bella**, 706 2nd Avenue. Downtown, pizza, homemade bread.

**Hot Licks**, 3549 College Road (near University Avenue), 479-7183. Great homemade ice cream, frozen yogurt, soup, and bread.

**Pike's Landing**, Mile 4.5 Airport Road, 479-6500. Open 11:30 a.m.–11 p.m. Huge deck on Chena River.

**Pizza Bella**, 1694 Airport Way. Italian, Greek, and American. Near Alaskaland and movie theaters.

**Thai House**, 526 5th Avenue, Fairbanks, AK 99701, 452-6123. Open Monday–Saturday, 11 a.m. to 10 p.m.

## NENANA

*Location/Climate:* At confluence of Nenana, Teklanika, and Tanana Rivers, 50 miles southwest of Fairbanks on George Parks Highway. 12"/yr. precip., 49"/yr. snowfall, below zero°F–high 60s°F.
*Population:* 490 (47.8 percent native, mainly Athabaskan and Eskimo).
*Travel Attractions:* Access to Tanana River, Alaska Railroad Museum, visitor center.
*Getting There:* Scheduled rail service from Anchorage and Fairbanks; vehicle access via George Parks Highway.
*Information:* Visitor Center, A Street and Parks Highway, Nenana, AK 99760, 832-9953, www.alaskaone.com/nenana/bells.htm.

Located at the confluence of the Nenana and Tanana Rivers, "Nenana" derives from the Athabascan word "Nenashna," which roughly translates, "point of camping at two rivers." The Army Signal Corps established the town in 1903 as a base for running long-distance telegraph lines, while barge traffic plying the Yukon and Tanana during the gold rush period brought settlers. When the Alaska Railroad used the town as its northern terminus from 1918 to 1923, Nenana's population reached 5,000. Today the town is an interesting mix of non-natives, Tanana Athabascans, and Eskimos. The economy is based largely on transportation services, both highway and river barge, as well as government jobs, tourism, and subsistence.

One great Alaska tradition is the **Nenana Ice Classic**—the annual contest to guess when the Tanana River ice will break up at Nenana. Local residents erect a large log tripod on the ice in the middle of the river, attached by a cord to a clock that stops when the tripod begins to move and the cord is pulled. Entrants purchase $2 tickets, writing in the date and time they believe the big event will occur, then wait for the fateful moment. Hundreds of thousands of dollars in prize money was shared by the winners. They take this contest very seriously in the northland!

Dogsled races are held at about the same time as the expected ice breakup, partly in commemoration of the race to take serum to Nome in 1925 during a diphtheria epidemic. Serum was rushed to Nenana by train, then taken by dogsled to Nome via the route of the old telegraph lines. That event led to the creation of the Iditarod Race.

## Things to See and Do in Nenana

**Alaska State Railroad Museum**—Where A Street meets the river, this small museum preserves artifacts from the days of the building of the Alaska Railroad. It's housed in the old train depot on Front Street with a B&B upstairs, 832-5500. Open late May–late September daily 8 a.m. to 6 p.m., free.

**Nenana Valley Visitor Information Center**—You can't miss this little log cabin as you drive north on the Parks Highway where it meets A Street just south of the river. Inside, you'll find the usual pamphlets, but also friendly folks who will give you the local lowdown (832-9953). Open in summer daily 8 a.m. to 6 p.m.

**Railroad Roller Bridge**—The Alaska Railroad bridge over the Tanana is "the largest single-span expansion bridge on rollers ever built." When the temperature changes radically and rapidly, you can hear the bridge moving on its rollers as the metal expands or contracts.

**Saint Mark's Mission Church**—Built in 1905 by early missionaries, the church was once paired with a mission school that held as many as 50 native students from throughout the area. The school closed in 1951, but the church still holds regular services.

### Where to Stay and Eat in Nenana
**Bed and Maybe Breakfast**, in the old rail depot on Front Street, 832-5272.

## CHENA HOT SPRINGS ROAD
*Road Conditions and Attractions—60 miles. Decent paved road. Trailheads, river running, Chena Hot Springs Resort.*

The route leaves the Steese Highway just north of Fairbanks, heads east through historic mining country, and climbs toward the divide between the Tanana and Yukon valleys. The country is quite lovely and opportunities for recreation abound, particularly hiking the trails in the Chena River State Recreation Area, canoeing the Chena River, and visiting the hot springs. The following milepost listings highlight the best of it.

**Tack's General Store and Greenhouse Cafe** (Mile 23.5), 488-3242. Open 8–8. Good food and a greenhouse.

**Chena River State Recreation Area** (Mile 26.1 to 50.7)—The Chena River is popular with kayakers, canoeists, and floaters. Five bridges over the river's north fork within the state recreation area (Miles 37.9, 39.5, 44.1, 45.7, 49) and a variety of other logical put-ins make it easy to devise a run to suit your situation. Moderate runs are found between the lower three bridges, while more challenging stretches are found upstream. Watch out for sweepers and log jams.

The **Rosehip State Campground** (Mile 27) and **Granite Tors Trail State Campground** (Mile 39.5) have nice sites along the river. Fishing, hiking, and river-running access are easy from the campgrounds.

The **Granite Tors Trail** (15-mile loop) offers access to the rock formations that inspired the name. Great views and some difficult trail sections. Through trail—2 days.

For a short, strenuous, and rewarding half-day hike, try the **Angel Rocks Trail** (3.5-mile loop) at Mile 48.9. Loop—half-day.

A long and nice route for backpackers is the **Chena Dome Trail** (29-mile loop, 2,000' gain) that starts at Mile 49.1. The loop roughly follows the ridgeline west above the north fork of the Chena River, reaching 3,000 feet in elevation before dropping north into the valley and returning to the trailhead. Through trail—3–4 days.

**Chena Hot Springs** (Mile 56.5)—The U.S. Geological Survey discovered these springs in 1904. All spring access is via the resort (see below). These are the region's most popular springs because they are the closest to Fairbanks, though many find the sulfur smell quite strong. There's an airstrip if you want to fly.

**The Resort at Chena Hot Springs** (Mile 56.5), (800) 478-4681, 452-7867, fax 456-3122. $75–$95 summer, $95–$115 winter, $40–$80 cabins, $10–$12 campsites. Indoor and outdoor pools, whirlpools, and tubs. Good restaurant. Day pass $8, $6 seniors and children 6–12, under 6 free. Volleyball, bikes, cross-country skiing. **BL**

## STEESE HIGHWAY (AK 6)—FAIRBANKS TO CIRCLE

*Road Conditions and Attractions—160 miles. Open year-round. The first 40 miles are paved, the rest is maintained gravel; the final miles have numerous sharp curves. Access to White Mountains National Recreation Area, Steese National Conservation Area, scenic passes above treeline, mining history, trailheads, river put-ins, Circle Hot Springs, Circle, and Yukon River.*

The Steese heads north from Fairbanks then quickly turns to the northeast, winding through the historic mining country of the Fairbanks gold strikes. Crossing over Cleary Summit, the road drops down to the Chatanika River and follows the boundary of the White Mountains National Recreation Area along the ridgeline to the north. Climbing above treeline to Twelvemile Summit, the route crosses from the Tanana into the Yukon watershed then climbs again to Eagle Summit

before dropping to the lowlands, the town of Central, and the turnoff to Circle Hot Springs. After the tortuous final miles, the Steese reaches the town of Circle, the Yukon, and road's end.

Most of the route winds through the twisting heart of the White Mountains, allowing access to mining sites, trailheads, river put-ins, and other recreational options. Services are available in Central and Circle. You'll see plenty of evidence of dredge and placer mining— old and new.

**Fairbanks** (Mile 0)—See above.

**Chena Hot Springs Road Junction** (Mile 4.9)—See above.

**Trans-Alaska Pipeline Viewpoint** (Mile 8.9)—This is one of the main viewing locations for visitors who wish to learn about the pipeline. The Alyeska Pipeline Service Company operates a visitor center here (open Memorial Day–Labor Day daily 8 a.m. to 6 p.m. 456-9391, www.mosquitonet.com/~ranchmotel/transack.htm).

**Goldstream Road Exit** (Mile 9.5)—Access to historic **Gold Dredge Number 8,** featuring mining relics and buildings, gold panning, a mastodon- and mammoth-bone display, museum, gift shop, snack bar, RV parking, tours, and, of course, the gold dredge. P.O. Box 81941, Goldstream Road, 457-6058, fax 457-8888. Open June–mid-September daily 9 a.m. to 6 p.m., $10.

**Steese-Elliott Junction** (Mile 11)—The expressway turns into the Elliott Highway while the Steese exits, turns east and heads into the hills.

**Felix Pedro Monument** (Mile 16.5)—This roadside monument remembers the man who discovered gold in Pedro Creek in 1902, setting off the gold rush that led to the founding of Fairbanks.

**Cleary Summit** (Mile 20.3, 2,233' elevation)—There are some good views from the summit area. There's also a small ski basin with a hilltop lodge.

**Old F.E. Gold Camp** (Mile 27.9), Chatanika, 389-2414. $60–$90. Food and lodging in a wonderful restored mining complex. Northern-lights viewing in winter.

**Chatanika Lodge** (Mile 28.6), Chatanika, 389-2164. Rooms $50–$65. Excellent classic Alaska roadhouse restaurant and bar. Take a look and then grab a bite. Walk to the gold dredge across the road (be careful to respect private property signs if posted). **RH**

**Upper Chatanika River State Recreation Site** (Mile 39)— Good river access. Campground with 25 sites, $8.

**Pavement Ends** (Mile 43.8)— Switch here to a good gravel road. Open year-round.

Paul Otteson

*Chatanika Lodge*

**Davidson Ditch and Nome Creek Road** (Mile 57.3)—In 1925 the 35-mile-long Davidson Ditch was built to carry water south from the higher reaches of the Chatanika River to an area not far from the settlement of Chatanika. The water was used to float the dredges that chewed away at placer deposits. Segments of large pipe were joined with tunnels and ditches to complete the project. Read the story and take a walk on the pipe.

From here, the road leads to the Nome Creek put-in for the **Beaver Creek** route (see White Mountains National Recreation Area and Steese National Conservation Area, below). Work is underway to lengthen this road to Ophir Creek.

**Cripple Creek BLM Campground** (Mile 60)—21 sites.

**Twelvemile Summit and Trailheads** (Mile 85.5, 2,982' elevation)—Pull off here for views and a short walk. The southern trailhead for the Pinnell Mountain Trail is here, as is the northern end of the Circle-Fairbanks Trail. The two can be linked into a very long route (see White Mountain National Recreation Area and Steese National Conservation Area, below).

**Birch Creek Canoe Trail Put-in** (Mile 94)—See White Mountain National Recreation Area and Steese National Conservation Area, below.

**Pinnell Mountain Trailhead** (Mile 107.1)—Not quite in the pass, this is the northern end of the route (see White Mountain National Recreation Area and Steese National Conservation Area, below).

**Eagle Summit** (Mile 108, 3,624' elevation)—This is the high point of the road and a great viewing area. Fine wildflowers in season.

**Central and Circle Hot Springs Road Junction** (Mile 127.8)— A few businesses are scattered near the junction along the short stretch of paved road that runs through town. You'll find food, gas, and lodging options. Turn south here for the 8-mile drive to Circle Hot Springs.

The town of **Central** (population 58) began as the Central Roadhouse in 1896, serving the Circle Mining District. It still serves as a supply center for the miners who work about 65 area claims. Visit the **Circle District Historical Society Museum** west of the junction on the north side of the road. This small, new museum features mining and area heritage exhibits. Ask about the great gold robbery of 1996, 520-1893. Open Memorial Day–Labor Day daily noon to 5 p.m.; $1, children under 12 50¢.

**Circle Hot Springs Resort** is my favorite of the three road's-end hot springs north of Fairbanks (Chena, Manley, and Circle). The water here is hot, unlike that in Manley; and only slightly aromatic, unlike that in Chena. There's a very large, clean outdoor pool in which you can find your spot and soak. The lodge itself is rustic and loaded with history. Enjoy the quiet ambiance of hot water, cool air, and easy living as contented people stroll amicably about. An airstrip allows charter air access from Fairbanks. Mile 8.3 Circle Hot Springs Road, Central, 520-5113. Open year-round, rooms $95–$125, cabins $85–$110, floor space for sleeping bags $20, restaurant and bar open all day, exercise room, library, massage therapy, and gift shop. Swimming for nonlodgers is $5.

**Circle** (Mile 162)—After enduring the final 35 winding miles of the Steese, you'll arrive at road's end, the Yukon River, and the town of Circle (see below).

# WHITE MOUNTAINS NATIONAL RECREATION AREA AND STEESE NATIONAL CONSERVATION AREA

*Location/Size:* Mainly north of Steese Highway (AK 6), northeast of Fairbanks, contiguous with Yukon Flats National Wildlife Refuge; southern unit of Steese National Conservation Area is south of the Steese Highway. White Mountain National Recreation Area, 1 million acres; Steese National Conservation Area, 1.2 million acres.

*Main Activities:* Hiking, hunting, fishing, snowmachining, river running, wildlife viewing.

*Gateway Towns/Getting There:* Fairbanks/vehicle access via Parks, Alaska, and Steese Highways; scheduled air service from Anchorage and other points. Park access: vehicle access to Steese via Steese Highway (AK 6), to White Mountain National Recreation Area via Elliott Highway (AK 2); charter air service from Fairbanks; foot access via trail; snowmachine access via winter roads.

*Facilities, Camping, Lodging:* Emergency winter shelters, summer trails, 200 miles of winter recreation routes. Reservable backcountry cabins in White Mountain National Recreation Area, designated campsites, mainly primitive camping.

*Headquarters and Information:* BLM Arctic District, 1150 University Avenue, Fairbanks, 474-2200, aurora.ak.blm.gov/WhiteMtns.

These contiguous parcels of BLM land spread north and east of the major historic and modern-day mining areas near the Steese Highway. White Mountains National Recreation Area is famous for winter recreation options via 200 miles of marked winter roads and paths. There are several reservable public-use cabins along these routes, offering shelter and comfort at the end of a day's travel. Good all-season hiking routes are described below.

**Beaver Creek**, a National Wild and Scenic River, has road access for a put-in at the confluence of Nome and Ophir Creeks, several miles southwest of Sourdough Camp on the Steese Highway. From there the creek never sees road again and drains all the way to the Yukon, just downstream from Beaver. The full 20-day route includes a segment on the Yukon with a take-out at Mile 56 of the Dalton Highway. Consult the BLM and outfitters about shorter trips.

The similarly sized Steese National Conservation Area has two units, one to the north of the Steese Highway and one to the south. Steese hosts an important caribou herd and provides habitat for many

Paul Otteson

*Tundra boardwalk in the
White Mountains*

other species. The northern unit features the excellent three-day ridge route of the Pinnell Mountain Trail (see below).

The southern unit of Steese National Conservation Area encompasses the drainage of **Birch Creek**, a National Wild and Scenic River featuring Class I–Class III waters. Birch Creek loops 125 miles through BLM wildlands between a put-in and take-out on the Steese Highway. Consult the BLM or outfitters about time, equipment, and shorter trip options.

Between the two preserves, the **Chatanika River** drains along the route of the Steese Highway before the road cuts south and the river crosses the Elliott, meandering through **Minto Flats State Game Refuge** to meet the **Tolovana River**. Outfitters serve short float trips on the Chatanika because of easy road access. Also found in this tumbled area of historic mines is the Circle-Fairbanks Trail, described below.

## Trails in White Mountain National Recreation Area and Steese National Conservation Area

Several White Mountain trails are intended for ATVs or snow-machines. Consult with the BLM in Fairbanks regarding cabins and trail conditions.

**Circle-Fairbanks Trail** (58 miles, 1,700' gain)—The muskeg, forest, and bog flats of the region's valleys sent early Athabascans to the ridgetops to search for travel routes. This segment of their original trail runs from Fairbanks Creek Road (4 miles from Cleary Summit Ski Area on the Steese Highway) to Twelvemile Summit at Mile 85.6 of the Steese. It's not actively maintained. Through trail—6–10 days.

**Pinnell Mountain National Recreation Trail** (27.3 miles, up and down along ridgecrests, 500' total gain northbound)—This is one of the best short backpack routes in the state. From Mile 85.6

to Mile 107.3 of the Steese Highway, the maintained path follows a ridgeline route entirely above treeline. Two emergency shelters are available. For a hefty 10-day route, you can link up with the Circle-Fairbanks Trail. Through trail—3–4 days.

**Ski Loop Trail** (5 miles, 500' gain)—This loop route begins and ends at Snowshoe Pass at Mile 28 of the Elliott Highway. Some sections may be wet or muddy. The route climbs to a summit then contours clockwise around the mountain and back to the pass. **RT**—half day.

**Summit Trail** (20 miles, 900' total, 1,800' return, 1,100' Wickersham Creek return)—From Snowshoe Pass at Mile 28 of the Elliott Highway, the trail follows the ridgeline to the north-northeast before dropping down a spur to Wickersham Creek. The return route along the stream is a winter trail and may not be suitable for walking. Consult the BLM office about options. **RT**—4–6 days.

## CIRCLE

*Location/Climate:* On Yukon River at end of Steese Highway (AK 6). 13"/yr. precip., 44"/yr. snowfall, -71°F–72°F.
*Population:* 94 (86.3 percent native).
*Travel Attractions:* Yukon River, Yukon Flats National Wildlife Refuge, Yukon-Charley Rivers National Park, interesting town.
*Getting There:* Vehicle access via Steese Highway; charter air service.
*Information:* Inquire at local businesses, www.ilovealaska.com/alaska/Circle/.

L. N. McQuestern opened a trading post here in 1887 to serve miners working claims along Birch Creek. His goods arrived via barge and riverboat after an 1,800-mile float up the Yukon. The founders mistakenly believed the town was on or very near the Arctic Circle and named it accordingly. You can walk upriver a bit to see the century-old graves at the little **Pioneer Cemetery** (ask for directions). Today this largely native community depends on subsistence, tourism, and limited government, construction, and retail work.

The best options for travelers involve float or powerboat trips on the Yukon River and access to remote villages. Circle is an ideal take-out point for a flight-free float trip beginning in Eagle. Along this stretch, the Yukon keeps to its banks, flowing through the hilly country of Yukon-Charley Rivers National Preserve. Downstream trips are possible as well, following the river as it meanders and

braids through the sprawling Yukon Flats, past Fort Yukon, Beaver, and the Dalton Highway. Guides, outfitters, and water taxis offer various options (see appendix).

Stop in at the trading post for a slow coffee and some talk. Camping is permitted on the riverside lot at road's end.

### Where to Stay and Eat in Circle
**Riverview Motel**, 773-8439, on the banks of the Yukon, three rooms and one apartment, $60 and up. Associated with Circle City Charters, which offers custom services up and down the Yukon River.

**Yukon Trading Post**, Mile 162 Steese Highway, 773-1217. Cafe, bar, store, gas, conversation. **RH**

## ELLIOT HIGHWAY (AK 2)—STEESE HIGHWAY TO MANLEY HOT SPRINGS
*Road Conditions and Attractions—150 miles. Open year-round, the first 28 miles are paved and the rest is good, graded gravel. Services in Manley Hot Springs. Access to White Mountains National Recreation Area, Manley Hot Springs, Tanana River, mining history.*

From its junction with the Steese Highway just north of Fairbanks, the Elliott (open year-round) heads northwest through mixed forests and hills, running between the Trans-Alaska Pipeline to the west and the boundary of White Mountain National Recreation Area to the east. The road crosses many minor divides including Snowshoe Pass, where you'll find trailheads for routes into the White Mountains.

At Livengood the highway swings southwest to run a bit more with the grain of the hills and valleys. Around Eureka and Manley near road's end, several small roads and paths lead off to the claims of the local mining district. There are services in Manley Hot Springs.

**Steese Highway Junction** (Mile 0)—The Elliott actually becomes the Steese, so if you're heading to or from Fairbanks you don't have to turn.

**El Dorado Gold Mine** (Mile 1.2)—This touristy attraction offers educational family fun. Visitors take a two-hour guided tour that features a ride on the Tanana Valley Railroad, a look at a working gold mine, a descent into a "permafrost tunnel," and a chance to pan for gold. For information, call 479-7613.

**Lower Chatanika River State Recreation Area, Olnes Campground** (Mile 10.6)—$8 sites 1 mile west of highway.

**Lower Chatanika River State Recreation Area, Whitefish Campground** (Mile 11)—$8 sites at the north end of the bridge.

**Snowshoe Pass and Trailheads** (Mile 27.7, 3,207' elevation)— Nice views above treeline. Trailheads for the Summit Trail and Ski-Loop Trail are here (see White Mountain National Recreation Area and Steese National Conservation Area, above).

**Livengood** (Mile 70.8)—Two miles up this road you'll find a highway maintenance station and the site of Livengood, a virtual ghost town that was once an active mining camp. Private-property postings discourage visitors from exploring too much. Most were placed by a large mining company that has hopes for the area.

**Dalton Highway Junction** (Mile 73.1)—Head north here to reach the Yukon River, Arctic Circle, Brooks Range, North Slope, and Arctic Ocean. Otherwise, turn left to stay on the Elliott.

**Minto Road Junction** (Mile 110)—Turn left and drive 11 miles to reach the Tanana Athabascan settlement of **Minto** (population 245, 97 percent native). Residents are occupied mainly with subsistence activities or government-based jobs. The town was originally on the Tolovana River but moved to its present site in 1969 due to flooding. The hunting and fishing lodge here has a restaurant and store.

Minto is at the edge of the **Minto Flats State Game Refuge**. The flats are covered with small lakes, ponds, bogs, and muskeg— ideal habitat for moose and waterfowl, and thus for hunters. Units of the refuge are found on either side of the Tanana River, north and east of Nenana. Units of the **Tanana Valley State Forest** lie adjacent to the flats and refuge, encompassing the hills and spruce, birch, and aspen forest of the taiga. Though currently closed to homesteading, state preserves are fully open to hunting, harvesting, and motorized vehicles.

**Manley Hot Springs** (Mile 151.2)— Manley Hot Springs (population 99, 15 percent native) was established in 1902 when John Karshner discovered the springs near the Tanana River and established a homestead. In the same period, an Army telegraph station and trading post were built to support local mining activity and river trade. The springs quickly became a famous local attraction, though the first resort, with its Olympic-size pool, burned to the ground in 1913. The last resort in Manley went bankrupt a few years ago. Today the Dart family accommodates respectful bathers in three greenhouse tubs of varying temperature on their property. Call before visiting (672-3171), and check in upon arrival before you head to the tubs. A contribution may be expected.

Manley's waters are naturally cooler than Circle's but not sulfurous like Chena's. Access to the Tanana River is a plus, as are the pleasant setting and friendly folks. A city campground has $5 sites.

**Manley Roadhouse (Manley Trading Post)** (Mile 151.2), Manley Hot Springs, 672-3161. Since 1906, an Alaska original. Food, bar, rooms, cabins, prehistoric and Alaskana artifact display. **RH**

# NATIONAL WILDLIFE REFUGES OF THE INTERIOR

Nine huge national wildlife refuges and part of a tenth are located south of the Brooks Range and north of the coastal ranges. Six of them are distinctly Interior in location and character, with lowland and foothill areas dominated by spruce forest. Three are associated with the largely treeless Arctic coastal eco-regions, fronting as they do on the Bering and Chukchi Seas. The tenth is the Arctic National Wildlife Refuge, which straddles the Brooks Range and includes coastal mountain and Interior lowland areas. Numerous smaller refuges, game preserves, and critical habitat areas are identified by the state and BLM.

The boundaries of the six Interior refuges almost can be seen as a large-scale topographic map of the heart of the state. Just about all of the land within them is lowland forest and wetlands, while elsewhere are rugged hills and low mountains. Each of the six refuges is associated with a river or confluence of rivers, floodplains, and characteristically Alaskan lake-dotted flats with willow-choked bogs and tufty muskeg.

Migratory birds from throughout the world come to Alaska by the millions to nest in the refuge wetlands. Some rest, feed, and move on, while others set up shop and get about the business of procreating. The seasonal rhythms and consistent wetness of the Alaskan bottomlands provide an essential anchor in the cycles of avian life.

Few people visit any of the refuges except wildlife harvesters, fish and game officials, researchers, and birders. All except the Tetlin are inaccessible by road, and none offer land routes for exploring outside of winter. Moose and bear hunters are frequent visitors, while sport fishers find freshwater species in abundance. Many residents of native villages subsist on the bounty of the refuge lands. The main activities for eco-travelers are birding and river trips in areas most often accessed by air drop-offs. Recommended river runs vary according to the seasons, water levels, challenges, and rendezvous points. Those planning river trips should consult outfitters, pilots, and refuge managers.

Difficult access, remoteness, and the attractiveness of other regions make the wet Interior basins uncommon destinations for visitors. Those who opt to spend time traveling through a refuge are likely to enjoy a truly Alaskan and very wild journey. Though there are many settlements in the remote parts of the Interior, the ones listed in this chapter are those that best serve as bases or transit points for access to the refuges and other areas.

## YUKON FLATS NATIONAL WILDLIFE REFUGE

*Location/Size:* Straddles Porcupine River and northernmost loop of Yukon River, centered by Fort Yukon, 150 miles north-northeast of Fairbanks, contiguous with Arctic National Wildlife Refuge, shares border with Canada. 8.6 million acres.

*Main Activities:* Canoeing and rafting, fishing, hunting, charter boat trips.

*Gateway Towns/Getting There:* Fort Yukon/river access from Circle, Eagle, and Dalton Highway, scheduled air service from Fairbanks; Circle/vehicle access via Steese Highway (AK 6), regular small-plane air service; Stevens Village, Chalkyitsik, Venetie, Beaver/regular and charter small-plane air service. Refuge access by charter air drop-offs;

*river access via Yukon, Porcupine, Sheenjack, Chandalar, and others; snowmachine access via winter roads.*
***Facilities, Camping, Lodging:*** *No facilities. Primitive camping. Limited facilities at several settlements within refuge bounds.*
***Headquarters and Information:*** *Refuge Manager, Federal Building and Courthouse, P.O. Box 20, 101 12th Avenue, Fairbanks, AK 99701, 456-0440, 456-0250, www.r7.fws.gov/nwr/yf/r7yflat.html, YukonFlats_Refuge@fws.gov (type "Attention Refuge Manager" on subject line).*

The main body of the refuge encompasses a 200-mile-long floodplain where spring meltwater spreads out relatively unconfined from the Yukon River, the Porcupine River, and their tributaries. The area hosts one of the highest densities of nesting waterfowl on the continent, including over 2 million ducks and geese that come and go via migratory routes that reach the lower 48. By August, many of the 40,000 lakes fill with molting adults and their young.

The Yukon River reaches its northernmost point near Fort Yukon in the heart of the refuge, just above the Arctic Circle. Athabascan Indians have long harvested wildlife here, hunting and constructing fish wheels to catch the king, coho, and chum salmon that are returning to Canadian streams to spawn. The refuge has several large inclusions of native and village corporation lands which are essentially private property. Several settlements along the rivers offer possible put-ins or destinations for river journeys.

River adventures are indeed the recreational option of choice in Yukon Flats since the flooded summer status of much of the refuge makes access in many areas problematic. Dawson City, Eagle, Circle, and the Dalton Highway offer points of road access to the shores of the Yukon. Outfitters offer combinations of motorboat and air shuttles, routes, guides, and rentals to suit most interests and schedules (see Appendix for listings).

## FORT YUKON

***Location/Climate:*** *On north bank of Yukon River at confluence of Yukon and Porcupine Rivers, 145 air miles northeast of Fairbanks. 14"/yr. precip., 44"/yr. snowfall, -76°F–80°F.*
***Population:*** *663 (85 percent native).*

*Travel Attractions: Native town, Yukon Flats National Wildlife Refuge access, river travel center, northern lights viewing.*
*Getting There: Charter riverboat from Circle; scheduled or charter air service.*
*Information: Contact one of the lodges below or a Fairbanks flying service (see Appendix).*

Situated on the Arctic Circle at the confluence of the Porcupine and Yukon Rivers, Fort Yukon was established by Alexander Murray in 1847 as the Hudson Bay Trading Company's outpost, about a mile upstream of its current location. Gwichin Athabascan Indians used the post as a trading center. Today, descendants of the Yukon Flats, Chandalar River, Birch Creek, Black River, and Porcupine River Gwichin tribes are the primary residents. Subsistence, government, and native and village corporation jobs occupy most residents, with tourism and visitor services a small segment of the economy.

With regular air service, Fort Yukon holds two primary attractions for visitors. It serves as a good base for several possible river trips, including a float from Circle. It is also known by winter visitors as a great place to view the northern lights. See the Appendix for outfitters who offer exploration possibilities.

## Where to Stay and Eat in Fort Yukon
**Betty's Bed and Breakfast**, 662-2558. The only option in this traditional native community. Northern lights viewing in winter.

## BETTLES AND EVANSVILLE
*Location/Climate: 180 air miles north of Fairbanks, west of the Dalton Highway, at the southern foot of the Brooks Range. 13.4"/yr. precip., 77"/yr. snowfall, below zero°F–70-plus°F.*
*Population: Bettles 34 (22 percent native), Evansville 30 (58 percent native).*
*Travel Attractions: Access to Brooks Range, Gates of the Arctic National Park and Preserve, river runs, backcountry lodging.*
*Getting There: Scheduled air service from Fairbanks; winter vehicle access to Dalton Highway via Hickel Trail.*
*Information: Bettles City Office, 692-5191.*

The settlement is named for Gordon Bettles, who opened a trading post during the 1899 gold rush at the northern terminus of the

Koyukuk River barge line. The navy built the Bettles Field airstrip in 1945, while Wilford Evans Sr. (for whom Evansville is named) built the Bettles Lodge in 1950. Both settlements are small, though the short road system reaches other area residences.

Small planes shuttle many summer visitors into and out of the Bettles area, most on their way to the Brooks Range or a river drop-off. Nearby backcountry lodges offer a foothills retreat with the option of further guided or outfitted explorations (see Appendix). The town is not the best choice as a backpacking base for the Brooks because it is far from the heights, but is better than Anaktuvuk Pass as a shuttle link from Fairbanks to Brooks drop-off spots.

River runners can put in here and float south on the **Koyukuk River**, or can fly to a drop-off upstream and float back down to Bettles. Upstream features rougher runs in scenic mountains while downstream offers easier floats through the Kanuti National Wildlife Refuge. Consult the Bettles rangers or lodge and tour operators about possibilities.

### Where to Stay and Eat in Bettles and Evansville

**Bettles Lodge**, P.O. Box 27, Bettles, AK 99726, (800) 770-5111, 692-5111. Historic old lodge built in 1950; now there's a new lodge, Jacuzzis, restaurant, and tavern.

## KANUTI NATIONAL WILDLIFE REFUGE

*Location/Size: Just west of the Dalton Highway, 150 miles northwest of Fairbanks, straddling the Arctic Circle, Kanuti River, and Koyukuk River. 1.4 million acres.*

*Main Activities: Hunting, fishing, wildlife viewing.*

*Gateway Towns/Getting There: Bettles/regular air service from Fairbanks. Refuge access by river from Allakaket and possibly from the Dalton Highway.*

*Facilities, Camping, Lodging: None.*

*Headquarters and Information: Refuge Manager, Federal Building and Courthouse, P.O. Box 20, 101 12th Avenue, Fairbanks, AK 99701, 456-0329, www.r7.fws.gov/nwr/kanuti/kanwr.html, kanuti_refuge@ fws.gov (type "Attention Refuge Manager" on subject line).*

The Kanuti Flats are an area where several small rivers come together, flowing into the Koyukuk, which eventually drains into the Yukon. Rolling plains are interspersed with lakes, ponds, and swampy flats. Canada and white-fronted geese and ducks nest in the refuge. Other wildlife in the refuge include moose, black bear, grizzly bear, wolf, and wolverine.

The **Koyukuk River, Jim River**, and **Bonanza Creek** offer good river runs, including road put-in options. Access to the **Kanuti River** is discouraged from mid-June through early July because of nesting activity. Check with the refuge manager on water levels and for general advice. See the Appendix for outfitters.

## NOWITNA NATIONAL WILDLIFE REFUGE

*Location/Size:* 200 miles west of Fairbanks, bordered by the Yukon River to the north. 1.56 million acres.
*Main Activities:* Nowitna River float trips, hunting, fishing.
*Gateway Towns/Getting There:* Galena and Ruby/regular small-plane air service from Fairbanks, river access via the Yukon. Park access by river via Yukon and lower Nowitna; charter air drop-offs.
*Facilities, Camping, Lodging:* No facilities. Primitive camping only.
*Headquarters and Information:* Refuge Manager, P.O. Box 287, Galena, AK 99741, 656-1231, www.r7.fws.gov/nwr/nowitna/ nownwr.html, r7kynwr@fws.gov (type "Attention Refuge Manager" on subject line).

Though established primarily to protect the wide wetlands of the lower Nowitna River valley south of the Yukon, the refuge includes a fair-sized area of rolling uplands in the south, as well as a narrow corridor surrounding the central Nowitna. The refuge hosts large concentrations of migratory waterfowl, black bear, moose, marten, mink, wolverine, beaver, and muskrat. Hunting and fishing are important subsistence and recreational activities.

A designated National Wild and Scenic River, the **Nowitna River** offers good opportunities for river trips. A standard 250- to 290-mile route puts in at the confluence with Meadow Creek, with take-out options at the confluence with the Yukon or 40 miles downstream in Ruby. The Nowitna Canyon is a highlight, though whitewater challenges above Class I depend on high water. Outfitters in Fairbanks and Galena are good sources for information on trips, as is the refuge manager.

 ALASKA

## KOYUKUK NATIONAL WILDLIFE REFUGE

*Location/Size:* Encompasses lower Koyukuk River and surrounding flats, just north of Galena and the Yukon River. 3.55 million acres (400,000 acres designated wilderness).
*Main Activities:* Moose hunting, fishing.
*Gateway Towns/Getting There:* Galena/regular small aircraft service from Fairbanks, river access via Yukon River. Park access by river via Koyukuk River from Galena; charter air or floatplane service to lakes or airstrips.
*Facilities, Camping, Lodging:* Landing zones. Primitive camping; cabins may be available.
*Headquarters and Information:* Refuge Manager, 656-1231, www.r7.fws.gov/nwr/koyukuk/kynwr.html, r7kynwr@fws.gov.

A vast wetland spreads around the meandering Koyukuk River north of its confluence with the Yukon, most included in the Koyukuk National Wildlife Refuge. Fourteen rivers, hundreds of streams, and over 15,000 lakes are encompassed by the refuge, as are the 10,000-acre **Nogahabara Dunes**. Spring floods saturate the lowlands, providing ideal nesting habitat for ducks, geese, and other water birds. By the end of the summer, 400,000 birds abandon the refuge on their annual migration to wintering grounds to the south. Black bear inhabit the forested lowlands while grizzlies roam the tundra and brush-covered uplands. The refuge is contiguous with Selawik National Wildlife Refuge to the northwest.

Rarely visited by anyone but fishers and hunters, opportunities include river travel, air drop-offs for dune camping or wilderness exploration, and charter flightseeing. The Koyukuk River can be floated from the Dalton Highway to the Yukon, or from river settlements in between. Contact the refuge manager and area outfitters and pilots for details.

## GALENA

*Location/Climate:* On north bank of Yukon River, 270 air miles west of Fairbanks. 13"/yr. precip., 60"/yr. snowfall, below zero°F–low 70s°F.
*Population:* 527 (45.3 percent Koyukon Athabascan).
*Travel Attractions:* Access to Yukon River and to Koyukuk, Innoko, and Nowitna National Wildlife Refuges.
*Getting There:* Scheduled air service from Fairbanks and other points; charter air; Yukon River.

*Information:* Contact a flying service in Fairbanks, or call the Galena City Office, P.O. Box 149, Galena, AK 99741, 656-1301.

As the largest village in the region, Galena serves as the logical gateway for visits to the Nowitna, Koyukuk, and Innoko Refuges. The airstrip was once used by the military and can handle large planes. The economy is mixed, with most residents involved in government, air transport, retail, or commercial fishing jobs. Fairbanks' flying services are good sources of information on the links needed to reach remote destinations via Galena (see Appendix).

### Where to Stay and Eat in Galena
**Yukon Cactus B&B**, 656-1728.

## INNOKO NATIONAL WILDLIFE REFUGE
*Location/Size:* 300 miles northwest of Anchorage in the central Yukon River valley. 4.25 million acres.
*Main Activities:* Innoko River float trips, fishing, hunting.
*Gateway Towns/Getting There:* McGrath/scheduled air service from Anchorage and Fairbanks; Galena/scheduled small-plane air service from Fairbanks. Refuge access by river via Yukon River; floatplane.
*Facilities, Camping, Lodging:* None. Primitive camping only.
*Headquarters and Information:* Refuge Manager, P.O. Box 69, McGrath, AK 99627, 524-3251, www.r7.fws.gov/nwr/innoko/innwr.html, r7innwr@fws.gov (type "Attention Refuge Manager" on subject line).

Bounded on the west by the Yukon River, this refuge is 80 percent wetlands. At least 250,000 waterbirds nest in the refuge, while the regular flooding in refuge streams nurtures the willow thickets that are the food source for a large population of moose. The best way to experience this refuge is by float trip down the **Innoko River** (see Appendix for outfitters). Exceptional viewing of birds, moose, and other wildlife is all but assured in season.

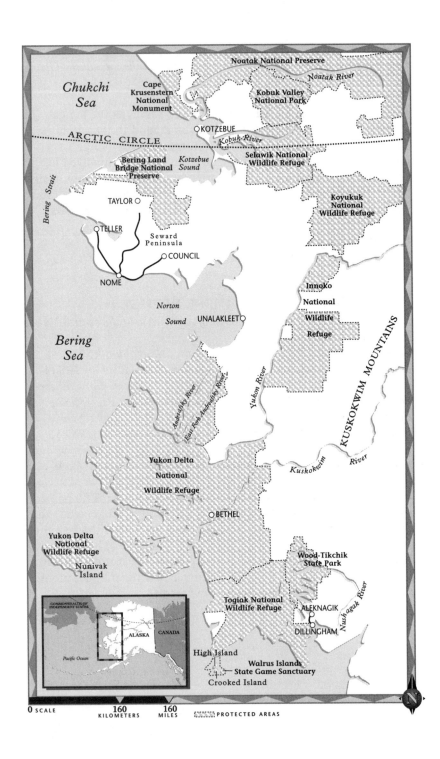

**Chukchi Sea**

Noatak National Preserve

*Noatak River*

Cape Krusenstern National Monument

Kobuk Valley National Park

ARCTIC CIRCLE

○ KOTZEBUE

*Kobuk River*

Bering Land Bridge National Preserve

*Kotzebue Sound*

Selawik National Wildlife Refuge

*Bering Strait*

TAYLOR ○

Koyukuk National Wildlife Refuge

○ TELLER

Seward Peninsula

○ COUNCIL

NOME ○

Innoko National Wildlife Refuge

*Norton Sound*

UNALAKLEET ○

**Bering Sea**

*Anvik River*

*East Fork Andreafsky River*

*Yukon River*

KUSKOKWIM MOUNTAINS

Yukon Delta National Wildlife Refuge

*Kuskokwim River*

○ BETHEL

Yukon Delta National Wildlife Refuge

Nunivak Island

Wood-Tikchik State Park

*Nushagak River*

Togiak National Wildlife Refuge

ALEKNAGIK ○

DILLINGHAM ○

High Island

Walrus Islands State Game Sanctuary

Crooked Island

COMMONWEALTH OF INDEPENDENT STATES

ALASKA  CANADA

*Pacific Ocean*

0 SCALE    160 KILOMETERS    160 MILES    PROTECTED AREAS

N

# WESTERN ALASKA

## 15

Though the division between the Interior and far west is arbitrary, the coastal region between the Alaska Peninsula and the western end of the Brooks Range has several distinct qualities. The region's climate is moderated by proximity to the sea. Forest coverage declines to the west until it is all but absent along the coast. The region is populated mainly by Eskimos, in contrast to the predominance of Athabascan Indians in the Interior.

In the south, the Kuskokwim Mountains fade into the lowlands on the north shores of Bristol Bay, a major salmon-harvesting center with Dillingham as its chief town. The central coast is dominated by the sprawling Yukon Delta, which hosts the mouths of the Yukon and Kuskokwim Rivers, swampy lowlands, thousands of lakes, and millions of waterbirds. Further north is Norton Sound, backed by the wide, low Nulato Hills and home of the coastal town of Unalakleet. The Seward Peninsula, site of Nome and Kotzebue, noses toward Russia and divides the Bering Sea from the Chukchi Sea.

Access to all areas is by air or via long-distance river travel. Only major towns and those useful for further explorations are described below. For further information, contact rangers, refuge managers, and the Alaska Department of Community and Regional Affairs (see appendix).

## WOOD-TICHIK STATE PARK

*Location/Size:* North of Bristol Bay between the Wood River Mountains and the Nushgak River. 1.6 million acres.

*Main Activities:* Fishing, hunting, boating, canoeing and kayaking, wilderness exploration, hiking.

*Gateway Towns/Getting There:* Dillingham/regular air service from Anchorage, possible boat access via Bristol Bay. Park access via the Wood River from Dillingham, via Lake Aleknagik from Aleknagik (road from Dillingham), jet boat shuttle, charter air drop-off.

*Facilities, Camping, Lodging:* No facilities. Five private lodges and several cabins are found on private land inclusions in the park. No drop-in services are available. Consult park headquarters for listings and reservation information. Primitive camping only.

*Headquarters and Information:* Headquarters (late May–late September), P.O. Box 3022, Dillingham, AK 99576, 842-2375; www.dnr. state.ak.us/parks/units/woodtik.htm. Headquarters (October–May 15), 3601 C Street, Suite 1200, Anchorage, AK 99503-5921, 269-8698.

Established in 1978, Wood-Tikchik is the largest state park in the nation. It features a series of long, deep "finger" lakes, their west ends nestled in deep valleys of the tundra-covered **Wood River Mountains** and their eastern shores along the Nushgak lowlands. The **Wood River** watershed drains the southern lakes while the **Tikchik River** and **Nushagak River** play the same role in the north. Powerboats are commonly used by fishers and hunters staying at the lodges on the southern lakes, while the wilder north offers greater challenge and solitude. The park is contiguous with the Togiak Wilderness of Togiak National Wildlife Refuge to the east.

Access is via Dillingham by air from Anchorage and Bethel. Floatplane shuttles drop you and your watercraft wherever you like. Most water travelers fly in and paddle out. Multiday floats in the south take the Wood River to Dillingham, avoiding the need for two flights. Northern trips require a lake or village pick-up—or a very long trip to Dillingham via the Nushagak. It's possible to drive from Dillingham to Aleknagik to put in at Aleknagik Lake—though only the upper end of the lake is in the park and long upstream legs are needed to reach the other lakes.

A few park summits reach over 5,000 feet, though most are in the 2,000- to 3,000-foot range. Brown bears are seen throughout the park, while moose and black bear prefer the forest and brush of the lowlands.

Contact park rangers for information on the five private lodges in the park.

## TOGIAK NATIONAL WILDLIFE REFUGE

*Location/Size: Encompasses north coast of Bristol Bay and Ahklun Mountains, contiguous with Yukon Delta National Wildlife Refuge and Wood-Tikchik State Park. 4.1 million acres (2.3 million acres designated wilderness).*

*Main Activities: Salmon and trout fishing, wildlife observation, rafting, coastal kayaking, wilderness exploration.*

*Gateway Towns/Getting There: Dillingham/scheduled air service from Anchorage; Togiak, Goodnews Bay, Quinhagak, Manokotak, and Platinum/regular small-plane and charter air service from Dillingham. Refuge access: coastal charter boat and sea kayak, air drop-offs.*

*Facilities, Camping, Lodging: No facilities. Primitive camping. Limited facilities in settlements within refuge bounds.*

*Headquarters and Information: Refuge Manager, P.O. Box 270, Dillingham, AK 99576, 842-1063, www.r7.fws.gov/nwr/togiak/tognwr.html, r7tonwr@fws.gov (type "Attention Refuge Manager" on subject line).*

This region of rough, low mountains, glacier-cut valleys, and wetland flats includes breeding areas for waterbirds returning from wintering locations around the Pacific. Spotted seals and seven species of whale are found in the coastal waters, while 1,500 miles of spawning rivers and streams are a vital link in Southwestern salmon fisheries. Several good water routes originate in the **Ahklun Mountains**, a couple with convenient coastal take-outs.

The **Walrus Island State Game Sanctuary** is contiguous with Togiak N.W.R., encompassing four main islands, several smaller islands, and a stretch of coastline east of Togiak Bay. Each spring, **Round Island** hosts up to 12,000 male walruses that gather on the beach well into July. Steller sea lions also bask ashore and 450,000 seabirds nest on the rugged isles. A permit is required to visit the sanctuary and strict rules apply. You'll pay about $200 for a round-trip flight from Dillingham to the town of Togiak, then $300 for the charter boat to Round Island. There you'll enjoy restricted camping and observation with a handful of others for several days.

For details and an application, contact the Alaska Department of Fish and Game, Division of Wildlife Conservation, P.O. Box 1030, Dillingham, AK 99576, 842-2334. An application form and general information may be found on-line at www.state.ak.us/local/akpages/ FISH.GAME/wildlife/region2/refuge2/rnd-isl.htm.

## DILLINGHAM

*Location/Climate: On Nushagak Bay of Bristol Bay, 380 air miles west-southwest of Anchorage. 26"/yr. precip., 65"/yr. snowfall, 4°F–66°F.*
*Population: 2,243 (55.8 percent native).*
*Travel Attractions: Wood-Tikchik State Park, Togiak National Wildlife Refuge, and Bristol Bay.*
*Getting There: Scheduled air service from Anchorage and other points.*
*Information: Chamber of Commerce, P.O. Box 348, Main Street, Dillingham, AK 99576, 842-5115, www.nushtel.com/~dlgchmbr.*

Dillingham is the regional center of trade and transport for Bristol Bay. Located on the west shore at the head of Nushagak Bay and the confluence of the Wood and Nushagak Rivers, the area has long been populated by Sugpiak Eskimos. In 1818 Russian fur traders erected the Alexandrovsky Trading Post across the bay at the settlement of **Nushagak**. A mission was established in 1837 and a school was built at the present townsite around 1900. A dozen canneries were in operation in the early 1900s before the influenza epidemic of 1918–19 killed all but about 500 residents of the region. The **Sam Fox Museum** preserves regional history (Seward and D Streets, 842-5610).

Today fishing dominates the economy; more than 300 residents hold commercial licenses. The **Peter Pan Cannery** runs daily tours of historic cannery buildings at 1 p.m. (842-5415). Travelers can take advantage of relatively inexpensive flights from Anchorage to Dillingham to gain access to Wood-Tikchik State Park, Togiak National Wildlife Refuge, and Walrus Islands State Game Refuge. Air and boat shuttle services offer flightseeing, boat tours, drop-offs, and pick-ups (see appendix). A road runs about 20 miles north to the town of **Aleknagik** on the shores of Lake Aleknagik near the south boundary of Wood-Tikchik State Park (see above).

### Where to Stay and Eat in Dillingham
**Beaver Creek Bed and Breakfast**, 842-5500 weekdays, 842-

5366 evenings and weekends. Breakfast, airport pick-up, *magi* (Alaskan sauna).

**Bristol Inn,** 104 Main Street, 842-2240. Rooms $110–$135. The nicest place in town.

**Camilla's Fisherman's Cafe,** 842-2929. Breakfast, lunch, and dinner.

**Muddy Rudder,** 100 Main Street, 842-2634. Breakfast, lunch, and dinner.

**Ricardo's of Dillingham,** 842-1205. Pizza and Mexican, bar.

# YUKON DELTA NATIONAL WILDLIFE REFUGE
*Location/Size:* Encompasses the deltas of the Yukon and Kuskokwim Rivers and coastal wetlands along the Bering Sea. 19.6 million acres (1.9 million acres designated wilderness).
*Main Activities:* Fishing, river travel, coastal exploration, Nunivak Island visits, wildlife observation.
*Gateway Towns/Getting There:* Bethel/scheduled air service from Anchorage, river access via Kuskokwim River. River access via Yukon and Kuskokwim; coastal access via charter boat and personal watercraft; interior access via charter air and regular small-plane air service to settlements.
*Facilities, Camping, Lodging:* Exhibits and information at visitor center in Bethel. Primitive camping, limited services in several settlements throughout refuge.
*Headquarters and Information:* Refuge Manager, P.O. Box 346, Bethel, AK 99559-0346, 543-3151, www.r7.fws.gov/nwr/yd/ydnwr.html, r7ydnwr@fws.gov (type "Attention Refuge Manager" on subject line).

Larger than Rhode Island, Connecticut, Delaware, Hawaii, and Massachusetts combined, the Yukon Delta National Wildlife Refuge is the largest designated preserve in America. Thousands of lakes dot this largely treeless, 28,000-square-mile refuge, dominated by the mouths of the Yukon and Kuskokwim Rivers. Seasonal or year-round residents include more than 750,000 swans and geese, 2 million ducks, and 100 million shore- and waterbirds.

Hills to the north and east host grizzly and black bear, moose, caribou, and wolves.

Though vast in scale, there are many substantial native land inclusions. The area has long been the home of Yup'ik Eskimos, most of whom still depend upon the bounty of the delta for subsistence hunting and fishing. Forty-two villages are within the refuge, several serving as good bases for exploration or as put-in points or destinations for river travel. A 20-mile road connecting Mountain Village and Saint Marys is the refuge's longest.

Twenty miles offshore, **Nunivak Island** is home to an introduced, but now virtually wild herd of musk ox—once practically eliminated from the state. Members of the herd are periodically removed to other locations to reestablish populations across its original territory. Reindeer introduced to the island provide a source of food and income for residents.

Two forks of the **Andreafsky River** north of St. Marys are designated National Wild and Scenic Rivers and offer river-running options. They flow through a hilly and forested area in the **Yukon Delta Wilderness** portion of the refuge. Access is difficult. Consult the refuge manager, outfitters, and local pilots when designing a trip.

## BETHEL
*Location/Climate:* At mouth of Kuskokwim River, 90 miles from Bering Sea, 400 air miles west of Anchorage. 16"/yr. precip., 50"/yr. snowfall, -2°F–62°F.
*Population:* 5,195 (63.9 percent native, mainly Yup'ik Eskimo).
*Travel Attractions:* Yukon Delta National Wildlife Refuge.
*Getting There:* Scheduled air service from Anchorage and other points.
*Information:* Chamber of Commerce, P.O. Box 329, Bethel, AK 99559, 543-2911, www.bethelchamber.com.

With about 5,200 residents, Bethel has grown from its roots as a Yup'ik Eskimo village into the largest Alaskan town with no access by road or ferry. It's situated near the mouth of the Kuskokwim River, 90 estuarine miles inland from the Bering Sea. The Yup'ik name "Mumtrekhlogamute" ("Smokehouse People") was changed to Bethel when the Moravian Church established the Bethel Mission in 1885.

Yup'ik traditions live on in town. Many residents continue to speak the native language, and subsistence wildlife harvesting remains economically important. With the town's status as a regional hub for 56 delta villages, many are employed in government, transport, shipping, medical, and native corporation jobs.

Cheap air service from Anchorage makes Bethel the logical base for explorations of the Yukon Delta National Wildlife Refuge and Nunivak Island. About seven flights connect Anchorage and Bethel daily. Reeve Aleutian flies from Bethel to Saint Paul Island three times a week, while Yute Air links Bethel and Dillingham daily. Regular air-taxi flights serve a number of delta villages while charter services offer tour, drop-off, and pick-up options (see appendix).

### Things to See and Do in Bethel
**Yup'ik Cultural Center**—Heritage exhibits include clothing, figures, ivory carvings, tools, and other artifacts. The center is adjacent to the community firehall.

**Moravian Church and Bookstore**—Built in 1959, this now unsound structure hearkens to Bethel's colonial heritage. It was Moravian missionaries who gave the town its modern name. The **Moravian Bookstore**, 543-2474, is a good stop for unusual gift items (open Monday–Saturday 11 a.m. to 5 p.m.). Both are found at 3rd and Main.

### Where to Stay and Eat in Bethel
**Alice's Restaurant**, center of town, 543-2272. Friendly and tasty, but you won't find Arlo Guthrie.

**Bentley's Porter House Bed & Breakfast**, 624 1st Avenue, Bethel, AK 99559, 543-3552. Very clean rooms $90–$120.

**Datu Place**, 272 Tundra Street, 543-2216, features tasty Chinese food at decent prices.

**Gloria's Deli**, center of town, 543-4403. Located at the Alaska Commercial Co. grocery.

**Pacifica Guest House**, 1200 Chief Eddie Hoffman Highway, 543-4305. Rooms $100–$160. Easily my favorite lodging choice in Bethel. Features **Diane's Cafe**, the nicest place to eat in town.

# SEWARD PENINSULA

This distinct thumb of land projects west from the mainland, separating the Chukchi Sea and Arctic Ocean to the north from the Bering Sea to the south. About 25 miles from Wales on the tip of the peninsula, the U.S.-Russia border passes through a narrow channel between Little Diomede Island (U.S.) and Big Diomede Island (Russia). Several small mountain ranges roughen the landscape, divided down the middle by the Koyuk River, which flows west to the sea at Port Clarence and the town of Teller.

Gold brought non-native settlers to the peninsula in 1898. On arrival, they found well-established settlements of Malemiut, Kauweramiut, and Unalikmiut Eskimos. The area's history dates back thousands of years and is today in evidence at several locations including the Bering Land Bridge National Monument, which protects sites from the last ice age. The land and culture of the Seward Peninsula have been shaped in the last century by the collapse of caribou herds, the rise and fall of gold, the influenza epidemic of 1918, and World War II.

Nome is the clear base of operations in the region. Originally a gold-boom town, Nome now serves the surrounding villages and centers Alaska's largest independent road system (not connected to the continental network). Kotzebue is the main town on the north coast. Visitors can enjoy mountain scenery, gold history, active native culture, parks, refuges, hot springs, and more.

## NOME AND VICINITY

*Location/Climate:* On south coast of Seward Peninsula, 510 air miles west-northwest of Anchorage. 18"/yr. precip., -3°F–65°F.
*Population:* 3,984 (52.1 percent native, mainly Eskimo).
*Travel Attractions:* Seward Peninsula, Bering Land Bridge National Park, Iditarod race finish and history, mining history, museum.
*Getting There:* Scheduled air service from Fairbanks, Anchorage, and other points.
*Information:* Nome Convention and Visitors Bureau, P.O. Box 251, Nome, AK 99762, 443-5535, www.nomealaska.org.

"There's no place like Nome!" shouts the city's motto—and it's true. When gold was found in the sands near the mouth of Anvil Creek east of town in 1898, yet another of Alaska's gold rushes was on. By the turn of the century, 20,000 miners were working the beaches of Norton Sound and upstream placer deposits—one-third of Alaska's non-native population at the time. By 1905 the rush faded and the population stabilized at around 5,000, where it remains to this day. Gold history litters the region, including the ghost town of Solomon, the abandoned locomotives of "the train to nowhere," and several rusting dredges.

In the winter of 1925, Nome was struck by a diphtheria epidemic, necessitating that medical supplies be brought overland from Nenana. Mushers and their dogs made the 674-mile trip in about 128 hours, inspiring the creation of the **Iditarod Sled Dog Race**. The race follows much of the historic Iditarod route that brought miners to the region from Seward during the gold rush. Nome is thrust onto the world stage for two weeks every March as the racers follow the modern route from Anchorage.

Related events include the **Bering Sea Ice Golf Classic** (March), in which competitors hit orange balls toward dyed "greens" on the frozen Bering Sea. On Memorial Day you can join the crazies who think 35°F is about right for a dip at the annual **Polar Bear Swim**.

Alaska Tourism Marketing Council

*The Iditarod Sled Dog Race is held each March.*

337

From Nome, you should be able to access Bering Land Bridge National Preserve by air. Regular flights go to Kotzebue, Saint Lawrence Island, several native villages, and to Nome's sister city of Provideniya, Russia—one hour away by air. Nome is a good town for walking, exploring, and meeting people—and it's as Alaskan as you can get!

## Things to See and Do in Nome

**Carrie M. McLain Memorial Museum**—Located in the basement of the library, the collection includes natural history, native and gold-rush artifacts, and gold-rush-era photographs. Kegoayah Kozga Library, Front Street, 443-2566. Open Monday–Saturday 1 p.m. to 7 p.m. (closes at 6 p.m. Saturday), call to confirm hours; free.

**Dogsled rides**—The dogs need something to do in the summer. Inquire at the Visitor Information Center or call the Burmeisters at 443-2958.

**Visitor Information Center**—Scrapbooks, photo albums, and historic displays flesh out this source for information on Nome and its environs. Front Street at Division, 443-5535.

## Where to Stay and Eat in Nome

**Fat Freddies**, Front Street east of Bering Street, 443-5899, is right on the water. It's connected by a long hallway to the Nugget Inn, which is nice when the weather is rough. Tasty seafood offerings.

**Golden Sands Guest House**, 411 Alley Way, 443-3900. The $55 single and $65 double rooms include a continental breakfast. "Sleeping-bag space" is available for $25.

**No Place Like Nome Bed-N-Breakfast**, Steadman Street and E. 5th Street, 443-2451, singles $60, doubles $70. A full sourdough-pancake breakfast is included.

**Nugget Inn**, Front Street and Bering Street, 443-2323. This Nome classic offers ocean-view rooms in the heart of town. It's clean and has character, with an entertaining lobby and a waterfront lounge. Rooms $85–$95.

**Pizza Napoli**, Front Street at Lanes Way, 443-5300. Decent pizza and other goodies at a fair price.

**Polar Cub Cafe**, Front Street and Federal Way, 443-5191. This local favorite has the best breakfast in town.

**Ponderosa Inn**, Spokane Avenue and E. 3rd Street, 443-2368. Enjoy a homey feel. Singles, doubles, and full-kitchen suites $64–$120.

**Twin Dragon**, Front Street between Lanes and Federal, 443-5552. Nome's center of international cuisine.

*Boardwalk in Nome*

## Nome-Area Roads

Plan on renting a vehicle in Nome. More than 280 miles of maintained roads branch out from town, enabling access to mountains, hot springs, gold sites, wildlife viewing, and native settlements. If you travel with a partner or two and take advantage of free camping, the cost of rental can be reasonable. Pick-ups can be rented at Stampede Rent-A-Car (443-3838) or Alaska Cab Garage (443-2939). Rates are about $80 a day, gas goes for around $2 per gallon. Sites worth visiting along the three main highways are described below. Allow at least five hours for a round-trip on any of these good gravel routes.

**Nome-Teller Highway** (Teller Road/72 miles)—Heading northwest from town, the route crosses through rolling tundra and grasslands and passes through the western end of the Kigluaik Mountains. The road ends at the native village of **Teller** (population 274, 87 percent Eskimo), once a gold-boom town of 5,000 but now oriented toward commercial fishing and subsistence wildlife harvesting. A herd of more than 1,000 reindeer grazes in the area; some of the

herd is harvested by the residents. Look for signs of some local disaffection with the federal government. Stop in at the store for a chat.

About halfway from Nome to Teller, Wooley Lagoon Road cuts a short way south to the beach, homes, fish camps, and wetlands of **Cape Wooley.**

**Nome-Taylor Highway** (Kougarok Road/89 miles)—This route provides access to the splendid Kigluaik Mountains—an underappreciated feature of the peninsula. A campground is located at **Salmon Lake** (Mile 38), not far from the pass through the range. About 65 miles out from Nome, a road branches to the west for about 8 miles to **Pilgrim Hot Springs.** Inquire at the visitor center about the status of the springs, which are on church-owned land.

Beyond the Kougarok Bridge at Mile 89, the road ends, becoming an ATV trail and a winter road to **Taylor.** Inquire about conditions.

**Nome-Council Highway** (Council Road/73 miles)—From Nome, the Council Road heads east along coastal flats and bars, and then continues inland at Dickson and on to **Council,** a traditional seasonal camp for the Fish River Eskimos. At Mile 36, you'll come to the ghost town of **Solomon** where many remaining structures hint at the town's thriving gold-rush past. Just beyond Solomon, to the right of the road, you can't miss the three wonderfully rusted, turn-of-the-century locomotives from the long-defunct **Council City and Solomon Railroad.** During the gold rush, Council was home to as many as 15,000 people; today there are a number of vacation homes and only about eight permanent residents. Don't try to drive across the stream at road's end into Council unless you've scouted the current ford carefully or can follow a local.

## BERING LAND BRIDGE NATIONAL MONUMENT
*Location/Size:* *100 miles north of Nome, 50 air miles from Kotzebue. Northwest coast of the Seward Peninsula. 2.78 million acres (94 percent federal).*
*Main Activities:* *Camping, hiking, backpacking, coastal kayaking, historic observation.*
*Gateway Towns/Getting There:* *Nome/scheduled air service from Anchorage and Fairbanks. Monument access via charter air or coastal boat in summer; via snowmobile, dogsled, or skis in winter.*

**Facilities, Camping, Lodging:** *Visitor center in Nome. Six public-use shelters or cabins, bunkhouse at Serpentine Hot Springs; primitive camping elsewhere.*
**Headquarters and Information:** *Headquarters, P.O. Box 220, 240 Front Street, Nome, AK 99762, 443-2522, www.nps.gov/bela.*

During the last and previous ice ages, the lowering sea level exposed much of the Bering seafloor, creating a land now known as Beringia. A remnant of this "land bridge" to Asia is preserved in the monument, where researchers study native history, flora, and fauna. The main attractions for the visitor are birding, wildlife observation, and access to the coastlands and lagoons. Musk ox and reindeer are found here, as are grizzlies, moose, wolves, wolverines, foxes, and smaller species. Many of the Seward Peninsula's 170 bird species are found within the monument.

**Serpentine Hot Springs** concentrates monument visitors. Located north of Taylor within the park's southern boundary, there is primitive camping and a bunkhouse that sleeps about 11, with additional floor space for sleeping bags. Expensive charter flights serve the springs from Kotzebue, and perhaps again from Nome. It's also possible to ride or hike to Taylor from the end of the Kougarok Road (Taylor Highway), and then hike an additional 8 miles to the springs.

## SELAWIK NATIONAL WILDLIFE REFUGE
**Location/Size:** *Bounded to the north by Kobuk Valley National Park and to the west by Hotham Inlet of the Chukchi Sea; straddles Selawik River and Arctic Circle. 2.15 million acres (240,000 acres of designated wilderness).*
**Main Activities:** *Rafting on the Selawik River, sport fishing.*
**Gateway Towns/Getting There:** *Selawik and Noorvik/regular small-plane air service from Kotzebue. Refuge access: coastal access via Hotham Inlet from Kotzebue; stillwater access via Selawik Lake; river access via drop-offs, Selawik, and Noorvik.*
**Facilities, Camping, Lodging:** *Primitive camping. Limited facilities in Noorvik and Selawik within refuge bounds.*
**Headquarters and Information:** *Refuge Manager, P.O. Box 270, Kotzebue, AK 99752, 442-3799, www.r7.fws.gov/nwr/selawik/selnwr. html, r7snwr@fws.gov (type "Attention Refuge Manager" on subject line).*

This nearly treeless refuge is surrounded by sloping tundra and encompasses a wide basin of estuaries, lakes, rivers, and deltas, including the sprawling Kobuk River delta. The **Selawik**, a designated national wild and scenic river, flows from its origin in the Purcell Mountains to Selawik Lake. The settlements of Selawik and Noorvik are located on native corporation land within the refuge boundaries.

## KOBUK VALLEY NATIONAL PARK

*Location/Size:* 1.71 million acres, approximately 75 miles east of Kotzebue.

*Main Activities:* Camping, hiking, backpacking, wildlife observation, rafting, canoeing, kayaking.

*Gateway Towns/Getting There:* Kotzebue/via scheduled air service from Anchorage, Fairbanks, and Nome. Park access: scheduled air service to Kobuk River villages (Kiana, Kobuk, Ambler), then up or downstream by river; chartered small aircraft; via snowmachine in winter.

*Facilities, Camping, Lodging:* No facilities. Primitive camping only.

*Headquarters and Information:* Headquarters, P.O. Box 1029, Kotzebue, AK 99752, 442-8300, www.nps.gov/kova. Public Lands Information Center, P.O. Box 1029, Kotzebue, AK 99752, 442-3890 (open 8 a.m. to 6 p.m. daily in summer).

Contiguous with Noatak National Preserve in the north and Selawik National Wildlife Refuge to the south, Kobuk Valley National Park preserves the heart of the **Kobuk River** valley, the low **Waring Mountains** in the south, and a portion of the **Baird Mountains** of the Brooks Range in the north. The Waring Mountains are protected by the parallel strips of the park's **Kobuk Valley Wilderness** and Selawik National Wildlife Refuge's **Selawik Wilderness**. The **Salmon River**—a designated national wild river well suited to kayaking and canoeing—flows from near the crest of the Baird Mountains south to the Kobuk. The towns of Ambler to the east and Kiana to the west are both on the relatively placid Kobuk River, providing ideal put-in and take-out points for floats through the length of the park.

The famous **Great Kobuk Sand Dunes** are located a moderate hike south of the Kobuk River in the heart of the park. Along with the **Little Kobuk Sand Dunes** and other smaller dune areas, these dunes cover about 25 square miles of parkland and reach heights of

100 feet. The dunes are maintained and moved about by the high winds that frequent the valley. Relict plant species dating to the Pleistocene are found in the park where conditions are similar to those of the recent ice age. Prepare for wet, windy, and wild conditions if you plan a visit. Consult with park officials, outfitters, and pilots about routes, float distances and times, and access. Remember to respect subsistence activities, camps, fishnets, and other gear of the native people who use the area.

## KOTZEBUE

*Location/Climate:* On tip of Baldwin Peninsula of the Seward Peninsula, near mouths of Noatak and Kobuk Rivers, 549 air miles northwest of Anchorage. 9"/yr. precip., 47"/yr. snowfall, -52°F–85°F.
*Population:* 2,947 (75.1 percent native, mainly Inupiaq Eskimo).
*Travel Attractions:* Kobuk Valley, Noatak, and Bering Land Bridge National Parks; Cape Krusenstern National Monument; and Selawik National Wildlife Refuge.
*Getting There:* Scheduled air service from Anchorage and other points via Nome.
*Information:* City of Kotzebue, P.O. Box 46, Kotzebue, AK 99752, 442-3401, www.ptialaska.net/~skinner/otz.html.

Located near the mouths of the Kobuk and Noatak Rivers on a narrow peninsula in Kotzebue Sound, Kotzebue has been home to Inupiaq Eskimos for at least 600 years. Traditionally named "Kikiktagruk," the camp was a center of Arctic trade long before German lieutenant Otto Von Kotzebue discovered it for the Russians in 1818.

Today, largely native Kotzebue is the service and transportation hub for villages throughout the region. Its unique site and importance as a base and headquarters for northwestern public lands make Kotzebue a good choice for a visit. From here, you can easily reach points in Noatak National Park and Preserve, Kobuk Valley National Park, Cape Krusenstern National Monument, and Bering Land Bridge National Monument.

### Things to See and Do in Kotzebue

**Northwest Alaska Native Association Museum of the Arctic—** This is where you can see the famous blanket toss—one of Alaska's

defining native images. There is also dancing, a multimedia presentation, and heritage displays. 2nd Street, open daily in summer, 442-3301, 8:30 a.m. to 5:30 p.m., $20 and worth it (considering the local cost of living).The museum is included in area tours offered by NANA's Tour Arctic, 442-3301.

## Where to Stay and Eat in Kotzebue

**Bayside Restaurant**, 303 Front Street, 442-3600. A cozy spot with a good mixed menu.

**Ice Cafe**, Shore Avenue between Tundra and Lagoon. Features delicious ice cream, desserts, and fast food.

**Nullagvik Hotel**, Front Street and Tundra Way, 442-3331. This is Kotzebue's only notable lodging choice and a surprisingly good one. The fairly new and recently renovated hotel has very nice rooms and an excellent restaurant.

## CAPE KRUSENSTERN NATIONAL MONUMENT

*Location/Size:* On the Chukchi Sea, 10 miles north of Kotzebue across Hotham Inlet. 659,807 acres (94 percent federal).

*Main Activities:* Arctic coastal environment, fishing, sea kayaking, archaeological investigation, bird watching.

*Gateway Towns/Getting There:* Kotzebue/via scheduled air service from Nome, Fairbanks, and Anchorage. Monument access via air from Kotzebue; boat or kayak from Kotzebue, Sheshalik, or Kivalina.

*Facilities, Camping, Lodging:* No facilities. Primitive camping only.

*Headquarters and Information:* Kobuk Valley National Park and Noatak National Preserve, Kotzebue, 442-8300 (headquarters). Public Lands Information Center, Kotzebue, 442-3890, www.nps.gov/cakr.

Located beyond the western end of the Brooks Range on the Chukchi Sea, Cape Krusenstern preserves archaeological sites along a succession of 114 lateral beach ridges. Sites of Eskimo communities dating back as far as 4,000 years are found among the ridges and the one-time shoreline of the Chukchi Sea. Even older sites are located inland along the foothills.

In summer, a rich display of wildflowers appears on the beach

ridges and nearby hills. Subsistence hunting of marine mammals
and inland game is permitted. Other possible activities are bird
watching and archaeological observation, but for many, witnessing
the wild land of the Arctic coast is enough. A road crosses the
northern boundary of the unit to reach the Red Dog zinc mine.

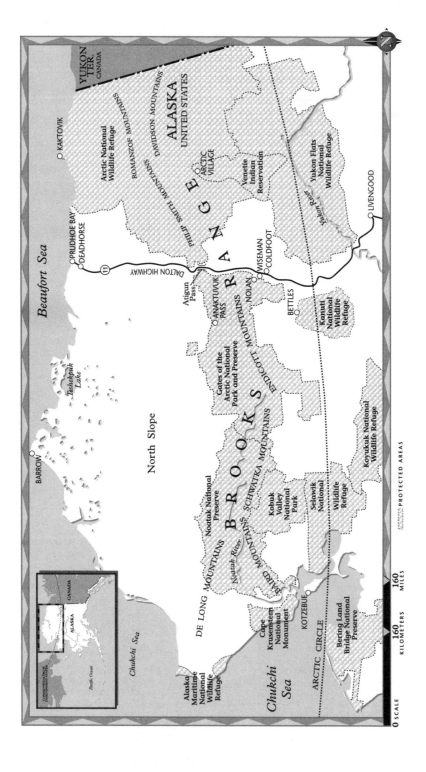

# 16

# THE FAR NORTH

For much of the year, Alaska's Far North is inhospitable and fore-boding. Located entirely north of the Arctic Circle, the sun doesn't rise over this vast region for up to two months every winter. Thin surface soil overlies a continuous layer of permafrost, thawing only for brief weeks during the summer. Arctic Ocean pack ice closes with parts of the coastline in the cold months, blocking boat and barge routes, while fog, wind, and darkness hinder even the boldest pilots.

Wildlife is thoroughly adapted to the challenge of the Arctic. Tundra plants burst into life in the endless June daylight. Animals give birth, feed, and mate during the intense months before winter. Migratory birds flee south after a brief feast.

Geographically, the Far North encompasses the Brooks Range—northernmost extension of the Rocky Mountains—and the north-draining foothills and tundra plains of the North Slope. The treeline at the northern edge of the taiga spruce forests demarks the region clearly from the Interior. The Brooks Range is barren, well-drained, and relatively dry, while the tundra-covered lowlands in the north show many features of the freeze-thaw cycle that affects all surface soils, including large domes called *pingos* and polygonally patterned dikes that separate lakes and bogs.

It is difficult to comprehend how wild the Brooks Range and North Slope truly are. Only nine permanent settlements with a combined population of 9,215 are located within a region nearly the size of Montana. All are encompassed by the North Slope Borough—the world's largest municipality and Alaska's least populated.

Visitors to the Far North will surely sense this emptiness. No village street can mask it. No motorized vehicle can dominate it. Even in the profoundly altered landscape around Prudhoe Bay, the impression is always one of briefly interrupted wilderness. The Arctic is my favorite region in the state, in part because it is so wild, but also because of the strange potency of Arctic light and the desperate intensity of the short growing season. Journeys to the Arctic require preparation, commitment, and some extra money, but the rewards are among the richest to be had.

## THE BROOKS RANGE

This wide band of mountains stretches from east to west across the entire northern tier of Alaska, effectively walling off the Arctic from the rest of the state. The southern slopes have trees at elevations up to 3,000 feet, but the high country and northern slopes are treeless. Compared to the southern mountains, the Brooks are relatively dry. Significant glaciation is found only around the 8,000- to 9,000-foot summits of the **Romanzof Mountains**—highest and easternmost in the range.

Cyclists on the Dalton Highway

Most of the Brooks Range is protected in three federal areas. In the east, the Arctic National Wildlife Refuge encompasses the migration range of the 110,000-member Porcupine caribou herd. The Philip Smith Mountains and Romanzof Mountains run through the heart of the refuge. The rugged Endicott Mountains in the central Brooks are protected in Gates of the Arctic National Park and Preserve. To the west, the Noatak River splits the Brooks lengthwise, separating the Baird and Schwatka Mountains to the south from the

De Long Mountains to the north. Noatak National Preserve encompasses the wide river basin and much of the mountainous watershed. These wildest of Alaska's mountains offer numerous opportunities for climbing, backpacking, fishing, and river running. Walking and mountaineering routes are fairly easy to develop in the Brooks Range, though daily mileage is often limited by the brush and tufty tundra. Unless you opt to hike out directly from the Dalton Highway, count on an expensive bush-plane link or a much more expensive guided trip; there are precious few bases for adventuring. Anaktuvuk Pass is the only year-round settlement in the higher reaches. Bettles, Arctic Valley, and river villages of the far west offer access to the southern foothills, but there are no settlements at all in the northern foothills.

## JAMES DALTON HIGHWAY (AK 11)— LIVENGOOD TO PRUDHOE BAY

*Road Conditions and Attractions—415 miles. Good, graded gravel road built to handle heavy truck traffic; occasional washboards, frost heaves, mud, ice, and snow. Arctic Circle, Wiseman, Atigun Pass, and the amazing wilderness of the Far North.*

Long known as the "Haul Road," the Dalton Highway begins at its junction with the Elliott Highway (AK 2) near Livengood and shoots north 413 miles to the oilfields of Prudhoe Bay. Until 1995, the highway was open only to vehicles involved in oil extraction and pipeline service. Travelers can now drive all the way to Deadhorse, a few miles from the Arctic Ocean.

The Dalton passes north through the hilly forest lands of the Interior, then follows the Middle Fork of the Dietrich River into the Brooks Range and crosses into Alaska's Far North over 4,739-foot Atigun Pass. Following the valley of the Sagavanirktok (Sag) River, the road drops gradually down the North Slope through tundra lands, low hills, and some canyon formations to the oilfields. Paralleling the Dalton for its entire length is the Trans-Alaska Pipeline—now to the left, now to the right; sometimes above ground, sometimes buried. There are many places you can stop for a look, but remember not to block gates and access roads.

There is no wilder drive in America than the Dalton Highway. You may see grizzlies bounding across a tundra whitened by a summer snow, or glimpse a herd of musk ox munching contentedly. You will certainly feel the growing presence of the Arctic as you head north, heralded by the strange behavior of light and sky as the sun's circling path flattens. You can sample the realities of resource exploitation in a hard place when you reach the ugly industrial sprawl of Prudhoe Bay. And when you arrive at the general store in Deadhorse and inquire about a bar or restaurant where you might relax after your long drive, the clerk will laugh out loud—there are none. The North Slope is dry and the only restaurants are the fixed-menu meals served during limited hours at the hotel.

Don't tackle the Dalton unprepared. The road is good, graded gravel, hardy enough to handle two passing semis—but those same semis have to pass you. Slow down as you approach oncoming trucks and stay to the right to avoid too much damage from flying gravel. Some folks use headlight screens and protectors for their windshields. Consider carrying an extra spare and five or more gallons of gas—there's one 240-mile stretch with no services at all. Stop at every roadhouse for gas and a break, and carry survival gear and a warm sleeping bag. If you have trouble, stay with your car.

**Elliott Highway Junction** (Mile 0)—Junction is at Mile 73.1 of the Elliott.

**Yukon River Crossing** (Mile 55.6)—This is the only bridge over the Yukon in Alaska and the first bridge downstream of White-horse. It's a good place to take a look around.

**Yukon Ventures Alaska** (Mile 56) Gas, food, information, lodging, car service, showers, and towing. Inquire about river cruises and floats. **RH**

**Arctic Circle Wayside** (Mile 115.3)—Here you'll find an over-look and display marking the road's crossing of the Arctic Circle. North of this point, there is at least one day a year when the sun never completely sets, and one day when it never completely rises. By the time you get as far north as Barrow, that number is up to 84 days. There is an undeveloped camping area.

**Coldfoot** (Mile 175)—Self-billed as "the farthest-north resort in the world," I wouldn't be at all surprised to find out that it's true—

though if gas, lodging, and gift shops make a resort, the people
in Barrow might have a case to make. It does have, however, the
farthest-north bar in the United States!

Coldfoot was once a bustling supply center for hopeful miners,
but now it doesn't even qualify as a town. You'll need to stop here
for gas—this is the last source of gasoline until you reach Prudhoe
Bay.

Don't miss the **Coldfoot Interagency Visitor Center** where
printed and oral advice on the public lands of the Far North can
be had for the asking. P.O. Box 9034, Coldfoot, AK 99701, 678-
5209, aurora.ak.blm.gov/arcticinfo. The office is open June 1–
September 10 daily 10 to 10 Evening slide programs are offered.

**Coldfoot Services and Arctic Acres Inn** (Mile 175), 678-5201.
Lodging, bar, restaurant, gift shops, and frontier attitude. Rooms
start at $135. **RH**

**Marion Creek Campground** (Mile 180)—Developed but primitive sites are available for $6 at this BLM campground. There are
27 sites, fire rings, tables, and restrooms.

**Wiseman and Nolan Road Junction** (Mile 188.6)—These two
settlements, along with Coldfoot, were centers of mining activity a
century ago. Today, **Wiseman** (population 28) hosts a hearty
group of residents eager for the frontier life. The town is reached
via a spur road from the Dalton along the stretch where it runs
west of the Koyukuk River. A small B&B, museum, and public
phone are found here, though there is no gas. Be sure to take a look
at this historic village.

**Wiseman Bed-and-Breakfast** (Mile 188.6), Igloo #8 (follow the
signs), Wiseman, 678-4456. As rustic and frontiersy as they get—
possibly my favorite lodging in the state. $90 includes breakfast.

**Treeline** (Mile 235)—Take a last look at the spruce trees.

**Atigun Pass** (Mile 244)—At 4,739 feet above sea level,
Atigun Pass is the highest year-round road pass in Alaska and
the farthest-north road pass in the world. This is also the continental divide between the Pacific and Arctic Ocean watersheds. The

pass can be snowy and icy at any time of the year. Use caution, particularly when descending. Though there are few turnouts, the sparse traffic allows plenty of time for pictures.

**Toolik Lake** (Mile 284.3)—A road leads west to the **Toolik Lake Research Camp** where University of Alaska researchers work on Arctic biology projects. There are no services or public facilities, but you can drive in and take a look. Someone might be around for a chat.

**Arctic Wilderness Lodge** (Mile 334), Prudhoe Bay, 659-2955, winter 376-7955. Fishing and viewing packages from about $300. Flying-service drop-offs, raft rentals, rustic. At the time of publication, lodging was not an option, but a facility may be reopened when you visit. Call ahead.

**Deadhorse/Prudhoe Bay** (Mile 414)—Private vehicles are still not permitted to drive all the way to the Arctic Ocean. Instead, follow the obscure signs to Deadhorse Center (the group of buildings just north of the airport; see Deadhorse, below).

## ARCTIC NATIONAL WILDLIFE REFUGE

***Location/Size:*** *Far northeastern Alaska, encompassing eastern Brooks Range and North Slope. 19 million acres (8 million acres designated wilderness—the second-largest national wildlife refuge in the nation).*
***Main Activities:*** *Wilderness exploration, backpacking, mountaineering, river running, coastal kayaking, fishing.*
***Gateway Towns/Getting There:*** *Deadhorse (Prudhoe Bay)/vehicle access via Dalton Highway, scheduled air service from Fairbanks and Barrow; Kaktovik/charter air service from Deadhorse; Arctic Village/charter air service from Fairbanks and other points. Park access by coastal kayak and cargo boat; charter air from Deadhorse, Fort Yukon, and Kaktovik; foot access from Dalton Highway and Arctic Village.*
***Facilities, Camping, Lodging:*** *No facilities. Primitive camping only.*
***Headquarters and Information:*** *Refuge Manager, P.O. Box 20, Room 266, Federal Building and Courthouse, 101 12th Avenue, Fairbanks, AK 99701, 456-0250, www.r7.fws.gov/nwr/arctic/r7arctc.html.*

America's second-largest and northernmost wildlife refuge, the Arctic National Wildlife Refuge is a national treasure. Commonly known by its acronym, ANWR (AN-wahr) encompasses virtually the entire northeastern corner of Alaska—an area larger than West Virginia. The four highest peaks and most of the glaciers of the Brooks Range are within the refuge, as are the calving grounds of the Porcupine caribou herd (named after the Porcupine River, which flows through the southern end of the refuge). At least 180 species of birds and 36 species of land mammal are found within ANWR, including all three bear species. Nine marine mammal species frequent the coasts.

All access to ANWR is via air or water, or by extended trekking through the Brooks Range from the Dalton Highway. Bush planes regularly fly in hunters, fishers, and wilderness adventurers, landing on gravel bars for drop-offs then returning to a designated rendezvous days later. Kayak and raft outfitters have identified several routes, including a couple that follow rivers from the Brooks Range to the Arctic Ocean. In general, however, pilots and outfitters are at the service of adventurous travelers who have their own ideas about explorations. Expect to spend upwards of $300 per hour for shuttle flights, remembering that distances are great in the refuge—a drop-off and pick-up could easily cost your party over $1,200. Fully outfitted and guided multiday trips will run several thousand dollars.

Only two settlements are in close proximity to the refuge, both offering air-link possibilities. **Arctic Village** (population 132, 94 percent Neets'aii Gwichin Athabascan) is in the Interior on ANWR's southern boundary, closer to the high-peaks areas than any other access point, though still 40 to 70 air miles away. There are no services. The Eskimo town of **Kaktovik** is on the Arctic Ocean (see below). The pack ice breaks up near the coast by mid- to late July, enabling kayak access to lagoons along the shore. Many who visit ANWR base their expeditions in Fairbanks and fly directly to drop-off points or to smaller towns for further shuttles. Others drive the Dalton to settlements and private airstrips. See the appendix for outfitters and air services.

Of the 18 major rivers that drain through the refuge from the Brooks Range or Canadian mountains, three are designated as national wild rivers: the **Wind River** and **Sheenjek River** flow south from the Brooks toward the Yukon, while the **Ivishak River** drains northward. Most rivers draining north are too rough for open canoes.

## ANWR Oil

*The ever-simmering debate over oil exploitation on the North Slope continues to heat up and will soon spill over. Geologists have good reason to believe that oil (perhaps a huge quantity) lies beneath the coastal region of the refuge—an area not designated as wilderness. The same argument is ultimately used by both sides in the debate— that ANWR is vast and wild. Depending on your perspective, it's either big and wild enough to have room for oil extraction, or it's so big and wild that it's all the more special as wild land. Even if our thirst for black gold eventually overcomes preservationist sensibilities, ANWR certainly represents a watershed case in the relatively recent American valuing of wilderness.*

*If you get a chance, fly out over ANWR and take a look. Words like "picturesque," "beautiful," or even "magnificent" don't seem sufficient to describe it. Words can't touch it—it's another world.*

Visitors must be completely self-reliant. Consult your bush pilot or outfitter, as well as refuge officials.

## GATES OF THE ARCTIC NATIONAL PARK AND PRESERVE

*Location/Size:* Central Brooks Range, 200 miles northwest of Fairbanks. National park, 7,523,888 acres (96 percent federal land); national preserve, 948,629 acres (99 percent federal land); designated wilderness, 7,052,000 acres.

*Main Activities:* Hiking, backpacking, climbing, kayaking, rafting, fishing, wildlife observation, horsepacking, winter snowmachining.

*Gateway Towns/Getting There:* Anaktuvuk Pass, Bettles/via scheduled air service; Wiseman, Atigun Pass/via Dalton Highway. Park

*access: direct overland foot travel from Dalton Highway; charter air service to drop-offs from Anaktuvuk Pass, Bettles, and Fairbanks.*
**Facilities, Camping, Lodging:** *Administration office in Anaktuvuk Pass. Primitive camping only. Limited commercial facilities in Anaktuvuk Pass.*
**Headquarters and Information:** *Headquarters, 201 First Avenue, Fairbanks, AK 99701, 456-0281; Bettles Ranger Station, 692-5494; Anaktuvuk Pass Ranger Station, 661-3520; www.nps.gov/gaar.*

Situated entirely north of the Arctic Circle across the central Brooks Range, Gates of the Arctic is the second-largest unit of the national park system after Wrangell–St. Elias. The park is characterized by rugged peaks with few glaciers, isolated, well-drained valleys, wild rivers, and numerous lakes. The southern slopes are forested to about 2,000 feet, while the high country and northern slopes fall from barren ridges to sheltered brushlands and tundra. Parts of six national wild rivers are within the park and preserve, including the **Alatna, John, Kobuk**, part of the **Noatak**, the north fork of the **Koyukuk**, and the **Tinayguk**. The **Killik River** is also good for float trips. Together with adjacent Kobuk Valley National Park and Noatak National Preserve, Gates of the Arctic constitutes one of the largest park areas in the world.

Visitors most commonly come to backpack through the high valleys and passes or to raft or kayak the rivers. Access is generally by air from Fairbanks to Bettles and Anaktuvuk Pass, or via charter drop-off to lakes, gravel bars, or airstrips. The Dalton Highway comes within about 5 miles of the park, though there are no roads at all within park boundaries. You can save bushflight costs if your backpack trips into the park begin or end at the Dalton Highway or Anaktuvuk Pass. John and Tinayguk River trips can end in Bettles (see the appendix for air service and outfitter listings, or consult the park headquarters).

Gates of the Arctic is strictly a wilderness park; travelers should be fully competent in outdoor skills. A backcountry registration program may be in operation by the time you arrive. Contact the Bettles Ranger Station before you begin hikes or river runs. Reservations are recommended for all visitor services from area businesses. Several outfitters, guides, and air services offer trips and route advice (see appendix).

## ANAKTUVUK PASS
**Location/Climate:** *In central Brooks Range, 60 miles west of Dalton Highway. 11"/yr. precip., 63"/yr. snowfall, -14°F–50°F.*

ALASKA

*Population:* 292 (85 percent Eskimo).
*Travel Attractions:* Gateway to Gates of the Arctic National Park and Preserve.
*Getting There:* Air taxi from Fairbanks, Deadhorse, and other points; tundra "cat-trains" in winter.
*Information:* City Office, P.O. Box 21030, Anaktuvuk Pass, AK 99721, 661-3612, www.ilovealaska.com/alaska/AnaktuvukPass.

Located in the divide between the John and Anaktuvuk Rivers, the village of Anaktuvuk Pass sits at 2,200 feet in the heart of the Brooks Range. Semi-nomadic Nunamiut Eskimos (inland northern Inupiaq Eskimos) long used the pass as a camp while following the caribou migrations. With the collapse of the herd and the introduction of Western lifestyle opportunities, the Nunamiuts disbanded in the region. Subsequently, Chandler Lake and Killik River Nunamiuts returned and established a permanent settlement here.

Subsistence hunting and trapping are important economically, as are guiding services, arts and crafts, and corporation services provided by oil revenues. Anaktuvuk Pass is becoming a somewhat popular jumping-off point for expeditions into the Brooks Range. There is also commerce from gambling.

If you're waiting for a plane or guide, visit the **Simon Paneak Memorial Museum**. Billed as America's farthest-north museum, various artifacts and educational displays recall the heritage of the Nunamiut Inupiat Eskimos. Several artifacts were produced by residents using traditional methods that date back thousands of years. P.O. Box 21085, Anaktuvuk Pass, AK 99721, 661-3413.

### Where to Stay and Eat in Anaktuvuk Pass
**Nunamiut Corporation Hotel**, 661-3220. $170 (includes three meals), $125 in winter (no meals available). The only place in town, mainly a work camp. Restaurant, store, camping, cable TV.

## NOATAK NATIONAL PRESERVE
*Location/Size:* In Western Brooks Range, 100 miles north-northeast of Kotzebue. 6.5 million acres.
*Main Activities:* Rafting or kayaking the Noatak, backpacking, wilderness exploration.
*Gateway Towns/Getting There:* Kotzebue/scheduled air service from

*Nome and Anchorage. Park access: charter air access to drop-offs, ridge walking, river running.*
**Facilities, Camping, Lodging:** *No facilities. Primitive camping only.*
**Headquarters and Information:** *Northwest Alaska Areas, P.O. Box 1029, Kotzebue, AK 99752, 442-8300; Kotzebue Public Lands Information Center, 442-3890, www.nps.gov/noat.*

The **Noatak River** flows 430 miles from its source high in the Brooks Range to Kotzebue Sound and the Chukchi Sea. The headwaters are protected in Gates of the Arctic National Park, while all but the final miles flow through the Noatak National Preserve. Park protection extends from the crest of the **Baird Mountains** and **Schwatka Mountains** to the south, to that of the **De Long Mountains** to the north. The preserve is virtually treeless, in marked contrast to the Kobuk valley immediately to the south.

River running is the activity of choice on the Noatak. Most of the river within the preserve is a very manageable Class I to Class II, though flash flooding from sudden rains can raise the stakes a notch. It's not uncommon to be dropped off at the first navigable stretch, then to float and paddle 400 miles to the village of **Noatak** (population 418, 97 percent Inupiat Eskimo), or perhaps another 80 miles to Kotzebue. Shorter trips are more common. The river cuts the 65-mile **Grand Canyon of the Noatak**, which should be included somewhere in a float itinerary.

Backpacking is also an activity of choice in the preserve, as is a combination float/hike trip. On several stretches, riverside terrain is walkable and close to the high country. Loop routes from and to a river camp can take you to the ridge tops. Kotzebue and Bettles are good bases for trips. Consult the preserve headquarters, outfitters, or pilots for recommendations (see appendix).

## THE NORTH SLOPE

North of the Brooks Range, the land sweeps down and to the north to the shores of the Arctic Ocean. No trees interrupt the view across the barren miles of coastal plain and low, rolling hills. Wide, shallow rivers and their lesser tributaries meander north, depositing broad gravel bars. Wildlife including grizzlies, musk ox, arctic foxes, Porcupine caribou, and polar bears roam at will.

*Caribou graze on the North Slope.*

Until very recently, travel to the region was enjoyed only by the well-funded. A few tourists visited Barrow for its northernness, while all others flew in for research, work, hunting, fishing, or major adventures—or because they lived on the slope. With the opening of the Dalton Highway to general traffic, access to the North Slope is now possible for any intrepid traveler with a good vehicle, a successful thumb, or a sturdy bike and no fear of flying gravel.

Wildlife populations are sparse due to the challenging environment, though animals are easily spotted in the open terrain. The locations of herding musk ox and caribou are well known though only occasionally observable from the road. Grizzlies roam actively and can pop up anywhere—including your free camp spot on the shoulder of a pipeline access road. Polar bears don't come too far inland, but are frequent summer visitors to areas of the coast.

The BLM manages most of the eastern lands of the North Slope, much of it in the vast **National Petroleum Reserve** south of Barrow (which does not, by most accounts, reserve much oil). To the west, the slope narrows as the Brooks Range and Arctic Ocean converge. The Arctic National Wildlife Refuge (see above), administered by the U.S. Fish and Wildlife Service, encompasses all of this region—though the Arctic Slope Native Corporation controls 92,000 acres around Kaktovik. The central area of the slope, including the Prudhoe Bay oilfields, is state-controlled land. All are similarly wild, though the scarring of tundra from overland vehicles, mineral extraction, and oil exploration is more prevalent west of ANWR.

## KAKTOVIK (BARTER ISLAND)

*Location/Climate:* North shore of Barter Island, on coast of Beaufort Sea, 120 miles east of Prudhoe Bay. Arctic, 5"/yr. precip., 20"/yr. snowfall, -56°F–78°F.
*Population:* 210 (85 percent Inupiaq Eskimo).
*Travel Attractions:* Arctic coast, Arctic National Wildlife Refuge, polar bears, native culture, subsistence whalers.
*Getting There:* Charter air from Deadhorse, Barrow, Fairbanks, and others; coastal access via boat; winter access via snowmachine.
*Information:* City of Kaktovik, P.O. Box 27, Kaktovik, AK 99747, 640-6313.

Few people ever visit the only permanent settlement on the North Slope portion of the Arctic National Wildlife Refuge. Until the late nineteenth century, Kaktovik (the Eskimo word for "Barter Island") was a trade center for natives from Alaska and Canada. During the Cold War, the U.S. military maintained a listening and communications station here, the remnant structures of which are still in place.

The Arctic Slope Regional Corporation receives an allotment of permits for subsistence whaling in the Arctic Ocean and one or two whales are usually killed by Kaktovik hunters in September. A collection of bleached whale bones decorates the beach near the airstrip. Polar bears occasionally come ashore from the pack ice, attracted by the scents of whale, fish, caribou, and other edibles.

As in some other remote villages, non-native visitors are received awkwardly, though rarely with hostility. It is best to be respectful with regards to touring and photographing. Kaktovik is an interesting place to visit when flying in and around ANWR.

## Where to Stay and Eat in Kaktovik

**Waldo Arms,** 640-6513. This is the only place in town and is most often home to construction workers and other intrepid types. Great company, solid food, classic atmosphere! $150, meals included, laundry available. Call for flight/stay packages.

## DEADHORSE (PRUDHOE BAY)

*Location/Climate:* At end of Dalton Highway, Prudhoe Bay oilfields, 625 miles north of Anchorage. 5"/yr. precip., 20"/yr. snowfall, -56°F–78°F.
*Population:* 25
*Travel Attractions:* North Slope, Arctic National Wildlife Refuge, Arctic Ocean, Dalton Highway services.
*Getting There:* Scheduled air service from Fairbanks and Anchorage; vehicle access via Dalton Highway (Haul Road).
*Information:* Consult local businesses, tour companies, outfitters, park rangers, or refuge managers.

The newer oil-extraction facilities of Prudhoe Bay are among the most technologically advanced in the world. To reduce destruction of the fragile tundra, the gravel pads needed for construction over permafrost are kept to a minimum size. Drill holes skew off at various angles and to various depths from the pads, allowing oil from a wide area to be funneled to a compact extraction point. Arco and British Petroleum—the field operators—are under a legal obligation to remove all traces of their presence when the oil is finally out. Their extraction techniques make the daunting task somewhat easier.

Still, you have only to look around to see how extensive the operation is and how many square miles of tundra and coastline are, for the present at least, given over to industrial sprawl. I've tried to find a strange beauty in the long pipes, tank farms, pumphouses, and processing plants, but I can't. The area is as ugly as they come. Take a look, then take a plane—puzzling over the irony that all that ugliness is required to fuel your escape.

Until the opening of the Dalton Highway in 1995, the town of **Deadhorse** existed solely to meet the various needs of the oil business. Truck repair shops, equipment rental yards, and industrial contractors are scattered along the haphazard roads. A general store and post office serves the workers. A "hotel" built of Atco units commonly hosts consultants, contractors, and short-term employees—though it has a cooperative venture with Princess Cruise Lines, serving the few who opt for a North Slope bus tour. There are no bars or other civic entertainments. Prepared food can be purchased in the hotel, but there is no menu—only the chef's daily special (which can be delicious).

The store and hotel of Deadhorse are located near the moderately busy airport. Beyond Deadhorse, the road is still closed, so you can't actually drive to the Arctic Ocean. Stop at the Prudhoe Bay hotel to book a $25 van tour if you want to stick your toes in the water, though don't bother if you're heading to Kaktovik, Barrow, or another coastal village.

*Oil pipes in Prudhoe*

Paul Otteson

### Where to Stay and Eat in Deadhorse
**Prudhoe Bay Hotel**, Prudhoe Bay, 659-2449. $110 single, $180 double (private bath); $75 single, $130 double (shared bath). Basic rooms, price includes three meals; meals available to non-guests (call for times).

## BARROW
*Location*: *10 miles south of Point Barrow, Chukchi Sea coastline, 180 miles west-northwest of Prudhoe Bay. Arctic, 5"/yr. precip., 20"/yr. snowfall, -56°F–78°F.*
*Population*: *4,234 (65 percent Inupiaq Eskimo).*
*Travel Attractions*: *Northernmost community on continent, midnight sun, air access to North Slope.*
*Getting There*: *Regular air service from Anchorage, Nome, and Fairbanks; small aircraft from elsewhere; coastal boat; winter overland access possible.*

*Information: City of Barrow, P.O. Box 629, Barrow, AK 99723, 852-5211, www.wintersolstice.com/barrow.html.*

This traditional Inupiaq Eskimo village is the center of government and economy for the Arctic Slope Native Corporation and North Slope Borough. The modern settlement was named for Sir John Barrow, second secretary of the British Admiralty. Ukpeagvik is the native name for the town, which roughly means "a high place for viewing"—so named because Cape Smythe achieves the lofty local elevation of about 30 feet. Oil support services, government, subsistence, and tourism occupy most workers. Barrow is where Will Rogers and Wiley Post died in a plane crash in 1935.

Barrow is a tourist destination of choice because it represents the northern tip of the United States and the northernmost community on the continent. Some travelers erroneously believe that they must go to Barrow to experience north country phenomena like the midnight sun, which occurs at least one day a year anywhere north of the Arctic Circle; and the aurora borealis, which is easily viewed in Fairbanks and can even be seen in the continental United States. Still, there is something special about standing at the tip of Point Barrow at midnight on summer solstice.

At 71 degrees north latitude, Barrow enjoys 84 continuous days of sunlight in the summer and suffers 67 continuous days of darkness in the winter. The reason those numbers aren't the same relates to the thickness of the sun. If one looks at when the midline of the sun is on the horizon at its lowest or highest point, the numbers would be an equal 75.

Other than a trip to the point and the natural wonders of being in the Arctic, there are no specific attractions here—though guided tours include native demonstrations. See the appendix for tour options.

## Where to Stay and Eat

**Top of the World Hotel,** (800) 882-8478, (800) 478-8520 (AK only), 852-3900. Modern, full-service hotel and restaurant. Tourist-rate rooms $160–$180.

# APPENDIX
## INSIDE ALASKA

---

- 907 is the area code for all numbers unless otherwise listed.
- An asterisk (*) after a company name indicates membership in the Alaska Wilderness Recreation and Tourism Association.

---

## AIR TRANSPORT COMPANIES

Many smaller flying services offer drop-offs and pick-ups at remote sites. Inflatable kayaks and rafts can often be accommodated—canoes, kayaks, and bikes occasionally.

Information is the best available at the time of publication. A listing here implies no specific guarantees or recommendations.

### MAJOR AIRLINES & IMPORTANT REGIONAL CARRIERS

**Alaska Airlines**
(800) 426-0333, (800) 468-2248 (tour packages), www.alaskaair-lines.com. The top carrier in Alaska, and to Alaska from western North America. Seattle is a year-round gateway. Direct summer flights are available from San Francisco, Los Angeles, and Phoenix. Anchorage is a hub for several routes. Alaska Airlines has commuter partners including Reeve, PenAir, and ERA.

**Bering Air Inc.**
Scheduled service to 32 northwestern towns from Nome, 443-5464 and (800) 478-5422 (AK only), or

Kotzebue, 443-5464, info@ beringair.com, www.beringair.com.

**Continental Airlines**
(800) 525-0280, www.continental.com. Scheduled service to Anchorage via Seattle.

**Delta Airlines**
(800) 221-1212, www.deltaairlines.com. Scheduled service to Anchorage.

**ERA Aviation ★**
Scheduled Flights (800) 866-8394, era-aviation.com—from Anchorage to Cordova, Homer, Iliamna, Kenai, Kodiak, Valdez, Seward, White-horse, and between Kenai and Homer.

**ERA Helicopter Flightseeing**
(800) 843-1947—based in Anchorage 266-8351, Juneau 586-2030, Talkeetna & Denali 683-2574, and Valdez 835-2595, era-aviation.com. Guided heli-hiking out of Denali.

**Frontier Flying Service, Inc. ★**
Based in Fairbanks, 474-0014, www.frontierflying.com. Scheduled service to Anchorage and towns throughout the Yukon valley, Brooks

Range, and Far North. Charters, tours, flightseeing.

**LAB Flying Service**
(800) 426-0543, 766-2222, www.haines.ak.us/lab. Scheduled service to Kake, Juneau, Skagway, Haines, Sitka, Hoonah, Petersburg, and Gustavus, most based out of Juneau or Haines. Flightseeing, charters, rafting and kayaking support.

**Northwest Airlines**
(800) 225-2525, www.nwa.com. The top carrier to Alaska from midwestern and eastern U.S. Scheduled service to Anchorage with non-stops from Minneapolis and Detroit. Non-stop service to Fairbanks from Minneapolis.

**PenAir (Peninsula Airways)**
(800) 448-4226, 243-2485, www.penair.com. Scheduled service from Anchorage to McGrath, Unalakleet, St. Mary's, Aniak, Dillingham, King Salmon, Sand Point, Dutch Harbor, St. Paul and St. George. Regional routes served from the hubs of Dillingham, King Salmon, Bethel, Kodiak, Cold Bay and Dutch Harbor.

**Reeve Aleutian Airways**
(800) 544-2248, www.reeveair.com. Scheduled service from Anchorage to Adak, Bethel, Cold Bay, Dillingham, Dutch Harbor, King Salmon, Port Heiden, Sand Point, and St. Paul with intermediate links. Tours to Russia and St. Paul island.

**Taquan Air ★**
(800) 770-8800, (888) 474-0088 (Sitka), www.alaskaone.com/ Taquanair. Scheduled service from Ketchikan to Prince of Wales Island,

Hyder, Prince Rupert, Metlakatla. Scheduled service from Sitka to Angoon, Hoonah, Kake, Tenakee and regional towns. Charters, flightseeing, rafting support, drop-offs.

**United Airlines**
(800) 241-6522, www.ual.com. Scheduled service to Anchorage with non-stop from San Francisco.

**Warbelow's Air Ventures, Inc.**
474-0518, www.akpub.com/fhwag/ warbe.htm. Scheduled flights from Fairbanks to Eagle, Circle, Fort Yukon, Bettles, Galena, and throughout the Interior.

**Yute Airways**
243-7000, www.yuteair.com. Frequent scheduled service between Anchorage and Kenai. Bush service to numerous communities from bases in to Aniak, Kotzebue, Bethel, Dillingham, King Salmon. Float plane tours in Dillingham.

*SOUTHEAST ALASKA—
SOUTHERN PANHANDLE*

**Misty Fiords Air and Outfit/Ketchikan**
225-5155. Charters, guiding, and outfitting in the Southeast.

**Nordic Air Inc./Petersburg**
772-3535. Air taxi, custom flightseeing, LeConte Bay, Petersburg region.

**Promech Air/Ketchikan**
225-3845. Scheduled flights to Prince of Wales Island communities and Metlakatla. Misty Fiords flightseeing, charters.

**Sunrise Aviation Inc./Wrangell**
(800) 874-2311, 874-2319,
www.pnw.com/sunrise. Charters,
float trip support and packages,
flightseeing, Anan Bear Observatory,
Stikine River, Shakes Glacier, Shakes
Hot Springs, drop-offs.

## SOUTHEAST ALASKA—
## NORTHERN PANHANDLE

**Coastal Helicopters Inc./Juneau**
789-5600, www.alaskaone.com/
coastal. Flightseeing, glacier landings, drop-offs, and short charters.

**Haines Airways/Haines**
766-2646, www.haines.ak.us. Scheduled service connecting Juneau,
Haines, and Skagway. Charters,
flightseeing, rafting and kayaking
support.

**Mountain Flying Service/Haines**
(800) 954-8747, 766-3007,
www.haines.ak.us/mtnfly. Glacier
Bay and Wrangell-St. Elias flightseeing, glacier landings.

**Temsco Helicopters/Skagway,
Juneau**
789-9501 (Juneau), 983-2900 (Skagway), www.temscoair.com. Flightseeing, glacier landings, heli-hiking,
drop-offs, custom tours.

**Wings of Alaska/Juneau**
789-0790, wingsofalaska.com.
Scheduled flights to Angoon, Cube
Cove, Gustavus, Haines, Hoonah,
Skagway, Tenakee. Juneau Icefield
flights, Taku Lodge packages, flightseeing, charters.

## COPPER BASIN & PRINCE
## WILLIAM SOUND

**Copper Delta Aero/Cordova**
424-7274. Flightseeing, glaciers,
Copper River Delta.

**Cordova Air Service/Cordova**
424-3289. Charters in Prince
William Sound region.

**Ellis Air Taxi/Gulkana**
(800) 478-3368 (AK only), 822-
3368. Service to Anchorage,
Gulkana, and McCarthy. Charters,
Wrangell-St. Elias flightseeing.

**Fishing and Flying/Cordova**
424-3324. Fixed wing and helicopter. Fishing, outfitting and flightseeing trips, drop-offs, helicopter
charters. Prince William Sound and
North Gulf Coast.

**Ketchum Air Service,
Inc./Valdez, Cordova, Anchorage**
(800) 433-9114, 243-5525,
www.ketchumair.com. Columbia
Glacier, flightseeing, air tours,
regional charters, drop-offs, float
trips.

**McCarthy Air/McCarthy**
(888) 989-9891, 554-4440,
mccarthyair.com. Wrangell-St. Elias
drop-offs and flightseeing.

**Wrangell Mountain Air ★
/McCarthy, Glenallen**
(800) 478-1160, 554-4411,
www.wrangellmountainair.com.
Wrangell-St. Elias flightseeing, drop-
offs. Regular service to Chitina and
McCarthy. Charters to Anchorage,
Glenallen, Valdez.

## ANCHORAGE, TURNAGAIN ARM & MATSU

**Alpine Air, Inc. */Girdwood**
783-2360, www. alaska.net/
~alpinair. Flightseeing, glacier landing, drop-offs, charters.

**Alyeska Air Service/Girdwood**
783-2163. Flightseeing, Prince William Sound, Denali, charters.

**Bear Air/Wasilla**
373-3373. Flightseeing, Denali, Talkeetnas, charters.

**Bush Airventures/Anchorage**
279-9600. Flightseeing, Denali, drop-offs, extended charters.

**Ellison Air/Anchorage**
243-1959, www.alaskaoutdoors.
com/Ellison. Float plane air tours, glacier tours, fly-out dining, Katmai bear viewing, Denali, Anchorage basin.

**Ketchum Air Service, Inc./ Valdez, Cordova, Anchorage**
(800) 433-9114, 243-5525,
www.ketchumair.com. Columbia Glacier, flightseeing, charters, drop-offs, float trips.

**Rust's Flying Service/Anchorage**
(800) 544-2299, 243-1595, www.
flyrusts.com. Float plane, bear viewing, flightseeing, fly-in fishing, float trips.

**Sound Aviation/Anchorage**
229-7173. Fixed wing, floatplane. Southcentral flightseeing charters.

**Vern Humble Alaska Air Adventure/Anchorage**

349-4976. Statewide air taxi service, associated with Rainy Pass Lodge.

**Willow Air Service/Willow**
(800) 478-6370, 495-6370, willowair@matnet.com. Float planes, drop-offs, rafting and kayak support, flightseeing, Denali, Knik Glacier.

## KENAI PENINSULA

**Bald Mountain Air Service * /Homer**
(800) 478-7969, 235-7969,
www.alaska-vacations.com/Baldmtn.
Katmai bear viewing, flightseeing.

**C Air/King Salmon**
246-6318. Alaska Peninsula charters. Brooks Camp shuttle flights. Katmai.

**Egli Air Haul/King Salmon**
246-3554. Alaska Peninsula charters. Brooks Camp shuttle flights. Katmai.

**High Adventure Air/Soldotna**
262-5237, www.alaska.net/
~haac/inform.htm. Charters, bear watching, raft support, flightseeing, remote packages.

**Hughes Air/Homer**
(888) 299-1014,
www.hughesair.com. Floatplane. Homer-based charters, shuttles to Brooks Camp, Katmai, bear-viewing, fishing and flightseeing packages. Lower Cook Inlet region.

**Kachemak Bay Flying Service/Homer**
235-8924,
www.xyz.net/~decreeft/fly1929.htm.
Float and wheeled planes,

Kachemak Bay flightseeing, charters, drop-offs.

**Katmai Air Service/King Salmon**
246-3079. Alaska Peninsula charters. Brooks Camp shuttle flights. Katmai.

**Kenai Air Alaska, Inc./Kenai**
(800) 284-7561 (in AK), 283-7561. Flightseeing, tours, and charters.

**Kenai Aviation/Kenai**
283-4124. Fixed wing. Charters, flightseeing over Redoubt Volcano, Harding Icefield, and more.

**Maritime Helicopters/Homer**
235-7771, www.xyz.net/~marheli. Glacier tours, heli-hiking, heli-fishing.

**Scenic Mountain Air, Inc./Moose Pass, Seward**
(800) 478-1449, 288-3646. Wheel and float planes. Flightseeing, charters, Kenai Fjords, Harding Icefield, fly-in hikes, fishing, drop-offs.

*KODIAK, SOUTHWEST, ALEUTIANS & BERING SEA ISLES*

**Branch River Air Service/King Salmon**
246-3437. Air taxi, flightseeing, float trips, to Bristol Bay, Alaska Peninsula, Katmai, Kodiak, Togiak.

**Iliamna Air Taxi/Iliamna**
571-1248. Scheduled mail/passenger flights to regional villages. Charters to Lake Clark, Bristol Bay, lake Iliamna region.

**Maritime Helicopters/Kodiak**
486-4400, www.xyz.net/~marheli. Glacier tours, heli-hiking, heli-fishing.

**Island Air Service/Kodiak**
486-6196, www.abn1.net/islandair. Wheeled planes. Scheduled flights to all 6 Kodiak Island villages, charters.

**Sea Hawk Air Inc./Kodiak**
(800) 770-4295, 486-8282. Float plane. Bear viewing, flightseeing, rentals, tours, drop-offs, charters.

**Tikchik Airventures/Dillingham***
842-5841, www.nushtel.com/~grant/tikchikair.html. Charters in Southwest Alaska for kayakers, rafters, canoeists, hikers and fishers to Wood Tikchik SP, Togiak NWR, Nushagak and Mulchatna rivers.

**Uyak Air Service/Kodiak**
(800) 303-3407, 486-3407, www.alaskaoutdoors.com/Uyak. Great guaranteed bear viewing, Kodiak and Katmai, flightseeing, drop-offs, charters, kayak and rafting support, fishing.

*TALKEETNA, DENALI & ALASKA RANGE*

**Denali Air/Denali (Parks Highway, 8 miles south of park entrance)**
683-2261. Denali flightseeing.

**Denali Wings/Healy**
683-2245. Denali flightseeing, charters to Anchorage or Fairbanks.

**Doug Geeting Aviation/Talkeetna**
(800) 770-2366, 733-1000, www.alaskaairtours.com. Climbing support, glacier landings, Denali flightseeing.

**Hudson Air Service & Sons, Inc./Talkeetna**
(800) 478-2321, 733-2321, www.hudsonair.com. Denali, climbing support, glacier landings, charters, drop-offs.

**K2 Aviation/Talkeetna**
(800) 764-2291, 733-2291, www.flyk2.com. Denali flightseeing, tours, drop-offs, expedition support, glacier landings, Ruth Glacier, mountain house drop-offs.

**Kantishna Air Taxi/Kantishna**
683-1223, www.katair.com. Kantishna shuttles, statewide charters. Kantishna-based Denali flightseeing, fly-in hiking. Day excursions to Arctic Circle, Manley Hot Springs, etc.

**McKinley Air Service/Talkeetna**
(800) 564-1765, 733-1765. Flightseeing, climbing support, Denali area charters, glacier landings.

**Talkeetna Air Taxi */Talkeetna**
(800) 553-2219, 733-2218, alaskan.com/vendors/flytat.html. Denali flightseeing, glacier landings, mountaineering courses, rafting and kayak support.

*THE INTERIOR, BROOKS RANGE & FAR NORTH*

**40-mile Air/Tok, Fairbanks**
883-5191, fortymi@ptialaska.net. Wheeled and float planes. Scheduled flights between Tok, Delta Junction, and Fairbanks. Service to Healy, surrounding villages, charters, flightseeing, long-distance charters.

**Alaska Flyers/Kaktovik, Prudhoe Bay**
659-2544. North Slope, Arctic NWR, Brooks Range, Kaktovik.

**Bettles Air Service/Bettles**
692-5111, www.alaska.net/~bttlodge. Float and wheeled planes. Brooks Range and Interior charters, fly-in backpacking, float trip support, flightseeing.

**Brooks Range Aviation/Bettles**
(800) 692-5443, 692-5444, www.brooksrange.com. Float and wheeled planes. Brooks Range and Interior float support, flightseeing.

**Cape Smythe Airlines/Nome, Barrow**
443-2414 (Nome), 442-3020 (Barrow), csas-ome.capesmythe.com. Scheduled and charter service to Far North communities from Nome, Kotzebue, Barrow, Deadhorse, and Koyuk. Flightseeing, drop-offs, expedition support.

**Larry's Flying Service/Fairbanks**
474-9169, www.larrysflying.com. Regular flights to Fort Yukon, Anaktuvuk Pass and lower Yukon Valley. Arctic Circle tours, Denali flightseeing.

**Midnight Sun Aviation/ Fairbanks**
452-7039. Flightseeing, tours, charters, bush flights.

**Northwestern Aviation * /Kotzebue**
442-3525, www.alaskaonyourown.com. Wheeled, float, and ski operation. Flightseeing, river trips, drop-offs, charters in northwest Alaska.

## FERRY, RAIL, BUS & SHUTTLE COMPANIES

**Alaska Backpacker Shuttle**
(800) 266-8625, 344-8775. Van service between Portage, Anchorage, Denali, Fairbanks, and points between.

**Alaska Marine Highway System**
(800) 642-0066, 465-3941, www.akferry.com. Coastal ferry service with numerous ports from Bellingham, WA to Dutch Harbor.

**Alaska Railroad Corporation**
(800) 544-0552, 265-2494, www.akrr.com. Service connecting Seward, Portage, Anchorage, Wasilla, Talkeetna, Denali, Fairbanks, and points between.

**B.C. Ferries**
(250) 386-3431, (888) 223-3779 (in B.C.), www.bcferries.bc.ca. Service in Vancouver region and coastal waters to Prince Rupert.

**Backcountry Connection**
822-5292. Van service connecting Glenallen, Chitina, and McCarthy.

**Caribou Cab**
683-5000. Parks Highway taxi service based in Denali. Chartering to Anchorage, Fairbanks, and elsewhere.

**Cordova Airport Shuttle**
424-3272. $9 shuttle between Cordova and Cordova airport, meets every flight.

**Denali Overland Transportation**
(800) 651-5221, 733-2384, denaliak@alaska.net. $40 van shuttles

between Talkeetna and Anchorage (4 passengers or more), other destinations, lodging booking.

**Denali Taxi**
683-2504. Parks Highway taxi service, Denali vicinity.

**Gray Line Alaskon Express**
(800) 544-2206, www.grayline.com. Serves all main highway routes. Buses can be flagged down midroute. Independent travelers share buses with tour groups and enjoy sightseeing stops.

**Homer Stage Line**
399-1168. Bus service between Homer and Anchorage, and Homer and Seward.

**Kachemak Bay Transit/Homer, Anchorage**
(877) 235-9101 toll free, 235-3795. Daily bus or van transport between Anchorage and Homer with stops on Sterling and Seward highways. Kenai Peninsula, Anchorage.

**Seward Bus Line**
563-0800 (Anchorage), 224-3608 (Seward). Daily bus service between Anchorage and Seward, $30 oneway, charters and tours.

**Talkeetna Shuttle Service**
(888) 288-6008, 733-1725, www.alaska.net/~tshuttle. Daily shuttles between Anchorage and Talkeetna in summer.

**VANtastic**
683-7433. Parks Highway shuttles based in Denali.

**Wrangell Mountain Bus**
554-4411. $5 one-way, Shuttle between McCarthy and Kennicott.

## OUTFITTERS, GUIDES, TOUR COMPANIES & RENTALS

Companies are grouped based on their primary area of service, which may not match their home or contact locations.

Listings were as accurate as possible at the time of publication.

If "drop-offs" are listed, "pick-ups" are implied.

The listing of a company here does not imply a recommendation or guarantee from the author or publisher.

### *MULTI-REGION AND STATEWIDE PROVIDERS*

NOTE—Other companies that provide multi-region or statewide trips are found in the Anchorage and other regional listings.

**Adventure Alaska Tours, Inc.** *
Hope—(800) 365-7057, 782-3730, www.AdvenAlaska.com. Custom trips, rafting, canoeing, sea kayaking, sightseeing, dog sledding, wilderness stays, cabins/lodging in Hope. Alaska, Yukon, Northwest Territories.

**Adventure Quest** *
Eagle River—694-1457, www.adven turequestinc.com. Booking agency for outfitters, lodges and trips. Statewide.

**Alaska Discovery, Inc.** *
Juneau—(800) 586-1911, 780-6505, www.gorp.com/akdisc.htm. Custom and scheduled guided trips, kayaking, canoeing, rafting, camping in

Tongass, Glacier Bay, Yakutat, and Icy Bay, Admiralty Island, Wrangell-St. Elias , Arctic NWR, and Gates of the Arctic, Noatak, Kongakut rivers.

**Alaska Natural History Expeditions** *
Anchorage—562-5838, www.alaska. net/~gowild. Outdoor education, flora & fauna, ecology studies, hiking, backpacking, rafting. Statewide.

**Alaska Photo Tours** *
Talkeetna—(800) 799-3051, 733-3051, www.alaska.net/~photoak. Photography trips statewide.

**Alaska River Adventures** *
Cooper Landing—(800) 224-2525, 595-2000, info@alaskariveradv.com. Sea kayaking, river trips, fishing, B&B's, winter trips. Statewide: Denali, Katmai, Bristol Bay, Kenai Peninsula.

**Alaska Sightseeing Cruise West** *
Seattle—(800) 426-7702, (206) 441-8687; Anchorage—276-1305; Juneau—586-6300; www.cruisewest. com. Cruises, small ship cruising, tourboats, bus tours, accommodations. Southeast, Denali, Fairbanks, Prince William Sound.

**Alaska Travel Adventures/Juneau**
(800) 791-2673, (800) 478-0052 (AK only), 789-0052, www. alaskaadventures.com. Glacier float trips, mountain lake canoeing, salmon bake, sportfishing, sea kayaking, gold panning and history, hiking tours. Juneau, Sitka, Ketchikan, Southeast.

**Alaska Welcomes You!** *
Anchorage—(800) 349-6301, 349-

6301, alaskan.com/vendors/ welcome.html. Custom trips, outdoor education, hiking, birding, wildlife, "getaways for the physically challenged". Anchorage, Chugach State Park, Upper Cook Inlet, Valdez, Denali, Kenai Fjords, Barrow, Nome.

**Alaska Wildland Adventures** *
Girdwood—(800) 334-8730, 783-2928, www.alaskawildland.com. Natural History Safaris, wilderness lodges, wildlife viewing, rafting, sportfishing. Prince William Sound, Kenai NWR, Chugach NF, Kenai Fjords, Denali, Kantishna, Wrangell-St. Elias.

**Alaska Wilderness Journeys** *
Talkeetna—(800) 349-0064, 733-2230, www.alaska.net/~journeys. Hiking, guiding, rafting, wildlife, birding, outdoor education. Statewide: Denali National Park, Ruth Glacier, Talkeetna Mountains, Arctic National Wildlife Refuge, Wrangell-St. Elias, Talkeetna, Tana, Copper, Susitna, and Hula-Hula rivers.

**Alaska Wildtrek**
Homer—235-6463, www.alaskawildtrek.com. Hiking, river trips, guiding and wildlife, van tours. Statewide, Brooks Range, Arctic NWR, Gates of the Arctic NP, Noatak NP, Kobuk Valley NP, Lake Clark NP, Kenai Peninsula, Denali NPP.

**Alaska Windsong Lodges** *
Anchorage—245-0200, www.alaskalodges.com. Booking agency for cruise ships, tourboats, flightseeing, historical/cultural inter-

pretation, photography, rafting, river trips, transportation, wildlife viewing. Interior and Southcentral: Denali area, Seward and Trail lake.

**Chinook Tours** *
Anchorage—346-1414, www.alaska.net/~chinookt. Booking Agency for backpacking, guiding, hiking, kayaking and canoeing, lodging, rafting and river trips, wildlife viewing, winter activities. Statewide.

**Equinox Wilderness Expeditions***
Anchorage—274-9087, www.alaska.net/~equinox. River trips, sea kayaking, birding, backpacking, wildlife, all-women trips. Statewide and Far North: Arctic NWR, Gates of the Arctic, Kenai Fjords, Wrangell-St. Elias, Glacier Bay, Denali, Katmai. Walrus Islands, Tongass NF.

**Kayak and Custom Adventures Worldwide**
Anchorage—(800) 288-3134, 258-3866, www.alaskan.com/kayak/. Sea kayak instruction, tours, and rentals, from Anchorage, Whittier, and Seward. Kenai Fjords, Prince William Sound, Aleutians, Hawaii, Thailand.

**Linblad Special Expeditions**
Seattle—(800) 397-3348, (212) 765-7740, www.expeditions.com. Small ship cruises. Inside Passage.

**National Outdoor Leadership School** *
Palmer—745-4047x335, eleanor_huffines@nols.edu. Outdoor/wilderness education and leadership, low impact camping and wilderness skills, mountaineering, backpacking, kayaking. Statewide:

ALASKA

Tongass NF, Chugach NF, Denali, Wrangell-St. Elias NPP, Gates of the Arctic NPP, Arctic NWR, Noatak Preserve, Alaska and Talkeetna Ranges, Prince William Sound.

**Nova River Runners ★**
Chickaloon—(800) 746-5753, 745-5753, www.novalaska.com. River trips, outdoor education, hiking, kayaking, sport fishing, outfitting, sea kayaking, adventure tours. Statewide and Southcentral: Wrangell-St. Elias, Chugach NF, Prince William Sound, Talkeetna Mountains, Gates of the Arctic NPP.

**Ouzel Expeditions, Inc. ★**
Girdwood—783-2216, www.alaska.net/~ouzel. Hiking, river trips, birding, wildlife, guiding, outfitting, fishing. Bristol Bay, Arctic NWR, statewide, Russia, lower 48.

**Soft Adventures, Outdoor Guidance and Education ★**
Eagle River—694-3648. Hiking, backpacking, outdoor education, bicycle tours. Statewide: Chugach SP, Denali, Talkeetna Mountains, Wrangell-St. Elias, Chilkoot Trail, Haines-Skagway area, Seward Peninsula.

**Whitt's Alaskan Adventures ★**
Cantwell—768-2662, www.whittsadventures.com. 2-week tour includes Juneau, Tracy Arm, Glacier Bay, Kluane Lake, Denali NPP, and points between.

**Wilderness Alaska ★**
Anchorage—345-3567, www.gorp.com/wildak. Outdoor

education, backpacking, rafting, kayaking, birding, wildlife. Brooks Range, Arctic NWR, Prince William Sound, Kenai Fjords NP.

**Wilderness Birding Adventures ★**
Anchorage—694-7442, wildbird@alaska.net. Birding, outdoor education, backpacking, river trips, sea kayaking, fishing. Statewide: St. Lawrence Island, Nome, Colville River, Copper Basin, Brooks Range, Arctic NWR, Wood-Tikchik SP, Prince William Sound, Shuyak island.

*SOUTHEAST ALASKA—SOUTHERN PANHANDLE*

**AK-Natural Offshore Adventures★**
Point Baker—489-2233, www.angelfire.com/ak2/aknatural. Charter boat, 5-day custom bird watching, wildlife viewing, kayaking, fishing, schooner cruises. Forrester and Hazy Islands, Prince of Wales, Kuiu, and Coronation Wilderness areas.

**Alaska Angling Inc. ★**
Petersburg—772-4499. Custom small group cruises, spring flyfishing for steelhead, summer whale watching, photography, sea kayaking, hiking, wildlife viewing and sport fishing in both salt and fresh water. Inside Passage, LeConte Glacier.

**Alaska Cruises ★**
Ketchikan—225-6044, akcruise@ptialaska.net. Tour and charter boats, kayak drop-offs, wildlife viewing. Southeast, Misty Fiords.

**Alaska Island Voyages ★**
Petersburg—(888) 772-8588, 772-

4700, www.yachtalaska.com. 65'
motor yacht, custom itineraries for
groups up to 10, gourmet dining, all
inclusive. Inside Passage.

**Alaska Passages \***
Petersburg—772-3967, www.alaska.
net/~akpassag. Small cruises with
whale watching, sea kayaking, fishing, hiking, birding, glacier viewing,
wildlife. Inside Passage.

**Alaska Vistas \***
Wrangell—874-2429, www.alaska
vistas.com. Fishing, kayaking, jet-
boat tours, flightseeing. Stikine
River, South Etolin Wilderness,
Wrangell region.

**Alaskan Aquamarine Experi-
ence, Inc.**
Ketchikan—225-8886, 225-2343.
Fishing, guided kayak trips,
kayak/camping packages. Misty
Fiords, Ketchikan area.

**Blue Jacket Trading Company \***
Port Alexander—568-2266,
www.portalexander.com. Charter/
tour boat, sailing/motoring, kayaking
mothership, fishing, marine education, trips for 2-6 guests. Baranof
and Prince of Wales Islands.

**Breakaway Adventures**
Wrangell—874-2488, www.
breakawayadventures.com. Fishing,
wildlife. Stikine-LeConte Wilderness, Stikine River, Anan Bear
Observatory.

**Coastal Island Charters**
Wrangell—874-2014, www.
alaskacic.com/seabird4.htm. Cruises,
tourboats, birding, fishing, hiking,

canoeing, kayaking, wildlife. Inside
Passage.

**Haida Charters**
Craig—530-7029, www.akusa.com/
haidacharters. One-day and overnight fishing trips, whale watching,
wildlife and ocean photography, 46'
boat. Craig, Prince of Wales region.

**Hindman Charters**
Petersburg—772-4478, www.alaska.
net/~hinchrtr/. Fishing, dinner
cruises, whale watching. Petersburg.

**Kaleidoscope Cruises \***
Petersburg—(800) 868-4373, 772-
3736, www.alaska.net/~bbsea. Whale
watching, glacier ecology tours,
charters, marine bird watching,
kayak transport. LeConte Bay,
Thomas Bay, Frederick Sound,
Lower Stephens Passage, Wrangell
Narrows, Summer Strait.

**The Pedalers**
Ketchikan—225-0440. Bike Rentals
for Ketchikan area.

**Sea Wind Charters \***
Petersburg—772-4389, www.
petersburg.org/seawind. Sail charters
with kayak excursions. Inside Passage from Petersburg.

**See Alaska**
Petersburg—772-4656. Van tours,
boat charters, guided hikes, fishing.
Petersburg.

**Southeast Exposure \***
Ketchikan—225-8829, burd@
ptialaska.net. Sea kayaking, bicy-
cling, outdoor education, guiding.
Misty Fjords, Prince of Wales
Island, Ketchikan area.

**Southeast Sea Kayaks**
Ketchikan—(800) 287-1607, 225-1258, www.ktn.net/sekayaks. Easy, guided kayak paddles at Ketchikan, Misty Fiords adventures. Ketchikan region.

**Tongass Kayak Adventures ★**
Petersburg—772-4600, tonkayak@ Alaska.net. Kayak outfitting, birdwatching, guiding, base camps, drop-offs. LeConte-Stikine Wilderness, Kupreanof and Kuiu Island.

*SOUTHEAST ALASKA—*
*NORTHERN PANHANDLE*

**58° 22' North Sailing Charters ★**
Juneau—789-7301, www.alaska sailing.com. Sailing charters in the Southeast.

**Adventure Sports**
Juneau—789-5696. Sea kayak rentals. Juneau.

**Alaska Cross Country Guiding and Rafting ★**
Haines—767-5522. Guiding, bird watching, hiking, lodging, mountain guides, photography, rafting and river trips, skiing, winter activities. Chilkat Bald Eagle Preserve, Kluane National Park, Tsirku Valley, Takhin Valley, Chilkat Valley, Endicott Wilderness, Tatshenshini/Alsek Provincial Park.

**Alaska Fly 'N Fish Charters ★**
Juneau—790-2120, www.alaskabyair. com. Floatplane charters, guided ground excursions, Pack Creek Bear viewing, wildlife viewing, freshwater fishing, guided hiking, flightseeing, charters. Admiralty Island, Lynn Canal, Glacier Bay, Point Adolphus,

Chichagof and Baranof Islands, Juneau Icefield, Tracy Arm.

**Alaska Nature Tours**
Haines—766-2876, www.kcd.com/ aknature. Outdoor education, hiking, birding, wildlife, cross-country skiing in upper Lynn Canal, Chilkat Valley, Chilkoot Valley from Haines.

**Alaska on the Home Shore ★**
Deming—(800) 287-7063 code 01, (360) 592-2375, www.homeshore. com. Charter vessel, whale watching, wildlife viewing, vessel-based kayaking, fishing, hot springs, hiking, ruins, week-long custom tours for up to five. Southeast, outer coast between Sitka and Pelican, St. Lazaria, West Chichagof-Yakobi Wilderness.

**Alaska Premier Charters, Inc.**
Sitka—(800) 770-2628, 747-8883, www.ptialaska.net/~apcinc. Boat tours, birding, wildlife, guiding, fishing, and lodging. Sitka, Crawfish Inlet, Khaz Bay, Hoonah Sound, Sitka Sound, Salisbury Sound.

**Alaska Rainforest Tours ★**
Juneau—463-3466, www.alaska.net/ ~artour. Central booking for small cruises, wilderness lodging, adventures. Southeast and statewide.

**Alaska Research Voyages ★**
Juneau—463-5511, sskaggs@ ptialaska.net. Sailing vessel based small group independent trips, custom trips, natural history, photography, research project opportunities. Sitka to Cape Spencer, east to Petersburg and Haines, Prince of Wales Island.

**Alaska Spirit Sailing Charters** *
Auke Bay—789-8945, www.
angelfire.com/ biz/AlaskaSpirit Sails.
Sailing adventures, ecotouring,
whale watching, kayaking, charter
boats, wildlife viewing. Southeast.

**Alaska Up Close** *
Juneau—789-9544, www.stikine
country.com. Photography tours,
wildlife viewing, bird watching.
Stikine River Country.

**Allen Marine Tours**
Sitka—747-8100, www.alaskaone.
com/amtsitka/. Sightseeing boat trips.
Sitka Sound, Silver Bay, Salisbury
Sound, Juneau, Taku Inlet, Auke Bay.

**Alaska Waters Inc.**
Wrangell—(800) 347-4462, 874-
2378, www.alaskawaters.com. Boat
tours, Anan Observatory, Stikine
River, Telegraph Creek mining village, sportfishing. From Wrangell.

**Anytime Cruises** *
Juneau—(800) 342-6538, 789-0609,
www.anytimecruises.com. Multi-day
cruises, fishing, dinner cruises, whale
watching. Cross Sound, Icy Straits,
Tracy Arm, Admiralty Island.

**Auk Nu Tours**
Juneau—(800) 820-2628, 586-8687,
www.auknutours.com. Auke Bay to
Glacier Bay ferry, boat tours in Icy
Strait and Tracy Arm.

**Auk Ta Shaa Discovery** *
Juneau—(800) 820-2628, 586-8687.
Canoeing and rafting trips, sea
kayaking, natural history and cultural emphasis. Mendenhall Lake
and Mendenhall River, Channel
Island.

**Bear Creek Outfitters** *
Juneau—789-3914, www.alaska.net
/~bearcrk. Freshwater and saltwater
flyfishing, wildlife viewing. Juneau
area waters, Admiralty Island.

**Berry Island Adventures** *
Sitka—747-5165, www.ptialaska.
net/ ~berryisl. Sailing, lodging, fishing, kayaking, charters, wildlife viewing, sailing. Sitka Sound, Baranof
and Chichagof islands, Glacier Bay,
Hoonah Sound.

**Chilkat Guides Ltd.**
Haines—766-2491, www.raftalaska.
com. Rafting trips, hiking, guiding,
canoe trips, winter trips. Yukon,
British Columbia, Haines region.

**Deishu Expeditions**
Haines—(800) 552-9257, 766-2427,
www.kcd.com/akkayak/. Quarter-day
to 10-day+ guided sea kayak trips,
kayak rentals and instruction, from
Haines.

**Dolphin Jet Boat Tours** *
Juneau—(800) 770-3422, 463-3422.
Wildlife, boat tours near Juneau:
Stephen's Passage, Lynn Canal,
Chatham Straits.

**F.I.S.H.E.S.** *
Hoonah—945-3327, fishes@
seaknet.alaska.edu. Fishing, sightseeing, wildlife. Icy Straits and Port
Frederick.

**Gary Gray, Registered Guide** *
Yakutat—784-3451. Lodging, fish-
ing, birding, rafting, and sightseeing.
Southeast.

**Glacier Bay Sea Kayaks**
Gustavus—697-2257. Park conces-

sionaire, sea kayak rentals, remote drop-offs. Glacier Bay NP.

**Glacier Bay Tours and Cruises ***
Juneau (also booking in Haines, Skagway)—(800) 451-5952, (206) 623-7110, 586-8687, www.glacier baytours.com. Point Adolphus whale watching, Juneau-Gustavus ferry, tours. Glacier Bay National Park, Admiralty Island, Inside Passage waters, Tongass National Forest.

**Glacier Guides, Inc.**
Gustavus—697-2252, www.glacier-guides.net. 38' boat-based park excursions, iking, guiding, outfitting, fishing, tourboat, wildlife. Glacier Bay NP.

**Greatland Guides ***
Juneau—463-4397, www.empnet. com/greatland. Sea kayaking, wildlife viewing, outdoor education. Lynn Canal, Chilkat Peninsula, Channel Islands, Endicott Arm.

**Gustavus Marine Charters ***
Gustavus—697-2233. Tourboat, bird watching, wildlife, fishing. Glacier Bay, Admiralty Island, Chichagof-Yakobi Wilderness region.

**Hoonalulu Kayaks**
Hoonah—945-3608. 1- and 2-person kayak rentals. Hoonah.

**Howard Charters ***
Pelican—735-2207, www.Howard Charters.com. Fresh and salt water fishing, sightseeing, hot springs, kayaking and canoeing, whale watching, hiking, wildlife viewing, lodging, transportation. Chichagof and Yakobi Island Wilderness, White Sulphur Hot Springs, Gulf Coast

from Sitka to Cross Sound, Icy Straits, Pelican, Elfin Cove, Hoonah, Gustavus.

**Icy Strait Adventures ***
Elfin Cove—239-2255, jcraig@ ptialaska.net. Marine charters, guiding, hiking, wildlife, whale watching, backcountry cabin, fishing. Icy Strait, Inian Islands, Mud Bay, Idaho Inlet, Cross Sound, West Yakobi, Glacier Bay.

**Kittiwake Charters**
Juneau—780-4016, www.alaskaone. com/kittiwake. Fishing, whale watching, wildlife, daily or overnight trips. Juneau area.

**Klondike Water Adventures, Inc.**
Skagway—983-3769. Guided 2.5-hour sea kayak trips from Skagway, combination tour with train. Skagway area.

**Marine Adventures Sailing Tours ***
Juneau—789-0919, www.alaska.net/ ~mast. Outdoor education, hiking, kayaking, sailing, wildlife, fishing. Glacier Bay, Inside Passage through Queen Charlotte Islands.

**McCormick Charters, Inc. ***
Haines—(800) 330-7245, 766-2450, www.sailak.com. Sailing eco-tours, guided groups, fishing charters, salmon and halibut fishing, whale watching, wildlife viewing, remote hiking. Upper Lynn Canal, Chilkoot Lake.

**Mountain Gears**
Juneau—586-4327. Bike rentals.

**Out of Bounds Adventures**
Juneau—789-7008. Customized

adventures, kayaking, rafting, mountain biking, glacier treks, heli-skiing, snowboarding. From Juneau.

**Packer Expeditions** ★
Skagway—983-2544/ Hiking, wildlife viewing, photography, winter trips, cross-country skiing. glacier trekking. Skagway, Northern Tongass.

**Pelican Charters** ★
Auke Bay (Juneau)—735-2460. Hiking, wildlife, birding, fishing, cabin rentals, charter boat, skiff rentals, drop-offs. Lisianski Inlet and Straits, West Chichagof, Yakobi Island, Icy Straits, Pelican, Gustavus, Elfin Cove, Hoonah, Juneau.

**Raven's Backyard** ★
Ketchikan—247-2836, corvus@ alaska.ktn.net. Hands on learning adventures, edible and medicinal plants, nature drawing, wildflowers and natural history via kayak, charter boat, trails or roads. Ketchikan.

**Raven's Fire, Inc.** ★
Sitka—747-5777. Outdoor Education, tourboat, wildlife, fishing, drop-offs, whale watching, day or multi-day trips. Inside Passage, Sitka, and Baranof Island region.

**River Adventures**
Haines—(800) 478-9827 (in AK), 766-2050, www.alaskarivertours. wytbear.com. Jet boat and rafting tours. Chilkat Bald Eagle Preserve.

**Sea Otter Kayak Glacier Bay** ★
Gustavus—697-3007, www.he.net/ ~seaotter/. Sea kayak rental, local transportation, lodging. Glacier Bay National Park and Icy Strait.

**Seawolf Wilderness Adventures** ★
Gustavus—697-2416, www.seawolf adventures.com. Charter/tour boat, private yacht, custom overnight wilderness adventures, kayaking, fishing, birding, whale watching. Glacier Bay National Park, Icy Strait, Outer Coast, Inside Passage.

**Silver King Marine** ★
Auke Bay—789-0165. Charter boat, sportfishing, consultant, wildlife viewing. Juneau, Auke Bay, northern Southeast.

**Sitka Sound Ocean Adventures**
Sitka—747-6375. Guided kayak trips, two hour to multi-day, kayak rentals, wilderness lodge packages. Sitka Sound.

**Sitka's Secrets** ★
Sitka—747-5089. Charterboats for whale watching, bird watching, fishing, guiding, wildlife viewing. Sitka Sound

**Skagway Float Tours**
Skagway—983-3508. Rafting, biking, hiking, day and part-day trips. Skagway, Klondike Gold Rush NHP, Taiya River.

**Sockeye Cycle/Alaska Bicycle Tours** ★
Haines—766-2869; Skagway— 983-2851, www.haines.ak.us/ sockeye/. Mountain and road bike tours, from Haines and Skagway, bike rentals in Haines and Skagway. Southeast, southeast Yukon and British Columbia.

**South Passage Outfitters** ★
Elfin Cove—385-3417, spo@olympus.net. Skiff rental, backpacking,

fishing, hiking, kayaking, lodging, wildlife viewing. Icy Strait, Cross Sound, Glacier Bay, Dundas Bay, Outer coast to Icy Point, Yakobi Wilderness.

**Southeast Alaska Ocean Adventures** *
Sitka—747-5011. Birdwatching, fly-fishing (catch and release), guiding, hiking, kayaking, canoeing, kayak shuttles, lodging, sailing, wildlife viewing, multi-day trips. Sitka Sound, off-shore Baranof, Kruzoff and Chichagof Islands.

**Spirit Walker Expeditions, Inc.** *
Gustavus—(800) 529-2537, 697-2266, www.he.net/~kayak. Guided hiking, kayaking, wildlife, outdoor education. Northern Inside Passage, Tongass.

**Time Line Cruises (Bird's Eye Charters)**
Juneau—586-4481, artour@alaska. net, puffin.ptialaska.net/~timeline. 16-person tourboat cruises to Tracy Arm.

**The Travel Connection**
Haines—(800) 572-8006, 766-2681, www.alaska4you.com. Specializing in custom trips statewide. Booking service for tickets, tours, rafting, fishing, salmon bakes. Haines.

**Whale Tail Charters (booked through Puffin Travel)**
Gustavus—697-2260, www.puffin travel.com/. Full and half-day cruises, whale watching, fishing. Glacier Bay NP.

**Wilderness Swift Charters** *
Juneau—463-4942, www.alaska.net/ ~tongass. Wilderness charters, drop-offs, outdoor education, kayaking, tourboat, wildlife. Northern Inside Passage, Pack Creek, Tracy Arm, Seymour Canal, Admiralty Island.

**Yeshua Guided Tours**
Haines—(800) 765-2556, 766-2334, www.haines.ak.us/yeshua/. Hourly and day tours, off-highway tours, eagle viewing, fishing, from Haines.

*COPPER BASIN, CHUGACH MOUNTAINS & PRINCE WILLIAM SOUND*

**Alaskan Angler Charters** *
Valdez—835-5090, www.alaska. net/~alaskanangler. Boat rentals, tackle rentals, charter boats, guiding, wildlife viewing, winter activities, marine transportation. Port Valdez, Valdez Arm.

**Alaska Trail & Sail Adventures**
Anchorage—276-2628. Custom sail-ing and kayak trips, kayak rentals, custom tours. Prince William Sound from Whittier.

**Alaskan Wilderness Sailing and Kayaking** *
Valdez—835-5175, www.alaska.net/ ~awss. Skippered sailing, guided kayaking, wildlife, outdoor educa-tion. Valdez, Prince William Sound, Chugach, Columbia Glacier.

**Anadyr Adventures** *
Valdez—(800) 865-2925, 835-2814, www.alaska.net/~anadyr. Ship-, camp-, or lodge-based kayaking trips, outdoor education, guiding, outfitting, hiking, fishing, wildlife. Shoup Glacier State Marine Park, Prince William Sound, Chugach

National Forest, Columbia Glacier, Port Valdez, Duck Flats.

**Auklet Charter Services** ★
Cordova—424-3428, www.auklet charters.com. Day and overnight charter boat, research and adventure cruises, wildlife viewing, bird watching, hiking, kayak trip support. Prince William Sound, Chugach National Forest, Cordova, Valdez, Whittier.

**Babkin Charters** ★
Anchorage—272-8989, www .alaskan.com/babkin_charters/. Bird watching, charterboats, fishing, hiking, kayaking, natural history interpretation, photography, skiing, wildlife viewing, winter activities. Prince William Sound.

**Capt'n Ron's Alaska Adventures**
Homer—235-4368 (winter), Whittier—472-2393 (summer), www. alaskawebs.com/captainron.htm. Fishing and sightseeing charters from Whittier.

**Copper Oar Rafting**
Glenallen—(800) 523-4453, 554-4453, www.alaskan.com/vendors/copper_oar.html. Rafting, backpacking and wilderness trips. Wrangell-St. Elias, McCarthy, Copper River Basin.

**Cordova Alaskan Adventures & Outfitters**
Cordova—800-881-7948, www. cordovaalaskan.com. Fishing, mountain biking, backcountry camping, photo safaris, hiking. Prince William Sound.

**Cordova & Northwestern Tours**
Cordova—424-5356. Copper River Delta bus tours, Million Dollar Bridge, Childs Glacier.

**Cordova Coastal Outfitters** ★
Cordova—(800) 357-5145, 424-7424, www.cdvcoastal.com. Boat, bike, canoe and sea kayak rentals, guided tours. Cordova and Copper River watershed.

**Discovery Voyages** ★
Cordova—(800) 324-7602, 424-7602, www.discoveryvoyages.com. Multi-day guided voyages, shore hikes, wildlife viewing, charter boats, bird watching, cruise ships and tourboats, fishing, hiking. Prince William Sound, Copper River Delta.

**Earth Odysseys** ★
Seattle—(800) 484-6904 code: erth, (206) 937-6092, www.earth odysseys.com. "Ed-ventures", custom tours, retreats, team building experiences, kayaking and canoeing, natural history interpretation.

*PRINCE WILLIAM SOUND*

**Honey Charters** ★
Whittier—(888) 477-2493, 472-2493, www.honeycharters.com. Booking agency, 4 boats in operation, sightseeing, fishing, drop-offs, whale watching from Whittier: Blackstone Glacier, Barry Arm, Prince William Sound.

**Kayak Tours of Alaska**
Soldotna, Whittier—260-3103, www.alaska.net/~kayak. Six-day kayak trips in Prince William Sound from Whittier. Transport from Anchorage included.

**Kennicott-McCarthy Wilderness Guides**
Kennicott—(800) 664-4537, 554-4444, www.alaskaoutdoors.com/kennicott/. Guided hiking, rafting, wildlife, winter activities. Wrangell-St. Elias National Park.

**Keystone Raft and Kayak Adventures, Inc. ★**
Valdez—835-2606, www.alaska whitewater.com. Rafting, kayak trips, fishing, wildlife, hiking. Keystone, Tsaina, Tonsina, Tana, Chitina, Tazlina, Klutina, and Copper rivers.

**Lazy Otter Charters, Inc. ★**
Whittier—(800) 587-6887, 472-6887, www.alaska.net/~lazyottr. Individual and group charters for kayakers and campers, drop-offs, pick-ups, wildlife viewing, whale watching, SCUBA diving adventures. Western Prince William Sound from Whittier.

**Northern Magic Charters and Tours**
Valdez—(888) 835-4433, 835-4433, www.akohwy.com/n/normagic.htm. Boat tours, fishing, custom cruises, drop-offs, kayak support, from Valdez.

**Nuliaq Alaska Charters ★**
Fairbanks—474-0040, nuliaq@alaska.net. Custom tourboat trips, fishing, wildlife, birding. Prince William Sound.

**Osprey Expeditions ★**
Copper Center—882-5422, www.alaska.net/~ospreyex. Guided wilderness raft trips. Wrangell-St.

Elias, Copper River Basin, Chitina, Copper, and Tana rivers.

**Outer Limits Charters ★**
Anchorage—562-1745, www.alaska One.com/outerlimits. Bird watching, cruises and tour boat, hiking, lodging, wildlife viewing, fishing, Northern Lights viewing. Kayak Island to Prince William Sound.

**Phillips' Cruises & Tours**
Anchorage—(888) 655-4723, 277-4676, www.see-alaska.com/phillips/. Glacier cruises in Prince William Sound from Anchorage and Whittier.

**Prince William Sound Kayak Center**
Anchorage—276-7235, 472-2452 (Whittier). Guided kayak tours, sea kayak rentals. Prince William Sound from Whittier.

**Raven Sailing Charters & Berth and Breakfast ★**
Valdez—835-5863, www.alaska.net/~ravenchr. Sailing charters, lessons, wildlife, kayak support, drop-offs, berth and breakfast in the harbor. Prince William Sound from Valdez.

**River Wrangellers ★**
Gakona—(888) 822-3967, 822-3967, www.alaskaoutdoors.com/wrangeller. Raft trips, fishing, bird watching, low impact camping, transportation. Raft, canoe, and gear rental. Copper, Tana, Klutina, Tazlina, Tonsina, and Chitina rivers, Wrangell St. Elias, Gakona, Glenallen, Copper Center.

**Sage Charters ★**
Cordova—424-3475. Charter boats,

bird watching, fishing. Cordova, Prince William Sound.

**Sound Eco Adventures ★**
Whittier—(888) 471-2312, 472-2312, www.alaska.net/~sea/seasite.html. Biologist-guided marine wildlife and nature tours with beachable boat, fast water taxi, winter activities, bird watching, charter boats, kayaking, canoeing, winter activities. Prince William Sound from Whittier.

## ANCHORAGE, TURNAGAIN ARM & MATSU

NOTE—See the "Large Tour Companies" list above for several Anchorage-based tour providers and outfitters.

**Adventure Ecostyle ★**
Anchorage—(800) 764-7795, 258-7793, www.alaska.net/~sitesea. Small group natural history hiking and sea kayaking tours, glaciers, bird watching, wildlife viewing, charter boat tours, fishing, riverboat tour, ground transportation. Anchorage, Matanuska Valley, Prince William Sound and Whittier.

**Alaska Mountaineering and Hiking ★**
Anchorage—272-1811. Gear rentals and sales: kayaks, climbing gear. Anchorage.

**Alaska Travel Company**
Anchorage—258-7477, 224-7277 (Seward), www.aktravel.com. Tour and travel agent, statewide tours.

**Birch Trails Sled Dog Tours ★**
Chugiak—688-5713. Dog mushing,

bird watching, hiking, kayaking, canoeing, lodging, northern lights viewing, rafting, river trips, winter activities. Beach Lake Park, Chugach State Park, Iditarod trail, Matanuska-Susitna Valley.

**Castle Mountain Outfitters**
Chickaloon—745-6427, cmorides@mtaonline.net. Trail rides, horsepack trips. Talkeetnas.

**Class V Whitewater, Inc.**
Girdwood—783-2004, www.alaska.net/~classv. Kayak and raft trips. Sixmile River, Portage River. Extended fly-in trips.

**Great Alaska Gourmet Adventures ★**
Anchorage—346-1087, www.alaskan.com/akadventures. Guided backpacking trips, etc. Chugach State Park, Denali, Alaska Range, Hatcher Pass.

**Hunter Creek Outfitters ★**
Palmer—745-1577, www.huntercreekoutfitters.com. Airboat shuttle, flightseeing, camping, hiking, wildlife viewing, kayaking, rafting, glacier viewing. Knik Glacier region.

**Knik Glacier Adventures**
Palmer—746-5133. Airboat tours, cabin rentals, llama trek. Knik Glacier.

**Lifetime Adventures ★**
Anchorage—(800) 952-8624, 746-4644, adventures@matnet.com. Kayak trips, bike and kayak rentals. Bike, kayak, and backpack trips, winter activities. Eklutna Lake, MatSu valley, Katmai NP, Katmai coast.

**Lucky Husky Racing Kennel**
Willow—495-6470. Summer kennel visits and sled rides, winter sled trips. Iditarod Trail, Denali foothills.

**Midnight Sun River Runners ★**
Anchorage—(800) 825-7238, 338-7238, www.sinbad.net/~msrr. Rafting, river tours, kayaking, wildlife viewing. 1/2 to 10 day trips. Statewide & Southcentral: Eagle River and Chugach State Park, Talkeetna River, Yukon River from Eagle to Circle.

**Nomad Travel Planners**
Anchorage—(888) 345 0313, 243-0313, www.nomad-travel.com/about.htm. Custom trips, Alaska, Kamchatka, Mongolia, worldwide.

**North Star Treks ★**
Sutton—745-4527, www.akcache.com/northstar. Guided hikes, cross-country ski trips, dog mushing, snowmobiling, all-women trips, custom adventures. Southcentral year-round, Interior in fall and winter.

**Northern Lights Snowmobile Tours ★**
Willow—Guided winter tours. Trapper Creek, Hatcher Pass, Willow area.

**Rafter T Ranch Trail Rides**
Palmer—745-8768, 354-8768. Trail rides, winter dog mushing, sleigh rides. Hatcher Pass area.

**St. Elias Alpine Guides ★**
Anchorage—277-6867. Mountaineering, backpacking, rafting, glacier hikes, ice climbing, historical tours. Wrangell-St. Elias.

**Sound EcoAdventures ★**
Anchorage—333-8209. Outdoor education, hiking, wildlife, winter trips, adventure tours, charters, drop-offs, "unique wheelchair accessibility." Southcentral.

**Susitna Expeditions**
Big Lake—(800) 891-6916 (AK only), 892-6916, kayaker@mtaonline.net. Kayak rentals and tours, hiking tours, ski tours and expeditions. Susitna basin, Nancy Lake, Meadow Creek, Little Susitna, Tanaina Lake, Denali SP.

**Tippecanoe ★**
Willow—495-6688, www.alaska.net/~canoeak. Canoe and raft rentals. Nancy Lake and Willow Creek State Recreation Areas, Little Susitna River, Deshka River, Moose Creek.

**U Choose Charters & Tours ★**
Anchorage—(800) 764-7795, 258-7793, www.alaska.net/~sitesea. Custom boat trips, wildlife and glacier viewing, birdwatching, guided fishing, hiking and beachcombing, kayaking, drop offs, ground transportation. Anchorage, Matanuska, Prince William Sound, and Whittier.

*KENAI PENINSULA*

**Alaska Kayak Camping Co.**
Seward—224-6056, www.seward.net/kayakcamp. Kayak and gear rentals, guided kayak trips, guided hiking, air tours. Resurrection Bay, Kenai Fjords.

**Alaska Rivers Co.**
Cooper Landing—595-1226,

www.summitlakelodge.com/thingsto
do/alaskariverco.htm. Kenai River
guided float trips, Kenai Canyon,
fishing. Kenai Peninsula.

**Allen Marine Tours**
Seward—(888) 305-2515, 276-5800,
www.AlaskaOne.com/wildlifequest.
Kenai Fjords NP tours on catamaran-
style tourboat. Lunch, snacks &
drinks included in tour. Kenai Fjords.

**Bay Excursions-Water Taxi
& Tours ***
Homer—235-7525, www.xyz.net/
~bay. Water taxi, drop-offs, tours,
custom services. Kachemak Bay
region.

**Central Charter Booking
Agency, Inc.**
Homer—(800) 478-7847, 235-7847,
www.central-charter.com. Booking
agent for Kachemak Bay region:
fishing charters, tours, guided trips,
kayaking.

**Center for Alaskan Coastal
Studies, Inc. ***
Homer—235-6667, chopin.bme.
ohio-state.edu/eherderi/acs. Outdoor
education, hiking, tourboat, wildlife
viewing, guided natural history
tours. Kachemak Bay.

**Danny J Tours**
Halibut Cove—(800) 478-7847,
235-7847. Ferry, tours. Exclusive
service to Halibut Cove and Saltry
Restaurant. Halibut Cove, Gull
Island, Kachemak Bay.

**Glacier Quest Ecotours ***
Seward—224-5770, glacierquest@
hotmail.com. Personalized small
group adventures with a focus on

natural history interpretation. Exit
Glacier, Kenai Fjords, Harding Icefield, Southcentral.

**Great Alaska Fish Camp and
Safaris ***
Sterling—(800) 544-2261, 262-
4515. Fishing, hiking, kayaking,
wildlife, bear viewing, mountain
biking, flightseeing, lodging. Kenai
Peninsula, Katmai NP, Denali NP,
Lake Clark NP.

**Fishin' Hole**
Soldotna—262-229. Canoe rentals,
fishing gear, etc. Soldotna, Kenai
Peninsula.

**Jakolof Ferry Service**
Homer—235-2376, www.jakolof
ferryservice.com. Ferry service,
kayak support, remote cabin support. Kachemak Bay, Homer, Seldovia, Halibut Cove, Jakolof.

**Katmai Coastal Tours**
Homer—(888) 733-2327, 235-8796,
www.netalaska.com/bears. Three-
day+ trips on 73' boat, outdoor education, hiking, birding, wildlife,
flightseeing. Homer, Katmai,
Kodiak, Barren Islands, Cook Inlet.

**Kayak'atak/Alaskan Paddling
Adventures ***
Seldovia—234-7425, www.alaska.
net/~kayaks. Kayaking. Seldovia
region.

**Kenai Canoe Trails/Northlite**
Anchorage—(888) 655-4723, 277-
4676, www.see-alaska.com/northlite.
The author of "The Kenai Canoe
Trails" leads trips in the Swan Lake
and Swanson River canoe trail
wildernes areas. Kenai Wilderness.

**Kenai Fjords Tours** *
Seward—(800) 478-8068, 224-4563, www.kenaifjords.com. Large tourboat day trips, overnights, sea kayak support. Resurrection Bay, Fox Island, Kenai Fjords NP.

**Litzen Guide Service** *
Kenai—776-5868. Guide service, fishing, flightseeing, air taxi, hiking, kayaking and canoeing, photography, wildlife viewing. Custom packages in the summer. Southcentral, Mount McKinley Lodge, Southwest, Statewide.

**Major Marine Tours**
Anchorage, Seward—(800) 764-7300, 274-7300, www.major marine.com. Large tourboat trips in Resurrection Bay, Kenai Fjords, Prince William Sound.

**Rainbow Tours**
Homer—235-7272, www.rainbow tours.net. Boat tours, Gull Island bird rookery, Seldovia, Kachemak Bay, from Homer.

**Renown Charters of Alaska**
Seward—(800) 655-3806, 224-3806, www.renowncharters.com. Large tourboat trips. Resurrection Bay, Kenai Fjords NP.

**Spirit Charters** *
Homer—235-3978, www.alaska. net/~captmike. Charter boat, fishing, wildlife. Cook Inlet, Kachemak Bay, Gulf of Alaska.

**Sunny Cove Sea Kayaking** *
Anchorage—345-5339, www.sunny cove.com. Sea kayaking adventures, wildlife viewing, outdoor education, hiking, kayak rentals, cross country and backcountry skiing. Seward, Resurrection Bay, Fox Island, Caines Head State Recreation Area, Kenai Fjords National Park, Chugach SP, Chugach NF.

**Trails-End Horse Adventures**
Homer—235-6393. One hour to multi-day, trail rides, cowboy poetry! Kenai Peninsula, Homer area, head of Kachemak Bay.

**True North Kayaking** *
Homer—235-0708, kayak@xyz.net. Kayaking, natural history interpretation, wilderness skills, day and multi-day kayaking excursions. Kachemak Bay, Kenai Fjords NP.

**Weigner's Backcountry Guiding**
Sterling—262-7840, www.alaska. net/~weigner. Guided canoe trips in the Kenai Wilderness. Kenai NWR.

*KODIAK, SOUTHWEST, ALEU-TIANS & BERING SEA ISLES*

**Afognak Adventures** *
Kodiak—(800) 770-6014, 486-6014, adventure@afognak.com. Booking agency for Muskornee Bay Lodge, Afognak Adventure Cabins, and Dig Afognak (archeological field camp), bird watching, fishing, kayaking, photography, wildflowers, wildlife viewing. Afognak Island.

**Alaska Alpine Adventures** *
Port Alsworth—AkAlpine@aol.com, www.AlaskaAlpineAdventures.com. Scheduled 10-day backpacking trips, 14-day expedition style treks, 7-day float trips, custom tours. Lake Clark NP.

**Alaska Rafting Adventures ★**
Dillingham—842-4303, AKraftadv@
aol.com. Rafting, Wood-Tikchik SP,
Dillingham region.

**Custom Tours of Kodiak**
Kodiak—486-4997. Booking agent
for bear viewing, flightseeing, kayaking, fishing, remote lodges, boat
tours. Kodiak, Katmai region.

**Eruk's Wilderness Float Tours ★**
Anchorage—(888) 212-2203, 345-
7678, www.alaska.net/~erukwild/
erukhome.html. Birdwatching, fishing, guiding, rafting and river trips,
wilderness skills. Lake Clark NP,
Wood-Tikchik SP, Alaska Peninsula,
Aniakchak Caldera NM, Yukon
River.

**Johnson Maritime/Walrus Island
Expeditions ★**
Dillingham—842-2102, www.alaska
walrusisland.com. 2-6 day trips on a
50' motor yacht. Walrus, whale, bear
and seabird viewing, natural history
interpretation, beachcombing,
botany, hiking. Round Island and
Cape Pierce, Togiak NWR, Togiak
Bay.

**Kodiak Island Ultimate
Adventures**
Kodiak—487-2700, www.kodiak
adventure.com. Booking agency for
wildlife, kayaking, charter boats,
sightseeing, tours, lodges, flightseeing. Kodiak Island, Afognak Island,
Shelikof Straits, Kodiak region.

**Kodiak Kayak Tours**
Kodiak—486-2722. Guided half-day
kayak trips, extended trips, instruction. Kodiak region.

**Kodiak Treks**
Kodiak—487-2122, www.alaskan.
com/kodiaktreks. Wildlife, guided
backpacking, hiking, birding, bear
viewing, Aleut Island Lodge. Kodiak
NWR, Katmai NP.

**Mythos Expeditions ★**
Kodiak—486-5536, mythosdk@
ptialaska.net. 2-6 person trips on 44'
Mythos, wildlife viewing, bears,
whales, seabirds, kayaking, hiking,
fishing, bird watching. Southwest
and Southcentral.

**Orion Outfitting/Alaska Sojourns★**
Wasilla—376-2913. Sea kayaking,
backpacking, fishing, float trips.
Kenai Fjords, Katmai coast, Wood
Tikchik, Togiak, Mulchatna.

**Reel Wilderness Adventures**
Dillingham—(800) 726-8323. Fly-
fishing packages. Wood-Tickchik
SP.

**Tanadgusix Corp./St. Paul Island
Tours ★**
Anchorage—278-2312, pribilof@
alaska.net. Pribilof Islands birding
tours. Outdoor education, tourboat,
hiking, birding, wildlife. Pribilof
Islands.

**Tikchik Riverboat Service**
Dillingham—842-4014. Boat based
fishing trips up into lower lakes of
Wood-Tickchik SP from Dillingham. Wood-Tickchik SP.

**Tikchik State Park Tours ★**
Anchorage—(888) 345-2445, 243-
1416, www.tikchik.com. Hiking,
kayaking, rafting and river trips,
wildlife viewing. Wood-Tikchik SP.

**Wavetamer Kayaking/Kayak Kodiak Adventures** ★
Kodiak—486-2604, wavetamer@gci.ne. Sea kayak trips, kayak bear viewing, kayak support, birding, winter trips. Kodiak, Katmai NP coast Shuyak Island SP.

## TALKEETNA, DENALI & ALASKA RANGE

**Alaska Backcountry Touring, LLC** ★
Ester—456-6091, www.mosquito net.com/~abt. Eco-adventure, wilderness tours, hiking, backpacking, guiding, rafting, kayaking and canoeing, outdoor education, wildlife viewing, ground transportation, dog sledding, winter activities. Statewide, Interior, Far North.

**Alaska-Denali Guiding, Inc.** ★
Talkeetna—733-2649, www.alaska.net/~adg. Mountaineering, hiking, river trips, cross-country skiing. Denali-Talkeetna region.

**Alaska Raft Adventures**
Denali Park—683-2684. Whitewater rafting and float trips. Denali NPP.

**CGS Bicycles**
Talkeetna—733-1279, www.gmcrowley.com. Mountain bike rentals and tours. Talkeetna.

**Denali Floats**
Talkeetna—(800) 651-5221, 733-2384, denaliak@alaska.net. Day and overnight trips, tours, rafting, guided adventures. Susitna, Chulitna, Talkeetna rivers, Talkeetna region.

**Denali Foundation** ★
Denali—683-2597, denali@mosqui

tonet.com. Elderhostel sponsor. Hiking, historical/cultural interpretation, natural history interpretation, wilderness skills, wildlife viewing, winter activities. Interior/Far North: Denali NPP.

**Denali Outdoor Center**
Denali Park—(888) 303-1925, 683-1925, www.denalioutdoorcenter.com. Raft and inflatable kayak trips, mountain bike rentals, whitewater kayak school. Nenana River, Denali area.

**Denali Raft Adventures** ★
Denali—(888) 683-2234, 683-2234, www.denaliraftadventures.com. Rafting and river trips. Paddle rafts or oared rafts, transportation, flotation suits, rain gear and other equipment are provided. Nenana River at Denali NP.

**Denali Wilderness Safaris**
Cantwell—768-2550. Jetboat and airboat trips. Nenana River, Denali area.

**Malay's Riverboat Service**
Talkeetna—(800) 736-2210, 733-2223, www.alaskan.com/mahays. Susitna, Talkeetna, and Chulitna rivers small boat cruises, fishing, drop-offs, canoe rentals.

**McKinley Raft Tours, Inc.**
Denali Park—683-2392, www.AlaskaOne.com/mrtours. Raft trips. Nenana River, Denali area.

**Paxson Alpine Tours & Cabins**
Paxson—822-5972, www.alaskan.com/paxsontours. Float trips, cabins. Paxson Wildlife Reserve, eastern Alaska Range.

**Talkeetna River Guides** ★
Talkeetna—(800) 353-2677, 733-
2677, www.talkeetnariver
guides.com. Easy float trips,
extended floats, fishing. Talkeetna,
Denali area.

**Talkeetna Riverboat Service**
Talkeetna—733-3336, www.
gotalkeetna.com. Fishing charters,
river drop-offs, 8 to 10-day float trips,
snowmobile tours, dog sled rides,
remote camps, raft rentals, RV park
and storage yard. Talkeetna area.

**Too-loo-uk River Guides** ★
Denali Park—683-1542,
www.alaskaone.com/tooloouk.
Guided rafting, whitewater trips.
Statewide: Brooks Range, Alaska
Range, Wrangell-St. Elias, Denali,
Fortymile region.

**Tumbling B Ranch Trail Rides**
Healy—683-6000, www.tumbling
branch.com. Horse rides and pack
trips. Nenana River valley near
Denali.

*THE INTERIOR, BROOKS RANGE
& FAR NORTH*

**7 Bridges Boats & Bikes**
Fairbanks—479-0751, www.
alaska.net/~gables7/7bridges.htm.
Canoe and bike rentals, river drop-
offs. Fairbanks.

**ABEC's Alaska Adventures** ★
Fairbanks—457-8907, www2.polar
net.com/~abec/ABEC1.html. Backpacking, hiking, rafting, canoeing,
kayaking, river trips, wildlife. Brooks
Range, Gates of the Arctic, Arctic
NWR

**Alaska Best Wilderness**★
Tanana—366-7111, www.mosquito
net.com/~abwe. Small-group expeditions by dog sled, backpacking trips
in little known mountains north of
the Yukon. From Tanana. Yukon
River, Ray Mountains, Kokrine-
Hodzana Uplands.

**Alaska Fish and Trails**
Bettles—479-7630, www.ptialaska.
net/~aktrails/. Backpacking, canoeing, kayaking, rafting, fishing. Gates
of the Arctic, Koyukuk River,
Brooks Range.

**Alaska Tolovana Adventures**
Nenana—832-5569, www.Alaska
One.com/tolovana. River trips, birding, wildlife, guiding, fishing, lodge,
dog sledding, winter trips, drop-offs,
multi-day trips. Statewide and
Southeast.

**Arctic Treks** ★
Fairbanks—455-6502, www.gorp.
com/arctreks. Backpacking, rafting
trips, hiking, wilderness skills.
Brooks Range, Gates of the Arctic,
Arctic NWR.

**Awl Alaskan Kennels**
Fairbanks—389-6957. Dogsled
trips. Chatanika area.

**Back Country Logistical Services**
Fairbanks—457-7606, www.alaska.
net/~finstad/. River trips, outfitting,
fishing, drop-offs. White Mountains,
Alaska Range.

**Canoe Alaska**
Fairbanks—479-5183, www.
mosquitonet.com/~canoeak. Instruction, Guided canoe and raft trips on
the Delta, Gulkana, Chena, and

Fortymile rivers, and on Beaver and Chena creeks, and other Interior rivers. Interior, Alaska Range.

**Circle City Charters (S&S Ventures)**
Fairbanks—773-8439. Boat trips, kayak support, lodging. Yukon River basin from Circle.

**Eagle Canoe Rentals**
Eagle, Dawson City —547-2203. Canoe rentals, custom guided trips, also rents canoes at Dawson City youth hostel. Yukon River region from Eagle.

**Ester Dome Walking Society ★**
Ester—479-8300, dayates@igc.org. Walk game trails and historic mining roads through boreal forest. Natural history interpretation, outdoor education, photography, wildflowers and wildlife viewing. Ester Dome, Fairbanks area.

**Friends of Creamer's Field ★**
Fairbanks—452-5162. Bird watching, hiking, historical/cultural and natural history interpretation, skiing, wildlife viewing, outdoor education, naturalist walks, programs. Creamers Field Migratory Waterfowl Refuge, Fairbanks.

**Independent Rentals**
Fairbanks—456-6595, www.akpub. com/akbbrv/indep.html. Rentals. Inflatable rafts and boats, 17' canoes, bicycles, camping and fishing equipment, etc. Fairbanks.

**Interior A.K. Adventures ★**
Fairbanks—(800) 890-3229, 388-4193, www.akpub.fhwag/logan.html. Backpacking, mountaineering and mountain guides, rafting and river

trips, fishing, glacier hiking, Northern Lights viewing, photography, wildlife viewing, winter activities. Beaver Creek, Birch Creek, Wild, Chatanika, Chena, Koyukuk, Noatak, Nowitna, Kobuk, Delta, Clearwater, and Gulkana rivers, Wood Tikchik SP, Sagavanirktok. Statewide.

**Mackey's Happy Dog Kennel**
Nenana—832-1001. Dogsled treks. Nenana region.

**Mountain Trip ★**
Anchorage—345-6499, MtTrip@ aol.com. Mountaineering, guiding, climbing instruction. Mt. Hunter, Denali, Mt. Sanford, Little Switzerland, Ruth Glacier.

**Nature Alaska Tours**
Fairbanks—488-3746. Natural history, birding. Prudhoe Bay, Nome, Gambell, Kenai Fjords, Seward Peninsula, Denali, Denali Highway, Brooks Range.

**Northern Alaska Tour Company**
Fairbanks—474-8600, www. alaskasarctic.com. Tours to Anaktuvuk Pass, Prudhoe Bay, Barrow, Nome/Kotzebue, Arctic Circle. From Fairbanks.

**North Country Outfitters ★**
Tok—883-5506. Guiding, outfitting, fishing, wildlife, horseback rides and trips. Interior & Southeast: Chichagof Island and Game Management Units 4, 6,12,17,20.

**Sourdough Outfitters**
Bettles Field—692-5252, www. sourdough.com. Back-packing, fishing, flightseeing, air taxi, lodging, northern lights. Gates of the Arctic

NPP, Noatak NP, Kanuti NWR, Kobuk Valley NP, Selawik NWR, Arctic NWR, Brooks Range.

**Tundra Tours**
Barrow—(800) 882-8748, 852-3900, www.tundratours.com. Package tours of Barrow in partnership with Alaska Airlines, Arctic Ocean, Inupiat cultural demonstrations, midninght sun, northern lights. Barrow.

**VanGo Custom Tours & Alaska Places** *
Fairbanks—235-5431, akplaces@ alaska.net. "Off-the-beaten-track tours" through Fairbanks region, Interior.

**Wilderness: Alaska/Mexico** *
Fairbanks—479-8203. www2.polar net.com/~wildakmx. Hiking, backpacking, kayaking and canoeing, river trips, birding, wildlife. Arctic NWR, Gates of the Arctic NPP, Noatak NP.

**Yukon Adventure Company, LLC** *
Ruby—468-4463. Class I sea kayak tour of Yukon River and tributaries. Small group 4-14 day ecoadventures, dog sledding, Northern Lights viewing. Yukon River region.

**Yukon Raft Adventures**
Eagle—547-2355, www.wwwdi. com/yukonraft/yraft_14.html. Extended Yukon River float trips. Eagle, Dawson, Circle region.

**Yukon River Tours** *
Fairbanks—452-7162, www. mosquitonet.com/mdlacey/url.html. 43-passenger tourboat, river trips, birding, native culture. Yukon River

from Tanana to Stevens Village, Beaver.

**Yukon Starr Enterprises**
Tanana—366-7251. Boat tours. Yukon River from Tanana, air links.

## REMOTE & WILDERNESS LODGING

Includes true wilderness lodges, as well as options in isolated towns and villages. Other choices are found in the regional chapters.

**Afognak Wilderness Lodge**
Afognak Island—(800) 478-6442, 486-6442, www.afognaklodge.com. Lodge and cabins. Remote wilderness lodge with outdoor education, hiking, birding, outfitting, boat tours, fishing. Northeast Afognak Island near Kodiak.

**Alagnak Lodge** *
Alagnak River—(800) 877-9903, (808) 593-1144. Riverside fishing lodge on Alagnak River near Bristol Bay.

**Alaska Retreat** *
Ruth Glacier, Denali NPP—733-2414. The legendary mountain hut above Don Sheldon Amphitheater and Ruth Glacier in Denali NPP. Primitive. Reserve a year in advance.

**Alaska's Thayer Lake Wilderness Lodge** *
Admiralty Island NM—247-8897. Inside Passage, brown bear viewing, rainforest exploration. In Killisnoo Wilderness.

**Blue Heron Inn** *
Yakutat—784-3287. Small bayside inn in Yakutat, bird watching, guid-

 ALASKA

ing, outfitting, sportfishing, photography, boat rentals.

**Chelatna Lake Lodge**
Chelatna Lake—(800) 999-0785, 243-7767, www.alaska.net/~chelatna/Lodge.htm. Fishing, rafting, flightseeing in Denali region.

**Denali Wilderness Lodge** ★
Denali region—(800) 541-9779, 479-4000, www.AlaskaOne.com/dwlodge. Historic fly-in lodge with guided walks, rafting, horseback riding, flightseeing, birding and evening programs. Denali region.

**Earthsong Lodge** ★
Healy—683-2863, www.AlaskaOne.com/earthsong. Cabins, breakfast included, kennel tours, winter sled excursions, dog cart rides, evening programs, hike planning with experienced Denali ranger, Denali views, backroad accessible near Healy. Denali.

**Favorite Bay Inn** ★
Angoon, Admiralty Island—(800) 423-3123, 788-3123, favorite bayinn@juno.com. B&B, tours, hiking, fishing, canoe and kayak rentals, serving Admiralty Island, Killisnoo Island, Chatham Straight, Baranof and Chichagof Islands.

**Gold King Creek, The Alaska Range, of Course** ★
Northern foothills of Alaska Range—322-3614, messages at 459-8288, www.alaskarange.com. Remote wilderness lodge, winter activities and gourmet food in the Northern foothills of the Alaska Range.

**Granite Mountain Chalet** ★
Sutton—745-8974, www.alaska.net/~mich. Bicycling, bird watching, hiking, northern lights viewing, photography, skiing, wildlife viewing, winter activities. Matanuska Valley.

**Growler Island Camp/ Stan Stephen's Cruises** ★
Valdez—(800) 992-1297, 835-4731, www.alaska.net/~ssc/growlerisland.html. Remote heated tent cabins with day activities, kayaking, tours, tourboat transport from Valdez, across from Columbia Glacier in Prince William Sound.

**Hallo Bay Camp & Kodiak-Katmai Outdoors Inc.** ★
Katmai NP coast—(800) 762-5634, 486-2628, www.hallobay.com. Remote wilderness cabins and common building. Guided bear and wildlife viewing, birding and marine wildlife.

**Iniakuk Lake Lodge** ★
Brooks Range foothills—479-6354, www.gofarnorth.com. Remote wilderness lodge. Hiking, backpacking, fishing, flightseeing, birding in Brooks Range 50 miles west of Bettles.

**Kachemak Bay Wilderness Lodge**★
Kachemak Bay—235-8910, www.xyz.net/~wildrnes/lodge.htm. Remote lodge and 2 remote cabin camps. Hiking, kayaking, fishing, guiding. China Poot Bay on Kachemak Bay.

**Kenai Fjords Wilderness Lodge**
Fox Island, Resurrection Bay—(800) 208-0200, 245-0200, www.alaska parks.com/KFWL.html.

Tourboat, wildlife viewing, sea kayaking, drop-offs, fishing. Remote lodge near Seward, owned by Kenai Fjords Tours.

**Kiana Lodge ★**
Kiana, at confluence of Kobuk and Squirrel Rivers—333-5866, www.alaskaOutdoors.com/Kiana. Remote lodge offering fishing, guiding, native culture, Northern Lights viewing, rafting and river trips, snowmobiling, wildlife viewing.

**Kennicott Glacier Lodge ★**
Kennicott, Wrangell-St. Elias NPP—258-2350. Hiking, flightseeing, wilderness exploration in Wrangell-St. Elias NPP. Wonderful historic location. Accessible by short van shuttle from McCarthy.

**Laughing Raven Lodge ★**
Port Alexander—568-2266 Lodging with meals: wildlife viewing, hiking, fishing, beachcombing, fish smoking and packaging, skiffs and kayaks for rent, motor/sailer "Bluejacket" for charter. At southern tip of Baranof Island.

**Lisianski Inlet Lodge ★**
Pelican—735-2266, www.alaska ecoadventures.com. Rustic log cabin homestead. Lodging, charter boats, birdwatching, hiking, fishing, kayaking, wildlife viewing, whale and sea otter watching.

**McKinley Foothills B&B/Cabins★**
Denali, Trapper Creek—733-1454, www.matnet.com/mckinley. B&B, rustic and remote cabins on the south side of Denali. Cuisine with a touch of the Caribbean. 20 miles from the Parks Highway.

**Otter Cove Bed & Breakfast ★**
Pelican—735-2259, www.ottercove. com. Small town B&B, hiking, tourboat, birding, guided trips, near West Chichagof-Yakobi Wilderness and Glacier Bay.

**Peace of Selby**
Gates of the Arctic NPP—672-3206, www.gorp.com/selby/default.htm. River trips, birding, guiding, outfitting, winter trips. Near Upper Noatak and Kobuk rivers.

**Ravenswood Retreat Lodge ★**
Meyers Chuck—946-8204, www.ktn.net/ravenswood. Lodge, kayaking, backpacking, guiding, hiking, lodging, wildlife viewing. Inside Passage, Clarence Strait, Cleveland Peninsula, Ernest Sound.

**Sadie Cove Wilderness Lodge ★**
Kachemak Bay—235-2350, www.netalaska.com/sadie. Private cabins, full-service remote lodge surrounded by Kachemak SP, hiking, fishing, wildlife viewing, sea kayaking, Log Cabin Sauna. Sadie Cove Fjord, near Homer.

**Stephan Lake Lodge ★**
Stephan Lake, Talkeetna Mountains—696-2163, www.AlaskaOne. com/stephanlake. Recreational lodge, backpacking, guiding, fishing, hiking, rafting and river trips, photography, ecotourism, bear viewing.

**Tenakee Hot Springs Lodge ★**
Tenakee—736-2400. Full service, fully guided sport fishing lodge. Fresh and salt water fishing for salmon, halibut, trout. Comfortable 42-ft. boat.

**Tolovana Hot Springs, Ltd.** ★
Interior, near Fairbanks—455-6706,
www.mosquitonet.com/~tolovana.
Remote rustic hot springs with 2
fully outfitted cabins, 45 miles
northwest of Fairbanks. Guided trips
possible. Interior.

**Tutka Bay Wilderness Lodge** ★
Tutka Bay of lower Cook Inlet—
(800) 606-3909, 235-3905,
www.alaskan.com/vendors/tutka.
html. Flightseeing, sea kayaking,
birding, fishing, hiking, winter activities. Remote lodge near Homer.

**Weeping Trout Sports Resort** ★
Chilkat Lake—766-2827,
www.kcd.com/weepingt. Bird watching, fishing, flightseeing, lodging,
day and overnight trips, water
related activities. Remote lodge near
Bald Eagle Preserve and Haines.

**Whaler's Cove Lodge**
Killisnoo Harbor, Admiralty
Island—(800) 423-3123, 788-3123,
www.AlaskaOne.com/whalerscove.
Beachfront cabins, lodge, specializing in sportfishing. Kayaking, canoeing, hiking, near Angoon.

**Windsong Wilderness Retreat
and Adventures** ★
Lake Clark NP—260-5410,
www.alaska.net/~twinlake. Remote
log cabin rental in Lake Clark NP.
Hiking, wildlife viewing, photography,
sport fishing, river rafting. Guided
trips from base camp on Twin Lakes.

## INFORMATION RESOURCES: GOVERNMENT, NATIVE, INTERNET

See regional chapters for details on

contacts for specific parks, refuges,
ranger districts, wild and scenic
rivers, visitor centers, etc.

## ALASKA PUBLIC LANDS INFORMATION CENTERS

The best of all sources for information and reservations for public
lands and recreational opportunities
statewide.

Anchorage, 605 W. 4th Avenue—
271-2737.
Fairbanks, 250 Cushman Street—
451-7352.
Ketchikan (Southeast Alaska Visitor
Center), 50 Main Street—228-6214.
Tok, Richardson Highway & Tok
Cutoff—883-5667.

## BLM LANDS

**Bureau of Land Management**
Main Office, Anchorage—271-5960.
www.ak.blm.gov/
Anchorage Field Office (West,
Southeast, Southwest, MatSu,
Kenai)—267-1246.
Northern Field Office (Fairbanks,
Upper Yukon, Seward Peninsula,
Far North)—474-2300.
Glenallen Field Office (Copper
basin, Southcentral coast)—822-
3217.

## NATIONAL FORESTS

**Alaska Region**—www.fs.fed.us/r10/

**Chugach National Forest**
Main Office, Anchorage—271-2500,
www.fs.fed.us/r10/chugach
Glacier Ranger District (east PW
Sound, western Kenai, Portage)—
783-3242

Seward Ranger District (Kenai Peninsula)—224-3374
Cordova Ranger District (Copper delta, eastern PW Sound)—424-7661

**Tongass National Forest**
Main Office, Ketchikan—228-6202

**Supervisor's Offices**
Chatham Office, Sitka—747-6671
Stikine Office, Petersburg—772-3841

**NF Visitor Centers**
Forest Service Information Center, Centennial Hall, 101 Egan Drive, Juneau—586-8751
Mendenhall Glacier Visitor Center, Mendenhall Glacier, Juneau—789-0097
Petersburg Visitor Information Center, First and Fram, Petersburg—772-4636
Southeast Alaska Visitor Center, 50 Main Street, Ketchikan—228-6220

**NATIONAL PARKS, PRESERVES & MONUMENTS**

**National Park Service**
State Office, Anchorage—257-2690, www.nps.gov/parklists/ak.html

**Alagnak Wild River**—246-1105, www.nps.gov/alag
**Aniakchak National Monument & Preserve**—246-3305, www.nps.gov/ania
**Bering Land Bridge National Preserve**—443-2522, www.nps.gov/bela
**Cape Krusenstern National Monument**—442-3890, www.nps.gov/cakr

**Denali National Park & Preserve**—683-2294, www.nps.gov/dena
**Gates of the Arctic National Park & Preserve**—456-0281, www.nps.gov/gaar
**Glacier Bay National Park & Preserve**—697-2230, www.nps.gov/glba
**Katmai National Park & Preserve**—246-3305, www.nps.gov/katm
**Kenai Fjords National Park**—224-3175, www.nps.gov/kefj
**Klondike Gold Rush National Historic Park**—983-2921, www.nps.gov/klgo
**Kobuk Valley National Park**—442-8300, www.nps.gov/kova
**Lake Clark National Park & Preserve**—271-3751, www.nps.gov/lacl
**Noatak National Preserve**—442-8300, www.nps.gov/noat
**Sitka National Historic Site**—747-6281, www.nps.gov/sitk
**Wrangell St.Elias National Park & Preserve**—822-5234, www.nps.gov/wrst
**Yukon Charley Rivers National Preserve**—463-0593, www.nps.gov/yuch

**NATIONAL WILDLIFE REFUGES**

**U.S. Fish & Wildlife Service**
Anchorage—786-3357, www.r7.fws.gov
**Alaska Maritime NWR**—592-2406, www.r7.fws.gov/nwr/akmnwr/akmnwrt.html
**Alaska Peninsula NWR**—246-3339, www.r7.fws.gov/nwr/ap/apnwrt.html
**Arctic NWR**—456-0250, www.r7.fws.gov/nwr/arctic/r7arctt.html

**Becharof NWR**—246-3339, www.r7.fws.gov/nwr/bec/becnwrt.html
**Innoko NWR**—524-3251, www.r7.fws.gov/nwr/innoko/innwrt.html
**Izembek NWR**—532-2445, www.r7.fws.gov/nwr/izembek/iznwrt.html
**Kanuti NWR**—456-0329, www.r7.fws.gov/nwr/kanuti/r7kanwt.html
**Kenai NWR**—www.r7.fws.gov/nwr/kenai/kennwr.html
**Kodiak NWR**—487-2600, www.r7.fws.gov/nwr/kodiak/kodnwrt.html
**Koyukuk NWR**—656-1231, www.r7.fws.gov/nwr/koyukuk/kynwrt.html
**Nowitna NWR**—656-1231, www.r7.fws.gov/nwr/nowitna/nownwrt.html
**Selawik NWR**—442-3799, www.r7.fws.gov/nwr/selawik/selnwrt.html
**Tetlin NWR**—883-5312, www.r7.fws.gov/nwr/tetlin/tetnwrt.html
**Togiak NWR**—842-1063, www.r7.fws.gov/nwr/togiak/tognwrt.html
**Yukon Delta NWR**—543-3151, www.r7.fws.gov/nwr/yd/ydnwrt.html
**Yukon Flats NWR**—456-0440, www.r7.fws.gov/nwr/yf/r7yflt.html

**OTHER FEDERAL RESOURCES**

**U.S. Geological Survey**, Public Inquiries Office, Anchorage—786-7011, www.usgs.gov
**Alaska Wild and Scenic Rivers**—www.nps.gov/rivers/wildriverslist.html#ak
**Ecoregions of Alaska**—www.eros.afo.wr.usgs.gov/ecoreg/ecoregmap.html

## ALASKA STATE GOVERNMENT

**Alaska Department of Fish & Game**
Anchorage—344-0541, www.state.ak.us/adfg. Information on fishing regulations.

**Alaska Division of Tourism**
Juneau—465-2012, www.commerce.state.ak.us/tourism/

**Alaska Mainstreet Visitor Center**
Tok—883-5775.

**Alaska Office of History and Archaeology**
Anchorage—269-8721. References and information on Alaska history, gold rush, digs, and research projects.

**Alaska State Parks**
Department of Natural Resources/Division of Parks & Outdoor Recreation Anchorage—269-8400, www.dnr.state.ak.us/parks.

## ALASKA NATIVE CORPORATIONS AND INFORMATION

Information on native corporation lands, regulations, and permits. References to village corporations and other native organizations.

**Alaska Native Tourism Council**
Anchorage—274-5400. Information on native events, sites, and travel opportunities.

**Ahtna, Inc.**, Copper basin, Wrangell—822-3476.
**Aleut Corporation**, Alaska Peninsula west of Point Moller, Aleutian Islands, Pribilofs—561-4300.
**Arctic Slope Regional Corporation**, North Slope, northern Brooks Range—852-8633.
**Bering Straits Native Corporation**, Seward Peninsula, Norton

Sound, St. Lawrence Island—443-5252.
**Bristol Bay Native Corporation,** Bristol Bay, inner Alaska Peninsula, Wood and Tikchik Lakes, Mulchatna and Nushagak Valleys—278-3602.
**Calista Corporation,** Yukon Delta, lower Kuskokwim basin—279-5516.
Chugach Alaska Corporation, Kenai Peninsula, Prince William Sound, Copper River Delta, Yakutat, Icy Bay—563-8866.
**Cook Inlet Region, Inc.,** Cook Inlet, Kenai Peninsula, Lake Clark, MatSu, Talkeetna Mountains—274-8638.
**Doyon, Ltd.,** Interior, southeastern Brooks Range—452-4755.
**Koniag Inc.,** Kodiak and Afognak islands, south coast of Alaska Peninsula from Aniakchak to Becharof Lake—486-5725.
**N.A.N.A. Regional Corporation,** Kotzebue Sound, Kobuk and Noatak Valleys—265-4100.
**Sealaska Corporation,** Southeast—586-1512.

## COMMUNITY INFORMATION CONTACTS

Chambers of commerce, visitors bureaus, or other sources.

**Anchor Point**—235-2600
**Anchorage**—274-3531, www.ci.anchorage.ak.us
**Barrow**—852-5211
**Bethel**—543-2911
**Big Lake**—892-6109, www.biglake-ak.com
**Copper Valley** (region)—822-5555
**Cordova**—424-7260, www.ptialaska.net/~cchamber
**Delta Junction**—895-9941 (sum-mer), 895-4628 (winter), www.akpub.com/akttt/delta.html
**Denali (region)**—www.alaska.net/~denst1/DST.home.html
**Dillingham**—842-5283
Eagle River (and vicinity)—696-4636
**Fairbanks**—(800) 327-5774, 456-5774, www.polarnet.com/Users/FCVB, www.fairnet.org
**Funny River**—262-7711
**Glenallen**—822-5555
**Gustavus**—697-2358
**Haines**—(800) 458-3579, www.haines.ak.us, www.hainesak.com
**Healy**—P.O. Box 437, Healy AK, 99743 (no phone)
**Homer**—235-5300, www.xyz.net/~homer
**Hyder**—(604) 636-9148
**Juneau**—586-2201, www.juneau.lib.ak.us, www.juneau.com
**Kenai**—283-1991, www.visitkenai.com
**Ketchikan**—225-6166, www.ktn.net, www.visit-ketchikan.com
**King Salmon**—246-4250
**Kodiak**—486-4782, www.kodiak.org/kodiak
**Kotzebue**—442-3760
**MatSu Region**—746-5000, www.alaskavisit.com
**Metlakatla**—886-1216, 886-4161
**Nenana**—832-5541
**Nome**—443-5535, www.alaska.net/~nome
**North Peninsula** (Kenai)—776-8369
**North Pole**—488-2242, www.fair-net.org/npole/npole2.html
**Palmer**—745-2880, www.akcache.com/alaska/palmer

Petersburg—772-3975,
www.petersburg.org
Port William—www.alaska.net/
~mmansour/ptwilliam.htm
Prince of Wales Island (—826-
3870
Prince William Sound (region)—
344-1693
Seldovia—234-7890
Seward—224-8051
Sitka—747-5940,
www.alaskainfo.org/sitka.html
Skagway—983-2854, www.skagway.
org
Soldotna—262-9814, www.
visitkenai.com
Sutton—745-4527
Talkeetna—733-2330
Tok—883-5775 (summer), 883-
5887 (winter), www.TokAlaskaInfo.
com
Unalaska/Dutch Harbor—
581-1483
Valdez—(800) 770-5954, 835-
4636, www.alaskagold.com/valdez,
www.alaska.net/~valdezak
Wasilla—373-9071
Whittier—472-2327, 472-2414
Wrangell—874-3901,
www.wrangell.com

Alaska Tourism and Travel
Guide—www.alaskan.com/
Alaska Volcano Observatory—
www.avo.alaska.edu/
Alaskan Bookstore (in assoc. with
Amazon) www.akusa.com/books
Bed & Breakfast List—bbchan-
nel.com/USA/Alaska
Budget Travel Alaska (great
links)—www.budgettravel.com/
laska.htm
GORP Alaska Travel—www.gorp.
com/gorp/location/ak/ak.htm
Hostels.com (all Alaskan hostels)—
www.hostels.com
Motel/Hotel List—usa-lodging.com/
motels/alaska/akcities.htm
Private AK Campgrounds—
roomsplus.com/campgrnd/ak/alaska.
htm
State of Alaska—www.state.ak.us/
Travel Alaska—www.travelalaska.co

## ALASKA INFORMATION WEBSITES

Alaska's Best (links, info, trivia)—
www.alaskasbest.com
Alaska Internet Travel Guide—
www.AlaskaOne.com/travel/
Alaska Geophysical Institute—
www.gi.alaska.edu/
Alaska Humanities Forum—
www.akhf.org
Alaska Job Center—
www.jobs.state.ak.us
Alaska Outdoor Adventures (great
links)—www.alaskaoutdoors.com

# INDEX

## ABOUT THE AUTHOR

**Paul Otteson** has traveled throughout western North America, camera in hand, for more than two decades. His has covered thousands of miles on foot, exploring scores of parks and wilderness areas and more thana quarter-million miles on the highways and backroads of the West. He has spent many months in Alaska, traveling by land, air, and sea and immersing himself in the Alaskan experience while maintaining a traveler's eye.

Otteson's international journeys led to his first book, *The World Awaits: A Comprehensive Guide for Extended Backpack Travel,* which is fast becoming a classic for those planning independent travel overseas. His other works include the *Northern California Travel•Smart Trip Planner* and *Kids Who Walk on Volcanoes,* a children's book about the lives of kids in the Central American highlands.

Paul and his wife, Mary, currently reside in the San Francisco Bay area—though Alaska, where they met, will always be their second home. The author can be reached through John Muir Publications, or by e-mail at ottoworks@sfo.com. An extensive website featuring book and travel information, links, and a catalog of Paul's images can be found at www.sfo.com/~ottoworks.